The Cathedrals *of* Scotland

Peter Galloway

Photographs by Michael Turner

SCOTTISH CULTURAL PRESS

First Published 2000 by
Scottish Cultural Press
Unit 13d
Newbattle Abbey Business Annexe
Newbattle Road
DALKEITH
EH22 3LJ
Tel: 0131 660 4666 • Fax: 0131 660 6414
e-mail: scp@sol.co.uk

British Library Cataloguing in Publication Data
A catalogue record for this book is available from the British Library

The publisher acknowledges subsidy from the Scottish Arts Council towards the publication of this book

ISBN: 1 84017 026 3

Designed by *Neil Gowans and Avril Gray*
Typeset from author-generated discs by *Ann Gowans*

Printed and bound by
Cromwell Press Ltd., Trowbridge, Wiltshire

To

The Reverend Canon Edgar Wells
and the people of the Church of St Mary the Virgin, New York,
for their hospitality, generosity and kindness during many hot and humid summers.

Acknowledgements

I am grateful to the following individuals, who have contributed to this book in a variety of ways: The Reverend Charles Armour, The Very Reverend Canon Bernard J. Canning, The Very Reverend Canon Noel Carey, Mrs Jeanette Castle, The Right Reverend Mario Conti, The Reverend Gordon S. Cuvie, Mr Michael Davis, Mr Richard Devaney, Mr Gordon Drummond, Mrs Dorothy M. England, Ms Anne Escott, The Reverend Ronald Ferguson, The Reverend Malcolm E. Grant, Dr Christine Johnson, Mr Alastair R. Johnston, The Reverend K. McBride, The Very Reverend David McCubbin, The Reverend Colin I. McIntosh, The Reverend Robert K. Mackenzie, The Reverend Michael MacMahon, The Very Reverend Gilleasbuig Macmillan, The Very Reverend William J. Morris, Ms June Morrison, The Reverend John McMurray, Mrs D. O'Hara, Mrs S. A. Porter, Dr Christopher C. G. Rawll, The Reverend Walter M. Ritchie, Mr David A. Roberts, Mr John Saunders, The Reverend James A. Simpson, Mrs Alice Small, The Reverend Albert E. Smith, The Reverend Roland Walls, The Very Reverend David Wightman, Miss Barbara Wishart, and Mr Graeme Wilson.

The Reverend Alan Moses and The Reverend Bill Scott, both London-based expatriate Scotsmen, kindly read the text at proof stage. I am also grateful to everyone at Scottish Cultural Press for having faith in this project and taking it to publication. I owe a great debt of thanks to Michael Turner for all his kindness and patience in driving me around Scotland and its cathedrals in the summers of 1994 and 1996, and for taking the photographs used to illustrate this book.

Contents

Preface

The idea of a book devoted to all the cathedral churches of Scotland was conceived as a companion to my book on the cathedral churches of Ireland, the intention being to provide an historical, social, ecclesiastical and descriptive study of each of the thirty-five cathedrals or cathedral sites in Scotland. Some of the cathedrals, especially those ancient foundations that are now used as presbyterian churches – particularly St Kentigern's Cathedral in Glasgow – have been the subject of a number of scholarly monographs. Other more minor sites, from the obscure fragments at Skeabost, to the post Second World War cathedral at Ayr, are still awaiting the attention of antiquarian and architect to relate their history.

The text of the present work does not pretend to compete with any individual monograph; it aims to give a broad perspective of the history and development of Scotland's cathedral churches, including all those buildings which were cathedrals, but are no longer. In a strict ecclesiological interpretation of the word, Scotland's medieval cathedrals ceased to be cathedral churches when Scotland's bishops were expelled from their dioceses in 1689. But it seemed pointless to exclude their history and beauty from this book, especially as popular belief will insistently apply the title 'Glasgow Cathedral' to the great medieval building that stands in the shadow of the Royal Infirmary, although it is *not* a cathedral, but not to St Mary's Cathedral on the Great West Road, or St Andrew's Cathedral on the bank of the Clyde, both of which *are* cathedrals.

The Scottish Dioceses

The historic Scottish dioceses were thirteen in number: Aberdeen, Argyll, Brechin, Caithness, Dunblane, Dunkeld, Galloway, Glasgow, the Isles, Moray, Orkney, Ross and St Andrews; and to these was added Edinburgh, which was established as a separate diocese by King Charles I in 1634. The history of the Scottish episcopate is obscure until the twelfth century, and a territorial diocesan structure only begins to emerge in the reign of King David I (1124–53).

There was no archbishop in Scotland before the fifteenth century, principally because of the claim of the archbishop of York to exercise metropolitan jurisdiction over the Scottish bishops. Scotland was finally recognised as an independent province in 1192, though without an archbishop. The diocese of Galloway remained subject to York, while the dioceses of the Isles and Orkney, being Norwegian dependencies, were subject to the archbishop of Nidaros. The Isles were ceded to Scotland in the thirteenth century; Galloway became part of the Scottish Church in the fourteenth century, to be followed by Orkney in the fifteenth century. The Scottish Church acquired the normal panoply of a provincial structure in the fifteenth century, when the bishop of St Andrews was given the title of archbishop in 1472, and similarly the bishop of Glasgow in 1492.

Each diocese had a cathedral church, and those of Aberdeen, Argyll (at Lismore), Brechin, Caithness (at Dornoch), Dunblane, Dunkeld, Edinburgh, Glasgow, the Isles (at Skeabost and then at Iona) and Orkney (at Kirkwall), are still in use as presbyterian churches. The cathedrals of Galloway (at Whithorn), Moray (at Elgin), Ross (at Fortrose) and St Andrews are disused ruins of greater or lesser interest; that of St Andrews being an especially melancholy sight. The small ephemeral cathedral at Birnie (for the diocese of Moray before the construction of the cathedral at Elgin) is still in use as a parish church.

Since the expulsion of the bishops from their dioceses in 1689, the Church of Scotland no longer has the diocese as a unit of organisation, but the historic diocesan names are mostly continued by the Scottish Episcopal Church and the Roman Catholic Church.

The Scottish Episcopal Church has retained the names of the ancient dioceses, despite several amalgamations, but its cathedral churches are often not in any of the original see towns. The cathedral of the united dioceses of St Andrews, Dunkeld and Dunblane is at Perth; the cathedral of the united dioceses of Moray, Ross and Caithness is at Inverness; the two cathedrals of the united dioceses of Argyll and the Isles are at

Cumbrae and Oban (though both are quite close to Iona); and the cathedral of the diocese of Brechin is at Dundee. The church did not continue the use of the title of archbishop after the deaths of Archbishop Arthur Rose of St Andrews in 1704 and Archbishop John Paterson of Glasgow in 1708, and the primate of the church is elected from among the diocesan bishops and entitled 'the Primus'.

The Roman Catholic Church has continued to use some of the ancient titles, although it has suppressed the dioceses of Brechin and Dunblane (both subsumed within the diocese of Dunkeld), the dioceses of Caithness, Moray, Orkney and Ross (subsumed within the diocese of Aberdeen) and in the years after the Second World War, created the dioceses of Motherwell and Paisley. As with the Scottish Episcopal Church, the cathedrals are not always in the historic see towns. The cathedral of the diocese of Galloway is at Ayr; and the cathedral of the amalgamated dioceses of Argyll and the Isles is at Oban. The primate of the church is the archbishop of St Andrews and Edinburgh.

The following four categories are only an indication of the scope of the book. The cathedrals appear in the text in alphabetical order according to their geographical location, and not according to denomination or ownership.

The Church of Scotland

The study of Scotland's medieval cathedrals is inseparable from the upheaval of the sixteenth century reformation, the end result of which was the triumph of presbyterianism against episcopacy in the government of the Scottish Church, in 1689. The Church of Scotland is today still presbyterian in its organisation, and therefore has no 'cathedral' churches (from the Latin *cathedra* – the throne of the ruling diocesan bishop) in the full ecclesiological meaning of that word, since it has no bishops. Although it ceased to be an episcopal church in 1689, virtually all the historic Scottish cathedrals are used by the Church of Scotland as places of worship and, since the nineteenth century, the Church has begun again to use the style 'cathedral' for all these buildings, with the exceptions of the churches at Birnie and Lismore. The church at Birnie immediately pre-dated Elgin as the cathedral church of the diocese of Moray. The truncated church at Lismore was the cathedral church of the diocese of the Argyll, but seems to have been reduced to parochial status before the sixteenth century reformation.

Aberdeen	The Cathedral Church of St Mary and St Machar
Birnie	The Cathedral Church of St Brendan
Brechin	The Cathedral Church of the Holy Trinity
Dornoch	The Cathedral Church of St Mary and St Gilbert
Dunblane	The Cathedral Church of St Blane and St Laurence
Dunkeld	The Cathedral Church of St Columba
Edinburgh	The Cathedral Church of St Giles
Glasgow	The Cathedral Church of St Kentigern
Iona	The Cathedral Church of St Mary
Kirkwall	The Cathedral Church of St Magnus
Lismore	The Cathedral Church of St Moluog

The Scottish Episcopal Church

After the beginning of the sixteenth century reformation of the church, which can be dated to 1560, the Church of Scotland retained its bishops, although for the next one hundred and thirty years, their episcopal authority often sat uneasily alongside presbyterianism.

Wholly on political grounds, the bishops were expelled from their dioceses in 1689, and episcopacy was purportedly abolished in the Scottish church. Although the bishops officially disappeared from any role in the government of the church, many priests and congregations remained loyal to their authority, and an underground 'episcopal' church began to emerge. Bishop William Hay of Moray (1688-1707) was a much respected figure who retired to Inverness after his expulsion from the living of St Giles, Elgin, the pro-cathedral of the diocese of Moray. Hay never ceased to think of himself as bishop of Moray and was so regarded by congregations who remained loyal to the episcopate. After the deaths of Bishop Andrew Wood of Caithness in 1694, Bishop James Ramsay of Ross in 1696, and Bishop Andrew Bruce of Orkney in 1699, Hay became the last remaining bishop in the north of Scotland, and exercised episcopal oversight of the vacant dioceses as well as his own. Men travelled from as far as Orkney down to Inverness to seek ordination at the hands of the aged bishop. As late as 1706 the moderator of the synod of Orkney urged the presbytery of Forres and Elgin to report 'the pretended bishop of Moray' for continuing to ordain clergy.

This 'Episcopal Church' survived and continued strongly until 1746. Suspected of Jacobite sympathies and consequently severely persecuted in the aftermath of the 1745 Jacobite Rising, the Episcopal Church was forbidden by law to possess any churches or chapels or to hold any public services. Faced with such persecution, the Episcopal Church dwindled until it became, little more than 'a shadow of a shade', although an unbroken succession of bishops was maintained throughout the eighteenth century. Only with the relaxation of the Penal Laws in 1792 were Episcopalians allowed to worship freely and openly again, and the nineteenth century saw the construction of their cathedrals. These range in style from the exquisitely proportioned small island cathedral at Millport on Cumbrae, to the curious, architecturally muddled and unfinished cathedral at Oban, to the immaculate perfectionist splendour of the cathedral at Edinburgh.

Aberdeen	The Cathedral Church of St Andrew
Cumbrae	The Cathedral and Collegiate Church of the Holy Spirit
Dundee	The Cathedral Church of St Paul
Edinburgh	The Cathedral Church of St Mary
Glasgow	The Cathedral Church of St Mary
Inverness	The Cathedral Church of St Andrew
Oban	The Cathedral Church of St John the Divine
Perth	The Cathedral Church of St Ninian

The Roman Catholic Church

After the sixteenth century reformation took hold in Scotland in 1560, those who remained loyal to the authority of the Pope lived a furtive and underground existence, and worshipped as, when and wherever they could. Groups of Roman Catholics were said to worship within the ruins of Elgin Cathedral until early in the eighteenth century. With the relaxation of the Penal Laws in 1792, the Roman Catholic Church, like the Scottish Episcopal Church, embarked on a programme of church and cathedral building. The waves of Irish immigration to south-west Scotland in the nineteenth century caused a rapid increase in the Catholic population in those areas; and this in turn led to the creation of two new dioceses, Motherwell and Paisley after the Second World War. The earliest Roman Catholic cathedrals are the two early nineteenth century cathedrals at Dundee and Glasgow; and the most recent is the post-Second World War cathedral at Ayr. When compared with their contemporaries, the Roman Catholic cathedrals in Ireland, the architecture of the Scottish Roman Catholic cathedrals is generally restrained and untriumphalist.

Aberdeen	The Cathedral Church of St Mary of the Assumption
Ayr	The Cathedral Church of the Good Shepherd
Dundee	The Cathedral Church of St Andrew
Edinburgh	The Cathedral Church of St Mary
Glasgow	The Cathedral Church of St Andrew
Motherwell	The Cathedral Church of Our Lady of Good Aid
Oban	The Cathedral Church of St Columba
Paisley	The Cathedral Church of St Mirin

The Greek Orthodox Church

There is one Greek Orthodox cathedral in Scotland. This cathedral, in Glasgow, was built in 1876-7 for a congregation of the United Presbyterian Church. It was closed in 1961 and purchased by the Greek Orthodox Church; it was raised to cathedral status in 1971 for the Greek Orthodox community in Scotland, under the dedication of Saint Luke.

The Ruined and Disused Cathedrals

'It cannot be denied', in the words of one observer, 'that the spirit of the reformers...chose precisely the most glorious of our national possessions among which to run amok'. Another, who felt more strongly, spoke of 'the reckless outrage which cloaked its violence under the guise of religious zeal... The pretence (for it was often nothing else) of "cleansing the sanctuary" not only robbed the Church of many a priceless possession, but begat, in the popular mind, a ruthless disregard of the sacred associations of places where generation after generation had worshipped God'.

Both comments are all too sadly true. The wanton destruction visited on some of the most foremost pieces of Scottish architecture in the sixteenth century and afterwards, under the principles of the reformation, leads the observer to wonder seriously whether the disadvantages of that movement did not in fact outweigh its benefits. The still magnificent ruins of Elgin and the wreckage of the once-magnificent cathedral of St Andrews remain today as silent witnesses to a campaign that was marked by much unreasoned hatred.

Other cathedrals in the 'ruined' category include the obscure remains at Birsay and the forgotten fragments at Skeabost on the Isle of Skye, both of which were probably abandoned rather than systematically destroyed. A more recent tragedy is the conflagration that destroyed the Roman Catholic pro-cathedral at Dumfries in 1961. Because of a highly questionable decision to abandon the site and move the see to Ayr, the building was demolished, and all that remains today are two forlorn and dilapidated towers, the very redness of the stone from which they were constructed seeming to serve as a reminder of the flames that destroyed the cathedral. Another red stone cathedral, that at Fortrose, has lost its chancel and nave, and only a yawning gap divides the complete south aisle from the isolated chapter house. The much-altered and diminished nave of the partly demolished cathedral at Whithorn, is a sad little reminder of the memory of Columba, the great saint of the border.

Birsay	The Cathedral Church of Christ
Dumfries	The Pro-Cathedral Church of St Andrew
Elgin	The Cathedral Church of the Holy Trinity
Fortrose	The Cathedral Church of St Peter and St Boniface
Skeabost	The Cathedral Church of St Columba
St Andrews	The Cathedral Church of St Andrew
Whithorn	The Cathedral Church of St Martin of Tours

The text of this book is based on visits to the Scottish cathedrals during the summers of 1994 and 1996, but cathedrals are places of living worship and changing liturgy, and it is no longer possible to guarantee that an altar, a statue, a chest or a painting will remain in the same position in perpetuity. With that caveat, I hope that the following survey of Scotland's cathedrals will bring these interesting buildings to the attention of a wider audience, and contribute a measure of understanding to their place in Scottish history and to the sometimes complex, emotional and radical developments of Christianity in Scotland.

Peter Galloway

Aberdeen

The city of Aberdeen, a royal burgh since 1179, lies on the east coast of Scotland, at the confluence of the River Don and the River Dee (*aber*: estuary; *deen*: Dee), 209km to the north-east of Edinburgh. The site of the city is ancient, and shows evidence of prehistoric, Roman and Pictish settlements. Aberdeen has three cathedrals: the nineteenth century cathedrals of the Scottish Episcopal Church and the Roman Catholic Church, and the fifteenth century granite cathedral of St Mary and St Machar.

The Cathedral Church of St Mary and St Machar
(Church of Scotland)

St Machar's Cathedral lies in the district known as Old Aberdeen, 2.4km to the north of the main city with which it has been incorporated since 1891. As the Church of Scotland is presbyterian and not episcopal in its government, the Cathedral Church of St Mary and St Machar does not house a 'cathedra' – the throne of a diocesan bishop – and is, ecclesiologically, no more a cathedral than Westminster Abbey is an abbey. As with the other former cathedrals, now used as presbyterian churches, the title of cathedral is continued in courteous deference to history.

St Machar was a sixth-century Irishman who was baptised by St Colman and became a disciple of St Columba at Iona. Sent with twelve disciples to convert the Picts, Machar was instructed to stop and build a church where a river would bend like a pastoral staff. The windings of the River Don provided an ideal setting and he built a church near the spot on which the present cathedral stands; the conjectured date is thought to be about 580 but there is no firm evidence. Machar is said later to have gone to Rome, and then to have been appointed bishop of Tours in France where he died. His feast is kept on 12 November.

Nothing remains of Machar's foundation, and very little is known of the history of the site until King David I (1124–53) abolished a see at Mortlach and replaced it with one at Aberdeen in 1132.

Mortlach, about 0.8km south of Dufftown, is said to have originated with a foundation of St Moluog in 566. Tradition claims that, to celebrate a victory over the Norsemen, King Malcolm II (1005–34) ordered the church at Mortlach to be lengthened by a measure of three spears and established a bishopric there. The names of four bishops are known: Heyn (c.1012–24), Donericus in the mid-eleventh century, Cormac in the late eleventh century, and Nechtan in the early twelfth century but, as with all the Scottish bishoprics before the twelfth century, the history of Mortlach is very obscure. The present church at Mortlach is essentially twelfth century, although rendering conceals the medieval stonework. The chancel lancets are thirteenth century and the north aisle is twentieth century.

The first known bishop at Aberdeen was Nechtan (1132–6), and a cathedral was certainly in existence on the present site by 1157 when the next known bishop, Edward (1151–71), was given permission by Pope Adrian IV to turn the cathedral into a monastic foundation. In 1256 there were thirteen canonries, including that of the dean and that held by the bishop. The solitary remnant of this cathedral is the lozenge-decorated base of a capital supporting one of its architraves, which can be seen in the charter room.

The cathedral was rebuilt at the instigation of Bishop Matthew (1172–99), but demolished by Bishop Henry le Chene (1282–1328) who proposed to build a larger church. Bishop le Chene swore fealty to King Edward I of England (1272–1307) when that monarch launched an attempt to conquer Scotland in 1296, but after the rise of Robert Bruce (King Robert I of Scotland, 1306–29) he fled, fearing retribution. Le Chene eventually made peace with

The Cathedral Church of St Mary and St Machar

Bruce, and was restored to his diocese with a grant of money and instructions to rebuild the cathedral. It is thought that his work was limited to the demolition of the short Romanesque chancel and apse and its replacement by a more spacious choir to accommodate stalls for the twenty-nine canons who then comprised the chapter.

With the arrival of Bishop Alexander de Kininmund (1355–80), a serious attempt was made to rebuild the nave. All that remains of his cathedral are parts of the ruined transepts and two of the pillars which once supported the central tower. Carved from red sandstone they are now mostly buried in the modern east wall of the nave. Bishop Henry de Lychton (1422–40) embarked on a further building programme, and the present nave, western towers and north transept date from his episcopate. His successor, Bishop Ingram de Lindsay (1441–58), paved and roofed the cathedral. Bishop Thomas Spens (1458–80) built the tabernacle of the altar and presented choir stalls and vestments.

Bishop William Elphinstone (1483–1514), generally regarded as the greatest bishop of Aberdeen, extended the chancel eastwards and started work on the south transept. He also constructed the central tower and spire (completed c.1511) and, in 1489, 'furnished it with 14 tuneable and costly bells, three whereof were very great… They hung on great oak trees a little from the said steeple, which stood upon four arch pillars, pended above very high. There was a battaline round about the said steeple, which was built four square, and four story high above the said pend [an arched space], for from it, were 24 steps of a ladder to a little four cornered chamber; and above it a square tower, with a stang on the top of it five ells in length, with a great globe of brass above the first cross of said stang; and above the second cross was a cock, an ell in length of brass, and the breast of copper, which stang, globe and cock Mr David Corse, a presbyterian minister of this church disposed of. In the said pend was an oval vacuity, through which came a rope from the bells, down to the church floor, wherewith the beadle rung one of the said bells to sermon, after the reformation.'[1]

Bishop Elphinstone also founded King's College (he is buried before the altar of the college chapel) and compiled the Breviary of Aberdeen. The college, founded in 1495, was subsequently joined by the later foundation of Marishcal College, to form the University of Aberdeen.

Bishop Gavin Dunbar (1519–32) completed the cathedral during his episcopate, by finishing the south transept, where he is buried, replacing the original cape stone roofs of the western towers with squat sandstone spires, and erecting the fine wooden ceiling of the nave. The bishop had a great love of heraldry and his coats of arms can be seen on many buildings in Aberdeen, but the nave ceiling of his cathedral church represents the fullest flowering of his love of the subject. The cathedral reached the zenith of its life during Bishop Gavin's episcopate.

The arrival of the sixteenth century reformation in Scotland was a disaster for St Machar's Cathedral as it was for so many other cathedrals. In July 1559, Bishop William Gordon (1545–77), fearing the ransacking of the cathedral, entrusted some of its treasures to the safe-keeping of the canons, and the remainder to the earl of Huntly. His fears were well-grounded. In December 1559, an army was sent north by the Protestant leaders (who called themselves the Lords of the Congregation) to impose the principles of the reformation on a reluctant Aberdeen. The army bore down on the cathedral in January 1560 with a destructive frenzy. The precise extent of the damage is impossible to calculate; but there followed the usual smashing of windows and woodwork, tearing down of altars, images and hangings, and the defacing of paintings – and, worst of all, the destruction of the cathedral library. It was only the arrival of the earl of Huntly and an armed force that saved the cathedral from greater enormities.

It was only a temporary respite, and the cathedral was eventually systematically denuded of anything that was not strictly required by the new reformed liturgy. The kirk session decreed 'that the organs, with all expedition be removed out of the kirk, made profit of to the use and export of the poor; and that the priest's stall and backs of altars be removed out of the places where they now remain, and situated in the parts of the kirk where men may be most easily sat to hear the sermons and such things that serve for that use to be otherwise disposed of or made money of'.[2]

St Machar's Cathedral never really recovered from the sacking of 1560. The chancel, the Lady Chapel, and the north and south transepts fell into disuse after that date, and it was later suggested that the chancel had been deliberately destroyed by the reformers. As the most sacred and ornate part of a church, chancels and their contents were usually a prime target for the anti-Catholic hatred of the reformers. Other opinions hold that the chancel may not have been completed at the time of the sacking in 1560. Although Bishop Elphinstone began extending the chancel, there is no evidence that it was completed by his successors. Some have argued that because the chancel was still incomplete in 1560 the reformers wasted no time on it. Whichever theory is accepted, it is certain that the effects of time, and the recycling of the stone work for other buildings probably caused the gradual demolition of the chancel, although substantial parts of it were still standing in the middle of the seventeenth century.

In 1568, the earl of Morton, regent of Scotland for the young King James VI, ordered the cathedral roof to be stripped of its lead to raise money to pay his troops. A certain William Birnie, a burgess of Edinburgh, was dispatched to Aberdeen to undertake the task. Birnie exceeded his brief by removing the bells as well as most of the lead. He took the bells and some of the lead to be sold in Holland, but about half a mile off shore the ship – probably overloaded – sank, and Birnie was among those drowned.

Some temporary roofing must have been put up to replace the pillaged lead, but there is no evidence of slate roofing until 1607. Alexander Scroggie arrived as parish minister in 1621 to find the cathedral in some disrepair. In December 1638, he sold the north transept to the marquess of Huntly for 400 marks as a burial place for the peer and his family, and argued that he was forced to do this in view of the dilapidated state of the structure. Through 'iniquitie of tyme' and lack of money 'ane part of the fabrick and staitlie ediface of the said kirk of Sanct Macher is alreddie fallin doun to the geround, so that there is scarss memory of the samen'. As to 'the rest of the said kirk quhilk is yit standing with the stepillis and pricketis thairof', the cost of maintaining it was so great that the parishioners were unable to afford even to keep it water- and wind-proof; there was a danger that the building would 'uterlie fall in ruin and decay, to the gryte greif of all charitabill myndit christians within this kyngdome'.[3] 'As also the said marquess obliged himself to pay all the burial-lairs that should be interred in said isle, which should be employed for upholding and maintaining said isle. All which is done by a charter which the session hath in custody to this day; and upon the account it is now called the Gordon's isle. There was a dyke but six quarters high to distinguish it from the church'.[4]

However good his intentions, Scroggie's ministry ended in 1640 when he was deposed by the General Assembly of the Scottish Church meeting in Aberdeen. The assembly had abolished episcopacy in 1638, and deposed and excommunicated the bishops. However, Bishop Adam Bellenden of Aberdeen (1635–8) ignored the sentence and continued to preach and celebrate communion in the cathedral. With the arrival of a covenanting army in Aberdeen in 1639, the bishop thought it prudent to seek refuge in England. Scroggie remained at his post, refused to sign the covenant and was removed from office.

The assembly launched a dreadful campaign to eradicate every last vestige of the Catholic faith from Aberdeen. Crucifixes, images of Christ, the Blessed Virgin, the saints and other such religious symbols, were sought out and destroyed. The consequential orgy of destruction reached the nadir of triviality and absurdity when representations of the wounds of Christ and the instruments of the Passion were discovered on the tomb of Bishop Dunbar, and carefully chipped away by a mason. Nothing was spared. 'The General Assembly… ordained our Blessed Lord Jesus Christ His arms to be hewn out of the front of the pulpit [rood loft], and to take down the portrait of our blessed Virgin Mary, and her dear son baby Jesus in her arms, that had stood since the upputting thereof in curious work under the sill-ring [ceiling] at the west end of the pend, whereon the great steeple stands. The Master of Forbes caused a mason to strike out Christ's arms in hewn work on each end of Bishop Dunbar's tomb, and likewise chisel out the name of Jesus, drawn cypher-wise, IHS, out of the timber wall on the foreside of Machar aisle, before the consistory door'.[5] The rood screen was also removed at this time.

Scroggie was succeeded by William Strachan (1640–53), who began a substantial programme of repairs, chiefly by spending the funds raised during the time of his predecessor. The nave was re-roofed with new lathes and slates in 1642–4, and similar work followed on the aisles, the south transept and the tower. The north transept was also re-roofed, but presumably at the expense of Lord Huntly since it was now his family burial ground. The work was finished by 1646 leaving the kirk session deeply in debt.

Strachan did carry out one piece of destruction, admittedly at the instruction of the presbytery of Aberdeen, but tragic nonetheless; the tall canopied wooden reredos behind St Katherine's altar on the east wall of the south transept was taken down and burnt. The story of the destruction of the reredos was recorded as follows: 'Upon the 16th December 1642 Dr Guild and Mr William Strachan, our minister, began the down-taking of the back of the high altar upon the east wall… as high near as the ceiling, curiously wrought of fine wainscot, so that within Scotland there was not a better wrought piece. It is said that the craftsman would not put his hand to the down-taking till our minister first laid his hand thereto, which he did, and then the work began, and in down-taking of one of the three timber crowns, which they thought to have gotten down whole and unbroken, it fell suddenly upon the kirk's great ladder, broke it in three pieces, and itself all in blads, and broke some pavement with the weight thereof. Now our minister devised a loft going athwart the church south and north, which took away the stately sight and glorious show of the body of the whole kirk; and with this back of the altar he decored this beastly loft'.[6] The 'beastly loft' was a gallery across the west end of the nave.

Further destruction occurred when Cromwell's soldiers came to Aberdeen in 1650 and quarried stone from the chancel and transepts, and demolished the remains of the bishop's palace, to build a fort on Castle Hill. This probably led to the humorous comment of Richard Franck, who visited Aberdeen in 1656 and saw 'an old weather-beaten cathedral, that looks like the times, somewhat irregular'.[7] The work of Cromwell's armies is thought to have led to the collapse of the central tower in 1688 during a storm. The structural weakness of the central tower had been recognised in 1687 when the king's mason advised the construction of buttresses on the east side of the tower. He also advised that no foundations should be dug within five paces of the tower wall to avoid further weakening. His advice was ignored and the tower began to move. On 9 May 1688 the two cathedral bells were carefully lowered to the ground and moved out of the cathedral and as they reached the west door, the tower collapsed. Most of the masonry fell to the east on to the site of the chancel, but certainly enough masonry fell to wreck the north transept. The collapse of the tower sealed the fate of whatever remained of the chancel and transepts. The archway leading into the crossing at the east end of the nave was walled off at a cost of 2,000 marks, and the chancel and transepts were left to time and the weather. Lack of funds may have influenced the decision to abandon the eastern part of the cathedral, but it was not the age for costly church building programmes, and the reconstruction of a chancel and a central tower would have been superfluous to presbyterian forms of worship. The central tower is thought to have been 45.7m high; an engraving of 1668 shows that it had a saddle-back roof and three windows on each side. The same picture also shows the south transept complete, with its roof in place. The extent of damage caused to the south transept by the collapse of the tower is less clear, and it may have been minimal. In 1725 the authorities of King's College 'caused workmen to take down the top of this isle, to help build anew the south side of the college'.[8]

The collapse of the tower was not the only problem to afflict the cathedral. 'At this time, there was a beadle of this church called William Gall, who in the night time had sifted the ashes of the dead, to get rings and other pieces of gold, whom Dr Keith, then minister, severely reproved for so doing, one Sunday before the congregation; and it was observed that the said beadle never prospered one day after so unchristian an act'.[9]

With the restoration of the monarchy in 1660 came the restoration of episcopacy, and four further bishops ruled in Aberdeen. But the departure of King James VII (James II of England) in November 1688, and the expulsion of the bishops by the Scottish Parliament in May 1689, finally confirmed the transformation of St Machar's from episcopal cathedral to presbyterian church.

The nave of the cathedral has remained complete and in use as a parish church since the sixteenth century reformation, although in the early nineteenth century its appearance was ruined by double galleries which ran along its north, south and west walls. In 1814 the north aisle was 'ceiled', and in the following year galleries were inserted in the north and south aisles to match the 'beastly loft' on the west wall. In 1815, the two westernmost bays of the north aisle were walled off to form a meeting room for the kirk session. The north aisle was clearly causing problems and the 'ceiling' of 1814 was replaced by more drastic action in 1824. The external wall was raised and surmounted by a crenellation; the windows were heightened, and the medieval lean-to roof was replaced by a flat roof. At the same time, the session room was removed, and the whole interior was lathed and plastered to the approval of at least some observers. 'Being now plaistered in the stile of the building a very great improvement in appearance and comfort is produced'.[10] The medieval pulpit was consigned to the sexton's store and, in 1844, given to King's College Chapel where it still remains.

By the middle of the nineteenth century, the cathedral was in a poor state of repair and, in 1866, the kirk session called a public meeting to decide on its future. The meeting resolved to launch an appeal for restoration, but the appeal was stillborn when it was argued that any funds raised should be used first to pay off a debt incurred by the cathedral some twenty-five years previously.

In 1867 a report on the state of the cathedral fabric was prepared by Mr McAndrew, a local architect. McAndrew reported that the medieval roof was in danger of collapse and should be replaced; that the ground levels around the cathedral should be lowered and drains installed; that all walls should be repointed; that the glass in the west end, clerestory and south aisle windows should be replaced; that the galleries should be removed and new pews provided; that the room over the south porch should be removed; that the frame supporting the bell and the clock in the south tower should be renewed; and that measures should be taken to deal with the periodic cascades of water from the flat roof of the still troublesome north aisle; all at a cost to be £2,300.

Substantial repairs were undertaken during a fifteen-month period in 1867–8 and not all of it in the best interests of the ancient fabric. It was long thought that the work was done to the designs of Sir George Gilbert

Scott, but this is not so. Scott was certainly consulted and submitted a report, but before it was considered, the work of repair had already begun, and so had the work of destruction. Had Scott's advice been heeded, more medieval fabric would have been retained. He had recommended that the fifteenth century fir roof, from which the heraldic ceiling was suspended, could and should be preserved, but the contract for replacing the medieval roof of the nave had already been placed and, consequently, much of the backing of the heraldic ceiling, was lost. The ceiling itself was coated with varnish, and the heraldic panels, bosses and finials were repainted and regilded. Scott also advised that the transepts should be rebuilt and, if not, then the eastern wall should be taken down and rebuilt to the east of the former chancel arch, to expose and preserve the sandstone capitals. Scott's efforts were largely in vain, and a rare opportunity was lost. The only item of Scott's report that was implemented was the removal of the 1824 lath and plaster on the walls, to reveal the older irregularly plastered and lime-washed rubble surfaces. Scott recommended that this plaster should be retained, and it was for a while, only to be removed in 1928. The repaired cathedral was re-opened in September 1868. No further major work took place for fifty years, although a large window by Rowland Anderson was inserted in the east wall in 1884, causing damage to the already damaged medieval sandstone carvings.

Further restoration, causing the closure of the cathedral, took place during the early months of 1928, and the congregation joined with St Mary's United Free Church for a period of four months. The nave and south aisle roofs were re-slated and felted. Scott had successfully argued in 1867 against the removal of the old plaster; but it went, sixty tons of it, in 1928. The removal of the plaster has given the cathedral a rough, rugged and quite medieval interior, not unlike the cathedrals at Trim and Killarney in Ireland, but it manages to evoke a strangely warm feeling at the same time. Permanent choir stalls were placed near the east window, and the present communion table, a gift from the Irvine family of Barra Castle, was installed. The room at the base of the north tower was brought into use as the minister's vestry. In 1937, the east end of the south aisle was converted into the present Mitchell Chapel and, in 1943, when St Mary's United Free Church united with the cathedral congregation, their lectern and prayer desk were brought to the cathedral for use in this chapel. Anderson's east window of 1884 was damaged in an air raid in 1943, and replaced by the present triple lancets in 1953.

During the 1960s an ambitious plan to rebuild the ruined transepts was considered, and a restoration committee was appointed to superintend the work. The plan was initiated at a time when it seemed that the university of Aberdeen was about to double in size, and would need accommodation [presumably for ceremonial occasions] of a sort which an expanded cathedral could provide. The scheme was suspended in 1970 partly because the projected expansion of the university did not materialise, and partly because the rebuilding of the organ became a major preoccupation. The disbanding of the restoration committee, in 1977, was a tacit declaration that, at least for the time being, the plan would have to be shelved. Whether it will ever be revived at a more propitious time in the future is debatable but, unless a generous benefactor can be found, the time for such building work has probably passed.

In 1979 a successor scheme envisaged the demolition of the east wall and the construction of a shallow apse beyond, on the site of the demolished chancel. 'Only by removing this new wall, and the surround to the Victorian traceried window which still exists, can the beauty of the original be restored to its proper appearance and dominance. The objective of the proposals… is, therefore, to clear away all newer stone work, revealing the old arch in full relief as once it was, and to reuse the fine stained glass in the new and more suitable setting of the apse end. The apse provides and appropriate termination to the present basilican form without excluding for future generations the prospect of reconstructing the original cruciform church'.[11]

The estimated cost of the 1979 scheme was £475,000; within two years inflation had pushed it to £675,000. An appeal was formally launched in 1981, and by 1991, £500,000 had been raised, but the plan for the construction of the apse proved to be something of a pipe dream, and it was admitted from the first that it would require one or two major benefactors. As the 1970 plan had been abandoned in 1977, so the 1979 plan was abandoned in 1984, and the money already raised was used to fund a major restoration of the building as it stood. The work, undertaken in the decade 1981–91, including re-pointing and replacement of decayed stonework on the towers and the west front. The pews in the north and south aisles were removed in 1985 and the floors in these aisles were paved with new granite slabs to match those laid in the nave several years earlier. The removal of the pews has given the cathedral a feeling of great spaciousness and an indication of what it must have been like in the medieval period. The removal of the plaster dado in the north aisle revealed a walled-up medieval piscina complete with iron hook from which a water kettle could be suspended. The interior of the cathedral, including the heraldic ceiling, was cleaned in 1990.

As seen today, St Machar's Cathedral is the fifteenth century aisled five-bay nave of the medieval cathedral, 38.4m long by 20.4m wide. There is no substantial trace of the chancel which, with the crossing, was possibly 21.3m long, or of the central tower. The two ruined transepts can be seen, although their walls survive only to a height of about 3m.

The cathedral is built mostly of granite, like much of the city that surrounds it. As Sir John Betjeman had written, 'No one can go to Aberdeen and not become interested in granite'.[12] Granite is a hard stone and difficult to carve, and consequently there is very little evidence of carving on St Machar's Cathedral, and the cathedral is, in the words of one visitor, 'massive rather than elegant'.[13] Instead of shafts supporting the west door there are merely rounds and hollows; instead of elaborately carved capitals there are simple flat blocks, from which springs a round arch enclosing two pointed doorways. Under the round arch and between the doorway heads is a vesica-shaped niche with pedestal which may have held a statue of St Machar. Similar niches may also be seen in the west doorways of the cathedrals of Elgin and St Kentigern's, Glasgow, and are usually thought to have contained an effigy of the patron saint of the church. In the case of St Machar's Cathedral, also dedicated to the Blessed Virgin Mary, the niche may well have contained an effigy of the Virgin and Child. Aberdeen's Roman Catholic cathedral has what is believed to be a replica of the effigy.

Above the west doorway are seven tall, narrow windows, flanked by two towers with broach spires, each totalling 33.8m in height. The towers, almost windowless and with machiolated parapets, present an image of stern fortification. The armorial bearings of Scotland and Bishop Dunbar can be seen on the spires, but apart from this, the rest of the exterior is extremely plain. There is a south porch with crow-stepped gables and several niches. In 1968 a charter room was created in the space above the porch and this is approached by a wooden stair. A list of the bishops of Aberdeen is attached to the staircase; it begins in 1132 and finishes with the expulsion of Bishop George Haliburton in 1689 (although he continued to exercise his episcopal ministry to those congregations that remained loyal, until his death in 1715, and a succession of bishops has been maintained since that date). Among other records, the charter room contains a selection of the cathedral's medieval charters dating to 1383.

The Gothic nave arcades rest on simple round granite Romanesque-style piers. The tiny clerestory has a passage in the thickness of the walls, and the placing of the windows is independent of the arcade below. The clerestory is unbalanced with eight windows on the north and ten windows on the south.

The most impressive sight in the cathedral is Bishop Dunbar's ceiling, erected in 1520 to the design of James Winter from Angus. It is a remarkable heraldic catalogue of anyone who was anybody in Europe and Scotland in 1520, displaying forty-eight shields in three rows. On the north side are the armorial bearings of the Holy Roman Emperor, the kings of France, Spain, England, Denmark, Hungary, Portugal, Aragon, Cyprus, Navarre, Sicily, Poland and Bohemia; the dukes of Bourbon and Guelders, and lastly the city of Old Aberdeen, depicted by a pot of lilies. On the centre row are the armorial bearings of Pope Leo X; the archbishops of St Andrews and Glasgow; the bishops of Dunkeld, Aberdeen, Moray, Ross, Brechin, Caithness, Galloway, Dunblane, Argyll, Orkney and the Isles; and the prior of St Andrews (representing the religious houses of Scotland), and King's College (representing the Scottish centres of scholarship). The armorial bearings on the south side represent the location of power in Scotland: King James V of Scotland (1513–42), St Margaret of Scotland, the duke of Albany, the earls of March, Moray, Douglas, Angus, Mar, Sutherland, Crawford, Huntly, Argyll, Errol, Marischal and Bothwell, and the city of New Aberdeen (representing the burghs of Scotland). The shields, the ribbing, the applied leafwork and almost all the carving on the frieze is original. The scrolls placed beside the shields, together with all the visible lettering, both on the scrolls and on the shields, date from the refurbishment of 1867–8. One can only be thankful, if surprised, that the ceiling was spared by the reformers of 1560 and by Cromwell in 1650, presumably either because they could not reach it or because it was functional.

The west end of the nave has a gallery (which is not the original 'beastly loft'), and an unusual and striking window of seven lights occupying nearly the whole of the west wall. The glass is by Clayton and Bell and was inserted in 1867; it depicts Christ and the twelve apostles, each bearing an emblem of their martyrdom. The present east wall that blocks the crossing arch dates from 1953. It is pierced by a triple lancet window containing glass by William Wilson. The crucified Christ is shown in the central window, and on either side, the Scottish saints: Machar, Columba, Ninian, Mungo, Cuthbert and Margaret, with Andrew, the patron saint of Scotland. The north transept window, immediately to the left of the Wilson window, and the adjacent window in the north aisle are the work of Daniel Cottier.

The windows in the north aisle date from the period after the Second World War. The first two windows are by Marjorie Kemp, and the next three windows are by her

ABERDEEN: *The Cathedral Church of St Mary and St Machar*

ABERDEEN: *The Cathedral Church of St Mary and St Machar*

ABERDEEN: *The Cathedral Church of St Andrew*

partner, Margaret Chilton. On the north wall is a tablet to the Paton family. On the floor are effigies of an unknown fifteenth century canon, wearing an almuce of a style unknown in England, perhaps indicating dependence on France; and of Bishop Henry de Lychton (1422–40) who was buried in the north transept. A shallow arched recess contains the effigy, also wearing an unusual almuce and carved from Morayshire sandstone, of Walter Idill, the official of the diocese of Aberdeen, 1446–68.

The organ, in the north aisle, is a three-manual Henry Willis instrument of 1891, with forty stops and 2,170 pipes. It was originally installed in front of the great east window, dominating the church until it was removed to its present position in 1928. It was rebuilt by Rushworth and Dreaper in 1929. Further alterations and extensions were made in 1956, and it was rebuilt again in 1973 at a cost of £20,000. The 1953 font, a tapering cylinder of Aberdeen granite set on a wide circular granite plinth, is by Hugh Lorimer and shows St Machar baptising converts in the River Don. It formerly stood at the east end of the aisle before the organ, but when the pews were removed from this aisle in the restoration of the 1980s, the font was placed here in this prominent position. The plinth dates from this period and was the result of the advice of Lorimer himself. An aumbry and piscina can still be seen in the north wall.

In the south aisle is the present nineteenth century pulpit with a 1987 tester. The previous pulpit, removed in 1824, was given to the cathedral by Bishop Stewart about 1540 and is still in use in King's College Chapel; the panel at the back, which supports the tester, is shaped to fit the round pillars in the nave of the cathedral.

At the west end of the south aisle is the elaborate monument of Bishop Patrick Scougal (1664–82), showing emblems of mortality crowding in. In the same aisle, towards the west end, hang the colours of the Scots Guards and the Gordon Highlanders. The three east windows and the two small windows behind the organ, all by Daniel Cottier in the pre-Raphaelite style, were installed between 1864 and 1876 and are typical of the romanticism of the Gothic Revival.

The small 1754 memorial to the right of the embarrassingly tiny communion table commemorates William Strachan (minister of the cathedral 1640–53) who died in 1666. At the east end of the south wall is an unusual memorial, with bas-relief effigy, to Canon Simon Dods (d.1496), one of Bishop Elphinstone's administrators. Beneath it is a smaller memorial to Alexander de Rynd (d.1492), nephew of Bishop Henry de Lychton. Three of the windows contain glass by Douglas Strachan. Before the aisle clock is the Leslie memorial window of 1913, depicting the story of St Machar and his mission from Iona and illustrating three great building bishops; another, the Crombie memorial window, dates from 1908; the third window is a war memorial of 1924 depicting St Michael and the Dragon. The memorial tablets below were designed and decorated by Cromar Watt. They record the names of the fallen of the cathedral and of St Mary's United Free Church. The clock by Charles Lunan of Aberdeen, decorated in black and gilt chinoiserie, is a good example of a tear drop tavern wall timepiece and dates from 1765.

From 1799 until 1987, the cathedral possessed a solitary bell in the south tower. It was made by Thomas Mears of London by recasting two older bells which formerly hung in the tower. In 1987 a new peal of eight bells was added as the result of a gift, and re-dedicated on 14 November. The peal had formerly hung (from 1906) in the tower of St Stephen's Church, West Ealing, London, which closed in 1986. St Stephen's had suffered from structural problems which had begun before the bells were ever installed there. The south tower of the cathedral was dark, dirty and empty; there were no floors and nothing but a void existed beneath the clock and its single bell high up in the spire. A new floor and a cage of steel girders were inserted in the empty tower to hang the new bells.

Outside the cathedral, beyond the east wall, can be seen the ruins of the transepts and crossing, the main blocking wall of 1953 and two blocked Romanesque arches leading to the north and south aisles. Both arches have blocked doorways, that on the south showing evidence of much alteration, and each has jambs with weathered carved capitals. The much more clearly defined crossing piers, also with carved capitals, can be seen partly buried in the 1953 wall. The south transept, known as St John's Aisle, has the monument of Bishop Henry de Lychton and the tomb of Bishop Gavin Dunbar. The extensive graveyard to the south dates from the seventeenth century and is choked with tombs.

With the exception of the north side, where ground falls steeply away to the Don, the cathedral was surrounded by a walled precinct, known as the Chanonry, containing the bishop's palace (to the east), and the canon's houses (to the north and west), and the courtyard housing the choir chaplains (to the south-east). A description survives of the bishop's palace: 'A large court, having four towers, one in every corner of the close, and a great hall and chambers… On the south side of the close were an outer and an inner part; in the middle a great deep well. He also had a passage by an iron gate, from the lodging into the chancel… which was easy and convenient for him. This court also had a water gate to go to the water of the Don, and the ward, which was on the north side of the lodging, surrounded with a strong saill-dyke in which is the hay yard, yet to be seen... His garden was at the south-east side of his close, which yet remains entire, lying betwixt the court and the chaplain's chambers. In the middle, upon the west dyke, there was a summer house, three stories high; so that upon the top of it one could see the town and all the fields about it. This garden hath high dykes; and in the north dyke were several slits, which perhaps were made to let the good air of the garden come into the toosalls... The said court had an entry from it to go into the bishop's green, which was surrounded by a dyke on the north side whereof stood the bishop's dovecote'.[14] Nearly all of these have disappeared and been replaced by private houses. The canons' residences were pulled down about 1725.[15]

The bishops of Aberdeen also had a residence on an island in Loch Goule, now called the Bishop's Loch, about 3.2km from the Brig o' Balgownie. Some remains of the palace still exist on the island, which was reached by a drawbridge from the mainland.

Seen from outside, St Machar's Cathedral appears as a squat and solid little building with two overlarge and fierce-looking western towers, capped with short square spires that resemble straightened rhinoceros horns. Others have been enraptured by St Machar's Cathedral: 'The aspect of its western end with its noble window of seven lights, flanked by lofty towers capped by those quaint old steeples, is singularly beautiful and striking – more especially when glowing in the mellowed ray of the western sun... None but the veniest clod of the valley can be uninfluenced by the spell which binds one in the rapt contemplation of so fair a scene of which the fascination is crowned by the swelling music of the Don'.[16]

Whatever the opinion of the exterior of the cathedral, the interior is spacious, surprisingly lofty, beautifully restored, well cared-for, and probably more in harmony with its medieval origins than at any other time since the onslaught of the sixteenth-century reformation.

1 Orem, William (1791): p. 59.
2 Brogden, W A (1986): p. 94.
3 Stevenson, David (1981): p. 9.
4 Orem, William (1791): p. 63.
5 Walcott, Mackenzie (1874): Volume 1, pp 98-99.
6 Lindsay, Ian Gordon (1926): pp 22-3.
7 Brown, P Hume (ed.) (1891): p. 204.
8 Orem, William (1791): p. 62.
9 ibid., p. 109.
10 Lindsay, Ian Gordon (1926): p. 3.
11 Alexander, J H and others (1981): pp 10-11.
12 Betjeman, Sir John (1952): p. 23.
13 Botfield, Beriah (1830): p. 65.
14 Orem, William (1791): p. 66.
15 ibid., p. 43.
16 Addis, M E Leicester (1901): p. 51.

The Cathedral Church of St Andrew

United Dioceses of Aberdeen and Orkney
(Scottish Episcopal Church)

The expulsion of the bishops by the Scottish parliament in May 1689, and the consequent presbyterianisation of the Church of Scotland, could not deprive the Scottish bishops of their sacramental orders. George Haliburton, appointed bishop of Aberdeen in 1682, continued to exercise his episcopal functions in relation to those congregations and individuals who recognised his authority, until his death in 1715. The see of Aberdeen then remained vacant for six years until the consecration of Bishop Archibald Campbell (1721–4), and a succession of bishops of Aberdeen has been maintained since that date. The diocese of Orkney was added to the diocese of Aberdeen in 1857 and the two dioceses have been united under the jurisdiction of a single bishop since then.

The early records of the Episcopal Church in Aberdeen have been lost, but it is known that Andrew Jaffey was appointed parish priest of the Aberdeen congregation in 1716, which at that time worshipped in a meeting house at the back of the Tolbooth. Because of their Jacobite sympathies, episcopalians were forbidden by the eighteenth century Penal Laws to build churches, and the size of their congregations was severely limited by the same laws. The episcopalian congregation worshipped in a succession of meeting houses in the city for much of the eighteenth century.

In 1776 John Skinner (1744–1816) arrived to succeed William Smith in charge of the episcopalian congregation, worshipping under the dedication of St Andrew. Skinner, the son of an episcopalian priest who had converted from presbyterianism, purchased a house in Long Acre, close to the site of the present cathedral, and converted the two upper floors into a chapel that could accommodate 500 people. In 1782 he was consecrated bishop coadjutor to Bishop Robert Kilgour (1707–90) and two years later he participated in the memorable consecration of Samuel Seabury as bishop of Connecticut. It was an event that renewed interest in the Scottish episcopalians, still hiding in the shadows from persecution. Seabury became the first episcopalian bishop in the newly independent United States of America. After the declaration of independence in 1776, British episcopal oversight of congregations in the newly independent nation became impractical and undesirable. Seabury was nominated by his fellow clergy in the state of Connecticut to travel to England with their blessing and seek consecration as a bishop. Although received by the archbishop of Canterbury, Seabury was informed that it was not legally possible for him to be consecrated in England, because bishops were required to take an oath of allegiance to the monarch. The archbishop then suggested that Seabury might travel to Scotland and raise the matter with the Scottish bishops who, not being part of an established church, would not have the same difficulty as their English colleagues. Seabury accordingly journeyed north to Scotland to seek the conferment of the apostolic succession from the bishops of the Scottish Church. He received a sympathetic hearing and was consecrated in Aberdeen on 14 November 1784, by Bishops Kilgour and Skinner, and Bishop Petrie of Moray and Ross. The choice of the northern city of Aberdeen, rather than Glasgow or Edinburgh, was due to the position of Bishop Kilgour as the primus of the Scottish Episcopal Church.

Bishop Kilgour resigned as bishop of Aberdeen in 1786 and as primus in 1788; in both offices he was succeeded by Skinner. The new primus was quick to instil a change of direction for his church. Episcopalians had long, and rightly, been accused of Jacobite sympathies by their opponents. In some ways, the very raison d'être of the church was its loyalty to the Stuart dynasty after the overthrow of King James II and VII in November 1688, and the church continued to be loyal to the exiled king until his death in 1701. Their loyalty was then naturally transferred to his son, the de jure King James III and VIII (until his death in 1766) and then to his son, the de jure King Charles III. On 31 January 1788, Prince Charles Edward Stuart, King Charles III to the Jacobites, died. The death of Bonnie Prince Charlie, as he is popularly remembered, caused a radical change of direction for the Scottish Episcopal Church. The new Stuart 'king' was a Roman Catholic cardinal, Henry Benedict Stuart, styled King Henry IX. He was a bachelor and the last surviving legitimate heir of King James II and VII. The House of Stuart was almost extinct and Jacobitism was almost defunct. If the Episcopal Church was to survive, it had to break free from a hopeless cause. On 24 April 1788, three months after the death of Bonnie Prince Charlie, a synod of the bishops and deans met at Aberdeen with Skinner as president. The synod resolved that, from Sunday 25 May 1788, the clergy should now pray for King George III (1760–1820). It was a significant decision that cut loose the Episcopal Church from the events of 1688 and brought it back into the mainstream of Scottish religious life, and, some would say, in touch with political reality.

Bishop Skinner now had a base from which he could negotiate the repeal of the Penal Laws. With the bishops of Edinburgh and Brechin, he went to London early in 1789 to begin the campaign for repeal. Opposition was mounted chiefly by clergy of the Church of England working in Scotland and the archbishop of Canterbury was less than supportive of Scottish bishops; but, in a touching gesture, the episcopalians were warmly supported by many leading presbyterian clergy. Skinner remained in London to watch the progress of the repeal legislation until it was given the royal assent on 15 June 1792.

The Cathedral Church of St Andrew

After the repeal, a new chapel was built next to Bishop Skinner's house, where the congregation worshipped until 1817. The chapel was consecrated in 1795, and an organ by Samuel Greene installed on 5 August 1796 at a cost of £185 1s 1d.

Bishop John Skinner died in 1816 and the clergy of the diocese promptly elected his son William (1778–1857) to be their new bishop. The choice of a son succeeding his father was not looked upon kindly by Bishop George Gleig of Brechin, the new primus, who sent a stern reproof to the clergy. The gesture was fruitless and William Skinner was consecrated bishop at Stirling on 27 October 1816. Like his father, he served as primus of the Scottish Episcopal Church, being elected in 1841 on the death of Bishop James Walker.

The origin of the present cathedral church lies in the construction of St Andrew's Church in King Street in 1816–17, at the beginning of Bishop William Skinner's long episcopate (1816–57). The church was designed by Archibald Simpson, the planner of Edinburgh New Town, whom Sir John Betjeman described as 'an architect of genius… someone head and shoulders above the men of his time'.[1] The church that opened on 25 July 1817 consisted of the present nave, a small apsidal east end, and galleries on the west, north and south sides. Kennedy's *Annals of Aberdeen* described it as 'by far the most elegant space of public worship in the town'.[2]

Exactly five months after it was opened, disaster struck the new church on Christmas Day. 'Just as the Communion Service had begun, a most alarming fire took place in St Andrew's Chapel, King Street, which at one time seemed to threaten the total destruction of that beautiful Gothic building. The fire was occasioned by the overheating of the stoves, the flues of which having got red, communicated with the other casing, and from thence to the pipes which pass under the organ gallery for the heating of the chapel. On the first alarm, the congregation retired, without any accident; but by the time the fire engines were brought, the flames had burst out from under the organ gallery, and ascended more than half the height of the instrument; it is impossible to describe the feelings of the congregation driven in an instant from the most sublime part of divine service, nor of the immense crowd of people who had assembled on the street… The damage is but trifling in comparison to what was intended'.[3] Fortunately, the damage was not great and the chapel was insured. The 1795 organ was destroyed, but a new organ, by James Bruce of Muir, Wood and Co. of Edinburgh, was installed on 30 August 1818. When Beriah Botfield visited St Andrew's in 1829 he described the church as 'a new and elegant Gothic structure'.[4]

In 1861, the construction of another episcopal church in Aberdeen [under the dedication of St Mary] was under discussion. George Gordon, a native Aberdonian and at that time British envoy to the court of the king of Wurttemburg, urged Skinner's successor, Bishop Thomas Suther (1857–83), to use the opportunity to launch an appeal for £10,000, to build a cathedral, and to employ George Edmund Street as the architect. 'The right moment appears to have arrived for urging upon your lordship… the absolute necessity… of an appropriately planned and adequately sized and dignified church, to serve as the mother church of the Aberdeen diocese, and the idea of adding to the plan and funds subscribed for St Mary's Church, so much as would be requisite, in order to give the contemplated edifice the type and size of a cathedral church'.[5] The suggestion appears not to have been seriously considered at that time and St Andrew's remained the mother church of the diocese. Being free of all debts, it was solemnly consecrated on 23 August 1864.

In 1871, the 1818 organ was rebuilt and enlarged to three manuals by Bryceson of London. Bishop Suther preached at the first service at which this 'new and powerful organ' was played and expressed the hope that, now the organ was complete, the congregation would continue their efforts to carry out the original design of the chapel, and build the chancel. The bishop's admonition did not fall on deaf ears and, in 1880, the apse was demolished and replaced by a choir and chancel to the designs of George Edmund Street. To commemorate the consecration of Bishop Seabury, a new east window was inserted in 1884; the window survives but is now to be seen in the Suther Chapel to the south of the chancel.

The three galleries were removed in 1909. In 1910 a carved screen (also now in the Suther Chapel) was erected at the entrance to the choir. The west porch was added in 1911 to a design by Sir Robert Lorimer, and in 1914 St Andrew's was formally declared to be the cathedral church of the united dioceses of Aberdeen and Orkney. (The diocese of Orkney had been detached from the diocese of Caithness and added to the diocese of Aberdeen in 1857, probably because of the ease of transportation between Aberdeen and the Orkney islands.)

The proposal for a new purpose-built cathedral surfaced again in the 1920s, when plans were drawn up for the construction of a cathedral in Broad Street where St Nicholas House now stands. Sir Ninian Comper, whose father had been an episcopal priest in the diocese of Aberdeen, was the chosen architect. The intention was to open the new cathedral in 1934 on the one hundred and fiftieth anniversary of the consecration of Samuel Seabury, and it was hoped that the new cathedral would be largely funded by American Episcopalians as a memorial and thanksgiving. In 1929 the bishop and provost crossed the Atlantic to raise funds for the project but their arrival coincided with the Wall Street financial collapse which put an end to any prospect of substantial American funding. Their hopes of a new cathedral dashed, the two men decided on the enlargement and embellishment of St Andrew's to designs by Comper. The work began with the decoration of the north and south aisles in 1935. Work on the extension of the east end began in 1938 and was completed in 1948.

The charmingly domestic-sized Tudor-style facade ornamented with four pinnacled turrets is unusual in Aberdeen, in being of polished Leith sandstone and not of granite. Wedged between terraced housing, it deserves a better location. The other three external walls of the cathedral are rough granite and can be seen by walking through the side passages right around the building. At the rear is the John Skinner Centre, housing cathedral offices, and a small garden, inspired by Freda Darwent, wife of Bishop Frederick Darwent (1978–92). The cathedral has no tower, though one was included in Comper's design for the proposed new cathedral in Broad Street.

Sir John Betjeman called the cathedral 'Aberdeen's best modern building' and described the interior in his inimitable way. 'You go in by a rather dingy entrance to a flat Perpendicular-style building...You push open the door and your heart gives a leap – there stretching away as in an old Dutch oil painting is Comper's superb renovation of the interior. Far away at the east end is a great baldachin over the altar in burnished gold with a spire like that on King's College Chapel. And beyond the gold of the baldachin, intensely gold in this blazing whiteness, you see the deep blue tints, the green and red of Comper's east window'.[6] His description is apt; the exterior, if not quite dingy, is certainly unpromising, and hardly prepares the visitor for the beauty of the interior.

The cathedral is a beautifully light and spacious building with high arcades and tall Tudor-style windows typical of early Gothic Revival. One can only be thankful that the removal of the galleries in 1909 has created such a beautiful space. The arcades have no capitals except where one shaft of each column runs up to meet the vaulting, which is plaster throughout the cathedral. The pews are modern and undistinguished. With the exception of the three eastern windows, the other windows have wooden tracery.

In the north aisle, the octagonal font, now sadly covered with white paint, is c.1865 and has the emblems of the four evangelists. On the west wall is a monument to Lieutenant Colonel R W T Gordon (d.1885) with standing figures by Stevens of Bayswater. The flags include one of American combat regiments presented by President Eisenhower, and one of the Episcopal Church in the United States of America. At the east end of the north aisle is the Lady Chapel; the reredos is by Sir Robert Lorimer (1917) and the modern Madonna by Maxime Duff. The ceiling of the aisle was decorated in 1935 with the arms of the (then) forty-eight states comprising the United States of America (Alaska and Hawaii were admitted to the union in 1959, but not to the north aisle of St Andrew's Cathedral, Aberdeen). They appear, in angel-held wreaths, in alphabetical order, eight to each bay. On the wall can be seen a fabric memorial in the shape of a mitre. It was presented by Bishop Frederick Darwent on his retirement as bishop of Aberdeen and Orkney in 1992, and was worked by his wife.

The ceiling of the south aisle is decorated with the arms of the forty-eight families who remained loyal to the Episcopal Church during the eighteenth century, when the Penal Laws were most fiercely implemented. With only five bays available, eight extra shields have been slipped in at the east end of each. In the south aisle is a memorial window to William Browning, second parish priest to the congregation of the new chapel, who died in 1843. At the west end stands a statue of Bishop John Skinner by Flaxman. Behind is a plaque brought from the previous church and recording its consecration by him in 1795.

The brass lectern is dated 1889. In the chancel are the choir stalls with the chapter stalls at each end, all undistinguished nineteenth century Gothic in style. The throne and prebendal stalls are labelled as follows:

High Altar

The Cathedra	
S. Drostan	S. Machar
S. Magnus	S. Kentigern
S. Moluag	S. Ninian
[5 unlabelled stalls]	[5 unlabelled stalls]
Samuel Seabury	John Skinner
S. Ternan	S. Nicholas

The chancel vault has large star ornaments with more royal and episcopal armorial bearings. The arms of the diocese of Connecticut can be seen over the Seabury stall on the north side. On the ceiling are the arms of King George VI, Queen Elizabeth, and Frederic Deane, who was bishop of Aberdeen and Orkney (1917–43) at the time of the extension to the chancel.

Betjeman's gasp at his first sight of the sanctuary is understandable. Everything here is dominated by the great gilded Comper baldachino, with its golden columns and surmounting 'crown'. Behind the baldachino is the 1942 east window of blue and yellow, with a majestas at the apex. The glass was given by Harry Jackson King of Auchenhove in memory of his wife. The window shows the Blessed Virgin Mary at the Annunciation, escorted by an angel carrying a shield emblazoned with the national flag of the United States of America. To the north of the high altar is the foundation stone of the Seabury Memorial laid in 1938 by the American Ambassador, Joseph Kennedy. The ambassador was accompanied by his twenty-one year old son, John, later president of the United States (1961–3).

The Suther Chapel, on the south side of the chancel, is named after Bishop Thomas Suther (1857–83). The chapel is entered through Sir Robert Lorimer's 1909 chancel screen; it was moved here in 1963 and had to be folded to fit the narrower width of the chapel entrance. The chapel window is the Seabury Centenary window, formerly (1884–1938) the east window of the chancel; it was removed here as part of Comper's redecoration. The altar mensa dates from 1880 and was made free-standing in 1976 when the chapel was redesigned. The blessed sacrament and holy oils are reserved here.

The organ is located in a special chamber on the north side of the chancel. Plans were made for a new organ in 1964, but insufficient funds were raised, and minor work was carried out in 1970. The organ was rebuilt again in 1984 by Hill, Norman and Beard.

Those who pass by St Andrew's Cathedral could mistake it for a fairly ordinary commonplace church, because the exterior, although pleasing, is not outstanding. Archibald Simpson's facade is there to conceal and protect the glory of Ninian Comper's interior; those who see it will not easily forget its beauty.

1 Betjeman, Sir John (1952): p 28.
2 Kennedy, William (1818).
3 Morrisson, H R & Turbet, R B (1981).
4 Botfield, Beriah (1830): p.66.
5 Gordon, George (1861).
6 Betjeman, Sir John (1952): p.21.

The Cathedral Church of St Mary of the Assumption

Diocese of Aberdeen
(Roman Catholic Church)

In August 1560, the Scottish Parliament formally abolished the authority of the pope in Scotland, adopted a reformed confession of faith and forbade the celebration of the mass. Officially, that was the end of the Roman Catholic Church in Scotland; but the real situation was very different and not dissimilar to that in England and Ireland. The church simply went underground and maintained a furtive but continuous existence until such times as Roman Catholics could again worship openly. A number of priests refused to adopt the reformed confession and continued to celebrate the mass according to the pre-reformation liturgy. Before their numbers had died out in the early seventeenth century, they were joined by the Jesuits, and the thread of Catholicism, in Scotland and especially in Aberdeen, remained unbroken.

There is evidence of a regular series of priests in charge of the Roman Catholics of Aberdeen from 1687. From 1694 a temporary hierarchy came into place for Scotland's Roman Catholics. Initially there was one vicar apostolic (a bishop without residential see), then two (from 1727), one for the so-called Lowland District, and one for the so-called Highland District. In 1827 these two districts were divided into three – the Northern District (which subsequently became the diocese of Aberdeen with the addition of Kincardineshire), the Eastern District (being largely what remained of the Lowland District) and the Western District (being the former Highland District with the addition of Glasgow and Galloway).

Two chapels, one staffed by the Jesuits, were in existence through most of the eighteenth century. In 1772 Bishop James Grant bought two houses and a garden at Justice Port on which St Peter's Church and presbytery now stand, and this was the bishop's principal chapel until the consecration of the present cathedral in 1860. The new chapel was opened in 1782 and after the suppression of the Jesuits it became the only Catholic church in Aberdeen. The chapel was within the area of the present presbytery, part of which was demolished in 1804 in order to build the present St Peter's Church. Here, on 19 August 1804, was celebrated the first sung high mass in Scotland since the sixteenth century reformation.

St Peter's Church was primarily the work of the remarkable Charles Gordon, ordained in the old chapel in 1795, and parish priest of Aberdeen for sixty years until his death in 1855. Beriah Botfield visited Aberdeen in

1829 and spoke of 'the few Catholics sprinkled away among the population, creep quietly to their secluded altar in a dingy alley'.[1] St Peter's has hardly changed since Botfield's description, although the alley is perhaps less dingy than it was in Botfield's day. Designed by James Massie in 1803, it was extended by Harry Leith in 1814 and can still be seen, discreetly hiding in Chapel Court off Justice Street, and entered through the gateway of a tenement of 1843.

The growth of the Catholic population of Aberdeen during the first half of the nineteenth century demanded a much larger church, but no one wanted to tackle the issue while Charles Gordon was still alive, since it would have meant the abandonment of St Peter's, the church that he had built. After his death in 1855, the way became clear to build a new and much larger church on a different site.

A new site was acquired in Huntly Street, and construction of the new church began in 1858 to the designs of Alexander Ellis. The site was that of a former episcopalian chapel dedicated to Saint John the Evangelist, which probably accounts for one of the main side altars in the present cathedral being dedicated to that saint. The body of the church was complete in 1860, and the tower and spire were added in 1876–7 by Ellis' partner, Robert G. Wilson. It was not generally thought of as a pro-cathedral until after the death of Bishop James Kyle in 1869, when his successor came to live in the city. It became a full cathedral in 1878 when Pope Leo XIII re-established a hierarchy of bishops, and the vicar apostolic of the Northern District became the bishop of Aberdeen.

The style of the cathedral is Decorated Gothic. The plan is basically rectangular with an aisled nave and chancel and a tower and spire at the north west. The indented 'stepping' of the west front accommodates the building to the curve of Huntly Street. The slender granite tower with a recessed belfry and spire is 60.9m high and top-heavy with ornamentation. The tower is boldly inscribed 'J N AD1876'. This refers to Bishop John Macdonald who, before his transfer from a titular see to the restored bishopric of Aberdeen, had the title 'Bishop of Nicopolis'. The spire is clumsily cluttered with heavy ornamentation, as though the architect, restrained at lower levels, was unleashed on the spire.

The original interior was quite plain. There were four altars; the high altar dedicated to Our Lady of the Assumption, flanked by the altars of St John the Evangelist and St Patrick at the end of each aisle, and the altar of St Joseph on the ground floor of the tower, used as the mortuary chapel. A wall painting, illustrative of the dedication of each altar could be seen above. Over the high altar, the painting of the Assumption of the Blessed Virgin measured 15.2m by 4.5m.

In 1874 William Stopani was appointed parish priest, and in his twenty years' incumbency he did much to adorn the interior of the church which was still largely an empty shell. He completed the spire and installed a carillon of bells at a cost of £1,200, erected a reredos, opened the rose window, adorned the sanctuary arch with a rood, paved the floor with marble, lined the walls with statues, and filled every window with stained glass. The reredos, supplied by Mayer of Munich, was an elaborate arched and pinnacled affair, of a standardised kind typical in the second half of the nineteenth century.

The cathedral today is probably only slightly less plain than it was in its original state, due to a reordering in the period 1957–60, during the episcopate of Bishop Francis Walsh (1951–63). The word 'gutting' would perhaps be better description of Bishop Walsh's 'reordering'. Much of Stopani's work was swept away in a frenzy of destruction that would have done credit to John Knox. The central aisle was widened by cutting down the length of the pews. The high altar, reredos, rood screen and statues were removed. The stained glass was removed from the clerestory. The reredos was dismantled and largely destroyed, with the exception of the carved angels and saints which were scattered, some being taken to Pluscarden Priory. It has been alleged that the monks eventually used most of them to make a rockery,[2] although no trace of them has been seen in recent years. Other pieces of the discarded reredos were fitted into part of an interior wall. Amid such savagery, it is a wonder that the stained glass of the east and west windows was allowed to survive. Very considerable hurt was caused to the congregation by the extent of the destruction, though some later remembered the building to have been dark and dingy.

The interior of the cathedral is now exceptionally plain, though not quite as grimly austere as it must have been in 1960. There seems to be little doubt that responsibility can be laid squarely at the door of Bishop Walsh. References to 'the bishop's overall plan' and 'the bishop's vision' and 'the bishop's attempt to make the cathedral what it ought to be', seem to point the accusing finger at the prelate. What possessed him to allow such architectural destruction is unclear. Statements at the time refer to the cathedral now being 'what it ought to be: that is a building, the first and basic function of which is as a shelter for a worshipping community gathered round an altar'. Later statements sought to promote the changes to the cathedral as 'the first, anywhere in the British Isles, to anticipate the liturgical reforms of the Second Vatican Council'. Both statements sound hollow and unconvincing and there is some evidence that recent embellishments for the one hundred and twenty-fifth anniversary in 1985, have tried to undo some of the damage done by Bishop Walsh. One observer described the interior as 'so bare that it might almost conform to the austere requirements of "the sanctified bends of the bow"… [a reference to] an extremely strict Calvinist sect from the West Bow of Edinburgh'.[3]

Bishop Walsh himself came to an unusual end. He resigned in 1963 after refusing to dismiss his housekeeper, Mrs Mackenzie, who was the estranged wife of a Church of Scotland minister. Bishop Walsh was the victim of his own charity, in giving her a home when she had nowhere else to go, and he repeatedly quoted the passage from scripture, 'I was homeless and you took me in'. This evangelical trait was characteristic of Bishop Walsh and, linked as it was to a rather determined individual, it led him to act in a manner that was regarded as imprudent at the time. The times were not as ecumenical as they are today, and there was considerable scandal in a Roman Catholic bishop encouraging the wife of a presbyterian minister to 'turn to Rome', leave him and her children, and find refuge under his roof. Bishop Walsh died in Grantham, Lincolnshire in 1974 and is buried there.

The cathedral today is a hybrid – an exterior from the 1850s and an interior from the 1950s. The seven bay aisled nave has a clerestory of three lights above each bay, and Gothic arcades resting on plain heptagonal columns without capitals, bases or plinths. The aisle walls, painted blue, have lean-to roofs supported by a network of struts, and dormer windows. In 1985 the spandrels of the nave arcades were embellished with six low reliefs (three on each side) by Ann Davidson illustrating incidents in the life of the Blessed Virgin Mary. Although good of their kind, they are small, and lost in the surrounding acres of magnolia paint. Beneath the centre relief on each arcade are the armorial bearings of Pope John Paul II (north side) and those of Bishop Mario Conti (south side). These were commissioned by Bishop Conti and made possible by various donations, including one from the bishop himself in memory of his parents, the one immediately above his armorial bearings.

The oak-panelled chancel has the bishop's throne against the east wall. It was formerly backed by a red curtain but, since the changes of 1985, this has been replaced by a tapestry by Fiona Forsyth, depicting various scenes from the life of the diocese, including an oil rig, a distillery, a harbour, a sheep, fields and heather moorland. The eagle is from the bishop's coat of arms and on its breast are three intertwined salmon from the seal of the diocese. On either side of the throne are chapter stalls. A row of shields on the chancel panelling displays the armorial bearings of former bishops of the diocese. Above the throne and below the rose window is a fibre glass rood, the work of Charles Blakeman. The ambo and the lectern are open iron frames. The 1960 altar is of Norwegian granite. This bare structure, resting on three pillars, is allowed a short tapestry superfrontal, also by Fiona Forsyth. The chapter stalls are labelled as follows:

B.V.M. de Aberdonia	B.V.M. Assumpta
S. Joseph	S. Andreas
S. Margarita	S. Clemens
S. Nicolaus	S. Columba
S. Macarius	S. Joannes Ogilbeus

To the south of the high altar is the chapel of St Nicholas, formerly the chapel of St Patrick, housing the City Patrons' altar. The painting above, by Felix McCullough, depicts Saints Andrew, Machar, Clement, Nicholas and Margaret, all of them patrons of Aberdeen or Scotland. A frontal conceals the altar behind which is a carving of the Last Supper that, amazingly, survived the destruction of 1957–60. To the north of the high altar is the chapel of the Blessed Sacrament, formerly the chapel of St John the Evangelist; here again the original altar survived Bishop Walsh. The painting of Christ, in which the Lord resembles an Anglo–Saxon king (in fact the likeness of Bishop Walsh), is also by Felix McCullough, The chapel has a modern brass tabernacle, and a brass standard sanctuary lamp. Above the altar is a curved canopy with representations of various eucharistic themes: a dove, loaves and fishes, a monstrance, a pelican feeding its young, and wheat and grapes.

The McCullough paintings were originally in reverse position, the one of the seated Christ in the south aisle and the patrons in the north aisle. Closer examination of the way in which the artist has painted the shadows indicates that they were intended for their original positions and not where they are now. The reason for the change was that the Blessed Sacrament altar – originally intended to be in the south aisle – was later moved for the convenience of the clergy to the side nearest the presbytery.

The iron-balustraded west gallery houses the organ, with elaborately painted pipes, another survivor of Bishop Walsh; it was built in 1887 by James Connacher of Huddersfield. Minor changes to the specification were made in 1978, but otherwise the organ is much as Connacher built it. The two halves of the organ flank the west window which depicts the fifteen mysteries of the rosary. Beneath the gallery is the shrine to St John

Ogilvie, with engraved glass by David Gulland. It was erected in 1978 to mark the centenary of the revival of the hierarchy. A contribution from funds left over from the celebrations marking St John Ogilvie's canonisation in 1976 was made by the Scottish bishops. The grey-green granite font, standing centrally at the end of the nave, had a brass cover by Gunning and was placed here in 1978.

Along the wall of the north aisle are the 1969 mosaic Stations of the Cross by Gabriel Loire of Chartres. Angular, grey and sombre, they are fine examples of their kind and typical of their date. In their favour, it might be said that perhaps they depict the way of the cross as it was, instead of the contrived sentimentality of many nineteenth century examples.

At the west end of the north aisle, beneath the tower, is the former chapel of St Joseph. Once used as the mortuary chapel, it is now the Lady Chapel. It has a plaster vault and a statue of Our Lady of Aberdeen, a replica of the medieval wooden statue of Our Lady of Good Success, now in the church of Notre Dame de Finisterre in Brussels. There are monuments here to four bishops: George Hay (vicar apostolic of the Lowland District 1811–28), James Kyle (vicar apostolic 1828–69), John Macdonald (vicar apostolic 1869–78 and bishop of Aberdeen 1878–89) and Colin Grant (bishop of Aberdeen for six weeks in 1889). The other wall monument in the chapel is to William Stopani, who did so much to embellish the cathedral. All these monuments were found buried in the vault under the tower. With the exception of the altar and the stained glass, this elegant little chapel with its crystal chandelier and wall lights might at first appear to be the only surviving remnant of the cathedral as it was. In fact it acquired its present appearance during the earliest years of the episcopate of Bishop Mario Conti (1977–).

Attached to the south-east corner of the cathedral is the chapter house which is used for weekday masses. On the south wall of the cathedral, near the entrance to the chapter room, is a list of the bishops of Aberdeen since the foundation of the see. Some observers would contemplate the interior of this cathedral today with a sense of depression. Whether in the cause of liturgical change or, as here, seemingly on the basis of episcopal whim, the extensive and savage destruction of Victorian Gothic is inexcusable. In fact it is difficult to see how a bishop would succeed in doing the same today against the wishes of the congregation and of the many interested conservation groups. This was the view of many people at the time of the re-ordering. Others hold the opinion that in removing the clutter of Victorian Gothic, Bishop Walsh has left a cathedral with the clean architectural lines of its original design more evident and reordered in a way which makes it a joy for the celebration of the liturgy of the Second Vatican Council.

1 Botfield, Beriah (1830): p. 66.
2 Anson, Peter (1960): p. 260. [In a curious note of irony, Anson dedicated this book to Bishop Walsh].
3 Fenwick, Hubert (1978) p. 262.

Ayr

The Cathedral Church of the Good Shepherd

Diocese of Galloway
(Roman Catholic Church)

Ayr (with a population of 50,000) is a large busy resort on the west coast of Scotland, at the mouth of the River Ayr, from which it takes its name. The town is 55km south-west of Glasgow, and close to Prestwick Airport.

After the destruction of St Andrew's Cathedral, Dumfries in 1962, Bishop Joseph McGee abandoned Dumfries and moved to Ayr, and the Church of the Good Shepherd became the cathedral church of the diocese of Galloway. The church is the newest of the Scottish cathedrals in terms of its bricks and mortar, although St Luke's Cathedral in Glasgow is the building in Scotland most recently raised to the status of a cathedral.

The cathedral stands at the junction of Dalmilling Road and Dalmilling Crescent in the suburban estate of that name, beyond the racecourse. The area is now entirely devoid of any antiquity, but Dalmilling was the site of a short-lived Gilbertine foundation in the thirteenth century. Founded in 1221 and disbanded in 1238, it is thought that the community had no more than two canons at any one time, and never matured into the double house of nuns and canons envisaged by the founder of the Order, St Gilbert of Sempringham. The land was subsequently transferred to Paisley Abbey, but whatever monastic buildings existed at Dalmilling probably vanished at an early date; a charter of King James VI (1567–1625) in 1587 speaks only of 'the lands of Dalmelling with the mill'.[1] The ephemeral existence of the Gilbertine house was sufficient for contemporary newspapers to record that the church was being built on the site of the monastery and in his sermon at the opening of the church the archbishop of St Andrews and Edinburgh remarked that, if the tradition was true, they were bringing back to life 'an old-time Catholic centre of worship'.

Plans to erect a church to serve Dalmilling and the surrounding district had been considered since the end of the Second World War, but formal planning permission was not sought by the diocese until August 1954. The foundation stone was laid by Bishop Joseph McGee on 29 June 1955 and bears the inscription: *Ecclesiae Domino Nostro Jesu Christo Pastori Bono dedicandae auspicalem hunc lapidem die xxix Junii Anno Reparatae Salutis MCMLV Josephus Candidae Casae Epus rite posuit* [On the 29th day of June in the year of grace 1955 Joseph, bishop of Galloway with religious ceremony laid the stone of great promise of the church to be dedicated to Our Lord Jesus Christ, the Good Shepherd]. The completed church was formally opened on 22 September 1957.

The new church was the second Roman Catholic Church in Ayr and represented the fruition of the labours of the 83-year old Mgr Joseph McHardy, parish priest of St Margaret's Church, who had long wanted to provide the Dalmilling district with its own church. Although the church itself was professionally built, the surrounding wall was built by the voluntary labour of the parishioners themselves, who had also raised the £35,000 cost of the church.

For five years, the Church of the Good Shepherd enjoyed the status of an ordinary parish church. Everything changed on the night of Ascension Day 1961 when the pro-cathedral church of St Andrew in Dumfries was gutted by fire. A little more than one year later, Bishop McGee announced that the Church of the Good Shepherd would replace St Andrew's as the pro-cathedral church of the diocese 'until circumstances change and finances permit the building of a new Cathedral Church'.[2] The decision to abandon St Andrew's and Dumfries caused a good deal of heartbreak to that church and town, but the die was cast. 'The destruction was so complete that after much consultation with the various experts and authorities, the decision has been reached that its reconstruction is impracticable and too expensive. In addition to the high cost of building a church suitable for a Cathedral, is the fact that Dumfries no longer occupies the central position in the diocese, which stretches from Gretna to Largs and embraces the four counties of Dumfries, Kirkcudbright, Wigtown and Ayr together with the islands of Greater and Little Cumbrae. This consideration weighed very materially in arriving at the conclusion that a more central location should be found, but where was this to be? Many parishes in Ayrshire were mentioned and considered and finally all authorities, ecclesiastical and lay, came to embrace the choice of the one most concerned and on whose judgement all relied, as being head of the diocese; and the Good Shepherd Church at Dalmilling was the choice of Bishop McGee. Naturally the Catholics of Dalmilling and Ayr are proud of the choice'.[3] On Sunday 17 June 1962, the church of the Good Shepherd was formally inaugurated as the cathedral church of the diocese of Galloway by Archbishop Gerald O'Hara, the papal apostolic delegate to Great Britain. The decree of the Sacred Consistorial

Congregation in Rome formally approving the choice declared that Ayr should now be 'an Episcopal City until such times as a new and more splendid cathedral is erected'.[4] The diocese is still waiting, but the time for such a scheme is now probably well past.

There is really not very much to be said about an architecturally undistinguished church that is only forty years old and was never intended to be a cathedral. The Good Shepherd Cathedral is an ordinary church, built in 1955–7 of Accrington brick to the design of John Fred Torry (c.1910–80) of William Cowie and Torry, a local architectural practice. The builders were Findlay and Sons. The cathedral is typical of its 1950s date and much like the buildings of the surrounding housing estate. The exterior is utterly unassuming and, without prior knowledge, no one would suspect that it was anything other than a nondescript post-war parish church; it has no pretensions or ambitions to be anything else. Even the low token tower with its chimney-like turret adds little prominence or dignity. The contemporary clergy house is attached to the north-east of the cathedral; and a later hall was added to the east.

From the entrance vestibule a door on the left leads to a vestry which was formerly the baptistery. Three central doors lead into the nave and aisles and a door on the right leads to the gallery stair. There are two black marble holy water stoups. The cathedral is rectangular with low red brick Romanesque arcades opening into narrow little corridor aisles. Above the arcades is a clerestory with tall, narrow square-headed windows; all the windows have standard metal frames. The Stations of the Cross are of parcel gilt lime set within square recesses in the spandrels of the nave arcades. The ceiling is wide, flat and plastered. At the west end of the nave, above the entrance doors, is a small minstrel-style gallery.

Both aisles lead eastwards into small shallow transepts. The north transept houses the Sacred Heart altar; the south transept houses the Lady altar. Both altars are of blue-flecked marble on a green marble base with side panels of pink marble and mosaic work around the top. The Sacred Heart altar, its front bearing the sacred monogram IHS (Jesus), houses a tabernacle with a brass door. The Lady altar displays the monogram MR (Mary Regina) on its front. Above the altars are ceramic representations of the Sacred Heart and the Virgin and Child respectively, both set in fields of gold mosaic. At the east end of the nave, close to the Sacred Heart altar, stands the green marble font on a single cylindrical pillar

The Cathedral Church of the Good Shepherd

Interior of the Cathedral Church of the Good Shepherd

of the same material. It has a brass cover which, curiously, has a fastener enabling it to be padlocked shut.

Below the Tudor-style chancel arch are four steps of red marble, paved with white marble. The present appearance of the sanctuary dates from a re-ordering in 1985. Photographs of the previous arrangement show the altar against the east wall, with a large crucifix on a panel on the wall above, and a very high tester. The Gothic-style altar is of white marble with pink marble panels and red marble colonettes. The ambo is of similar construction. Behind the altar, against the east wall, is the bishop's throne, flanked by an alarmingly and incongruously grand set of chairs, presumably either for concelebrants or for the cathedral chapter; all quite out of keeping with the commonplace style of an ordinary parish church. Remove the altar, and the sanctuary could be constituted an impressive court of ecclesiastical discipline. Each chair is set against a low panel of pink marble framed with grey marble. The bishop's throne is set against a matching but much taller panel of the same marbles, with a large crucifix in the centre. The whole panel is set within a wooden frame on which are carved the instruments of the Passion. The 1985 embellishment was largely facilitated by the recycling of materials from other churches. The marble was acquired from the subsequently demolished Roman Catholic church of St Robert Bellermine, Glasgow. The stained glass windows on the north and south sides of the chancel contain glass from the Church of Our Lady and St Margaret, Kinning Park, Glasgow. The north window depicts St Ninian, flanked by symbols of St Luke and St John. The representation of St Ninian is modern and was commissioned for the reordering. The south window depicts Christ as the Good Shepherd flanked by the symbols of St Matthew and St Luke.

The cathedral is set in the middle of a post-war housing estate and could, on the basis of its external appearance, almost be taken for the tenant's hall; but the interior tells a different story. Light, bright, pleasant, warm, friendly and unpretentious, this is the epitome of the parish church cathedral.

1 Easson, D E (1957): p. 89.
2 *The Ayrshire Post*, 18 May 1962, p. 7.
3 ibid.
4 ibid., 22 June 1962, p. 8.

Birnie

The Cathedral Church of St Brendan
(Church of Scotland)

Birnie is now a quiet and secluded little village 4km south of Elgin, with a small and much altered parish church. However, for thirty years in the second half of the twelfth century it was the see of the diocese of Moray, and the small parish church that survives today was the cathedral church of the bishop of the diocese.

The early records of the diocese of Moray were destroyed in the conflagration that wrecked Elgin Cathedral in 1390, but the diocese is thought to have been established early in the twelfth century. A bishop named Gregory is first recorded about 1114, but without territorial designation; from 1124 he was styled bishop of Moray. He died sometime after 1127, but no further bishop of Moray is known by name until William (1153–62), during whose episcopate the see of the diocese was established at Birnie; it remained there for only thirty years until moved to Kinnedar c.1184.

The early history of Birnie is obscure, but it is known that there was a church here in the Celtic period, dedicated in the name of St Brendan the Navigator. Brendan (c.486–c.575 or c.583) enjoyed a reputation as a voyager and, according to a much later legend, discovered America. He is one of the most famous saints in the history of Ireland and founded a number of monasteries there, principal among them being Clonfert. But whereas his work in Ireland is well recorded, the story that he established a foundation at Birnie is not supported by satisfactory evidence, and is almost certainly legendary. Brendan's fame spread far and wide and the dedication of the church at Birnie probably owes more to reputation than to personal contact.

The church at Birnie is built on a low mound and may have been surrounded by a marsh at one time. The circular form of the old churchyard to the south of the cathedral (the extensions to the north and north-west are modern) suggests that the site may have been a place of pagan ritual in prehistoric times.

Although much of the structure of the present church at Birnie dates from the twelfth century cathedral period, the title of 'cathedral' is not used today. The final establishment of the see of the diocese of Moray at Elgin, and the construction of the great cathedral church there in the thirteenth century, permanently overshadowed Birnie, Kinnedar and Spynie and reduced them to the status of parish churches. There is now nothing remaining at Kinnedar and Spynie from the cathedral periods, but at Birnie, the building that was once a cathedral church still stands.

The church is a very simple small rectangular nave and chancel Romanesque building of c.1140, though much altered and repaired, and it is difficult to determine precisely how much of the masonry is original twelfth century work. The church does not seem to have been seriously affected by the strife of the sixteenth century reformation, but there is a long history of patching and mending in the ninety years from 1644 to 1734. A visitation by the presbytery in 1644 reported that, 'The kirk somewhat ruinouse, ordined to be repaired'.[1] Another visitation in 1647: 'The minister and elders ar orderit to repair the kirk and kirkfloore'.[2] In 1659, 'The church of Birny needs repairs and wants a bell'.[3] After the restoration in 1660, it seems that all necessary repairs had been carried out, as the presbytery was able to report: 'The fabrick of the kirk is in sufficient order for the present'.[4] By the early years of the eighteenth century, the church was again falling into decay. In 1710 'The minister of Birney represents that not only the Kirk of Birney needs reparation and that there is no manse there at all except some old ruinous walls'.[5] It seems that a manse of sort was constructed but nothing appears to have been done to the church. In 1731, David Dunlop, the minister reported a very sorry picture: 'that the church of Birney was in a ruinous state in the gavels, doors, windows, and other places, the roof like to fall down, the pulpit needs to be renewed or at least much mended'.[6] The presbytery agreed to a request for funds in 1732 and substantial repairs were undertaken in 1734.

The work included the enlargement of the three windows in the south nave of the wall, and the rebuilding of the west wall from its foundations, including the provision of a small bellcote at the apex of the gable. The work completed, it was reported to the presbytery in 1737 that 'the fabric of the church is in a very good order… There is a loft in the west end of the kirk, newly built by the poor's money, which is to be let for the benefit of the poor'.[7] The 'loft' was presumably a gallery of some description, which has long since disappeared; it may have been removed in the repairs of 1891. The alterations to the church appear to have taken precedence of the problem of the manse, about which Alexander Murray (minister 1743–65) was forced to complain in 1751. 'The presbytery consider the melancholy circumstances of Mr Murray, living in a ruinous house for several years and no probability of the heritors doing anything… the floors will not bear people to walk on them, the walls are failing and the roof such that it is thought dangerous to live under it in winter'.[8]

In 1883 the church was reported to be in need of substantial repair and a preliminary meeting proposed the erection of a new church. Further proposals in 1890 called for the complete renovation of the church. With the generous help of the dowager countess of Seafield, the work was undertaken in 1891 by A Marshall Mackenzie. The walls of the church were completely stripped of whitewash. The wooden plastered ceiling was removed, and the present open timber roof was installed; a moulded string course of dressed stone was inserted around the top of the walls inside, separating them from the roof. The church was refurnished with new pews and a new pulpit. The heating stove and chimney, prominently sited at the east end of the chancel, were removed and placed on the north side of the church.

Further restoration was first considered in 1955, and the decision to go ahead was made in 1959. The work, chiefly the restoration of the three windows in the south wall of the nave, was implemented in 1962–3. The three large square windows were reduced in size and given round tops, to resemble what was believed to be their pre-1734 size. The windows were designed by John Wright of Elgin, a chartered architect and also treasurer of the church.

A sundial on the south wall of the church is dated 1793. The birdcage bellcote at the apex of the west gable dates from the rebuilding of 1734, as does the Georgian-style west window although its arch-shaped lintel could be much older. A cinquefoil headed window can be seen over the priest's doorway in the south chancel wall, and a doorway in the north wall, only visible from the exterior, blocked in 1891.

The nave measures 12.7m long by 5.6m wide; the chancel is 4.8m long by 3.9m wide. The open timber roof was erected in 1891. The pews are pine and a small Walker pipe organ of 1970 stands at the west end. On the north wall is a series of memorials. At the west is a 1900 memorial to George Gordon (1801–93), who was minister of Birnie 1832–89. Then a crudely engraved tablet to another minister, William Sanders, who died in 1670 – this tablet is a pedimented plaque flanked by small engaged columns supporting 'winged souls' as caryatids – the inscription reads: 'Here lies under this pulpit the corps of Mr Wm Sanders Lait minister of this Paroch who decesed the 13 May 1670 and of Katherine and Elspet Sanders his children'. The wording suggests either that the memorial was formerly elsewhere and put here, probably during the restorations of 1891, or that the pulpit once stood at this point. Then follows a memorial to the seventh earl (1815–81) and the eighth earl (1851–84) of Seafield. Then one to Joseph Anderson, minister of Birnie, 1766–1808. Lastly one to Lieutenant George Duff Gordon, who was killed in France in 1915 at the age of twenty, and was a grandson of George Gordon.

On the north side of the nave, close to the chancel arch, is the font, consisting of a possibly twelfth century plain bowl, standing on a spiral fluted pillar with square base, both presented in 1885 by the Ecclesiological Society of Aberdeen, who visited the church in 1884; the pedestal is carved from Auchindoir sandstone.

The chancel arch is twelfth century and has scalloped capitals, and leads into a small square and rather dark chancel. Light comes from two deeply-splayed lancets, one in the north wall and another in the south wall, and from a third window above the priest's doorway. The glass in the last-named window is by Crear Macartney and was inserted in 1965 in memory of the Petrie family. The glass in the other window on the north wall, also by Macartney and depicting St Brendan, was inserted in 1979. The glass in the south window, depicting St Ninian, was inserted during the restoration work of 1962–3. Behind a grill, enclosing the south window reveal, is kept a Ronnell Bell, a Celtic saint's bell, 33cm high. An unsubstantiated story says that the bell is of silver and copper, was made at Rome and blessed by the pope. In the same enclosure can be seen a Spanish goat bell for comparison and a 'hairy' Bible of 1773 bound in undressed calfskin. Bishop Simon de Tonei (1172–84) is said to be buried beneath the floor.

In 1846, Samuel Lewis noted: 'About a mile east of the church, on the side of the road, is a stone called the 'Bible Stone', having a figure of a book distinctly engraven on it'.[9] This stone, a granite boulder, was later moved to the west pillar of the north entrance to the churchyard, and built into the low wall surrounding the churchyard. By 1882 it had been placed in its present position at the entrance gate to the former glebe field, north-west of the church, and now used as an extension to the churchyard. The 'Bible Stone' is much weathered and probably of Pictish origin. Other stones can be seen set in the churchyard wall.

Lewis also noted that 'in the corner of a field once called Castlehill, the foundations of what is supposed to have been the ancient episcopal palace were dug up about half a century ago'.[10]

1 Cramond, W (1903): p. 13.
2 ibid., p. 14.
3 ibid., p. 16.
4 ibid.
5 ibid., p. 17.
6 ibid., p. 20.
7 ibid., p. 21.
8 ibid., p. 23.
9 Lewis, Samuel (1846): p.129.
10 ibid.

Birsay

The Cathedral Church of Christ

From the town of Kirkwall on Orkney's Mainland, a road winds through rolling pasture, skirting the occasional loch, to the north-west coast of the island. Here lies the parish of Birsay, 19.2km north of Stromness and site of the first cathedral church of the diocese of Orkney, and enjoying the claim to be site of Scotland's most northerly cathedral.

Thus far, the story is straightforward but, from here on, it becomes complicated. The problem is that Birsay has two distinct sections; a village on the mainland, and an island a short distance off the coast, known as the Brough of Birsay. The word 'brough' (pronounced 'brock') is of old Norse origin and means 'island'. Of these two parts of Birsay, the island is ecclesiastically more interesting than the mainland. It contains traces of a Pictish settlement from the seventh and eighth centuries, a Norse settlement of the ninth to twelfth centuries, and a twelfth century church and monastery. The mainland village contains the imposing ruin of a sixteenth century palace of the earls of Orkney, a much-altered parish church and not much else.

The *Orkneyinga Saga*, a Norse epic written c.1200, tells how Thorfinn, earl of Orkney 'had his permanent residence at Birsay, where he built and dedicated to Christ a fine minster, the seat of the first bishop of Orkney'. Although this statement is generally accepted, a question was raised in 1958 as to whether the *Saga* referred to the island or to the mainland as the site of the cathedral. The issue is open to debate, but the remains of the church on the island indicate a building too small to have been an important minster and by tradition its dedication is to St Peter rather than to Christ. Thorfinn's Christ Church was built in the eleventh century, whereas most historians would date the island church to the twelfth century.

The site of the mainland village, at the head of the Bay of Birsay, has a stronger claim to be the seat of the earlier Norse earls just as it was for the later earls in the sixteenth century. The ruins of the sixteenth century earl's palace still dominate the village and the present parish church, not far from the palace, stands on the site of an earlier building known as 'Christ's Kirk', that was demolished in the eighteenth century. There is also some archaeological and historical evidence for an episcopal palace here in the sixteenth century.

The parish church on the mainland

The monastic ruins on the island

Whether the cathedral was on the island or on the mainland, the Brough of Birsay was a place of importance throughout its history. The island church and its monastery remained a pilgrimage site into the post-reformation era, long after Birsay had suffered political and ecclesiastical eclipse by the building of St Magnus' Cathedral at Kirkwall in the twelfth century. It is certain however that Birsay (island or mainland) was the see of the bishop of Orkney from c.1050 to c.1160, and that Christ Church, Birsay, was the cathedral church during that period.

The first known bishop of Orkney was Henry (who is first recorded about 1035), an Englishman, who was also treasurer to King Cnut. Little is known of him beyond the facts that he recognised the jurisdiction of the archbishop of York, may have been active in Iceland and may be the same Bishop Henry who was appointed by the king of Denmark to the see of Lund in c.1060–1. A succession of bishops is known after his time – Turolf, John, Adalbert, Radulf, Roger and William the Old, most of them little more than names – and it was during the episcopate of the last-named that the see was moved from Birsay to Kirkwall and the present cathedral of St Magnus was built to replace Christ Church, Birsay.

The Brough of Birsay is a small tidal island of 21 hectares. It rises out of the sea like an irregular-shaped cake with a sloping top, from a high cliff on the west to a low cliff of about 6m on the east. The island is separated from the mainland by a rocky channel of about 50m. A narrow, modern, concrete causeway can be used to reach the island, but this is only usable for two hours on either side of low tide. There is nothing on the island apart from the ruins and a population of seafowl and rabbits. The ruins themselves can be clearly seen from the mainland, and were largely unexplored until the early 1930s.

The walls of the small Romanesque church survive to a height of only 8–10 courses, except the north wall of the chancel. There are traces of two windows, in the north wall of the chancel and in the apse. The church is a rectangular structure, built of grey whinstone, consisting of a nave, 9.7m by 5.7m, a chancel and an apse. There may have been a square tower at the west end, but the only traces above ground are the stones jutting out of the west wall of the church on either side of the entrance, where the walls of the tower were bonded into the church.

A stone bench runs around the walls of the nave, and a few stone slabs in the centre of the floor mark a grave which contained a male skeleton in the remains of wooden coffin. On either side of the step up into the chancel are semi-circular recesses, possibly designed to hold small altars, the bases of which can be seen. The altar itself is a reconstruction dating from 1934. It may originally have been in the apse, but a cross-wall or reredos was inserted between apse and chancel in medieval times, and the altar was moved into the nave; a shrine may have stood in the apse. A large wall cupboard can be seen in the north wall of the chancel.

Immediately outside the south wall of the nave are

ABERDEEN: *The Cathedral Church of St Mary of the Assumption*

BIRNIE: *The Cathedral Church of St Brendan*

BIRNIE: *The Cathedral Church of St Brendan*

BRECHIN: *The Cathedral Church of the Holy Trinity*

CUMBRAE: *The Cathedral and Collegiate Church of the Holy Spirit*

DORNOCH: *The Cathedral Church of St Barr*

traces of the foundations of an earlier building. Some have conjectured that this may have been an earlier church, but there is no evidence for this and the building may have been secular rather than ecclesiastical. The church and its graveyard give the impression of having been arbitrarily superimposed on an existing pattern, and it may be that earlier buildings were demolished to build the church in the twelfth century. On the north side of the church are traces of the monastic complex. A range of buildings form three sides of a courtyard, with the church itself forming the fourth. There are no surviving records of the monasteries in Orkney and Shetland, so it is impossible to state which religious order the Birsay monastery belonged to, but the twelfth century date would suggest Augustinian.

The mainland village of Birsay is dominated by the ruins of the courtyard palace (built 1569–74) of Robert Stewart, earl of Orkney. It consists of four ranges around an open courtyard, with projecting towers at three of the four corners; there were entrances at the south and the west and over the west door were the initials of Earl Robert and the date of foundation. The palace was used only occasionally by later earls of Orkney. It was described as 'a sumptuous and stately dwelling' in 1633 and, as late as 1700, a visitor found it 'a handsome and stately edifice and the ceiling of the hall to have been ornamented by paintings from scriptural subjects'.[1] The palace fell into decay and ruin in the eighteenth century, probably a victim of disinterest and the weather.

The nearby parish church, dedicated to St Magnus, was built in 1664 and enlarged in 1760. The church is a plain and undistinguished single-chamber building with harled walls. Recent work on the foundations has uncovered evidence of a twelfth century church, and there are traces of medieval work in the north and south walls; but without extensive archaeological excavation, it is impossible to say much more. A re-used lintel, bearing the inscription SBELLUS, is set into the south wall as the sill of a blocked lancet (Monsbellus was a name given to Birsay in the late sixteenth century). A number of seventeenth and eighteenth century tomb slabs with rustic inscriptions can be seen in the churchyard. The church contains a late medieval red sandstone font with an octagonal bowl. A tomb slab dated 1645 is set into the floor at the north-east corner.

Birsay is a lonely place, and wherever Christ Church stood, it was surely Britain's most northerly and remote cathedral.

1 Sutherland, Elizabeth, Countess of (1807): p. 12.

Brechin

The Cathedral Church of the Holy Trinity

(Church of Scotland)

Brechin (population 7,500) lies 106km north-east of Edinburgh and 35.3km north-east of Dundee, on a steep slope above the South Esk. Its name is of Gaelic derivation – 'the town on the hill of the grassy slopes' – and the geography of the surrounding area supports this. To the north and west lie the Grampian Mountains, to the south Burkle Hill and to the east, 13km distant, lies Montrose on the coast.

The earliest history of Brechin is obscure, but it belongs to the group of ancient Scottish sees – including also Elgin, Kirkwall and probably Dunkeld – whose origins are *not* linked in memory and history to any notable Celtic saint; unlike Aberdeen which has St Machar, Dornoch (St Bar), Fortrose (St Boniface Curitan), Glasgow (St Kentigern), Dunblane (St Blane), Iona (St Columba), Lismore (St Moluog) and Whithorn (St Ninian).

The earliest reference to Brechin is an entry in the *Pictish Chronicle*, which states that King Kenneth II (971–95) gave 'the great monastery of Brechin to the Lord' in the year 990 and founded a church dedicated to the Holy Trinity. The interpretation of this brief entry in the *Chronicle* is now impossible to determine. The king may have founded a Culdee settlement, or he may have recognised and endowed one already in existence, but nothing is known of its subsequent history. The one remaining structure from this shadowy period in the religious development of Brechin, is the Round Tower which stands adjacent to the virtually rebuilt cathedral. When the diocese of Brechin was founded c.1150 by King David I (1124–53), the prior and members of the Culdee community at Brechin formed the first cathedral chapter. They continued as such until the thirteenth century when a bull by Pope Innocent IV, dated 1249–50, transformed them into a college of secular canons. 'The brethren who have been wont to be in the church of Brechin were called Keledei and now by change of names are styled canons'.[1]

The first named bishop of Brechin was Samson (1150–72), and a succession of twenty bishops is known. The diocese was never large, consisting of about twenty parishes, mostly in north Angus, and was comparatively poor and undistinguished in medieval Scotland. The cathedral was administered by a chapter of between eleven and fourteen secular canons.

The last papal bishop of Brechin was John Sinclair (1565–6) who married Queen Mary and Lord Darnley in the chapel of Holyrood House in 1565. John Knox delivered a typically grim and unforgiving assessment of Sinclair: 'blynd of ane eie in the body, but of boithe in his saule'.[2] Bishop Alexander Campbell (1566–1606) was appointed by Queen Mary and received the revenues of the diocese, but his ecclesiastical role was non-existent and his office was purely titular like so many other Scottish bishops after the reformation in the sixteenth century. Bishop Andrew Lamb (1607–19), who presented to the cathedral the chandelier that now hangs in the chancel, was a cautious and tolerant individual. Bishop David Lindsay (1619–34) was a favourite of King Charles I and preached the sermon at his coronation as king of Scotland at St Giles' Cathedral in Edinburgh in 1633. In the following year, Lindsay became the second bishop of Edinburgh. Bishop Thomas Sydserf (1634–5) was at Brechin for little more than a year before his appointment as bishop of Galloway. Of all the Scottish bishops deposed by the Glasgow General Assembly in 1638, Sydserf was the only one to survive until the restoration of the episcopate in 1661; he was then appointed bishop of Orkney and died in 1663.

Bishop Walter Whitford (1635–8) loyally read the liturgy prepared for Scotland by King Charles I and Archbishop William Laud of Canterbury in 1637. He did so against the advice of the Privy Council: 'He being resolved to serve the King in a time when other feeble cowards couched, would not be counselled; but on the Sunday following went to the pulpit with his pistols, his servants and, as the report goes, his wife, with weapons. He entered early in the morning when there were few people, he closed the doors, and read his service; but when he had done, he could scarce get to his house; all flocked about him, and had he not fled, he might have been killed'.[3] The climax was reached in November of the same year: 'Mr Walter Whiteford [sic], bishop of Brechin, upon a Sunday within the kirk of Brechin, using this English service, as he had often times done before but [without] impediment in that kirk, the people got up in a mad humour, detesting this sort of worship, and pursued him so sharply, that hardly he escaped out of their hands unslain, and forced for safety of his life to leave his bishopric and flee the kingdom'.[4] With the other Scottish bishops, Whitford was deposed by the Glasgow Assembly in 1638 on a series of false charges, including drunkenness, adultery, and possessing a crucifix. The bishop and his family moved to London and lived there in poverty until King Charles I gave him a parish in

The Cathedral Church of the Holy Trinity (early 20th century postcard)

Northamptonshire. He died in 1647 and was buried in St Margaret's Church, Westminster. In the year of his death, Brechin itself suffered from an outbreak of plague; about two-thirds of the town's population died within four months.

The restoration of the monarchy brought the restoration of episcopacy and six further bishops ruled in Brechin in the years 1661–89, apparently without controversy, though their role in the government of the town was minimal. 'The bishops of Brechin of the second episcopate... were just an anachronism. They may have been the least effective and the least important of all the bishops who came to Brechin right from the reign of David I'.[5] The comment is partly true, but it was probably true of all the other Scottish diocesan bishops of the restoration period, as much as of Brechin; and whatever their reduced political role, their spiritual and pastoral role was as important as that of their predecessors. Bishop James Drummond (1684–95) preached for the last time in his cathedral church in April 1689 before his expulsion.

Any account of the history of Brechin Cathedral and its architecture faces one great difficulty; it was virtually reconstructed at the beginning of the twentieth century, albeit in a sympathetic style, and little remains from earlier periods. There is known to have been a Romanesque cathedral on the site, presumably contemporary with the foundation of the diocese in the mid-twelfth century but, although a few carved stones were found during excavations in 1900–2, there are no substantial remains. The Romanesque cathedral was demolished, probably to build something bigger and better, in the early thirteenth century; and some parts of this Gothic cathedral survive today, but mostly enveloped by twentieth century walls and roofs.

Brechin Cathedral is dedicated to the Holy Trinity, and the consecration stone can still be seen in its original position on the outer face of the south wall of the chancel. As with other Scottish cathedrals, the fabric of Brechin suffered during the sixteenth century reformation. The chancel was abandoned after about 1580 and the chancel arch filled in to form a new east gable. The rood screen was dismantled and the pulpit set up in the middle of the south arcade of the nave. Galleries were first erected in the cathedral about 1608, and allocated to various trades in the town. The merchants' gallery was erected against the blocked chancel arch and the skinners had a gallery in the middle bay of the south aisle. The cordiners' gallery was built against the west gable wall.

Separated from the nave, the chancel fell into ruin and quickly became a stone 'quarry' to repair the churchyard walls. By the end of the nineteenth century the north wall was covered with ivy, though displaying the mutilated remains of three tall lancet windows adjoining the chancel arch, and the south wall displayed a single lancet. Some repair work was undertaken in the seventeenth century. In 1649, after several hundred years of coping with an earthen floor, the floor of the nave was provided with stone paving at a cost of £100. The remainder of the cathedral was paved in 1661 at a cost of £38.

The present state of the cathedral is due less to the gradual demolition of the chancel than to thorough 'restorations' of the cathedral in 1806–8 and again in 1900–2.

Although it is commonly used, the word 'restoration' is scarcely appropriate to describe what was done to Brechin Cathedral in 1806–8. The cathedral was virtually reconstructed and a considerable amount of medieval fabric was destroyed in the process. The transepts were demolished. The walls of the north and south aisles were demolished and then rebuilt to a higher level, enclosing the clerestory, making the aisles wider and higher, to enable a single roof to cover the whole church, and to incorporate a section of the round tower in the south aisle wall. The walls were covered with whitewash, a flat plastered ceiling was inserted below the clerestory, and galleries were erected in the north and south aisles and along the west wall. The blithe destruction of so much medieval work was accompanied by a suggestion that the Round Tower should be demolished to provide materials for the reconstruction. The plan was opposed by Lord Panmure who threatened to hang the first man to lay hand on it.

By the mid-nineteenth century, fashions had changed – the juggernaut of the Gothic revival swept all else aside and what had been done to Brechin Cathedral was viewed with deep regret; and the roof in particular came in for considerable criticism. David Black, the nineteenth century historian of Brechin, described it as 'immense, abominably ugly'. From the descriptions of contemporary observers, the work of 1806–8 was typical of its date and totally out of keeping with what remained of the medieval stonework, and gradually it became an embarrassment. One observer delivered a disdainful assessment in 1900: 'Although the present building forms a comfortable parish church, it is by far the plainest and least attractive of Scottish Cathedrals',[6] and 'plain, even to baldness... The galleries, still in existence, and the pews, of the old-fashioned narrow and high-backed style'.[7] The galleries had become the preserve of the town guilds of Brechin, and their fronts were adorned with the armorial bearings of the guilds accompanied by an 'appropriate' scriptural text of dubious exegetical worth. The town magistrates had the ten commandments supported by Moses and Aaron; the scholars: "the law was our schoolmaster to bring us unto Christ" (Galatians 3:24) and "now learn of me for I am meek and lowly" (Matthew 11:29); the glovers and skinners: "present rams' skins dyed red and badgers' skins for an offering" (Exodus 25:5); the farmers: "they that sow in tears shall reap in joy" (Psalm 126:5); the tailors: "the hand of the diligent maketh rich" (Proverbs 10:4) and "they sewed fig leaves together and made themselves aprons" (Genesis 3:7); the wrights: "the righteous shall flourish like the palm tree" (Psalm 92:12); the weavers: "my days are swifter than a weaver's shuttle' (Job 7:6); the bakers: "present a cake of your first dough an offering to the Lord" (Numbers 15:20) and "man shall not live by bread alone" (Matthew 4:4); the smiths: "the smith drinketh no water and is faint" (Isaiah 44:12); the butchers: "rise, slay and eat"; the shoemakers: "and your feet shod with the preparation of the gospel of peace" (Ephesians 6:15). An unassigned gallery acquired the name of the believers' gallery; it was located behind the pulpit and those who occupied it would not be able to see the face of the preacher, and therefore lived by faith rather than by sight!

All this was swept away at the beginning of the twentieth century. After a long debate on the question of restoring the cathedral, a much more careful and sympathetic restoration took place in 1900–2 to a design by John Honeyman, and the cathedral was re-dedicated on 23 April 1902. The work of 1806–8 was removed and everything possible was done to return the cathedral to its medieval appearance. The ruined chancel was re-built, and the nave and aisle roofs resumed their original form with clerestory. The transepts were a notable exception to the general rule of recovering the medieval outline. Those demolished in 1806 had been little more than shallow expansions of the easternmost bays of the north and south aisles, each closed with a gable pierced by a large window. An illustration of the north transept in 1790 shows a high broad window of four lights with Decorated tracery. Honeyman's south transept was a partly conjectural restoration of the medieval south transept, but the north transept was replaced by an outer aisle, and the aisle galleries were removed. The three surviving lancets on the north wall of the chancel were restored, but the wall below was so eroded by ivy that it had to be rebuilt. The missing windows were then added so that there are now five tall lancets on each side. Honeyman's humorous gargoyles are the great delight of this restoration and not to be missed: there are forty-four on the south aisle parapet and thirty-four on the north aisle, and no two are alike.

The result of Honeyman's work is attractive in the sense that Brechin once again resembles a medieval cathedral, but the destruction of 1806–8 has ensured that, with the exception of the two towers, the exterior of the cathedral is almost entirely early twentieth century. The nave arcades and the weathered west doorway are the only remaining thirteenth century work; the square tower is thirteenth–fourteenth century and the round tower is tenth–eleventh century. The rest of the cathedral is mostly the work of Honeyman in 1900–2.

The plan is an aisled nave, with chancel, transepts and north-west tower. The 21.3m high square tower was completed during the episcopate of Bishop Patrick de Leuchars (1351–83), although construction took place over many years, and the base of the tower, up to the level of the first string course, is thirteenth century. Construction to the level of the battlemented parapet continued in the fourteenth century. A note in the session books of the outlying parish of Methnot records that the vicar of the parish 'in his fulfilment of his obligation delivered to Patrick, bishop of Brechin, a large white horse, and also a cart and horse to lead stones to the building of the belfry of the church of Brechin'.[8] The ground floor of the tower is a 4.1m square room with a groined vault and three narrow lancets; it served as the chapter house before the sixteenth century reformation; it is now used as a vestry.

At the north-east corner of the tower is a stair-turret, finished with a high octagonal roof. The tower houses a bell of 1780. In 1974 a new floor was provided on three steel joists to replace deteriorating timber joists. The spire, pierced by four lucarnes, houses the mechanism of the cathedral clock and contains two small bells to ring the quarter chimes. The present clock was donated by the Town Council in 1974, replacing a similar donation from the restoration of 1806–8, which had deteriorated to a point beyond repair.

The main entrance to the cathedral is through the north porch, entirely the work of Honeyman, which leads into the north aisle. The cathedral is constructed throughout of a mud-red sandstone, giving the interior a pinkish hue. The five-bay nave is 25.5m long but the two westernmost bays are blocked to the head of the arches to accommodate the organ loft. The pipes have been positioned on either side of the fifteenth century west window which has Decorated tracery. The stained glass, illustrating the Te Deum, and showing prophets, apostles, martyrs, saints, angels and archangels, is the work of William Wilson and was installed in 1958.

The nave arcades have eight pillars and four responds, in an interesting mixture of octagonal and clustered styles, which is totally asymmetrical. The four piers of the north arcade are alternately octagonal and clustered, but all four pillars on the south side are octagonal. The two responds at the east end of the nave are clustered, but the west responds are octagonal. The four piers and the west respond are more slender on the south side than their counterparts on the north. The theme of irregularity is continued in the clerestory where the windows, with plain reveals surmounted by a trefoil-headed arch are, unusually, positioned above the springing rather than the points of the arcades. The stained glass of the clerestory is the work of William Wilson and was installed systematically between 1954 and 1961. The windows of the south clerestory were installed in 1954–7 and depict Saints Andrew, Columba, Ninian and Cuthbert. The windows of the north clerestory were installed in 1957–61 and depict Saints Margaret, Mungo, Drostan and Columba. The timber roof of the nave dates from the Honeyman restoration; the pews are pine.

The aisle walls are 1900–2 and, although lower than their 1806–8 predecessors, are still higher than the medieval walls. At the west end of the aisle is a benefaction board erected in 1683 recording details of the cathedral benefactors from 1615 1772; by its side hangs a modern benefaction board of 1953. Close by is a window with 1952 glass by William Wilson, depicting Adam, Abraham and Isaac. The second window is a war memorial of 1949 by Douglas Strachan, depicting Moses, Melchizedek and David. At the east end of the north aisle can be seen a late twelfth or early thirteenth century coffin lid. The stones include a heraldic stone – possibly depicting the armorial bearings of Bishop George Sherwood (1454–62), a nephew of King James I (1406–37) – and a ninth or tenth century Northumbrian-style carved slab, showing Mary and the infant Jesus (excavated from a garden close to the cathedral). The twelfth century stone font was presented to the cathedral in 1964 and brought back into use in 1978.

At the east end of the north aisle, a screen partitions the aisle from the north transept, which breaks the traditional symmetry of transepts. Whereas the south transept (both north and south are the work of Honeyman) follows the medieval pattern, the north transept is much larger. The 1900–2 restoration did not include the replacement of the galleries and, instead of building a copy of the south transept, Honeyman designed a rectangular structure (opening from an arcade of two bays) to provide additional seating to replace that lost with the removal of the galleries. The north transept has a hammerbeam roof, springing from carved stone corbels, which rises above the level of the north aisle roof. Queen Victoria died (in January 1901) during the course of the building of the transept and, in the erastian tradition of the time, it was named the 'Queen's Aisle' in her memory. The transept was converted into a side chapel in 1951 and separated from the body of the cathedral by the wrought iron screen. The chapel contains a modern oak communion table and lectern, and pine pews. The 1977–8 west window is the work of Gordon Webster and depicts a representation of the Magnificat flanked by Elijah and the Widow to the left, and Ruth and Naomi to the right. The two north windows by William Wilson date from 1955 and show the prophets Jeremiah and Daniel. The rose window on the east wall, illustrating the Benedicite, is also by Wilson and was inserted in 1953. The transept also houses a nineteenth century octagonal Aberdeenshire granite font, brought here from Brechin's Maison Dieu Church which closed in 1992.

The medieval chancel is thought to have been 25.5m long, but the 1902 chancel is less than half that length. The thirteen windows contain stained glass by Henry Holiday of London. The east wall is entirely 1900–2 and includes three lancets to match those on the north and south walls. There is a small closed arcade at the apex with three rounded arches, of which the centre one is pierced with a rose window. In the centre of the chancel is an early sixteenth century brass Flemish chandelier, given to the cathedral by Bishop Andrew Lamb (1607–19) in 1615. The communion table, altar and pulpit are of pale oak; the pulpit has two figures of patinated brass in niches. There is an indifferent brass eagle lectern of 1951.

The south transept was rebuilt much as it had appeared in old engravings, with the intention of placing the organ there; but the area proved to be too small. The transept was used as a baptistery for some years, and houses a disused brown-veined onyx font and also the pre-1900 communion table. The south window, depicting Jesus with children, might have been intended as vague allusion to the original baptismal purposes of the transept. There are also three memorials to former ministers of the cathedral.

In the south aisle the centre window of 1932, depicting the apostles, is by Herbert Hendrie; the flanking windows are the work of Hugh Easton in 1952, and also depict apostles. At the west end is a bronze Art Nouveau tablet to David Carnegie (1871–1900) with a bas-relief bust (Carnegie, an explorer of Australia, was killed in the South African War). In the south west corner the Round Tower projects into the aisle and displays a doorway formed during the 'restoration' of 1806 but blocked in 1847 when the tower was transferred to the care of the state. There is also a collection of old carved stones including the Aldbar Stone, a standing Celtic Cross with interlace work; and the Brechin Hogback, a grave cover with a Norse animal carving and heads of about eleventh century.

The Round Tower, so typical of Irish ecclesiastical architecture, is one of only two in Scotland, the other being at Abernethy. The tower is 26.2m high to the base of the conical cap, 32.3m high to the apex of the cap and 4.5m in diameter at the base. Standing at the south-west angle of the cathedral, it was built of irregular blocks of red sandstone by Irish masons between 990 and 1012, but the top is fourteenth century. The cap was blown down in a storm in November 1683; the session ordered 'a hundred marks uplifted which was in the cordwiners' hands for the repairing the head of the Little Steeple, blown over on the 5th day of this month'.[9] In 1839, an examination of the interior showed that six ladders would be needed to reach the top. The lowest ladder rested on an earth floor, but two of the ladders had gone, and the other four were rotten and decayed. In 1842 the external door, previously blocked with rubble stonework, was opened. The tower had long been used as a tip, and rubbish, which had accumulated to the level of the first corbel, was removed to a depth of five feet. 'The bottom of the tower … had served as a general receptacle for all the odds and ends of the several beadles of the church, and the refuse of the nests of the owls and jackdaws… which, from time immemorial, had built on the top of the tower'. In 1847 the tower was transferred to the care of the state, and the two small bells, previously hung in it, were moved to the spire of the square tower; new ladders and floors were inserted in the same year.

The tower tapers uniformly outside but the internal diameter of 2.3m is constant. The round-headed doorway follows the later Irish tradition of being 1.8m above ground level. A representation of the crucifixion, showing Christ with uncrossed legs, is carved at the apex of the arch. Figures are carved on each of the inwardly inclined jambs. That on the left holds a pastoral staff of the type peculiar to the Celtic church; the other has a cross-headed staff with an open book resting upon it. On each side of the door at the foot is carved a grotesque beast. The top of the tower is capped with an octagonal roof with dormer windows on four sides. Although the tower is closed to public access, the summit can be reached by a series of internal ladders resting on semi-circular wooden floors. Samuel Lewis thought the tower to be 'an object of much interest. It is a lofty slender column of very ancient character, and in high easterly winds is observed to vibrate in a slight degree'.[10] In 1829 Beriah Botfield criticised the fact that the tower had been joined to the cathedral in the restoration of 1806–8 'by modern masonry, with somewhat questionable taste or purpose'.[11] Although still physically attached to the cathedral, the tower remains in the care of the state.

The bishop's palace stood on the north side of a lane called Bishops Close, to the north-east of the cathedral, but nothing remains. Its foundations were dug up in 1771 for the construction of a building which was itself demolished in 1850. There were also episcopal palaces at Farnell and Fearn, and the bishop was additionally the parish priest at Cortoquhuy. The chapter houses stood to the north of the cathedral in what is today known as Chanonry Wynd.

Walking around Brechin Cathedral today, one can be thankful for the work of John Honeyman and for the way in which he lovingly, gently and successfully restored and re-formed this delightful mud-red rustic barn of a cathedral.

1 Easson, D E (1957): p. 190.
2 Lindsay, Ian Gordon (1926): p. 33.
3 Thoms, David Boath (1972): p. 102.
4 ibid.
5 Thoms, David Boath (1977): p. 86.
6 Addis, M E Leicester (1901): p. 33.
7 ibid., p. 34.
8 ibid., p. 33.
9 Thoms, David Boath (1972): p. 63.
10 Lewis, Samuel (1846): volume 1, p. 153.
11 Botfield, Beriah (1830): p.50.

Cumbrae

The Cathedral Church of the Holy Spirit, Millport

United Dioceses of Argyll and the Isles (Scottish Episcopal Church)

The island of Great Cumbrae is 3.2km west of the town of Largs, and part of one of three island groups in the Firth of Clyde (Arran and Bute being the others). Great Cumbrae (usually known simply as Cumbrae – which derives from the Gaelic meaning 'a bold or steep coast arising abruptly from the sea') is 6.4km long and 3.2km wide. One road, 19.3km long, circles the island, passing through the small town of Millport (population 1,500), which is home to the smallest cathedral church in Britain. The island can be reached by a car and passenger ferry from Largs to Cumbrae Slip. It has been inhabited since the Stone Age and was the home of an obscure reclusive female saint named Maura, perhaps in the sixth or tenth centuries. Her cell is thought to have been at Millport, on the site where 'The Garrison' now stands (see below).

The origin of Cumbrae (or Millport) Cathedral lies with the influence of the nineteenth century Oxford Movement. While an undergraduate at Christ Church Oxford in the 1840s, George Boyle (1825–90), sixth earl of Glasgow from 1869, was strongly influenced by John Henry Newman, Edward Pusey and others, whose teachings produced the Oxford Movement – a movement that radically changed the liturgy and spirituality of the Church of England, reminding the Church of its catholic heritage and its pre-reformation history. Boyle, fired with enthusiasm, developed an ambition to build a church and a theological college on the island of Cumbrae, which he then owned. He was the only earl of Glasgow to reside on the island and purchased a house called The Garrison from the marquess of Bute – this long, low, crenellated folly of a mansion can still be seen on the shorefront at Millport. It was built in the late eighteenth century and given a Gothick facade in 1819. The Garrison was one of five fully-staffed houses that Lord Glasgow owned in Scotland.

The cathedral church that was formed on the island of Cumbrae was the flower of a seed of the Oxford Movement, first sown in the mind of a young and wealthy Scottish undergraduate at Oxford and then transplanted to a relatively obscure Scottish island simply because it was owned by the young undergraduate. In 1848, still only twenty-three years of age, Boyle invited the architect William Butterfield (1814–1900) to reconstruct some buildings in the grounds of The Garrison to provide a private chapel for his mother, the dowager countess of Glasgow. Butterfield was the foremost proponent of the Gothic Revival style of architecture (the architectural companion of the Oxford Movement); All Saints' Church, Margaret Street in London, and Keble College in Oxford are among his finest works. The choice of Butterfield probably originated with his design for the new cathedral at Perth (for the dioceses of St Andrews, Dunkeld and Dunblane) in 1847; Boyle was a member of the building committee at Perth. The private chapel at The Garrison, known as St Andrew's Church, was more than a private chapel; it could seat eighty people and later served an Episcopalian congregation for thirty years. Boyle was so pleased with Butterfield's work that, in 1849, he commissioned him to design a college and collegiate church on a hillside site in the grounds of The Garrison. The church and college are now separated from The Garrison by the intrusion of College Street. The result was a church, two college buildings (north and south of the church), a chapter house, a refectory and an open cloister. The foundation stone was laid on 29 May 1849. The south college was opened on 18 November 1850, and the north college on 9 October 1851.

The south college, structurally joined to the church, was used from its opening in 1850 as the house for the provost and the residentiary canons, and for clergy needing a rest or time for study or writing. The small bell turret above the south college is a clear indication of the monastic nature of the College of the Holy Spirit (as Boyle called it); it was rung to indicate the hours of rising and retiring, and also the liturgical hours of prayer in the church. Stalls were provided in the chancel of the cathedral for the provost and for the four residentiary canons; and there were six additional stalls provided for honorary (non-resident) canons; three were to be nominated by the bishop of Argyll and the Isles, and three by 'the founder', as Boyle came to be known.

The primary intention of the foundation was 'the frequent celebration of divine service by a collegiate body under circumstances favourable to religious learning', and the college was to consist of five canons (including the provost) and seven choristers. A two-volume office book, entitled *The Hours of Prayer*, was published by Boyle in 1851 and confirmed his intention that the canons should adopt a semi-monastic existence. Not only were they to remain celibate, but they were to recite daily in the choir of the church the offices of matins, evensong, and the day hours of the breviary. Also in 1851 Boyle produced a privately printed document entitled *Primary Constitution and Statutes of the Church and College of Holy Spirit*, which prescribed in detail the life he expected of the community of which he was virtually the Visitor and lay abbot. 'The earnest desire of the Founder is, that the ancient hours of Prayer may be devoutly observed day by day, for the more abundant setting forth of the glory of God, and for the increase of personal holiness and a spirit of recollection among the members of the College. It is the desire of the Founder that the Offices for the Day Hours... may never, even for the shortest period, cease to be in use'.[1]

The community based in the south college would consist of older priests who could no longer cope with active pastoral work, but would maintain the daily round of worship, and young priests who would serve the church in the diocese of Argyll and the Isles and who would relieve parish clergy in times of sickness. Seminarians would be trained for work in the Gaelic-speaking districts of the diocese; graduates would attend for one session and others for two. Undergraduates would come there during university vacations to read theology.[2] From 1850 to 1853 the north college was assigned for the use of the choir school and thereafter as residence for the undergraduates and seminarians. Life was somewhat Spartan: 'In food let there be plainness and moderation; and let all members of the College abstain from the use of wine and spirits (unless the necessity of health require it)'.[3] Early rising was to be a habit; the members of the college were to be out of bed by 6.30am at the latest.

Perhaps the most extraordinary indication of what Boyle hoped and expected from his little community, was the impossibly utopian standard that he set for the choir. The choristers, as far as possible, were to be 'such as from their very infancy have lived in accordance with their Baptismal grace, and kept their robe of innocence unstained by grievous known sins'.[4] Punishment awaited those who offended. 'If any are betrayed into sin... some penalty will be added, such as confinement at the hours of recreation';[5] and a solemn ceremony of deprivation was prescribed for those whose behaviour was deemed to be serious enough to warrant expulsion, including the removal of the chorister's surplice by the provost.[6] For all the strictness of these 'school rules', there was a limit. 'The Founder need scarcely add, that in no case whatever may bodily chastisement in any form be inflicted'.[7]

All this was the realisation of the dream of George Boyle. He certainly had the money to bring his dream to fruition and, while his money lasted, so did his dream. Sadly, the whole enterprise, for several reasons, proved to be a castle in the air and there were problems from the start. The college never really filled the role of a seminary for the diocese of Argyll and the Isles, let alone the entire Scottish Episcopal Church, and its significance substantially diminished after the growth of the Theological College at Edinburgh. Instead it became a resort during long vacations for those studying for ordination and also a centre for retreats. During its seminary days, there might have been as many as seven or eight clergy in residence at any one time, with about 18–20 students. One of the resident canons served as the parish priest of St Andrew's, Millport, while the organist and his wife educated the 6–8 resident boy choristers, and this little cathedral maintained the daily singing of matins and evensong until 1885. The canons lived a quasi cloistered existence and the Cumbria Statutes of 1850 did not permit the provost or any of the residentiary canons to marry; not that the accommodation would have been at all suitable for a married priest. George Cosby White, the first provost, resigned in 1853 in advance of his impending marriage.

The early days of the college were also difficult because of the attitude of Bishop Alexander Ewing of Argyll and the Isles (1847–73). Ewing, who declared himself a loyal protestant, detested the Oxford Movement and feared that it would cause a flood of those sympathetic to the movement into his diocese. Argyll and the Isles was a newly-revived diocese and Ewing was determined to keep it firmly under control.

With the departure of Provost White to be married and to be vicar of St Barnabas, Pimlico in London, the bishop promptly appointed himself as the new provost of the college, with the agreement of the founder, in an effort to bring this proprietary church and college more under his own control. He remained provost until his resignation in December 1866. A severe attack of bronchitis caused him to go to the sunnier climate of Palermo for three or four months from the beginning of 1867 and, by then, Ewing felt sufficiently confident enough to surrender the provostship to the vice-provost, John Gibson Cazenove.

It was only in 1875, after the death of Bishop Ewing and the arrival of the more sympathetic Bishop George Mackarness (1874–83), that George Boyle, by now earl of Glasgow, gave the church, the college and an endowment, to a body of trustees to hold the property on behalf of the Scottish Episcopal Church. Subsequent events were to prove that the terms of the endowment did not guarantee the site; but with ownership now belonging to the Church, the way was now clear to elevate the status of Cumbrae, and to provide the diocese of Argyll and the Isles with what it lacked – a cathedral church.

On 3 May 1876, the collegiate church of the Holy Spirit was solemnly consecrated as the cathedral church of the diocese of the Isles and the pro-cathedral church of the diocese of Argyll. Although the two dioceses had been united since 1819, the heady constructionist and expansionist days of the mid-nineteenth century gave rise to the expectation that the unions of dioceses would eventually be dissolved, and that a separate cathedral would be provided for the diocese of Argyll in due course. Although construction of a cathedral at Oban was eventually begun, membership of the Episcopal Church in this far-flung diocese has always been small, and the separation of the Isles from Argyll has never been a serious possibility. In 1920 St John's Church, Oban was declared the cathedral church of diocese of Argyll, and Bishop Kenneth Mackenzie intended that it should replace Cumbrae, but Cumbrae's Statutes were such that the cathedral's position could not be altered. So Oban became the cathedral church for both dioceses and Cumbrae was retained as a second cathedral church for the diocese of the Isles.

The consecration of Cumbrae as the cathedral church was attended by Bishop Robert Eden of Moray, Ross and Caithness, and primus of the Episcopal Church, who had himself been the instigator of the building of the cathedral in Inverness.

As the cathedral church of the diocese of the Isles, Cumbrae was an absurdity from the beginning. The island was at the southernmost tip of the diocese and the only convenient way of reaching it was to travel overland through the diocese of Glasgow to the town of Largs. But Lord Glasgow and Bishop Mackarness cherished their little cathedral and for nine years it continued merrily on the path that Lord Glasgow had set for it in 1849. As far as the bishop and the earl were concerned, Cumbrae could stand proudly beside York, Durham, Lincoln, or any of the great English cathedrals, in everything except history and size.

The life of the cathedral changed dramatically and irrevocably as a result of the Scottish banking crisis in 1885. Lord Glasgow, one of Scotland's wealthiest men, had funded the cathedral and college entirely from his own personal fortune. In 1885 he lost heavily in the collapse of the fraudulent City of Glasgow Bank and went bankrupt with debts of nearly £1,000,000. He had no choice but to sell the island of Cumbrae and over 60,750 hectares of land elsewhere. Only the estate of Kelburn, on the mainland, behind the town of Largs, remained to succeeding earls of Glasgow, and that only because of the generosity of his second cousin and successor, who sold his own land at Shewalton to purchase Kelburn. The Garrison and St Andrew's Episcopal Church passed to the third marquess of Bute, a leading Roman Catholic peer, and the local episcopal congregation was forced to move to a former girls' school in George Street.

Although the cathedral and college were safely vested in trustees, Lord Glasgow's endowment was found to be worthless. Part of it was lost through a legal defect in the deed of donation and the rest was not available for ecclesiastical purposes during Lord Glasgow's lifetime. Services in the cathedral were suspended, and Provost Frederick Noyes resigned and moved to the diocese of Salisbury; the collegiate staff was dismissed; the organist resigned and the choir school was dispersed, and the buildings were closed and locked. The dreams of 1849 disappeared overnight in 1885 and hard reality caught up with Lord Glasgow's cathedral.

At that point wiser and harder counsels would have taken the choice that now seems obvious; abandon the remote island cathedral and sell it to the highest bidder. The biographer of Bishop Alexander Chinnery-Haldane (1883–1906) summed up the dilemma that faced the bishop of Argyll and the Isles. 'What was he to do with this ruined institution? Some said, Let it go. It was known that Lord Bute was ready to give any sum that could be reasonably be asked for the buildings and grounds. The college had never in any notable way served the cause of the Church in the diocese, why not be content with securing little St Andrew's, which would serve all practically required purposes, and use the money gained by the sale of the college in any way that would best benefit the diocese'.[8] With hindsight, it might have been the best course to follow, but the bishop refused Lord Bute's offer for two reasons: firstly he had no desire to hurt the feelings of Lord Glasgow who had invested so much of his own money in establishing the cathedral; secondly, he was concerned about the negative publicity that might arise from the sale of an Anglican cathedral to a Roman Catholic peer. In the former respect he was being sensitive and thoughtful; and in the latter respect, the option of sale could not seriously have been entertained without damaging the image of the diocese of Argyll and Isles in particular, and the Scottish Episcopal Church in general. For all its inaccessibility, the church had been solemnly consecrated as the cathedral church of the diocese of the Isles only nine years earlier, and its closure would have been a humiliating loss for the confident Episcopal church that was still emerging from the shadows of persecution.

For the time being the costs involved in running the cathedral and the college were met by the bishop through the generosity of his wife. Anna Chinnery-Haldane had inherited a considerable fortune from her father, Sir Nicholas Chinnery, and the bishop had a good deal of money of his own; but that did not solve the problem of what to do with the place; paying the bills and maintaining the buildings was only a temporary management of the crisis. At first the bishop himself took on the role of provost and in 1886 a priest from the diocese of London arrived at the college, with the bishop's approval, having offered to train for ordination any candidate that the bishop sent him. The experiment was not a success and the priest grew weary of the work and resigned at the end of 1887.[9] Apart from four occasions in 1890–1, the church and college returned to a state of desolation and solitude for the next five years. On 30 April 1890, the cathedral was opened for what must have been a very poignant event: the funeral of its founder, the earl of Glasgow. It was opened at Pentecost in the same year for an ordination, and again in August for a meeting of the diocesan synod. In 1891 it was opened for a week for a clergy retreat.

Regular work only began in 1892 with the arrival of Provost Thomas Ball (1892–1916) who was also given charge of the little congregation of St Andrew's in the village. The congregation was invited to worship in the re-opened cathedral and continues to worship in the cathedral to this day – but under the title of St Andrew's – so continuing the tradition that a cathedral church does not have a resident congregation. The college was again opened for retreats, and a daily eucharist was again celebrated in the cathedral. Bishop Chinnery-Haldane had first summoned the clergy of his diocese to a retreat at the college in 1884, and he held an annual retreat in the college for the diocesan clergy in the years 1892–1905. Sir David Hunter Blair (1853–1939), the Roman Catholic baronet and Benedictine monk, visited the college during Ball's incumbency. He found the buildings 'looking like an Oxford college through the wrong end of a telescope. Provost Ball, whom I found at tea with his sisters, received me kindly and showed me the whole establishment, which looked rather derelict and neglected (I fancy there was very little money); and the college had been closed for some years'.[10]

After the departure of Provost Ball, another episcopal provostship occurred with Bishop Kenneth Mackenzie (1916–19). Retreat work expanded with the appointment of Provost Robert Taylor (1919–26), who was assisted by the surviving sisters of the Community of St Andrew of Scotland. They were invited to move from their home in Joppa, near Edinburgh, to occupy the north college to undertake sacristy and parochial work and to look after retreatants. The names given to the rooms in the north college, Faith, Hope, Charity, Joy, Peace, etc., date from the occupancy of the Sisters (1920–7). The community, founded in 1867, was never very large, perhaps with no more than six professed sisters at any one time. In 1927 the community moved back to Edinburgh and then in 1933 to the care of the All Saints Sisters at Oxford. The last sister of the Community of St Andrew died in 1949.

The north college has continued as a retreat house, in one form or another, until the present time. For a short while in 1946–7, a Test School was established in the buildings for the preliminary training of ex-service candidates for Holy Orders. After the closure of the Test School, the buildings were again used for retreats in a very small way during the incumbency of Provost George Douglas (1949–73). Douglas was a dignified and affable gentleman, though he could be irascible if the courtesies he expected were not accorded to him, and his obstinacy was proverbial. One who visited him shortly before his death found that, 'he was still maintaining regular services in the church, on weekdays as well as Sundays, still polishing the cutlery, airing the beds and keeping the library tidy and in order. He entertained guests to excellent coffee in his library'.[11]

After the death of Douglas in January 1973, the diocesan bishop, Richard Wimbush, appointed himself provost (1973–5). An invitation to the Society of Saint Francis (the Anglican Franciscans) to establish a house in the college was refused. The bishop then invited the Community of Celebration to occupy the vacant buildings. The community, led by Graham Polkingham, consisted of a group of about fifty young Americans, originally from a charismatic renewal parish in Houston, Texas, and was in residence for ten years (1975–85). Polkingham himself served as the cathedral provost, 1975–80. The experiment was a gamble on the part of the bishop and it was not a great success, principally because the community was essentially missionary, using Cumbrae as a base; and its members found, like others before them, that the island is difficult to reach. The community left in 1985, most of its members moving to Pennsylvania, and the college was again used as a retreat house from 1987 with the arrival of Provost David McCubbin (1987–94).

The departure of the community was followed by a thorough structural survey of the complex in 1989. It revealed that, although the buildings were structurally sound, much renovation work was needed. A restoration appeal committee was formed, including the present earl of Glasgow, and work on the first phase was begun and completed in 1991. The finial of the spire, which had become dangerous, was rebuilt; the bells, hung from an unsafe cradle, were removed from the tower; and urgent repairs were made to the roofs and gutters. The second phase, in 1995, involved repairing a lancet window in the north college, renewing part of the cloister roof, re-hanging the three original bells with five new additional bells, and re-instating the clock chiming. The bells were re-commissioned by the Princess Royal on 19 July 1995. The first two phases had cost a total of £110,000. The third phase of the appeal will involve repairing the dormer windows of the college, the remaining lancet windows, and restoring the decorative work of the chancel.

The buildings are now well concealed by the trees and undergrowth which have obliterated the once well-tended sloping lawn that separated the cathedral and college from Lord Glasgow's former home. The cathedral can be approached from the west by a long straight pathway that climbs through an overgrown wood to a series of flights of steps beside terraced lawns, or from the east past the two-sided cloister of the college. It sits on a grassy podium looking towards the mountains of Arran, and the harmony of the buildings and the landscape is an important element in the evident serenity of the place. Paul Thompson, Butterfield's biographer, described it thus: 'Nowhere is Butterfield's sense of landscape more impressive than at Cumbrae… It stands on a long, low, green island in the Clyde, hidden from the little town of Millport behind a thicket of trees and a long buttressed wall with heavy wooden gates under a stone arch. A wicket door opens to a path which climbs through the wood. The college stands on grass terracing at the crest of the hill, so that the first glimpse of its spire from below exaggerates its height. The picturesque qualities of the buildings are at once obvious. Each main range stands at right angles to one of another character: the bare north roof surfaces of the church contrasted to the richer handling of the chorister's house and the sheer verticality of the spire to the long roof of the canon's house… The spire marks one axis, the balancing canons' and choristers' houses the other. The buildings are thus a close group, yet fully open to the landscape. Seen from the east, the college is unforgettable, the sharp thrust of the spire and the simply battered chimney-breasts playing against the long line of slate roofs and grey walls, and beyond, the distant mountain silhouette of Arran across the Clyde'.[12] 'The situation is sheltered and charming in every possible way… Reposeful reticence is the key note of Cumbrae'.[13]

The cathedral and college are built of grey sandstone quarried on the island. The prominent slender tower with its square stone spire is 37.4m high. It has buttresses at three angles and triple lancets on each face of the upper stage, which contains three bells. The spire is surmounted by a large iron cross and a weather-cock. The base of the tower forms a porch to the lofty aisleless nave of the cathedral which has a high-pitched roof. On entering the cathedral it immediately becomes clear how small the building is; the nave is only 12.1m long by 6m wide, seats about 70 people and is quite plain apart from a partly tiled floor and some memorial brasses. It was originally illuminated by the light from a row of several hundred gas jets along the string course line, which produced a very devotional effect, even if the smoke darkened the walls.[14] There are no windows on the north wall. The octagonal font at the south-west corner of the nave was designed by Ernest Geldart in 1881. Behind, on the west wall, is a brass to John Gibson Cazenove (d.1896), vice-provost of the cathedral 1854–67 and provost 1867–75, in the form of a Celtic cross. By the font is a painting depicting the deceased Saviour, with St Mary Magdalene trying to stop the insertion of the lance; it was formerly the altarpiece of St Andrew's Church, Millport. The painting on the north wall is a copy of 'The Visitation' by Alvertinelli (sixteenth century); the smaller one behind the plain wooden Butterfield pulpit is an Italian pieta of c.1600. The eagle lectern on the south side is a memorial to Bishop Ewing.

The west window, by Wailes, was paid for by the workmen who built the cathedral, in thanksgiving for their safety during the construction period. It was severely damaged during a storm on 28 December 1879. An entry in the service register records the event. 'Evensong was interrupted by a great storm which blew in the West window of the church – the same storm blew over the Tay Railway Bridge'. The four stained glass windows on the south side of the nave, together with the east window, are by Hardman of Birmingham. The windows above the lectern are a memorial from Lord Glasgow to his friend and mentor John Keble (1792–1866) and depict Saints Ambrose, Jerome, Gregory and Augustine. Keble's famous Assize Sermon at the University Church in Oxford in 1833 had been hailed as the beginning of the Oxford Movement that was the progenitor of the cathedral. Keble had always regarded the Scottish Episcopal Church with deep reverence and accepted an honorary canonry of the cathedral in 1854 with great pleasure; he stayed at Millport in 1852. The other two windows depict Saints Cecilia, Catherine, Ignatius and Polycarp.

The unavoidably dominant feature of the cathedral is Butterfield's great stone screen with marble columns, which sternly guards the entrance to the chancel. It was modelled on the fourteenth century screen at Great Bardfield Church in Essex, but has marble columns, a cross instead of a rood and less tracery. It has bands of colour, brass quatrefoil tracery and polished brass gates. On either side of the gates are two pillars of Aberdeen granite which branch out and upwards into the stone tracery which has a large embossed stone cross high up in the centre. Around the arch is a pattern of red, green and black tiles. Two nineteenth century icons purchased by Provost Ball in 1891 are affixed to the brass railing which surmounts the septum. Inside the chancel on the left is a brass to

Canon William Robertson (d.1859) with his effigy depicted in prayer.

The chancel is almost as long and as high as the nave, though much more elaborately decorated. The walls are enriched by polychrome encaustic tiles, with spaces in Parian cement for the introduction of murals. The ceiling was painted in 1851 in orange and green, with representations of the wild flowers and ferns from the island. A candelabrum of six lights by Hardman is all that remains of the larger original. The east and south windows are also by Hardman. The oak stalls are by Butterfield and bear brass plates naming the titles of a long departed capitular body that collapsed and dispersed at the time of Lord Glasgow's bankruptcy.

VII St. Adamnus Clericus Synodi	Episcopus
II St. Ninian Canonicus honorarius	Canonicus honorarius
III St. Maura Canonicus honorarius	Canonicus honorarius
V St. Mungo Canonicus	Canonicus
IV St. Molocus Canonicus	Canonicus

VIII	VI	I	
St. Andrew	St. Colman	St Columba	*
	Decanus Diocesis	Praepositus	

**(stall not labelled)*

On the north side of the sanctuary is the cathedra (the bishop's throne), formerly the angel's throne from the Catholic Apostolic Church in McAslin Street, Glasgow; it was presented to the cathedral when that church was closed in 1950. Above the throne is a memorial tablet, framed in onyx, to Bishop Chinnery-Haldane, 'a faithful and beloved pastor whose wisdom and liberality at a time of distress preserved this cathedral and the adjoining college buildings to the Scottish Church. Remember him concerning this O God and spare him according to the greatness of thy mercy'. Adjacent to the bishop's throne is the aumbry housing the reserved sacrament. High up in the south-east corner is more evidence of the original purpose of the college, a lancet window which allowed the occupant of the infirmorum cubiculum, the infirmary room in the canons' house, to look down to the altar; all part of Butterfield's monastic plan. How much it was used as an infirmary is unknown, but Bishop Chinnery-Haldane always used it during his annual retreats at the college, as Provost Ball fondly remembered. 'I think I shall scarcely be startled if, on going into it, I shall some day see him, in purple cassock, seated at the table covered with books and papers, busily writing, the window wide open (whatever the weather or time of year) to let in a flood of the sweet fresh air from outside'.[15]

Butterfield's reredos was at some date replaced by an 'English' altar with riddel posts and his communion rail with a wooden substitute of 1931. On the south side of the chancel is the priest's door and above, a diamond-shaped ceramic memorial in the door arch to Bishop George Mackarness (1874–83).

A tall wide arch on the north side of the chancel, blocked by a Butterfield iron screen, leads into the ante-chapel, now partly occupied by the organ. The 1876 bishop's throne, in use until 1950, now stands here. There is also a collection of fragments of ancient Celtic stones found on the island and presented to the cathedral by Lord Glasgow. Among the cathedral treasures, but not on display, is a processional cross with bronze head thought to date from about AD1000, showing Christ and emblems of the evangelists. The ante-chapel has two small windows with twentieth century stained glass depicting the archangels Michael and Gabriel. The present organ, the second in the cathedral's history, was installed in 1930. The ante-chapel leads into the Lady Chapel with its own septum; the chapel adjoins the south college. The chapel, the first part of the cathedral to be completed, was formerly the chapter house and has St Andrew's Cross roof trusses and a tiled floor. The east window is by Wailes and has a geometric pattern with a small shield at the bottom of the left light with the date 1851.

To the west of the cathedral is a little walled graveyard and here lies buried George, sixth earl of Glasgow, whose enduring monument is the cathedral that still stands above his last resting place. In the other direction, the south wing of the college forms another arm of the cruciform group and terminates in the oriel window of the provost's study.

'The college indeed might be a part of an Oxford college transported to the little island that looks out upon the hills of Arran and Ailsa Craig. Modest, shy, retiring, it seems to recall Keble himself; in cloister, refectory and libraries, there is a quiet charm that recalls the sweet attractiveness of the author of *The Christian Year*, while the whole range of buildings, including the church with its lofty spire, suggests the confident security with which the influence of the Movement inspired the whole Church… The curious thing is that here is a frankly

Gothic-revival group of buildings, conceived in a revivalist atmosphere, which is simpler and more in keeping with the true Spirit of the early Middle Ages... than anything else created in Scotland in the nineteenth century, and a great deal more of the spirit of the old Iona than the revived Iona of today... Every detail is as plain and perfectly proportioned as could possibly be imagined, nothing is extraneous, thus making the architecture fully Gothic in structure as well as in appearance'.[16]

The purpose of the Church and College of the Holy Spirit was a confused mix from the start of the project. Part church, part choir school, part seminary, part monastery and part infirmary, it gathered together those strands in the religious revival that most appealed to the enthusiastic mind of a young and wealthy Scottish aristocrat; and he gave effect to his dreams by attempting to re-create Iona in his own back garden. Small, inaccessible and inconvenient, the cathedral is an ecclesiastical oddity, a product of the money and romantic dreams of the sixth earl of Glasgow. From the day in 1885 when he ceased to be able to fund the cathedral and the college, the dream was shattered, and the hard truth of the matter is that no one has really known quite what to do with the place. There is undoubtedly a place for an episcopalian presence on Cumbrae but, after 1885, the Episcopal Church was left with far more plant than it really needed. This established consecrated cathedral, with its accompanying monastery, on the very southern tip of the diocese of Argyll and the Isles, has defied the attempts of successive bishops to give it a raison d'être.

But for all that it represents an unrealised and impossible dream, there is something quite endearing about this beautifully-sited little cathedral, complete with its monastic precinct. There is a restful peace about the place which is perhaps more suited to the retreat house chapel than the cathedral church. All things considered, perhaps it was not a waste of money, nor an ill-chosen site.

1 Boyle, George (1851): p. 7.
2 Lochhead, Marion (1966): p. 89.
3 Boyle, George (1851): p. 12.
4 ibid., p. 33.
5 ibid., p. 35.
6 ibid.
7 ibid., p. 44.
8 Ball, Thomas Isaac (1907): p. 130.
9 Craven, J B (1907): p. 387.
10 Hunter Blair, David (1922): p. 101.
11 Fenwick, Hubert (1978): p. 272.
12 Thompson, Paul (1971): pp 318–9.
13 Fenwick, Hubert (1978): p. 269.
14 Anson, Peter (1973): p. 30.
15 Ball, Thomas Isaac (1907): p. 135.
16 Fenwick, Hubert (1978): pp 268–9.

Dornoch

The Cathedral Church of St Mary and St Gilbert

(Church of Scotland)

Dornoch is a small town with a population of about 1,000 in the former county of Sutherland, 323km from Edinburgh, high up on the north-east coast of Scotland. Its low-lying semi-coastal landscape, with sand dunes and gravel, is reflected in the name of the town which comes from the Gaelic *Tor-nach*, meaning 'pebbly place'.

A dignified but sleepy little place, Dornoch clusters around a wide and spacious centre, dominated by the squat cathedral church of St Mary and St Gilbert and an imposing fragment of the bishop's castle. In his *Topographical dictionary of Scotland*, published in 1846, Samuel Lewis described Dornoch as consisting of 'several spacious well-formed streets; the houses are of a very inferior order, little better than humble cottages, and though the county town, the place has only the appearance of an insignificant hamlet'.[1] Beriah Botfield, who visited the town in the summer of 1829 described its location as 'being neither on the coast nor on the post road, though within a gun-shot of both one and the other'.[2] His description is apt; Dornoch lies off the main road from Inverness to Wick, at the end of a road leading towards the Dornoch Firth and the sea.

The diocese of Caithness, with jurisdiction over Caithness and Sutherland, was founded between 1146 and 1150 with its see at Halkirk near Thurso. There is nothing today at Halkirk remaining from that period; the town is largely as it was planned by Sir John Sinclair in c.1800. There is a disused parish church of 1751–3; and the foundations of two very small buildings, probably of Pictish origins. There was a bishop's castle, but there is no remaining trace; it stood in the field adjacent to the Abbey Manse; and there is no trace of any building that might have been used as a cathedral church.

In 1223 the see of the diocese was transferred from Halkirk to Dornoch where there is alleged to have been a Culdee settlement, possibly founded as early as the sixth century under a saint named Barr or Finbarr. Evidence for the existence of this saint at Dornoch is slight and dubious. The seventeenth century historian of Sutherland, Sir Robert Gordon (1580–1656), repeated inaccurate folklore when he said that Barr had been made a bishop in 1079 by King Malcolm III (1058–93) 'who loved him dearly for his holy lyff and conversation'.[3] Other historians have confused Barr with the Irish saint, Fin Barre, describing

The Cathedral Church of St Mary and St Gilbert

him as 'a native of Caithness and bishop of Cork'.[4] Whoever Barr was, it would be difficult to identify him with St Fin Barre of Cork, who was a native of Connacht (not Caithness) and died c.623. A church dedicated to St Barr is said to have survived until the reign of King James VI (1567–1625);[5] a local tradition said that it stood to the east of the present cathedral in the centre of the present churchyard, about halfway between the cathedral and Tor-an-naurach, the high ground at the east end of the churchyard.[6] There is no reason to dispute the possible existence of an ancient Culdee settlement at Dornoch – this would have predisposed the site for the coming of the cathedral in the thirteenth century – but it seems clear that nothing reliable is known of its origin or history.

The first three known bishops of Caithness, Andrew (1151–84), John (1198–1202) and Adam of Carlise (1213–22) had their seats at Halkirk or Scrabster. In these early years of a monarchical and territorial episcopate, dispute and disorder were frequent occurrences in this remote part of Scotland. In 1198, Bishop John was involved in a bitter dispute with Earl Harold of Orkney over the collection of revenue. The bishop was attacked at Scrabster by the earl and his followers, who 'pulled out his toung and both his eyes, then killed him most cruellie'.[7] This account portrays the bishop as the innocent victim; other accounts suggest that Bishop John was not entirely blameless, and that his unpleasant death in 1202 might have been the culmination of a campaign against his financial irregularities; a papal mandate of 1198 to the bishops of Ross and Orkney required them to compel Bishop John to desist from interfering with the collection of Peter's Pence in Caithness, a tax which the earl was apparently willing to pay.[8]

King William the Lion (1165–1214) avenged the death of Bishop John by putting out the eyes of Thorfin, the son of Earl Harold, whom he had held as a hostage, and then prepared an expedition against the earl who promptly agreed to pay a fine of 2000lbs of silver. However, the church was not content with a simple fine. The bishop of Orkney laid the case of his brother bishop before Pope Innocent III, who ordered the earl to walk fifteen days in public through his estates with bare feet and scanty clothing, and with his tongue hanging out and fastened in that position. He was at the same time to be vigorously scourged with rods. At the conclusion of this discipline the earl was to set out for Jerusalem and fight for three years on crusade. Only when this penance was accomplished could the earl be restored to communion. It appears that the earl managed to evade this humiliating penance, saved probably by the remoteness of his possessions.

Bishop Adam of Carlisle (1213–22) suffered an equally gruesome fate. On 11 September 1222, a mob burst into his palace at Halkirk, and burnt him in his own kitchen. It was said to be the established custom in the diocese that for every score of cows, a span of butter should be given to the church. The bishop increased the demand to a span first for every fifteen cows, then for every twelve cows, and finally for every ten cows. The people assembled to consider what should be done. One exclaimed 'short rede, good rede; slay we the bishop' (few words are best; let us kill the bishop)'.[9] 'The inhabitants of Catteynes… entered the chamber of Bishop Adam in the town of Hackrick in Catteynes under silence of the night, because he had accused them for not paying of ther tithes. First they murthered a monk who was his companion; then they hailled and drew the bishop by the hair down to his kitching; and ther scourged him with rods; last of all theu fired the hous, and burned the bishop therin'.[10] Pope Honorius III issued a bull of excommunication against the murderers, accusing them of being 'degenerate sons' and 'raging like wolves' and 'rushing like the emissaries of the devil against Christ the Lord'.[11] Subsequently King Alexander II (1214–49) marched to Caithness with his army and executed four hundred of those responsible.

Into this unruly and perilous diocese, in 1223, came Gilbert de Moravia, archdeacon of Moray. Perhaps because of the unhappy experiences at Halkirk, Bishop Gilbert moved the diocesan see from Halkirk to Dornoch; but the choice of the town may have been governed by the fact that Gilbert was a kinsman of the earl of Sutherland and had received (c.1211) extensive lands from him in the vicinity of Dornoch. The new cathedral at Dornoch, previously served by a single priest, was given a chapter of ten canons by its new bishop, including himself and the abbot of Scone. Gilbert was a leading figure in the national and ecclesiastical affairs of Scotland in his day, and was described as 'one of the noblest and wisest ecclesiastics the medieval church produced'. He died on 1 April 1245, 'and was, according to his owne appoyntment, buried at the Cathedrall Church in Dornogh, wher his burial place is to be sein at this day, direct under the steiple'.[12] He was subsequently canonised and the day of his death is kept as his feast day.

After his consecration as bishop of Caithness and the transfer of the see to Dornoch, Gilbert began to build a cathedral at his own expense. Construction was far enough advanced for the first service to be held in 1239, when the remains of Bishop Adam were transferred from Halkirk. Built of sandstone the new cathedral was cruciform with an aisled nave.

In 1428, the pope granted an indulgence to all visitors to the cathedral who contributed to the restoration of the building, which was then said to be 'collapsed in its fabric, desolate and destitute and in need of costly repairs'.[13]

Apart from the usual destruction of altars, the cathedral survived the depredations of the sixteenth century reformation, only to succumb to a bout of clan feuding in 1570. Mackay of Strathnaver and the Master of Caithness set fire to the cathedral during the course of a feud against the Murrays of Dornoch. 'The master of Catteynes brunt the Cathedrall Church and the toun, in the night seasons, which the inhabitants culd no longer defend'.[14] The said John, master of Caithness, committed the unforgivable crime of opening the grave of Gilbert de Moravia and 'burst St Gilbert with his foot, and threw the ashes of that holy man with the wund'.[15] The event caused Bishop Robert Stewart (1541–86) to leave Dornoch c.1570 and take up residence at St Andrews. He doubtless felt that Skibo and Scrabster were becoming unsafe. He does not seem to have returned to his diocese, although he remained titular bishop of Caithness until his death.

After the burning of 1570, the cathedral remained roofless for nearly fifty years. Further damage was done in 1605, on the day of the discovery of the Gunpowder Plot, when a storm destroyed the north arcade of the nave. Being precisely contemporary with the Gunpowder Plot, the damage to the cathedral was enough for some to treat it as an omen of the devil's work. 'The Fyfth day of November 1605 years, the detestable powder treason of the Romane Catholicks of England wes miraculously discovered at London: a monstrous and divillish plot... The same verie night that this execrable plott should have been put in execution, all the inner stone pillars of the North syd of body of the Cathedrall Church at Dornogh (laiking the rooff befor) were blowen from the verie roots and foundation, quyt and clein over the outer walls of the Church; which walls did remain nevertheless standing, to the great astonishment of all such as hath sein the same. These great winds did even then prognosticat and forshew some great treason to be at hand: and the divell was busie then to trouble the ayre, so was he bussie, by these hiss fyrebrands, to trouble the estate of Great Britane'.[16]

Public worship in the years 1570–1614, might have been held in the ruined cathedral, though possibly in some part of the episcopal palace, which was now in the hands of the earl of Sutherland. The bishop of Caithness had in fact lost all his traditional residences, since the Gray family occupied Skibo and the earls of Caithness were living at Scrabster. Eventually, when the earl of Caithness fell into disfavour with the king, he surrendered the house at Scrabster to the bishop, together with some land in Caithness.

In 1614, John, earl of Sutherland, declared his intention to restore the cathedral, 'at the instigation and persuasion of Mr John Gray, Dean of Catteneys'.[17] He died in 1615 before much had been accomplished, but the task was continued by his brother Sir Robert Gordon of Gordonstoun, guardian for his young son, also named John. Work continued from 1614–17 and the chancel was covered with slate from a nearby quarry, 'as it were by the special providence of Almightie God'.[18] The nave and aisles remained roofless and were walled off, while the chancel and transepts were used as the parish church. In August 1623, the bishop held a synod of clergy at Caithness and ordered that each incoming minister within the diocese should pay the first year's profits from his benefice for the repairing and maintenance of the cathedral.

In 1625, Sir Robert Gordon's period of guardianship ended and he wrote a long letter of advice to his nephew discussing, among other things, his responsibilities with regard to the cathedral. 'Do not fail to repair and decore the south ile of the church... which is the sepulture of your ancestors. Erect ther a monument and a tombe for them and yourself, if be not performed to your hand, and cause paint about the inner walls of that ile, or upon the selerine thereof, the portraitours and pictoures of all the Earles of Southerland with the soume of ther lyfs from the beginning'.[19]

Gordon's advice was not followed for whatever reason and, possibly at his instigation, King Charles I wrote to the earl on 22 June 1634: 'hearing that the bodie of that church is as yet to sett vp, which will require the assistance of the most able and eminent persones in that diocie, wee haugh hereby thought fitt speciallie to recommend vnto yow to assist so pious a work by vsing the advise and direction herein of the reverend father in God, the bishop of Caithnesse, and by helping to make up such a general contribution amongst all the inhabitants of that diocie as wilbe sufficient to finish that work'.[20] Nothing seems to have been done, but there was a severe famine in the north of Scotland in 1634, and the prospect of major construction work on the cathedral may have been too much for the earl to contemplate.

Bishop John Abernethy (1616–38) was deposed, with all his fellow bishops, at the Glasgow General Assembly of 1638. The cathedral was again damaged by the Mackays in 1654, during the Cromwellian period. Bishop Andrew Wood (1680–95), the last bishop of Caithness to reside at Dornoch, left the town in 1690, and the building ceased to be a cathedral church.

In the second half of the seventeenth century the cathedral was again unusable. In 1677 Thomas Kirk found 'a pretty church, miserably ruinous; there is scarce any roof left upon it: we were told that about sixty years ago happened a great earthquake under the church, which raised up the pillars on the north side thereof and threw them over the wall without harming it'.[21] By the end of the century the resident minister was using a meeting house, apparently not the cathedral, somewhere in the town and complained that 'it can in no way be a fitt place to preach in'.[22] In 1708 the presbytery inspected the fabric of the cathedral and found that it was 'altogether decayed, without a roof, with crazes in the walls, so that it will be more easy to build a new church than repair the church, it being a large ruinous fabrick of a cathedral'.[23] In 1714, George Ogilvie, a mason, reported to the presbytery 'that no less than three thousand five hundred merks would repair the Isles of the Old Church, repair the steeple, and put the Kirk under Lock and Key making it a fitt place for Divine Worship, excepting only that he did not undertake to Glass the Church'.[24] Some half-hearted work appears to have been undertaken in the years 1714–16, but nowhere near a total restoration. A new steeple was begun in 1728, but was still unfinished by 1732.[25] The cathedral was partly in use, but the Reverend John Sutherland complained that it was 'so ruinous that unless it was repaired he and his congregation would have to desert it'.[26] Delay was inexcusable owing to 'the danger there was from the heavy grey slates on the most crazy part of the roof both to persons in Church and others without going past that way'.[27] In 1761 the minister complained to the town council that swine were constantly roaming the churchyard 'which is unfenced, and dig up graves and the bones of the defunct'.[28] In 1786 it was reported that there was 'ane midden within the west aisle of the broken kirk of Dornoch'.[29]

Well into the eighteenth century, the chancel and transepts were still being used for burials, as freely as the ruined nave. The seats of the congregation were placed on top of the gravestones, and one minister described the floor as 'nauseous and unhealthful'. He also complained that the cathedral was so 'vastly spacious, lofty and irregular as greatly to exceed the utmost exertions of the human voice'.[30] In 1775, a grant of £300 was obtained from the Exchequer towards repair and alterations. A wooden floor was inserted 2.1m above the existing floor, together with a gallery for dignitaries in the south transept. Small doors at ground floor level gave access to the area below the wooden floor, to allow the continuation of burials. A sketch of c.1776 shows that the south arcade, south aisle walls, and west end of the nave were still standing, though in a ruinous condition.

In 1760 Dornoch was visited by Richard Pococke, bishop (1756–65) of the Irish diocese of Ossory, who has left an inaccurate and confusing description of account of what he saw of the ruins of the cathedral. 'The church here is the body of the old Cathedral… it seems to be pretty near a Greek cross, tho' in the Eastern part, now uncovered, there are four arches on each side supported by round pillars with a kind of a Gothic Doric capital. In the body or nave are only three plain Gothic windows on each side; but what is most remarkable is a round tower within, joining to the south-west angle of the middle part. It is built for a staircase, and is about ten feet in diameter, with geometrical stairs'.[31] In fact the bishop mistook east for west and the chancel for the nave; and the staircase is at the north-east not the south-west. He is the only person who speaks of the existence of a round tower, and it may have been a stair turret or the steeple begun in 1728.

The ill-treatment of the cathedral was continued in the early nineteenth century. One last piece of destruction occurred in 1813 with the demolition of the remains of the chapter house, an oblong and vaulted structure that stood on the north side of the chancel. In 1816, the chancel being too small for the numbers attending the church, a gallery was erected, and access gained by an outside stone stair leading to a door in the north wall, about where the centre window now is. Finally, in the 1830s, a movement to restore the cathedral consolidated what remained of the old fabric and produced the attractive medieval pastiche that is Dornoch Cathedral today.

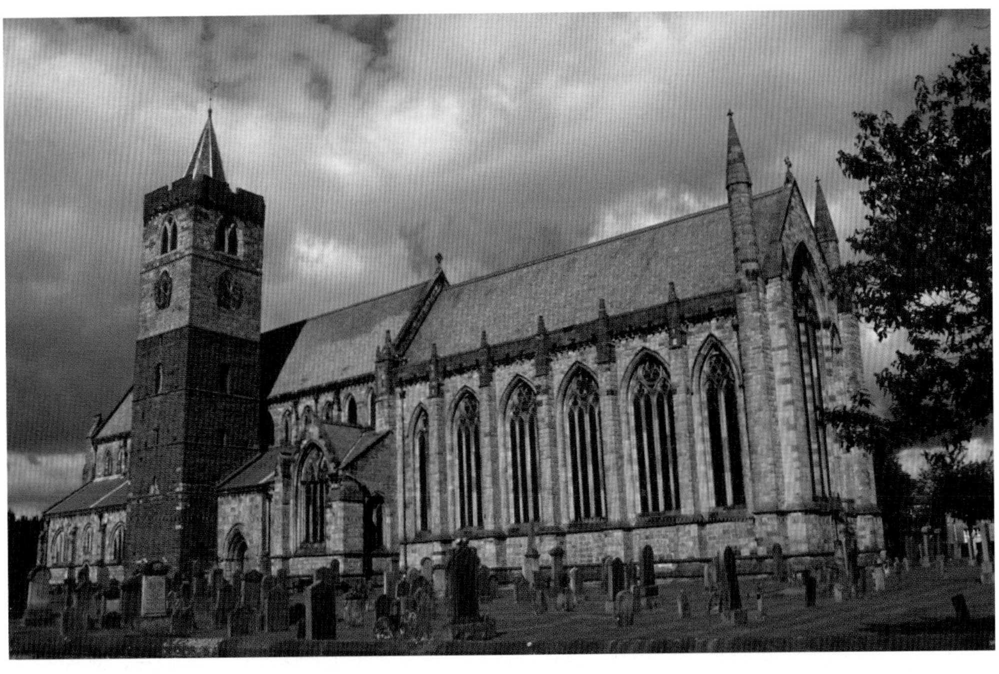

DUNBLANE: *The Cathedral Church of St Blane and St Laurence*

CUMBRAE: *The Cathedral and Collegiate Church of the Holy Spirit*

DUNBLANE: *Cathedral Church of St Blane and St Laurence*

DUNDEE: *The Cathedral Church of St Paul*

A meeting on 18 September 1834 formally sanctioned the drastic restoration of the entire cathedral in 1835–7, funded largely through the generosity of Elizabeth, duchess and countess of Sutherland (1765–1839). The earls of Sutherland had been the principal landowners in Caithness for generations and, in 1771, the title was inherited by Elizabeth who became countess in her own right. In 1785 she married George, marquess of Stafford, who was given a dukedom in 1833 and took the title of duke of Sutherland. In recognition of her possession of the ancient earldom, his wife styled herself duchess and countess of Sutherland.

The duchess-countess at first employed the architect William Burn to produce designs for the cathedral and he was previously thought to have been the architect of the restoration. In fact Burn's designs were disliked by the duchess and she dismissed him before work began. The man charged with responsibility for restoring the cathedral was Alexander Coupar, Superintendent of Works on the Sutherland estate, assisted by William Leslie. Advice was provided by Sir Francis Chantrey and sketches by the duchess-countess.

It was unfortunate that the restoration should have taken place in the infancy of the Gothic Revival when the treatment of medieval fabric was cavalier to say the least, and reactions were mixed. 'The ruined nave... with its pillars, aisles, end arches, and its detached chapel [to the south of the nave, and used in later years as the burial place of the Gordons of Embo] were cleared away with a ruthless hand. The grave stones with which its area was crowded were also unceremoniously cleared out, and the required level for the floor obtained by carting away hundreds of loads of soil mixed with human remains... The 'restoration' consisted of entirely rebuilding the nave, without aisles, doing away with the raised wooden floor and galleries in the remainder of the church, and opening up the whole building from end to end. The tower was repaired, the steeple [spire] practically reconstructed, and a round outside tower and stone stair built in the north-east angle, giving access to the central tower. The pulpit was placed against the north-east pillar [presumably of the crossing]. The greater part of the choir was railed off, and formed into a Sutherland family pew. The interior, even the fine shafted pillars and arches of St Gilbert's workmanship, supporting the tower, received a thick coat of ochre wash, and the whole place was given a spick and span appearance... Doorways were made in the gables of the transepts and nave, and the former doorways, with the outside stairs leading to them, cleared away'.[32] Having secured her wishes in every other respect, the duchess-countess was forced by public opinion to withdraw her intention to insert stained glass in the east windows of the chancel. In those unenlightened days, stained glass was a 'popish symbol' and to be firmly opposed. Petitions and remonstrances against the proposed glass were sent to the duchess-countess, who relented, and ordered the windows to be blocked up instead.[33]

In spite of the destruction or obscuration of so much medieval work, a gazetteer of 1847 claimed that 'the fine Church of Dornoch... is as nearly as possible a facsimile of the old Cathedral, the proportions and elaborate decorations having been carefully copied'. Samuel Lewis criticised the 'minute regard to original design', though 'it at present forms one of the most interesting religious edifices of the kingdom'.[34]

Dornoch Cathedral is today mostly as it was completed in 1835–7, although the internal rubble stonework was stripped of its lath and plaster during a further restoration in 1924–7. The cathedral is a simple cruciform building, consisting of nave, chancel, transepts and central tower, 36.6m high to the tip of the spire. The rubble stonework of the internal walls gives a quasi-medieval appearance, and belies the fact that the nave is almost entirely from the 1835–7 restoration. During the work of 1924–7, two piers of the medieval arcade were discovered, and these can still be seen at the east end of the nave close to the crossing piers and mostly buried in the nineteenth century nave walls. The crossing, tower, transepts and chancel are mostly thirteenth century, but both transepts were largely refaced in 1835–7. The transept porches, the tower newel staircase and the external buttresses to the east wall of the chancel are also 1835–7. The fawn-coloured plaster vaulting throughout the cathedral also dates from 1835–7. The central tower has a single lancet on each face and its machiolated parapet supported by corbels runs round the top, while at each corner is a small round turret. The tower contains a single bell bearing the inscription 'Wm. Mears of London, Fecit 1785'.

Entrance is normally through the doorway in the south transept, although the main entrance is at the west end of the nave. This is concealed by an internal wooden porch erected in 1980. An 1837 marble effigy of the first duke of Sutherland – who died in 1833 – once stood in front of the west door. The work of Sir Francis Chantrey (1781–1841), it formerly stood at the east end, on the site of the high altar. It was moved to the west end of the nave in the early twentieth century and then to Dunrobin Castle to allow construction of the new porch. In the wall above the porch is a tablet recording the restoration undertaken by the duchess-countess.

The tracery of the five-light west window is copied from an old design, but the window is comparatively short to allow for the west doorway below. At the south-west is the stone sarcophagus containing the remains of Sir Richard de Moravia, brother of Bishop Gilbert. Sir Richard was killed in battle in 1240 during the course of a Danish invasion and was assigned a burial place in the cathedral. His coffin, unlike that of his brother, survived the destruction of 1270. His crossed legs indicate that he was a crusader. The top of the head is chipped off, and the legs are in pieces. It was taken from its niche in the choir during the restoration.

One of the great attractions of Dornoch Cathedral is its rich and varied collection of twentieth century stained glass. The cathedral windows have been steadily filled since the beginning of the century and the result has been a beautiful transformation of the interior. The window on the south wall of the nave next to the crossing is by Francis Spear (1952) and depicts Saints George, Peter, Andrew, Hubert and Gilbert. The second window, in honour of St Peter, is by Charles Kempe (1905). The third window is by Gordon Webster (1972) and depicts Christ. The final window has yet to be filled with stained glass. The westernmost of the north wall windows also still has clear glass. The second window was inserted in 1993 and depicts Queen Margaret and her husband King Malcolm III; the queen is shown pointing her husband towards an extract from the prologue to St John's Gospel, 'And the Word was made flesh and dwelt among us'. The third window, by James Ballantine (1928) depicts the nativity and the presentation of Christ. The fourth window, also by Ballantine (1916), depicts Abraham.

The pillars and arches supporting the tower are of Dornoch sandstone, with capitals and arches of Embo stone. They are essentially thirteenth century, but were restored c.1925. The bases of these pillars can be seen to be about 45cm beneath the present floor level. The octagonal font, standing at the south-east of the crossing on five columns, four of red marble, is early twentieth century.

The south transept was long known as St James' Aisle, there being an altar under that dedication, endowed with a full-time chaplain in 1279 by William, earl of Sutherland. The transept was also used as the burial place of successive earls of Sutherland from 1247 to 1733. On the west wall of the south transept, close to the crossing is a small, blocked doorway containing a little skull and crossbones tablet, one of five so-called mortality slabs in the cathedral. The east wall of this transept is thirteenth century; the west wall is 1835. This wall in its original form could have had only one window due to the width of the nave aisles. The stained glass of the transept is, like that in other parts of the cathedral, an interesting mixture. The glass in the east window, closest to the crossing, is a First World War memorial by James Ballantine. The other window is by Percy Bacon and is on the theme of 'Suffer the little children'. On the west (opposite) wall, the window closest to the crossing is also by Bacon and shows the Blessed Virgin Mary holding the Christ child. The other window in this wall commemorates William Fraser, a member of Dornoch town council for sixty-seven years, and provost of the burgh for the last twenty-one years of his life. The glass of the south windows is an assortment; the eastern window is the work of Crear Macartney (1989); the centre window is by Morris and Co. (1930) and commemorates Rosemary Millicent, Viscountess Ednam, daughter of the fourth duke of Sutherland, and also her young son Jeremy; mother and child were killed in separate accidents in 1929–30. The western window is by G Maile (1947), a memorial to Eileen, duchess of Sutherland (1891–1943).

The north transept, like the south, shows thirteenth century work in the east wall and a much restored west wall. There is a piscina in the east wall. The cathedral organ was installed in the north transept in 1893, originally occupying its whole width. It was reconditioned and relocated in 1908 due to the generosity of Andrew Carnegie (1835–1919), the Scottish–American steel magnate who spent the happiest years of his life living at Skibo Castle, 6.4km to the west of Dornoch. His generosity was followed by that of his daughter Margaret who paid for the organ to be rebuilt in 1979 when the organ console was moved to the chancel. The three stained glass windows in the transept are by Heaton, Butler and Bayne, and depict Christ as the lover of children, the light of the world and the good shepherd.

The chancel is thirteenth century. The carved hexagonal oak pulpit, pews and communion table date from 1911. The windows have been framed into a dignified wall arcade resting on long shafts. As in the transepts, the shafts have disappeared but the arches remain. Beneath the floor is the (now sealed) nineteenth century burial vault of the Sutherland family. On the south wall is a piscina, whose basin is now level with the floor, which was raised to make room for the Sutherland vault below; and there are traces of a sedilia. In the floor behind the altar is a large marble memorial slab to Duchess-Countess Elizabeth, formerly attached to the then blocked central east window. The large memorial on the south wall, with a vesica-shaped panel in the base, is to William, earl of Sutherland, who died on 10 June 1766 at the age of thirty-two, and his wife Mary who predeceased him by nine days, at the age of twenty-six. The memorial is inscribed with a quotation from the second book of Samuel, chapter 1, verse 23: 'They were lovely and pleasant in their lives and in their death they were not divided'. Amid all this funereal Sutherland grandeur is the pleasant sight of a little stone set into the east wall with a charming inscription: 'Below this is Mrs Mackay's Grave as mentioned in ye inscription on ye north wall'.

There are several mortality stones set into the chancel walls. These eighteenth century tombstones were found in the ruined nave and incorporated into the chancel walls during the restoration. The skull, the spade for digging the grave, the coffin, the hour-glass and the bell to be rung at the funeral, reflect the eighteenth century obsession with death.

The three windows on the north side of the chancel are the work of Percy Bacon and were inserted in 1926 in memory of Andrew Carnegie. The windows commemorate themes that were closest to his heart: music, peace and learning. The east windows contain glass by Christopher Whall in memory of Cromartie, fourth duke and twentieth earl of Sutherland, who died in 1913. The easternmost window in the south wall is by Miss Haston and commemorates the second Viscount Chaplin (1877–1949). The centre south window is by William Wilson and commemorates Millicent, duchess of Sutherland (1867–1957); Dunrobin Castle, the ancestral Sutherland home, can be seen in the upper background. The third window, by Crear Macartney (1989) celebrates the life of the founder, Bishop Gilbert de Moravia, and shows him sailing from Moray to Dornoch.

To the south of the cathedral, across the road, is the much-altered Dornoch Castle, which is thought to have once formed part of the bishop's palace. The bishops also had residences at Skibo and Scrabster, neither of which survive. The castle records were mostly lost during the destruction of 1570, so its earlier history is unknown. It is thought that the castle was built in the fourteenth century and rebuilt and extended in the sixteenth century. The castle was again habitable by 1615 when the twelfth earl of Sutherland died there. Repaired in 1720, it was again ruinous by 1760. The castle was a large and stately building with three towers; that remaining being the square south-west tower with stair turret which probably dates from c.1500. The principal rooms were located in a wing where the west end of the Court House now stands. Other than a low vaulted former kitchen, nothing remains of the original internal layout. The wing, which had walls of fine ashlar, survived until demolition in 1813. Bishop Pococke saw it in 1760 and described it as 'a solid high building, consisting of four floors above the arched offices on which it was built'.[35] It was connected with the surviving tower by the kitchens, part of which, with vaulted roof and huge fireplace and chimney, still remains. The castle was surrounded by a high wall in which was a gateway facing north east. The gate appears to have been to the east of where the fountain in the square now stands. The tower was used as a court and county gaol from 1814. It was altered by William Fowler in 1859–60 to provide a residence for the sheriff of Sutherland. It was still being used as gaol in 1874, but was restored in 1881 as a 'quaint dwelling place for English sportsmen' (a shooting lodge in fact). It was reconstructed in 1925, and occupied privately until 1947, since when it has been a hotel.

From the light and charm of its cathedral and the quaintness of its castle, to something far less pleasant. There is a dark, horrible and infamous episode in the history of Dornoch that the town would probably rather forget. Here, in 1722, occurred the last burning in Scotland of a woman alleged to be a witch. The unfortunate victim was Janet Horn, a lady's maid who had travelled in Italy. She settled at Kintradwell, where, through ignorance or malice, 'the neighbours soon began to whisper among themselves that she indulged in the 'Black Art' and that the evil one kept company with her'. A series of preposterous allegations were made, including one that she had turned her daughter into a pony and then had it shod by the devil. She was put on trial at Dornoch, convicted, and sentenced to be rolled in tar, then in feathers, and then to be burned with fire.[36]

Dornoch has seen a fair amount of violence and cruelty in other ages, but all this is now well in the past, and today it resembles nothing so much as a neat and pleasant little market town. The cathedral, which sits squarely and prominently on rising ground in the centre of the town, is the epitome of a parish church and, without reading something of its history, the visitor would never guess that it was once the cathedral church of the diocese of Caithness. The vigorous nineteenth century 'restoration' under the auspices of the duchess-countess might be justifiably and fiercely criticised, in that it swept away so much that might have been saved, but the result is a clean, bright and confident building.

1 Lewis, Samuel (1846): volume 1, p. 286.
2 Botfield, Beriah (1830): p. 161.
3 Mackay, Hector M (1920): p. 2.
4 ibid., p. 3.
5 ibid., p. 2.
6 ibid., p. 3.
7 ibid., p. 6.
8 ibid., p. 8.
9 Walcott, Mackenzie (1874): volume 1, p 128.
10 Mackay, Hector M (1920): p. 7.
11 ibid.
12 ibid., p. 19.
13 Gifford, John (1992): p. 562.
14 Mackay, Hector M (1920): p. 46.
15 ibid.

16 Lindsay, Ian Gordon (1926): p. 53.
17 Mackay, Hector M (1920): p. 64.
18 ibid., p. 66.
19 ibid., p. 75.
20 Bentinck, Charles D (1926): p. 212.
21 Brown, P Hume (ed.) (1892): p. 34.
22 Mackay, Hector M (1920): p. 89.
23 Bentinck, Charles D (1926): p. 253.
24 ibid., p. 257.
25 ibid., p. 381.
26 ibid., p. 306.
27 ibid., p. 307.
28 Mackay, Hector M (1920): p. 114.
29 Bentinck, Charles D (1926): p. 311.
30 Mackay, Hector M (1920): p. 111.
31 ibid., p. 107.
32 ibid., pp 139-40.
33 ibid., p. 143.
34 Lewis, Samuel (1846): volume 1, p. 286.
35 Mackay, Hector M (1920): p. 107.
36 ibid., p. 93.

Dumfries

The Pro-Cathedral Church of St Andrew

Diocese of Galloway
(Roman Catholic Church)

The story of the Roman Catholic cathedral at Dumfries can be told entirely in the past tense, as it was gutted by fire on the night of 10–11 May 1961 and the ruins mostly demolished.

Dumfries, bisected by the River Nith, is a border town in south-west Scotland, about 119km south of Glasgow, and is now best known for its association with the poet Robert Burns (1759–96), who lived there for the last five years of his life. The origin of the name of the town is uncertain but is thought to mean either 'the ridge in the brushwood' or 'the fort in the brushwood'.

The former presence of a cathedral in the town is now only a faint memory for those of a certain age and above and, despite the fact that so little of the structure remains, there seemed to be no good reason to expunge the memory of St Andrew's Cathedral, Dumfries from its place among the cathedral churches of Scotland. For eighty-three years, it was the cathedral church (albeit with the official status of pro-cathedral) of the Roman Catholic diocese of Galloway, the predecessor of the present cathedral at Ayr; and the only cathedral in Dumfries. Beyond the two surviving towers, there is nothing left of the cathedral, and the following account relies on contemporary descriptions.

In 1811–13, at the instigation of Fr William Reid (1767–1845), John McCracken designed and built in Shakespeare Street, a plain church dedicated in the name of St Andrew, for the use of the Roman Catholic community of Dumfries. The foundation stone was laid on 4 April 1811 by Marmaduke Constable-Maxwell of Terregles, a local Roman Catholic landowner, and the church was formally opened by Bishop Alexander Cameron, Vicar-General of the Lowland District, on 9 May 1813. The church, built in the Classical revival style fashionable at the time, was described in 1834: 'The Catholic Chapel of Dumfries is a spacious and commodious building, erected in 1813. To external splendour or magnificence it can lay but little claim, being of the plainest and simplest order of Grecian architecture, and, until last year, its interior bore an equally plain and ornamented appearance. But, through the exertions of the Rev. Mr Reid, by whom this structure was raised, it has now been decorated in a style which, while it is highly ornamental, harmonises with the simplicity of the building and gives it an air of dignity and grandeur, which in places of public worship, is seldom surpassed. Over the Altar has been placed a highly finished copy of Vandyke's celebrated painting of the 'Descent from the Cross,' executed by Mr G. Lindsay from Edinburgh. The Altar and the finely fluted columns and pilasters by which it is surrounded, have been painted in imitation of Sienna marble. In appropriate niches, on each side of the Altar, are the statues of S. Andrew, the Patron of the Chapel, and of the Apostle S. Peter. The side walls and ceiling are painted after a beautiful design, and over the whole a mellow and chastened light is thrown by the stained glass of the windows. The spirit and taste with which the interior decorations have been executed, reflect the highest credit upon the talents of Mr J MacPherson of Dumfries'.[1]

A Roman Catholic school in Dumfries was first mentioned in 1836, and in 1842–3, a school and bell tower were built adjacent to the church at the north-west; and a carved stone from the front wall is still inserted at the base of the school bell tower. In 1849 the school tower was given four bells. Doubtless inspired by the school tower, the church, which was now thought to look bare and insignificant, was given its own tower in 1856–9; it was taller than the school tower and surmounted by an octagonal spire; the four bells were transferred to it. 'The whole height, including the cross which terminates the spire, is 44.9m. The design has been very much admired and it is admitted by all who have seen it to be superior to anything of the kind in or around Dumfries. The order of architecture is mixed Gothic. It is intended to hang in it the bells which are at present in a lower tower attached to the Schools. They are four in number and form a chime, but are not in a sufficiently elevated position to give full effect over the town to their fine tones'.[2] The porch at the base of the tower provided the principal entrance to the church.

The church was enlarged in 1871–2 to a design by George Goldie, architect of the contemporary Roman Catholic cathedral at Sligo in Ireland. Goldie's design turned the plain classical box church into an elaborate and fully cruciform building. The east wall, with the altar flanked by two vestry doors, was removed and replaced with a spacious chancel and apse, adding about 15.2m to the length of the church. Two transepts, housing altars of the Blessed Virgin Mary and the Sacred Heart, extended the width to 21.9m. The church was now beginning to look very elaborate. 'Splendidly sculptured panels, charged with religious emblems, relieved by inlays of grey polished granite, formed the sides of the chancel, inclosing two niches in which are life-sized statues of St Joseph and St Andrew. Two great-angel corbels, advancing across the open space over the lower altar steps, sustain a panelled architrave, behind which is the half-dome of the apse… Beneath the arched roof of the apse stands the high altar, entirely composed of richly-sculptured Caen stone and slabs of highly polished marble, the tabernacle in the centre having a metal door, richly gilt, engraved, enamelled, and set with agates, etc. The floor is a beautiful mosaic of encaustic tiles. The left hand transept contains the Lady altar which, like the high altar, is composed of Caen stone and marbles, richly carved. The other transept chapel is dedicated to the Sacred Heart, and has a sculptured altar… These chapels are separated from the chancel and the church by coupled arches, carried on splendid monolithic shafts of polished Dalbeattie granite. Low

The Pro-Cathedral Church of St Andrew

metal screens, with stone pedestals, crowned by great spheres of polished serpentine, and two lofty and elaborate gas standards of painted iron and brass foliage, separate the chapels from the church. Across the whole width of the chancel and chapels runs a sculptured communion rail of stone, inlaid with serpentine, and crowned with a slab of Sicilian marble. Gilt metal gates of handsome design close the entrances to the chancel and the chapels, and the whole space in front of this communion rail is richly paved with tiles. On the left hand side of the church is the pulpit on granite shafts, richly carved and inlaid with marble like the altars. A beautiful bas-relief of St Andrew, in white alabaster, forms the central feature of the front of the pulpit, and a statue of an angel bearing a scroll stands at the foot of the stairs. The windows of the Lady Chapel are filled with stained glass of unusual beauty, both for drawing and for colour. Various incidents in the life of the Blessed Virgin are represented under canopies in the Italian or Renaissance style. The opposite chapel has smaller rose windows containing the patron saints of the United Kingdom and of the Maxwell family. In the body of the old church nothing has yet been done but to clear away the old-fashioned pews, and to substitute new and elegant open seats with ornamented ends. Hereafter, we understand, the whole building is to be richly decorated in colour, and when it is done, there is no doubt that St Andrew's church will be one of the most striking ecclesiastical structures belonging to the Catholic body of Scotland'.[3] The newly extended and refurbished church was re-opened on 24 October 1872.

St Andrew's was indeed one of the most striking Roman Catholic churches in Scotland and, more than that, it was about to reach the zenith of its career. In 1878 Pope Leo XIII restored a hierarchy of archbishops and bishops for the Roman Catholic church in Scotland, the first since the sixteenth century reformation. Newly enlarged and refurbished, St Andrew's Church was declared to be the pro-cathedral church of the restored diocese of Galloway, taking the place of the old ruined cathedral at Whithorn. John McLachlan, vicar-general of the Western District, became the first bishop of the diocese (1878–93) and was solemnly enthroned in St Andrew's in June 1878.

Further redecoration of the interior took place in 1879: 'The walls are a very pale tint of green, and in three buff panels are emblazoned the arms of Pope Leo XIII, John, Bishop of Galloway, and Captain Alfred Peter Constable Maxwell... Round the windows is painted an arabesque design in various colours. In the sanctuary, the dome is painted blue, studded with gold stars. Of the five panels still to be finished, three are to be filled with ecclesiastical subjects. These are divided with a rich arabesque design painted in colours. In the Lady Chapel the ceiling is panelled with a very pale tint of grey, with fine leaves and fruit painted in natural colours. The walls are in different gradations of blue, with ornaments for the most part in white'.[4] In 1913 the cathedral celebrated the centenary of its consecration with the construction of two vestries on either side of the apse and a new baptistery at the rear of the north-east vestry.

The years after the Second World War saw a decline in the fortunes of the cathedral. In 1947 the boundaries of the diocese of Galloway were altered by the creation of two new dioceses – Paisley and Motherwell. The northern part of Ayrshire, formerly part of the archdiocese of Glasgow, but now cut off from it, was transferred to the diocese of Galloway, thus changing the balance of the Catholic population, most of whom now lived far from Dumfries. Before the Second World War, the construction of new houses on the outskirts of Dumfries made the provision of a new church and parish necessary, and in 1958 the church of St Teresa of Lisieux was built in Glasgow Street. At a stroke, the size of the congregation of the cathedral was reduced by half.

The life of St Andrew's Cathedral ended in the early hours of Ascension Day (11 May) 1961, when it was gutted by a fire thought to have been caused by arcing between an electrical conduit and a gas pipe. The total destruction of the organ loft and its contents pointed to this part of the cathedral as the origin of the blaze. The fire was seen by a passer-by, who noticed flames through windows at the west end of the cathedral, shortly after 11pm on the night of 10 May. When the fire brigade arrived and gained entry to the cathedral, the west gallery and steeply pitched boarded roof with its oak trusses were alight, and sixty per cent of the ornate ceiling had collapsed. A strong smell of gas indicated that jets of burning gas from melted gas piping increased the intensity of the fire and contributed to the rapid spread of the flames. A member of the congregation, who lived close by, hurried to the burning cathedral and then returned to her home heartbroken by the sight and unable to watch the conflagration any longer.

A photograph of the interior of the gutted cathedral indicates that although the ceiling was destroyed and the roof badly damaged, many of the large 35cm by 15.2cm oak roof trusses were still in position, though charred and, although the gallery had partially collapsed, the pews had hardly been touched by the fire, and the north, south and west walls at least were intact. Restoration within the existing walls might have been possible but, rightly or wrongly, it was considered that the cost of restoring the cathedral would have been prohibitively expensive. Although a new church was subsequently built on part of the site, the feelings of bereavement and grief felt by the congregation were not helped by the decision of Bishop Joseph McGee (1952–81) to abandon St Andrew's, and make the church of the Good Shepherd at Ayr, the new cathedral church of the diocese of Galloway. The alteration of diocesan boundaries in 1947, the construction of St Teresa's Church in 1958, and the cost of re-building the cathedral as it was, were cited as reasons for transferring the see to Ayr. The decision was formally approved by a decree of the Sacred Constitutional Congregation in Rome dated 12 March 1962.

Whatever the reasoning, the bishop's choice of a plain and nondescript modern church in a coastal town on the far side of his diocese, in preference to the challenge of building a new cathedral church in the ancient town of Dumfries, was questionable. It was said that the people of St Andrew's never forgave Bishop McGee for his decision.

The ruins of the old cathedral were subsequently demolished, and the most prominent remains today are two neglected and rather mournful-looking Italianate red stone towers. Both towers are square with round-arched doors, openings and recessed panels, clasping pilaster strips, louvered bipartite belfries in each top stage, and some arcaded corbel tables.

The 41.1m high south tower, built of red ashlar, is that of the cathedral, and has three tall stages. The lower part is by John H. Bell and was part of the extension work of 1843. The lucarned octagonal broach stone spire was added in 1858 by Alexander Fraser. A modern carved stone representation of St Andrew can be seen at first floor level on the east face of the tower. Although there is a passageway through the ground floor stage, now barred by grills, and what appears to be a trapdoor in the boarded ceiling, the tower is otherwise inaccessible and largely inhabited by pigeons.

The shorter four-stage north tower, part of the school and built in 1842, is said to have been designed by Marmaduke Constable-Maxwell of Terregles. He was a local landowner and is not otherwise known as an architect, and the tower is unlikely to have been entirely his design. On the south side is a cross set within a roundel, and above, the inscription A M D G with the date 1843. The tower is mostly constructed of red ashlar and has tall round-arched panels in the third stage. The roofline of the old school building can be seen on the south and east faces of the tower, and where the school abutted on the tower, the ashlar is replaced by rubblework. The tower has two doorways: a stone-blocked doorway opening on to Shakespeare Street and a bolted and padlocked wooden door on the east side. The tower is therefore, in theory, accessible, but the large numbers of pigeons that fly in and out of the louvered window at the summit of the tower, suggest that the interior is probably a most unpleasant place.

A section of the north wall and other low wall fragments of the cathedral can also be seen, together with the clergy and house and the hall at the east end of the site. There is also a memorial plaque to Fr William Reid the driving force behind the construction of the cathedral, on a section of wall adjacent to the new church. Across the courtyard to the rear of the towers can be seen St Andrew's Church, the plain, cheerless and functional successor to the cathedral. Designed by Sutherland and Dickie in the brutalistic warehouse-style of the time, it was built in 1963–4 and consecrated on 30 November 1964 as a parish church. It could easily have become the new cathedral church.

1 McCall, Peter (1991): p. 45.
2 ibid., p. 53.
3 ibid., pp 55–6.
4 ibid., p. 63.

Dunblane

The Cathedral Church of St Blane and St Laurence
(Church of Scotland)

Dunblane (population 7,000), is a town sprawled over the hills above the Allan Water, 8km north of Stirling and about 66km north-west of Edinburgh. The origins of the site are thought to go back to a foundation of St Blane c.600, but the facts are lost in the mists of time and the surviving stories about Blane are quite unreliable; even the years of his birth and death are not generally agreed. All that can be said with any certainty is that he was a disciple of the Irish saints, Comgall and Canice, and was buried somewhere in the vicinity of the town which now incorporates his name (*Dunblane* meaning 'the fort of Blane'). The rest of Blane's life is the subject of legend; but in the absence of verifiable fact, some of those stories may as well be given here as a representative collection of what was once believed about him.

Blane is alleged to have been born in Bute, perhaps about the year 565, a Briton of the kingdom of Strathclyde, and educated in Ireland for seven years. From there he went in a small boat, with neither sails nor oars, to be a missionary to the Picts in the north of Scotland. After this miraculous voyage he lit a lamp, which had been accidentally extinguished during the office of vespers, by means of fire and sparks proceeding from his finger tips. On his return through England from a pilgrimage in Rome, he raised a youth of noble birth from the dead and baptised him, calling him Columba (not to be confused with St Columba). Legend says that the boy is supposed to be buried somewhere within the precincts of the present cathedral. Blane himself died perhaps before the year 630. He was once thought to have been buried on the Isle of Bute, due to the presence on the island of a small twelfth century chapel dedicated in his name; but this is now thought to have been named after him rather than a commemoration of the site of his interment. Blane is generally accepted to have been a bishop and his feast day is 10 August.

Blane's foundation enjoyed a precarious existence, and there is no known succession of bishops at Dunblane after his death. The settlement was raided and burnt by the Britons of Strathclyde in 844 and 860, and again in 912 by the Danes. The oldest object at Dunblane today is the ninth century Pictish standing stone cross near the west door of the cathedral; it was found in 1873 underneath the floor of the chapter house.

By the twelfth century, Dunblane was of sufficient importance to be made the see of a territorial diocese, at the reorganisation of Scottish dioceses during the reign of King David I (1124–53). Construction of a cathedral was begun but not completed during the twelfth century, possibly during the episcopate of Bishop Laurence (1162–78), but the four lower stages of the cathedral tower are the only remains of that building.

The diocese had a troubled existence after the time of Bishop Laurence and there had been no bishop of Dunblane for two years until a Dominican friar named Clement was consecrated bishop of the diocese in 1233. Clement was received into the Dominican Order (the Order of Preachers) by St Dominic himself, and is credited with introducing the Order to Scotland; this cannot be verified. The Dominicans arrived in Scotland in 1230, it is said at the request of King Alexander II (1214–49). Other sources claim that they were brought to Scotland by William Malveisin, bishop of St Andrews (1202–38). Perhaps the three men together were responsible. Whatever the true facts, there is no doubting that Clement was a Dominican friar; but it is also true that there is no record of a Dominican friary at Dunblane.

On his arrival, Bishop Clement found a chaotic and poor diocese and a half-built cathedral. Much of the cathedral property had been alienated and Clement went to Rome at some date between 1235 and 1237 to appeal for the support of Pope Gregory IX in his efforts to put the matter right. 'Its rents were barely sufficient to maintain him for six months; there was no place in the cathedral wherein he could lay his head; there was no collegiate establishment, and that in this unroofed church the divine offices were celebrated by a certain rural chaplain'.[1] Clement returned to Dunblane with the full support of the pope and began a campaign to retrieve the diocesan revenues. In 1237 the bishops of Glasgow and Dunkeld were appointed to adjudicate between Bishop Clement and the earl of Monteith, who had seized a greater part of the church lands during the vacancy in see, and took the revenues from them; the bishop won the contest.

The present cathedral is due entirely to the decision of Clement not to finish the incomplete Romanesque cathedral. Everything but the tower was demolished and work began on the construction of the present cathedral. The chancel and the adjacent chapter house were the first to be started, and were completed during Clement's time. Work then began on the nave, but it was unlikely that it was finished before his death in 1258. Clement was beatified, although he has not been canonised; his feast day is on 19 March.

Dunblane Cathedral was completed by Clement's successor, Robert de Prebenda (1258 84), a French-speaking Anglo–Norman, but barely was the work finished than the new cathedral fell victim to the political turmoil that engulfed Scotland at the end of the thirteenth century. On the death of the young Queen Margaret (1286–90), the 'Maid of Norway', the throne of Scotland fell vacant and was claimed by several rival candidates. Bishop William of Dunblane (1284–91) declared his submission to King Edward I of England. It may have been an act of political prudence, but it did not save the cathedral. The king ordered the roof to be stripped of lead to provide material for the construction of siege engines against Stirling Castle; though he obligingly left a small portion of roof over each altar.

The subsequent life of the diocese was uneventful. Bishop Finlay Dermoch (1403–19) built the first bridge over the Allan in 1409; it was rebuilt in 1849 and that bridge can still be seen below the present enlarged structure. Bishop Michael Ochiltree (1429–47) crowned the six-year old King James II (1437–60), at the abbey church of Holyrood in Edinburgh, Scone – the usual place of coronation – being thought to be too near the scene of the murder of King James I in Perth. Bishop Ochiltree also raised the roof of the chancel and added the chapter stalls which can still be seen in the chancel. The tower was completed during the episcopate of Bishop James Chisholm (1487–1526) whose armorial bearings can be seen on the parapet.

The sixteenth century reformation brought less destruction to Dunblane than it did to many other cathedrals, and the damage was confined to the furnishings rather than the fabric of the building. In 1559 the cathedral was stripped of its ornaments and its ten altars by the earl of Argyll and the prior of St Andrews, who was to become earl of Moray and regent of the kingdom. They arrived one morning towards the end of June while the people were at mass. A priest was bold enough to ask why they had come and was informed that the cathedral was to be 'purified'. To gain time the dean said that the bishop would have to be consulted. 'Nay', said the earl, 'time presses, and I do not trust your bishop, but this condition will I make, that I do not come beyond the barrier into the choir'.[2] Then his followers cleared the nave of all its altars and the images of the saints. The fact that the furnishings of the choir were not destroyed at that time may account for the preservation of Bishop Ochiltree's fine chapter stalls.

With the exceptions of St Blane and the Blessed Clement, the best known of the bishops of Dunblane was Robert Leighton, who arrived at the restoration of the episcopacy in 1661. With humility, he chose Dunblane as the smallest and poorest see in Scotland. Leighton was far ahead of his time in his ideas of toleration. Ordained a presbyterian minister in 1641, he later became principal and professor of divinity at Edinburgh University. During his tenure of the see of Dunblane (1661–71) and then as archbishop of Glasgow (1671–4) he tried hard to bring presbyterians and episcopalians in a single church, but he was neither a typical episcopalian nor a consistent presbyterian and only aroused the suspicion and distrust of both sides at a time when extremism was the norm. Despairing of the task he resigned the see of Glasgow in 1674 and died in 1684. At his death he left his library to the clergy of the Dunblane diocese, and it can still be seen in the house built to receive it, situated in the street which leads to the cathedral.

After the imposition of the reformation, the chancel continued in use as the parish church. The nave was abandoned and its roof had collapsed by 1600; it remained roofless for nearly three hundred years and gradually came to be used as a burial ground. Richard Franck described the town in 1656 as 'Dirty Dumblaine'. 'Let us pass by it, and not cumber our discourse with so inconsiderable a corporation'.[3] 'I think it time lost, to survey the reliques of a ruinous heap of stones … there's nothing eminent but narrow streets and dirty houses'.[4] In 1689 Thomas Morer described the cathedral as 'a large church much abused by the wild Cameronians'.[5] About 1810 there was a report that 'some years ago the noblemen and gentlemen in this neighbourhood exerted themselves to arrest the rapid decay of this venerable building'. Nothing was done to the nave, and in 1829 it was described thus: 'the building of great length, the longest part roofless, but yet very entire, and still used as a burying ground. The great west window is singularly beautiful; but the eastern end of the building has been renewed, and fitted up as a parish church, neatly pewed with oak, the pulpit surmounted by an imperial crown. In the church are preserved the ancient prebendal stalls, of black oak, very curiously carved, the only remains of Popish furniture known to exist in any ecclesiastical structure north of the Tweed'.[6]

The chancel was repaired by Thomas Brown in 1861 and again by Sir George Gilbert Scott in 1872–3, but it was too small for the congregation and by the mid-1880s, it was in need of further work. In 1886 Alexander Ritchie was instituted as parish minister of Dunblane and decided that something more than patching and mending was needed. The nave, although in a good state of preservation, had been roofless for three hundred years. The chancel and chapter house, although roofed, were small and cramped, and were said to be leaky and draughty. The heritors of the parish, among whom was a

Mrs Janet Wallace of Glassinghall, had a legal obligation to provide a suitable parish church. Ritchie pressed them to come to a decision, but soon discovered that they saw no reason to share his sense of urgency. At one stage in the debate, it was suggested that the cathedral should be abandoned and a new red brick church built instead. The heritors were asked to contribute to the cost of the new church and Janet Wallace was said to be 'indignant in her refusal'. She stated that she would be glad to contribute to the restoration of the cathedral but nothing else and certainly not to its ruination. As Mrs Wallace was prepared to contribute the bulk of the cost, the momentous decision was taken to re-roof the nave, remove the dividing partition wall, and restore the whole cathedral to use.

The plan was not greeted with overwhelming approval. Opposition came from members of other denominations who, with some cause, objected to the Church of Scotland receiving so much help; and from those who claimed right of burial within the ruined nave. Opposition also came from the Society for the Protection of Ancient Buildings, a body whose members generally preferred picturesque and romantic-looking ivy-clad ruins. John Ruskin, the English art critic and writer, and a member of the Society, delivered a withering indictment of the proposed restoration: 'My dear Sir, Restorations are always either architects' jobs or ministers' vanities, and they are the worst sort of swindling and boasting. That of Dunblane Abbey, the loveliest ruin in Scotland (and, in its way, the loveliest in the world), would be the most vulgar brutality Scotland has committed since the reformation. I had rather hear she had run a railroad through it, and thrown the stones into the brook. Ever faithfully yours, John Ruskin'.[7] His opinion was partly justified, but no one who has seen the restored cathedral can doubt that the re-roofing of the nave has saved it from further inexorable deterioration.

Despite the negative comment, the proposed restoration plan attracted a good deal of enthusiasm and a planning committee started its deliberations in December 1888. Sir Robert Rowland Anderson (1834–1921), the dominant Scottish architect of his day, was given the task of supervising the work. After nine months of planning, work on the building started in September 1889. The congregation was able to continue worshipping in the chancel throughout most of 1890 when they moved to the recently built Victoria Hall in the town. There they remained until the first service held in the newly restored cathedral on 5 March 1893. The total cost of the restoration was about £26,000, of which £19,000 was contributed by Mrs Wallace and her family.

The nave was re-roofed and the whole cathedral brought back into use. Anderson reconstructed the windows, and designed the wooden screen between the nave and the chancel, the communion table and pulpit. Stained glass was soon re-introduced: the east window in 1901, the west window in 1906 and the south chancel windows in 1915. Further work on the chancel was done in 1914–15 to the designs of Sir Robert Lorimer. The result was the salvation of Bishop Clement's thirteenth century cathedral church.

Dunblane Cathedral is a long and handsome building situated in a wide churchyard which slopes down a steep bank at the west to the Allan Water, exuding an air of prosperous contentment. The plan is an aisled nave of eight bays, with the Romanesque tower out of alignment, looking like an incongruous insertion into the south nave aisle, and a six bay chancel with a chapter house attached to the north wall; there are no transepts. The nave is 39.3m long and 17.3m wide; the chancel is 24.6m long by 8.5m wide.

The west door, flanked by pointed blind arches, has twelve orders of shafts and mouldings; above are three lancets, each of two lights. The centre lancet has a cinquefoil head, the two either side have quatrefoil heads. In the gable is a vesica piscis, around which are carved leaves. Ruskin was enchanted by them: 'It is acknowledged to be beautiful by the most careless observer, and why beautiful? Simply because in its great contours it has the form of a forest leaf, and because in its decoration it has used nothing but forest leaves. He was no common man who designed that Cathedral of Dunblane. I know nothing so perfect in its simplicity, and so beautiful, so far as it reaches, in all the Gothic with which I am acquainted. And in just proportion to his power of mind, that man was content to work under nature's teaching, and, instead of putting a merely formal dog-tooth, as everybody else did at that time, he went down to the woody bank of that sweet river beneath the rocks on which he was building and he took up a few of the fallen leaves that lay by it, and he set them in his arch side by side forever'.[8] The window is now known as the Ruskin window.

The nave has a double clerestory but no triforium. The nave arcades are deeply moulded and rest on clustered columns. The double clerestory above has outer windows and an inner arcade with a passage between. Everything at this level is much weathered due to three centuries of exposure to the elements. The pattern of outer window and inner arcade with passage between is continued in the west window which appears deep-set behind a glass screen. The timber barrel roof dates from the restoration of 1893 and the bosses show the armorial bearings of the feudal patrons of the cathedral, followed by the royal arms. The series concludes above the chancel arch with the armorial bearings of Queen Victoria, in whose reign the restoration took place. Above the chancel arch can be seen twin openings looking through into the chancel; until the restoration, they were filled with glass. The Scots oak pews were designed by Sir Robert Lorimer, and the carved flower design on the end of each pew is unique. Lorimer was an outstanding designer in the early years of the twentieth century and the wood work at Dunblane is held to be among his finest achievements. The front pews of the nave, and those in the south-east corner, are decorated with carved animals, each said to represent a Christian virtue: e.g. the bloodhound for fidelity and watchfulness; the ox for patience and service; and the hare for zeal and eagerness. Each of the wrought iron pendants for the nave lights was made in 1935 and decorated with three flowers; again each design is unique.

The west window has glass by Clayton and Bell and represents the Tree of Jesse. It was presented in 1906 by the distinguished jurist Sir Robert Younger (1861–1946), later Lord Blanesburgh, in memory of his parents.

At the east end of the south aisle, in a tomb recess, lies a badly weathered effigy of a bishop, generally thought to be that of Bishop Michael Ochiltree. Two small adjacent recesses, one possibly a piscina and the other possibly an aumbry, indicate that an altar once stood at the end of this aisle.

The tower, which Bishop Clement incorporated into his church, projects awkwardly into the south aisle. The lower four floors of the tower are Romanesque and constructed of red freestone, the fourth has small Romanesque belfry windows, divided into two lights by a shaft. The fifth floor is yellow freestone and the sixth floor is grey freestone; both floors are probably late fifteenth or early sixteenth century. The red freestone parapet bears the arms of Bishop James Chisholm. The total height of tower and spire is 38.9m. The tower houses nine bells made by John Taylor of Loughborough and presented by Lord Blanesburgh in 1908; originally hung as a chime, in which stationary bells are struck by moving hammers, they were re-hung as a ringing peal in 1948, the cost being met by a bequest from Blanesburgh. A short flight of wooden stairs leads from the south nave aisle into the ground floor of the tower. The interior has a thirteenth century stone vault and a Romanesque arch in its east wall. A spiral staircase leads to the ringing chamber on the first floor, and then again to the clock room on the second floor, passing on the way a blocked doorway giving access to a removed floor. The clock was made by Hamilton and Inches and dates from 1908. From the clock room a ladder gives access to the bells and then to the roof.

The first two windows in the south aisle, past the intruding tower, are by Louis Davis, and date from 1917. The design is complex and mystical, but the broad themes are 'Departure' (the first window) and 'Arrival' (the second window). The windows commemorate James Webster Barty (1841–1915) and Anne Moubray Barty (1845–1914).

The circular font on a clustered stem, at the west end of the south aisle, is by Sir Rowland Anderson. Dating from 1879, it is carved with symbols of water and was given to the cathedral at the time of the restoration. Behind the font is a window depicting baptismal themes; the work of Douglas Strachan, and made in 1926, it was given in memory of John Duncan Nimmo and Robert Louis Nimmo. The silver sanctuary lamp above the font came from a Greek Orthodox church at Edessa and was donated to the cathedral in 1948. It had been given to J Hutchison Cockburn (minister of the cathedral, 1918–44), shortly after his appointment as Secretary to the newly-formed World Council of Churches at Geneva.

Steps in the south-west corner of the aisle, beyond the baptistery, lead to a tiny vaulted chapel once known as Katie Ogle's Hole. Katie Ogle is thought to have been a witch who awaited trial there and, in more primitive times, the room may have been used as a prison for witches. The 'hole' was restored and dedicated as the Clement Chapel in 1964 in memory of the cathedral's founder. On the wall of the entrance to the chapel, a small window made and given by Gordon Webster in 1964, depicts Bishop Clement. The chapel is a quiet peaceful place intended for private devotion; it has a modern bronze Majestas by Maxwell Allan.

On either side of the west door are sets of carved and canopied misericords, believed to date from the episcopate of Bishop James Chisholm (1487–1526).

At the west end of the north aisle, a door leads to a small vaulted chamber, from which a spiral staircase leads up to the passage between the west window and its arcade; here a fine view can be had of the restored nave. Also at the west end of the aisle is a Celtic Cross that was discovered under the nave during the restoration of 1893.

In the centre of the north aisle, by the doorway, can be seen a pair of medieval recumbent effigies said to commemorate Malise, eighth earl of Strathearn, and his countess. Of the two adjacent bells, the larger has a tediously precise inscription in which the bell presumes to relate its history. 'I was founded in Edinburgh 1612 by the care of William Blaikwood, Bailie of Dunblane, and stayed still so in my exercise till 1657 when I was broken by the unskillful direction and handling of some men, and by the care and expense of Harie Blaikwood, Bailie of Dunblane, the son of William. I am founded again at Brimen by M. Clavdigage, anno 1660. recast 1809 by T. Mears & Son of London, out of the funds of the kirk-session of Dunblane'. The other bell is dated 1687, and was given by Lieutenant General Drummond.

At the east end of the aisle, formerly the Lady Chapel, two notable local families, the Stirlings of Garden and the Stirlings of Keir, are commemorated by a large gilt, onyx and marble monument and various plaques. The large window in the north east corner was designed and made by Gordon Webster in 1968 and illustrates the theme of the compassion of Christ. In the last but one bay to the west is a recess containing a heraldic memorial to members of the Strathallan family, who by tradition are buried there. It was restored by the eighth Viscount Strathallan in 1893.

The pulpit is the work of Sir Robert Lorimer and is carved with representations of various saints. The screen which divides the nave and chancel is the work of Anderson and dates from the restoration. It represents the site of the wall which was constructed after the collapse of the nave roof. The screen is an unusual sight in a presbyterian church; but of all the 'presbyterian cathedrals' in Scotland, Dunblane represents the most thoughtful attempt to reconstitute the appearance of the medieval cathedral; to marry the reformed liturgy to the unreformed architecture. The sockets for the medieval rood screen can be seen on the north wall of the chancel immediately through the screen.

The woodwork of the stalls, organ case and reredos was designed by Lorimer, donated by John Graham Stewart and presented in 1914. After the restoration of 1893, an organ by Eustace Ingram of London was installed and given a case by Sir Rowland Anderson. In 1914 the organ was moved to the attic above the chapter house and given a new case by Lorimer, but the re-siting of the organ, in an area detached from the cathedral, proved to be acoustically unwise. A new heating system caused more problems and, by 1975, it was clear that the old organ had no future. The present organ, by the Dutch firm of Flentrop, was installed in Lorimer's organ case in 1989–90.

The reredos behind the communion table was designed to commemorate Bishop Robert Leighton (1661–71), who tried so valiantly to heal the bitterness between the presbyterian and episcopal wings of the church after the restoration of the episcopate. The reredos is designed to represent the seven corporal acts of mercy (Matthew 25:35). The east window above was designed by Charles Kempe and inserted in 1901.

On the north wall is the effigy of a bishop, once thought to be that of the early fifteenth century Bishop Finlay Dermoch. It is now generally agreed that such a prominent place of honour in the chancel would more likely be given to Bishop Clement, the cathedral's builder. A brass plate naming the effigy to be that of Bishop Clement was erected on 25 September 1983 to commemorate a visit by Queen Elizabeth The Queen Mother. Whether that will suppress all further doubt and debate about the identity of the effigy is another matter.

The magnificent collection of fifteenth century misericords, on the north and south walls of the chancel (three on the north and seven on the south), date from the episcopate of Bishop Michael Ochiltree, and mercifully survived the sixteenth century reformation. A square-headed recess on the south wall could conceivably have been the aumbry for the reservation of the Blessed Sacrament.

The six windows on the south side of the chancel are filled with stained glass illustrating the Benedicite. Designed by Louis Davis, they were presented by Sir Robert Younger in 1915. In the middle of the chancel floor are three large blue stones with brasses. The inscription on the centre brass reads: 'In memory of Margaret, eldest daughter of John, first Lord Drummond, by tradition privately married to King James IV (1488–1513), and poisoned at Drummond Castle with her sisters Euphemia and Sybilla by some of the nobles, who desired the King's marriage with the Princess Margaret of England. The three sisters were buried beneath these slabs in the choir of the Cathedral of which their uncle Walter Drummond was Dean, AD 1501'. Euphemia is on the south side and Sybilla is on the north. The stones are original; the brasses were presented in 1897 by George Drummond, earl of Perth and Melfort (1807–1902), and his daughter Lady Edith Drummond (1854–1937). The story of Euphemia and Sybilla Drummond is the stuff of family legend; although the Drummonds themselves believed it, there is no need for anyone else to do so.

The chancel is adjoined by a north aisle, also thirteenth century but older than the chancel and only connected to it by a small doorway. It is thought to have been built as a temporary church by Bishop Clement, while the cathedral was in the course of construction, and then subsequently used as the Lady Chapel and chapter house. The chapter houses at Dunkeld and Fortrose Cathedrals are in the same position on the north side of the chancel. The aisle has a groined vault and Scots oak panelling; the windows are filled with early twentieth century glass by Douglas Strachan and Gordon Webster. Above the aisle is a room that probably served as the cathedral library and is now used as the organ loft; it is lit by several small windows over those of the aisle below. The openings into the chancel are modern.

The slight remains of the thirteenth century bishop's palace are to the south of the cathedral on the edge of the bank that leads down to the Allan Water. Only grassed-over vaulted lower chambers remain.

Above the bank of the Allan Water, Dunblane Cathedral enjoys a location not unlike Dunkeld Cathedral above the Tay, although there is less natural beauty and no shrouding by trees; but there the similarity ends. The sad, half-ruined cathedral at Dunkeld needs to be veiled by the natural order to avoid the remorseless exposure of its tragic condition. Dunblane Cathedral has no need to be shielded from gaze or supported by natural beauty. The restoration of 1889–93 has renewed a strikingly visible and proudly eminent cathedral church, which lacks only a cathedra formally to authenticate its status. Nevertheless, Bishop Clement would probably be delighted to know that it was the indignation and the generosity of one woman – Janet Wallace – that has preserved his long and handsome cathedral church.

1 Butler, Dugald (1901): p. 48.
2 Lindsay, Ian Gordon (1926): p. 64.
3 Brown, P Hume (ed.) (1891): p. 194.
4 ibid., p. 195.
5 ibid., p. 287.
6 Botfield, Beriah (1830): p. 19.
7 Lindsay, Ian Gordon (1926): pp 67–8.
8 Addis, M E Leicester (1901): p. 64.

Dundee

Dundee lies on the north bank of the Tay estuary, 88km north of Edinburgh. The origin of the name of the city is obscure, but might be roughly translated as 'fort of fire'; perhaps a reference to the character of the chieftain whose fort it was.

Now a commercial and industrial city, and a port, Dundee was made a royal burgh c.1190 by King William the Lion (1165–1214), and developed into one of the principal towns of Scotland. It is the home of two cathedrals, one for the Scottish Episcopal diocese of Brechin, and the other for the Roman Catholic diocese of Dunkeld.

The Cathedral Church of St Paul

Diocese of Brechin
(Scottish Episcopal Church)

The episcopal cathedral is the successor of a number of chapels serving the diocese of Brechin after the episcopalians were forced to go 'underground' in 1689. Initially built as a parish church, it was raised to the status of the cathedral church of the diocese of Brechin in 1904.

The origins of the cathedral lie in the remarkable ministry of Alexander Penrose Forbes, bishop of Brechin (1847–75). Forbes had an early career with the East India Company, before entering Brasenose College, Oxford, in 1840. There, like so many of his undergraduate contemporaries, he was much influenced and inspired by the teachings of John Henry Newman and the other founding fathers of Oxford Movement. Abandoning his original intention to return to India, he was ordained in 1844; from that point onwards, his rise was meteoric. He was curate of Aston Rowant in Oxfordshire 1844–5, curate of St Thomas, Oxford 1845–6; incumbent of Stonehaven, Kincardine 1846–7, and then, from January to August 1847, vicar of St Saviour's Church, Leeds. The incumbency at Stonehaven was due to Forbes expressing an interest in working in the Scottish Church to Bishop David Moir of Brechin (1840–7). When Moir died in August 1847, Forbes was not unknown to the diocese, and his name was presented to the electors of the diocesan synod at the suggestion of the future prime minister, William Gladstone. Thirty years old and only three years in holy orders, Forbes was elected bishop of Brechin by a large majority over his rival W E Henderson, and remained there for the rest of his life.

Forbes was a learned and holy priest who was as much at home in the world of academics as he was in the dreadful slums of Dundee, but his episcopate was not

The Cathedral Church of St Paul

without controversy. His defence of the doctrine of the Real Presence, in his primary charge in August 1857, brought the accusation of encouraging eucharistic adoration, and he was criticised by the bishops of Edinburgh, Argyll and Glasgow. In May 1858, the other Scottish bishops issued a pastoral letter saying that they felt bound to resist the teaching of the bishop of Brechin on the disputed matter. In May 1859, a charge of erroneous preaching was levelled against the bishop by his defeated rival, W E Henderson, and by two vestrymen. Forbes was 'examined' by his brother bishops. In March 1860 they issued a declaration of admonition and censure, warning him to be more careful in the future, but he was not deprived of his see, and continued as bishop of Brechin until his death, a much-loved figure throughout his diocese.

After many years of ill-health, Forbes died at the age of only fifty-nine in 1875. The Oxford theologian, Henry Parry Liddon was pressed to accept the bishopric. Liddon was Dean Ireland Professor of Exegesis at Oxford University, and a canon of St Paul's Cathedral in London. He stood firmly in the tradition of the Oxford Movement and would have been an eminent and appropriate successor to Forbes, but he declined for much the same reason as John Mason Neale declined the deanery of Perth in 1850; he felt that he was needed more in England. 'In the evening Mr Nicholson, the Dean of Brechin, came here. He was most anxious to persuade me to accept the bishopric. He said that I should be elected unanimously by clergy and laity. He had written out several arguments to move me. I said 'No': (1) on the ground of nationality; (2) on that of its being necessary to abandon my stall at St Paul's, and my Professorship to Puritan and Rationalistic successors'.[1]

When Forbes was elected bishop, he moved the episcopal residence from the ancient but small rural town of Brechin itself, to the city of Dundee. Dundee in the 1840s was a grim place, crowded, squalid and impoverished. 'There was work enough in the jute mills, the ship-building yards, and the engineering works, but wages were low and so was the price of whisky. The slums were appalling... whole families lived in one room, foul and bug-ridden, thick with stench, devoid of sanitation. The only escape was in the pub'.[2] Dundee's episcopalian congregation worshipped, under the dedication of St Paul, in a large upper room in a bank house, furnished with green-baize covered pews and an altar draped in red velvet. On 'Communion Sundays' (the eucharist was not yet celebrated every Sunday), the rail was hung with white linen. The congregation numbered about three hundred and ranged from the county gentry to the very poor.

Forbes decided that this upper room, in use since 1812, was not a fit place for an episcopal congregation. As early as January 1848, he had begun to take practical steps to erect a church, with the intention of providing Dundee's episcopalian congregation with a beautiful church in which they could find relief from the squalor of most of their homes, a building of which they could be proud, and a building that would express a confident episcopalian presence. In an early sermon to his congregation, he urged them, 'to the great holy work of building to the glory of God a stately church... a builded prayer in stone and lime, a standing creed professing by its very form of architecture that we believe in the triune God and in the crucified Saviour'.[3] He began collecting money to build a church, and, by curbing his own expenditure, willingly included a good proportion of his own income. It was a measure of his vision, confidence and persuasiveness that Forbes was able to persuade his congregation, firstly to raise and spend £14,000 on a new church; and secondly, that it should be large enough to accommodate 800 people, when a church with half that capacity would have sufficed for Dundee's episcopalians.

The commission to design the new church was given to Sir George Gilbert Scott (1811–78). Influenced by the study of Augustus Pugin's work on medieval architecture, Scott was a principal exponent of the Gothic revival style of architecture, and undertook restoration work on a number of English cathedrals, including Ely, Lichfield and Salisbury. Among his other enduring commissions are St Mary's Episcopal Cathedral in Edinburgh, and the Albert Memorial and the Midland Grand Hotel (fronting St Pancras Station), in London.

St Paul's Church (it was not formally made the cathedral church of the diocese of Brechin until 1904), was erected in 1853–5 on one of the most historic sites in the city; the site of a castle demolished c.1314. Contemporary opinion was divided on the decision to build the church on a site which, for all its history, was neither capacious nor exposed enough to allow Scott's architecture to be seen to its best advantage. The *Building Chronicle* was critical; 'the new episcopal church on Castle Hill seems destined to form a striking instance of the prejudice a fine building may suffer from an ill-chosen site. It is hemmed in on the west by tall buildings with scarcely a footpath around it, while all around the other sides a glimpse can only be got of its elaborate features through rifts between houses'. Others thought that St Paul's was wonderful. When the hymnologist John Mason Neale visited Dundee in 1855, he thought St Paul's Church to be the finest he had seen since All Saints', Margaret Street, in London. All Saints was reckoned to be the 'model' church of the Ecclesiologists, the architectural wing of the Oxford Movement. *The Ecclesiologist* shared Neale's opinion. The church 'gains much by its unequalled site... The treatment is purely Northern and Teutonic, like the plan of the building itself. In it, everything fits into its own place and is in harmony with the remaining structure... St Paul's stands high among the Churches of the [Gothic] Revival. All concerned in the undertaking have to congratulate themselves on a rare success. In the nave everything is sacrificed to height, and the effect is worth the sacrifice'.[4]

There is no point from which to gain a good view of the whole cathedral, apart from the air. The site is cramped and crowded and the cathedral is hemmed in by buildings on the south and the east. One gains the strong impression of a building that, internally and externally, soars upwards to break free from the confines of its neighbours. Scott's 63.9m tower and spire is a prominent landmark in the city centre, and has eight bells, the tenor weighing more than one ton, cast by Mears and Stainbank of London in 1871. The total cost of the cathedral was £14,000. When the vestry was told that the spire would cost £700 they asked for the design to be changed to reduce the cost; Scott indignantly refused.

The cathedral, built in the Geometrical Decorated style, stands on Castlehill with its principal entrance in Nethergate. A flight of steep steps sweeps up through the vaulted ground floor of the tower. The interior is as lofty as the tower promises; the nave arcades rest on slender columns and support a steeply-pitched timber roof. The nave has no clerestory, although there is one in the transepts which are lower than the nave. The cathedral is 36.5m long and, although at first it appears to be a single hall, it is cruciform with a nave of five bays, shallow transepts, an apsidal chancel, tower and spire. It was intended that the chancel should be flanked by small chapels, and that the organ and choir should be accommodated in the gallery under the tower, but the plans were changed and the organ now occupies the north chapel; it was built by Hill of London in 1865, reconstructed by Rothwell in 1937, and reconstructed again, by Hill, Norman and Beard, in 1975.

All the windows have stained glass except one in the north aisle and the lower part of the high west window. The west window was at one time filled with stained glass depicting St Peter and St Paul. The lower part was blown out in a storm and has never been replaced. The pews are pine and typical of their date.

At the west end of the north aisle is the Lindores Cabinet; the panels, probably sixteenth century, are thought to have come from the choir stalls of Lindores Abbey. They were assembled in this setting in 1923. In the second bay of the north aisle is the vestry doorway, surmounted by a bust of Bishop Forbes who is buried below the chancel.

The north transept, known as St Roque's Chapel, contains the altar, reredos and war memorial from St Roque's Church, built in the Blackscroft area of the city at the beginning of the twentieth century, and closed in 1956. The reredos is a gilt and blue, vaguely Arts and Crafts construction with a representation of the Crucifixion. The altar was maliciously damaged by fire early in 1994 and subsequently restored. The steel and wood railings are modern.

The chancel has a stone vault and a clerestory above the bay containing the pale oak stalls. The stalls themselves have alternating plain and canopied seats in the back rows, and depict effigies of St Andrew, St Paul, King David I, St Margaret of Scotland, and St Modwenna, abbess of a local religious house. The stalls are labelled as overleaf:

BISHOP	DEAN
CANON	CANON
CANON	CANON
CANON	CANON
CHAPLAIN	CHAPLAIN
PRECENTOR	PROVOST

The brass in the centre of the chancel floor marks the tomb of Bishop Forbes. A recumbent white marble effigy of the bishop can be seen within a canopied recess on the north side of the chancel. The high altar is of black marble and the reredos above contains a trefoil-headed Italian mosaic panel by Antonio Salviati of Venice, depicting Christ in glory; it is framed by alabaster work and shafts of different marbles. The triple sedilia has marble canopies on free-standing columns.

The marble credence and aumbry on the south side of the altar is a memorial to Sister Margaret Mary of the Community of St Mary the Virgin and St Modwenna. The community, one of the dreams of Bishop Forbes, was founded in 1870 at King Street, Dundee. Forbes became the first Anglican bishop since the sixteenth century reformation to found a religious community, but his dream did not flourish. The little sisterhood never had more than a handful of members and was almost extinct by the end of the nineteenth century. The mother foundress died in 1900 and the convent in King Street was taken over by the Society of St Margaret in the following year. The Sister Margaret Mary commemorated by the aumbry was probably Miss Margaret Neish, one of the two original sisters of the community who died in 1887.

The Lady Chapel in the south chancel aisle is reached through the screen at the side of the stalls. Its altar and the mosaic panel of the Annunciation were transferred from an earlier chapel, dedicated to St Paul, which stood in Castle Street.

There are several brass memorials in the south transept. The most recent is that to Bishop John Sprott (1903–82) and his wife Freda Bone (1905–91). Sprott was provost of the cathedral 1940–59 and bishop of Brechin 1959–75.

In the south aisle is a pulpit of Caen stone with pink granite pilasters and a pale oak tester. There is a memorial to Patrick Chalmers (1819–91), son of James Chalmers, the (disputed) inventor of the postage stamp. Patrick did much to promote his father's cause and this memorial was erected by his daughters in 1919 on the centenary of his birth. There is also an oil painting of Bishop Forbes. On the window sill of the last bay in the aisle is a bust of Alan Don, provost of Dundee 1921–31 and dean of Westminster Abbey 1946–59. At the west end of the cathedral is the font; the bowl is by George Gilbert Scott; the pedestal is from Lindores Abbey and is medieval. The cover was donated by the Clunie family.

A nine-phase restoration of the cathedral and its adjoining buildings began in 1984 and is still to be completed. Funding has largely been provided through the generosity of Historic Scotland and the Heritage Lottery Fund. The stonework of the tower and spire have been fully restored, as has the north wall of the church, and about half of the stained glass, and it is anticipated that the interior of the cathedral will be refurbished in due course.

The restoration plan also includes the two buildings which share Castlehill with the cathedral: Castlehill House and the adjoining St Roque's Hall. Castlehill House, a Georgian town house of c.1760, but with nineteenth century alterations, served as the residence of Bishop Forbes and later of the cathedral provost. It has been fully restored inside and outside, the external walls having been harled and limewashed. By the way that Scott embellished all the external cathedral walls, including that which abuts Castlehill House, it seems clear that he expected the house to be demolished in due course. St Roque's Hall, designed by Alexander McCulloch, was built c.1888 as an Episcopal Church school known as Roodyard School. The school closed before the First World War and the building now serves as a base for the cathedral's offices.

1 Johnston, John Octavius (1904): p. 243.
2 Lochhead, Marion (1966): p. 112.
3 Perry, William (1939): pp 49–50.
4 McKean, Charles & Walker, David (1984): p. 19.

DUNKELD: *The Cathedral Church of St Columba*

EDINBURGH: *The Cathedral Church of St Giles*

EDINBURGH: *The Cathedral Church of St Giles*

EDINBURGH: *The Cathedral Church of St Mary*

EDINBURGH: *The Cathedral Church of St Mary*

The Cathedral Church of St Andrew

Diocese of Dunkeld
(Roman Catholic Church)

At the beginning of the nineteenth century, the entire Roman Catholic population of Dundee numbered only about fifty individuals, and for most of the eighteenth century there was no Roman Catholic priest resident in the city. William Pepper, the first resident priest since the sixteenth century reformation, arrived in 1782. The few Catholics in the city worshipped in a small room at 93 Hawkshill until 1792, when an upper floor of a house in Seagate was purchased. When part of the ground was required to improve the harbour, the congregation moved again, in 1813, to Meadowside.

Due to the large influx of Irish Roman Catholics seeking employment in the jute mills of Dundee, the Catholic population had soared to 5,000 by the 1830s. In 1825 there were thirty-nine baptisms at the chapel; by the following decade, the number had risen to an average of 250 each year. The chapel in Meadowside became inadequate and a site on which to build a new church was procured in Nethergate opposite South Tay Street. There was a certain risk involved in choosing such a prominent site. At a time when the Roman Catholic Church was still emerging from the shadows of persecution, courage was required to erect a Roman Catholic church in the visible expanse of Nethergate.

Building began on 1 June 1835 and the completed chapel was solemnly dedicated by the vicar apostolic of the Eastern District on 7 August 1836. The whole Roman Catholic population of Scotland had been put under the jurisdiction of a single vicar apostolic in 1694. The jurisdiction was divided into Highland and Lowland Districts in 1712; and into Eastern, Western and Northern Districts in 1827. With the restoration of the hierarchy in 1878, Dundee was placed in the diocese of Dunkeld, which embraced the three ancient dioceses of Dunkeld, Dunblane and Brechin (the latter two being suppressed) and a small part of the diocese of St Andrews. In 1886, during the episcopate of Bishop George Rigg (1878–87), the church was designated the pro-cathedral of the diocese.

St Andrew's Cathedral stands in Nethergate, a few hundred yards east of St Paul's Cathedral of the Scottish Episcopal Church. It was designed by George Mathewson, an eminent local architect and, with some alterations at the east end, it is much as he left it. The sanctuary was reconstructed as a war memorial in 1920–2 and was enlarged and extended to the south by cutting into the presbytery accommodation. It was also elevated from the floor and this is the work which can still be seen today. The architect of the extension was C G Menart. The newly-extended cathedral was re-opened on 5 February 1922 and less than a year later, on 14 January 1923, it was formally raised to the status of the cathedral church of the diocese of Dunkeld. In his book *The Cathedrals of Scotland*, published in 1926, Ian Lindsay, who had no great fondness for Scotland's Roman Catholic cathedrals, managed a slight compliment: 'The building belongs to the bad period of the beginning of the last century, but the flight of steps to the high altar is rather imposing, and the whole interior has a fresher appearance than most'.[1]

The cathedral is a really curious building and worth visiting if only to see how the architect made use of such a steeply sloping site. Because of this, the cathedral is aligned north-south rather than the traditional east-west. The only part of the building that is both visible, attractive and of architectural interest, is the north front (dismissed by *The Builder* as 'churchwarden's Gothic'), which provides the main entrance on Nethergate. The front, faced with ashlar, with its ogee-arched central doorway below a large perpendicular window, token embattlement, and four tall crocketed finials, is a quaint example either of late Gothick or of early Gothic Revival, according to opinion. Four empty niches still await resident saints.

The rest of the exterior of the cathedral is exceptionally uninteresting, and the long walk needed to view the south gable is not necessary except for the curious; as the cathedral is built on such a steep slope, it is in fact very difficult to view the other walls other than from a distance. From Nethergate narrow, dark and uninviting stepped side passages lead to the rear of the cathedral. Walking down the passage on the west side, the visitor could, until a few years ago, have seen a confessional projecting from the cathedral wall on a cantilever in a most alarming way. This has now been removed though the blocked opening can still be seen. A similar situation can be seen on the east side where the projecting confessional stands on a bridge over the passage way.

Appreciating the full oddity of the design of the building requires a walk down to and across the former railway yard (presently a car park) at the rear. From this view, any idea that the building is a church can be abandoned; all trace of Gothick or Gothic disappears, and the cathedral resembles nothing so much as a large shapeless ramshackle warehouse, with a four storey house built on to the south gable. It can be seen from here that the slope of the ground is so steep that the uppermost floor of the house is lower than the sills of the sanctuary windows, and that various rooms and a parish hall inhabit the space below the cathedral floor.

Through the main entrance on Nethergate is a lobby, with a stair on the east side leading up to the gallery. On the west side of the lobby is the baptistery, seen through a glazed door and a wrought iron screen. The baptistery was renovated in 1874, and the ornate Gothic font and the stained glass window, depicting the baptism of Jesus, both date from this time. The baptistery was further renovated in 1923.

The interior of the cathedral has an unusual layout. The sloping floor of the nave funnels towards a shallow V-shaped sanctuary which is 15.2m high, the high altar being reached by an astonishing flight of sixteen steps. This arrangement gives the interior the quite distinct feeling of a theatre, the nave and gallery representing the stalls and the grand circle; the chancel arch becomes the proscenium arch, and the sanctuary becomes the elevated stage. The arrangement is partly because of the sloping site and partly because of the elevation of the sanctuary in the alterations of 1920–2. Although a central altar has been introduced to conform to the liturgical decrees of the Second Vatican Council, the high sanctuary and the numerous steps preclude anything more, short of demolition and rebuilding.

The view towards the sanctuary is framed by five Tudor arches on slender posts, probably cast iron, that support a gallery. The main roof, a span of over 15.2m, rests on plaster imitation Tudor arches which spring from foliage corbels and a wall-arcade high on the side walls. What may be described as the chancel arch is similar, with angel corbels, but the sanctuary arch beyond is a weak and notional design. The cathedral is furnished with pine pews and the walls have a scumbled wooden dado. The cathedral is lit from circular bronzed electroliers each with four glass pendant fittings.

The north end of the nave is dominated by the First World War memorial. Represented by statues of the Holy Family, the memorial was erected during the alterations of 1920–2, and serves as a memorial to the families who lost members during the War.

The canopied Carrara marble pieta near the baptistery is a memorial to Bishop Angus Macfarlane (1901–12), and above is a large crucifix formerly carried in Good Friday processions.

Four stained glass windows in the body of the cathedral are by Mayer of Munich and were dedicated on 2 December 1928, together with the new organ and the re-modelled organ gallery. In a touching gesture, much of the expense was met by Mgr John Turner, administrator of St Andrew's Cathedral 1902–38, from the money he had received on the occasion of his golden jubilee to priesthood. The first window beyond the pieta depicts the Last Supper, then one depicting St Peter. The matching windows in the other wall depict St Theresa and the Conversion of St Paul.

The two further windows, closest to the sanctuary, on the east and west walls depict the mysteries of the Rosary and were inserted c.1880–90. The Sorrowful and Glorious mysteries can be seen on the east wall; the Joyful and Sorrowful mysteries on the west wall.

Between the stained glass windows on both side walls are four painted panels depicting St Catherine and St Andrew (on the east wall) and St George and St Margaret (on the west wall). They were painted by Alexander Christie and his pupils for the private chapel of a Roman Catholic family at Murthly in Perthshire. When the estate passed out of the family, the panels were acquired (c.1875) by St Mary's Cathedral, Edinburgh. After much negotiating, Mgr Turner acquired the panels for his cathedral and they were dedicated on 5 September 1932.

The Stations of the Cross are statuary in carved oak Gothic frames, and were dedicated on 27 September 1896. Enlargement (c.1986) of the ritual choir, to conform with the liturgical decrees of the Second Vatican Council, has entailed bringing new marble steps forward to the flimsy Gothic oak rail, reputedly carved by Mgr Robert Clapperton (1831–1906), administrator of the cathedral 1869–1901. The east end is a composition of marble, light oak and gilding, with walls largely in pale green. The flight of steps to the high altar is imposing but gives the sanctuary a very shallow appearance.

The windows on the east wall depict, south to north, the arms of the dioceses of Brechin and Dunblane, and the arms of the dioceses of Dunkeld and St Andrews, and the two Scottish saints, Columba and Margaret; and on the west wall, south to north, the armorial bearings of Bishops Angus Macfarlane (1901–12) and Robert Fraser (1913–14), the armorial bearings of Bishops George Rigg (1878–87) and James Smith (1890–1900), and the two Irish saints Patrick and Bridget (a poignant reminder of home to the many Irish immigrants who came to work in Scotland in the early nineteenth century).

The bishop's throne is an ornate oak chair dating from 1896, the work of Mr Bremner of Broughty Ferry. The windows above the throne display the armorial bearings of the four ancient dioceses (Brechin, Dunblane, Dunkeld and St Andrews), all or parts of which are now incorporated into the diocese of Dunkeld. The oak chapter stalls are perched behind the two green-grained marble ambos. The ambos have metal inserts of the four evangelists: Matthew and Mark on the east, and Luke and John on the west. Plaques commemorating the diocese and the chapter can be seen on the east and west walls.

The Cathedral Church of St Andrew

The high altar and gilded wooden reredos date from 1896. All the sanctuary windows date from 1922; the window above the altar depicts the martyrdom of St Andrew. The two solid brass sanctuary lamps on either side of the high altar are early twentieth century.

The chancel is flanked by two marble altars. On the north, the Sacred Heart altar, solemnly blessed on 29 September 1885 – the adjacent window depicts Christ and his mother, with St Matthew and St Michael. On the south side of the sanctuary, the altar of Our Lady of Perpetual Succour, inaugurated on 26 May 1889, has a wooden Gothic reredos. Above the tabernacle is a picture of the dedication. The base of the altar is a green, blue and white marble representation of the tomb of Christ. The adjacent window, dating from 1897, depicts the Holy Family at Nazareth, with the Blessed Virgin Mary and her parents Joachim and Anne.

At the side entrance in the west wall is a marble and brass memorial to Mgr Robert Clapperton. A black marble plaque beneath the west gallery records the 1988 celebration of the millennium of Christianity in Russia by Dundee's Ukrainian Catholic community.

St Andrew's Cathedral is not an architectural wonder, but it is an architectural curiosity and well worth a visit. Externally, on Nethergate, it looks like a church; from every other viewpoint, it could be anything.

1 Lindsay, Ian Gordon (1926): p. 247.

Dunkeld

The Cathedral Church of St Columba
(Church of Scotland)

In their survey of the ecclesiastical architecture of Scotland, published at the end of the nineteenth century, David MacGibbon and Thomas Ross were moved by the site of Dunkeld Cathedral. 'Situated in the beautiful, though rugged, glen which forms the pass to the Highlands from the fertile lowlands of Perthshire, this grey and venerable ruin adds an unexpected and charming interest to the lovely scene of the locality'.[1]

Dunkeld, 24km north-west of Perth and 88km north-west of Edinburgh, is a town with a population of about 1,000, standing on the bank of the River Tay, which is crossed at this point by a handsome bridge of 1809 designed by Thomas Telford. Although otherwise of no significance, Dunkeld has perhaps the most enchanting site of any cathedral in Scotland. The building itself is a little disappointing, consisting of a roofless nave and a dull chancel; but it stands in a most beautiful location, surrounded by tall trees, in the centre of an immaculate lawn that slopes gently down to the river that meanders through wooded mountains. The landscape, rather than the architecture, provides the beauty of Dunkeld.

The earliest history of Dunkeld is obscure. A Culdee settlement is said to have been founded here in the sixth century by St Columba and St Kentigern, or perhaps a century later by St Adomnán, but this is speculative. A monastic foundation was certainly established here before 729 by Celtic monks who had been driven out of Iona by the frequent Viking raids. The relics of St Columba were brought here from Iona about 850 when the island monastery was being regularly plundered. The monks' experience of the Viking raids at Iona may well have contributed to the nature of their new settlement at Dunkeld, a name which means 'the fort of the Culdees'.

Dunkeld Abbey occupied a prominent position in early medieval Scotland. Its first known abbot, Tuathal, who died in 865, was described as the chief bishop of Fortriu, but whatever ecclesiastical primacy he and his successors may have exercised in those early years, had passed to the abbot of St Andrews by the middle of the tenth century. The prominence of Dunkeld continued, and many of the later abbots were married laymen who were officers of state in the kingdom; they would have drawn an income from the abbey estates but had little involvement in the daily life of the monastic community.

Crinan, lay abbot of Dunkeld, who was killed in battle in 1045, was married to a daughter of King Malcolm II (1005–34) and their son was to rule as King Duncan I (1034–40) until murdered by his cousin and successor King Macbeth (1040–57). The income from the abbey was probably considerable enough for it to be used as a perquisite for members of the royal family. Ethelred (died before 1097), son of King Malcolm III (1058–93) and Queen Margaret, was the last lay abbot of Dunkeld.

Dunkeld may have been established as the see of a territorial diocese in the early twelfth century but the history of the Scottish bishops and bishoprics before the reign of King David I (1124–53) is obscure. Cormac appears as the first of a new line of bishops at Dunkeld, although he was not specifically styled bishop of Dunkeld until about 1127. The boundaries of the dioceses of the adjoining dioceses of Dunkeld, Dunblane and St Andrews were complicated, and the three dioceses often included detached plots of land wholly within the boundaries of the other two dioceses; the bishop of Dunkeld for example had jurisdiction over several detached territories along the shores of the Firth of Forth. The island of Inchcolm in the Forth also belonged to Dunkeld and most of the bishops chose to be buried there. The diocese at first extended across to the west coast but sometime between 1183 and 1189 the western part was detached to form the diocese of Argyll which, after 1236, had its cathedral at Lismore. The mid-fifteenth century chronicler, Walter Bower, said that this was done at the request of Bishop John Scot (1183–1203) who felt unable to help the Gaelic-speaking part of his flock. Heart-warming though the story is, and charitable though it would be to accept it, a more likely explanation is that the division was engineered by King William the Lion (1165–1214) to reduce the influence of a man who had not been his own choice for the bishopric of Dunkeld.

The last serious invasion of Scotland by an English army, led to its rout at the battle of Bannockburn in 1314. Smaller but less threatening raids occurred in subsequent years, and in 1317, a landing at Donisbristle on the coast of Fife created a panic. What followed was the stuff of courage and heroism, though possibly embellished. Bishop William Sinclair of Dunkeld (1309–37) was at Donisbristle at the time and determined to resist the invaders. He gathered a small fighting group of sixty men and led the assault on the English shouting, 'Turn, for shame, and let all who love Scotland follow me'. The English lost 500 men and were driven back to their ships. When King Robert the Bruce (1306–29) heard the story he said that Sinclair should be his own bishop, and Sinclair was long known as 'Bruce's own bishop'.

The age of Dunkeld Cathedral is more complex than might at first be apparent and nothing of the present building is earlier than c.1250. The chancel of the cathedral was long thought, on the evidence of a sixteenth century chronicler, to have been built entirely during the episcopate of Bishop Sinclair, who employed a mason known as Master Robert. But parts of the lower walls, and possibly much of the upper walls, are mid- to late-thirteenth century, and pre-date Sinclair. The architectural details of the wall arcade, which runs along the north and part of the east wall of the chancel, suggests a mid-thirteenth century date, though the great east window has Perpendicular tracery.

The nave of the cathedral was built in the fifteenth century. It was begun in 1406 by Bishop Robert de Cardeny (1398–1437), who also fortified the bishop's palace. He was buried in the chapel of St Ninian at the east end of the south nave aisle, where his tomb can still be seen. The nave was completed during the episcopate of Bishop Thomas Lauder (1457–75), who erected the south porch and began work on the chapter house on the

The ruined nave of the Cathedral Church of St Columba

north side of the chancel in 1457. He also began work on the north-west tower in 1467, but it was completed by his successor Bishop James Livingstone (1475–83), whose armorial bearings were placed near the top.

Bishop Lauder is also reported to have given many ornaments including vestments, six candlesticks, a chalice, a silver cross containing part of the true cross, a silver pyx, bishop's throne, chancel stalls, and a reredos for the high altar painted with representations of twenty-four miracles performed by St Columba. He also built the first bridge over the Tay at Dunkeld in 1461.

Being bishop of Dunkeld was by no means a safe and comfortable position. 'The prelates of Dunkeld were much exposed to the aggressions of the heads of the Highland clans in the vicinity of the diocese, with whom a constant state of warfare was maintained. The revenues of the see were frequently intercepted by armed bands who waylaid the bishop's officers, and carried them off by violence; and such of the lands belonging to the bishops as were contiguous to the estates of the Highland chiefs were either seized and appropriated to their own use, or plundered and laid waste. The bishops were assaulted even while officiating in their own cathedral; and those who ventured to resist, or bring to punishment, the leaders by whom these outrages were perpetrated, were beset by parties against whose hostile attacks they were compelled to defend themselves by a numerous retinue of armed attendants'.[2]

'In the reign of James II, the earl of Atholl, nephew of that monarch, assembled the canons of the abbey, and requested them to appoint his brother, Andrew Stuart, though not in full orders, successor to the see. With this request they thought proper, through intimidation, to comply; but the election was afterwards abrogated by Pope Leo X, and Gavin Douglas, uncle of the earl of Angus, was appointed, whose arrival to take possession of the see caused the servants of Stuart to fly to arms, and seize upon the palace and the tower of the cathedral, whence they discharged a volley of shot against the house of the dean, to which Douglas had retired to receive the homage of the clergy. On the following day, the city was filled with the armed adherents of both parties, and a dreadful scene of violence ensued; but at length, Stuart, finding it impossible to relieve his men in the palace, was compelled to abandon it, and, having no hope of retaining the prelacy, he retired on condition of being allowed to hold that portion of the bishop's rents which he had already received, and also the churches of Alyth and Cargill, on payment annually of a trifling acknowledgement'.[3]

Bishop Gavin Douglas (1515–21) is remembered for having first translated Virgil into Scots, a work done when he was still provost of St Giles' Church, Edinburgh. Douglas asked Archbishop James Beaton of Glasgow (1509–23) to mediate on a feud between the earls of Arran and Angus. The archbishop took the precaution of wearing mail armour under his rochet, and swore on his conscience that he knew nothing of the matter. As he struck his breast to emphasise the point, the mail rattled. Douglas replied, 'How now, my Lord, methinks your conscience clatters; to bear arms becomes not a priest'.[4] Bishop Douglas died in London, and is buried at the Queen's Chapel of the Savoy.

With the sixteenth century reformation came the usual story of destruction. The cathedral, now governed by a chapter of twenty-two secular canons, was desecrated in 1560 as the result of a letter sent by Lord James Stewart on behalf of the Lords of the Congregation to the lairds of Arntilly and Kinvaid. They were ordered 'to pass incontinent to the Kyrk of Dunkeld, and take down the haill images thereof, and bring forth to the kirkzayrd and burn them oppenly, and siclyk cast down the altaris, and purge the kyrk of all kinds of monuments of idolatyre. And this ye faill not to do, as ye will do us singular empleseur; and so committis to the protection of God. Faill not, but ze take guid heyd, that neither the dasks, windocks, not durriss be any ways hurt or broken – yther glassin work or iron work'.[5] The last clauses were not obeyed and the 'dasks, glassin work and iron work', went the same way as 'all kinds of monuments of idolatyre'. Some individuals were more than prepared to take advantage of the despoiled cathedral; the laird of Cardeny, for one, removed the roof of the nave, and it has remained unroofed since that time. There may also have been damage to the chancel roof, since it was repaired in 1600 by Stewart of Ladywell, and re-roofed again in 1660.

Repairs to the chancel were undertaken at various stages during the seventeenth to nineteenth centuries, by successive marquesses and dukes of Atholl. The cathedral was badly damaged during the dreadful battle of Dunkeld in 1689 which destroyed the town. The battle took place between the highland supporters of King James VII (1685–9) and the lowland supporters of King William III (1689–1702) and Queen Mary II (1689–94), and ended the cause of King James in Scotland. The first marquess of Atholl (d.1703) paid for the repair of the cathedral in 1691 and a memorial to him can be seen on the south wall of the chapter house. Further repairs in 1762 re-roofed the tower and replaced some of the tracery in the chancel and, at the same time, the second duke (d.1764) erected a sumptuous and ostentatious pew for himself and his family immediately in front of the pulpit. Henry Skrine, who visited the cathedral (c.1812), described the chancel as 'wretchedly fitted up', although he qualified this statement by adding, 'like the rest of the Scotch churches', which might indicate a rather fundamental and general bias.[6] A visitor in 1819 observed the partly ruined cathedral with pity: 'Few churches have passed through such stormy scenes as Dunkeld, and its ruined state is a melancholy testimony to the lawlessness of the tumultuous times which have left their mark upon its desecrated walls'.[7]

An extensive restoration of the chancel took place under the supervision of the architect Archibald Eliot in 1814–15. The £5,000 cost of the work was mostly borne by the fourth duke of Atholl (1755–1830), whose statue can be seen in the chapter house; the government contributed £996 18s. For historic reasons, the cathedral was not technically a parish church and the Eliot restoration was preceded by a period of bargaining between the Crown and the duke of Atholl on the question of responsibility for the maintenance of its fabric. When the necessity for extensive restoration became apparent, the Crown shrewdly attempted, in 1811, to present the cathedral to the parish for use as a parish church. The duke objected to this and a royal warrant in 1812 granted the chancel to the duke and his heirs. The dukes of Atholl continued to own the chancel until 1928, when a change was made possible by the terms of the Church of Scotland Properties and Endowment Act 1925.

The Eliot restoration involved the stabilisation of the ruined nave (but no more), presumably paid for by the government contribution. Only the three western bays of the chancel were used for worship, with the pulpit placed below the central window on the south side. Facing the pulpit, on the north side, was the Atholl pew, a large box with curtained sides and with three large openings looking towards the pulpit. Galleries on the east and west sides provided additional seating for the congregation. Much of the carved and moulded stonework was renewed and it seems likely that the window tracery seen today was inserted by Eliot in an attempt to recreate a more medieval appearance. The chancel was given a plaster vault, painted to give it the appearance of dressed stone.

Robert Southey, who visited Dunkeld towards the end of the restoration, managed a sarcastic compliment: 'The duke is now fitting it up at considerable expence, and in good taste – if we could forget that it is only in plaister work, and if we could forgive the defilement of four windows… two of them are disfigured by galleries, one by the grand seat of the Athols, and one by the pulpit… there is a crack down the tower which ought to be repaired in time'.[8]

The Eliot restoration was an attempt to insert presbyterian forms of worship into the renewed chancel of a medieval cathedral church designed for a very different liturgy. Eliot seems to have done his best with the information that he had to hand, but appreciation of the qualities of medieval architecture was still in its infancy, the Gothic Revival was yet to come, and the Ecclesiological Society was yet to be founded. As the nineteenth century progressed Eliot's work came to be regretted as a mistake.

A restoration plan was drawn up in 1900 by the architect Peter Macgregor Chalmers, but rejected by the seventh duke of Atholl (1840–1917) for reasons which are no longer clear. Some years later, the shipping magnate and former MP for West Perthshire, Sir Donald Currie (1825–1909), agreed to restore the cathedral at the request of his nurse, a local woman who knew and loved Dunkeld. The appointed architects were Dunn and Watson, who had worked on his estate at Glenlyon. The work was carried out during 1908 and the chancel was re-opened for worship on 16 October.

Dunn and Watson virtually gutted the chancel and returned to the east-west alignment of the medieval liturgy. The galleries, the plaster vaults and all the furnishings of 1814–15 were removed. The communion table was placed at the east end of the chancel and set against a carved and panelled screen with the pulpit on the north side; the oak communion table, stalls, screens and pews were designed by Sir Robert Lorimer. An organ gallery was erected at the west end and stained glass, by Burmeister and Fulks, was inserted in the east window. The barrel roof with its small bosses also dates from 1908. To eliminate the possibility of any future contention, the ownership of the tower and nave was transferred to the state, and ownership of the chancel was transferred from the dukes of Atholl to the parish, both in 1928.

The cathedral is approached from the village square by way of Cathedral Street, an immaculately restored set of little Georgian houses. They mostly date from the rebuilding of the village after the devastation caused by the battle of Dunkeld. They were in serious disrepair by 1950 and in danger of demolition. An appeal by the National Trust for Scotland succeeded in purchasing the houses which are now let to tenants.

At the far end of Cathedral Street an impressive set of wrought iron gates gives access to the grounds of the cathedral. Bearing the coronet and cypher of the dukes of Atholl, the gates were made about 1730 for the entrance to Dunkeld House and transferred here in 1832. Through the gates can be seen the east gable of the chancel of the cathedral.

The Cathedral Church of St Columba (early 20th century postcard)

The Chancel and Chapter House

The chancel is roofed and still used as the parish church of Dunkeld; it measures 31.6m by 8.2m. Along the north wall runs a thirteenth century trefoil-headed blind arcade used at one period as chapter stalls, but later covered up by the wooden stalls of Bishop Lauder. On the north wall of the chancel there are two twentieth century tablets: one to John, eighth duke of Atholl (1871–1942), and the other a war memorial to the Scottish Horse. The colours of the 42nd Royal Highlanders can be seen above. A third memorial commemorates James Stewart of Ladywell who died in 1636. Beyond is a priest's squint and then a doorway into the area behind the 1908 Lorimer screen.

The door on the north wall, to the west of the screen, leads into the fifteenth century chapter house. The armorial bearings above the door are those of the dukes of Atholl who made it into a mausoleum. The two-storey chapter house dates from 1457 and the ground floor was refurbished as a museum in 1994. It was constructed during the episcopate of Bishop Lauder and his armorial bearings can be seen on the buttresses. The chapter house has quadripartite vaulting and contains a number of relics relating to the history of the cathedral. On the left is the Great Curfew Bell, inscribed JOANNES MEIKL NOS FECIT EDINBURGH 1688 (John Meikl made us. Edinburgh 1688); the use of the plural probably indicates that the bell was one of a set. This surviving bell was hung in a special wooden belfry and rung daily at 6am and 8pm until the First World War; it was taken down for safety reasons in 1975. The cross-slab close by is perhaps eighth or ninth century and was re-used as a tombstone in 1779. Next to the slab is the tombstone of the fiddler Niel Gow (1727–1807); it originally stood in the churchyard at Little Dunkeld, where Gow lies buried, and was placed here for conservation purposes. The large, canopied but unfinished Atholl tomb dates from about 1600. A bust of Sir Donald Currie, benefactor of the 1908 restoration, who died in April 1909, can be seen set in the tomb. There is a note of irony here: Sir Donald symbolically claiming an Atholl tomb for doing what a duke of Atholl should have done.

The standing white marble effigy of John, fourth duke of Atholl (1755–1830), is by John Ternouth (1795–1849) and was carved in 1835. Ternouth is best known for the great bronze relief of the battle of Copenhagen at the base of Nelson's Column in Trafalgar Square. The adjacent wall tablet commemorates Lord Charles Murray (1799–1824), sixth son of the fourth duke, who died in Greece during the war of independence. The encyclopaedic monument on the south wall, with a Latin inscription flanked by thirty-two heraldic shields, commemorates the first marquess of Atholl (d.1703), whose small portrait medallion can be seen at the top of the left pilaster, matched by his wife on the right pilaster.

The chapter house also contains a printing curiosity known as the great 'she' bible of 1611. It is a copy of the Authorised Version of the Bible with Ruth 3:15 misprinted as 'and she went into the city', instead of 'and he went into the city'.

Last is a ninth or tenth century Celtic slab whose carving has been interpreted as Christ, in the symbolic form of a fish, and the twelve disciples; commonly known as the Apostles' stone, it is a fine example of Pictish art. It appears to depict a battle scene, Daniel in the Lion's Den, and the miracle of the loaves and fishes.

Back in the chancel and behind the Lorimer screen is the carved, though much damaged, effigy of Bishop William Sinclair (1309–37) on the north wall. The bishop is shown wearing an alb, tunicle, dalmatic and chasuble. Also, here is the tomb of the infamous Alexander Stewart (c.1343–94), the 'wolf of Badenoch' who burned Elgin Cathedral in 1390. The 'wolf' is appropriately depicted by a mailed effigy with mailed figures in niches around the sides; his feet rest upon a lion. There is also a white marble monument to Major-General Sir Robert Dick (d.1846) who fought at the Battle of Waterloo; and, centred on the east wall, the 1872 Black Watch memorial in white marble, depicting two dead soldiers, by Sir John Steell (1804–91). There are also memorials to two former ministers of the cathedral. The colours of the Black Watch, carried at Waterloo, hang on the north wall. The east window depicts the Christian virtues (fortitude, charity, prudence, justice, faith, hope, temperance and patience), five shepherds gazing at the angelic host, and St Columba preaching.

Through the south door of the screen, and back in the chancel, is a fourteenth century triple sedilia and two heraldic stones, and a brass to Thomas Rutherford, minister of the cathedral 1877–1926.

At the west end of the cathedral, above the gallery, can be seen the blocked fifteenth century chancel arch that led into the ruined nave. Also at the west end is the modern square font. The organ was reconstructed in 1975. On the north wall the rough cartouche with JSMM relates to the repairs of 1600.

The Nave

The ruined nave was begun in 1406 and completed in 1464. The south porch was added later in the fifteenth century. A major restoration of the nave was undertaken by the Office of Works in 1922–6. Although roofless, the nave is in reasonable condition, and even in its ruined and decaying state, it is still an impressive sight; it measures 36.5m long by 18.2m wide and consists of seven bays, with triforium and clerestory. The windows of the aisles have various designs, due perhaps to the lengthy period of fifty-eight years it took to build the nave and partly to the interests of different teams of masons. The nave was only roofed for one hundred years and has been exposed to the elements for four hundred years; the window tracery is badly weathered, although some has been replaced in recent years.

The nave is entered by way of the late fifteenth century roofless south porch. The grooves for the timber roof meet at a heraldic stone which, by virtue of its position, may have been inserted after the porch had become roofless.

The south aisle vaulting springers can still be seen which might indicate a stone vault, but more likely one of timber. Restoration work has been undertaken on the badly weathered window tracery, including sensitive replacement with completely new stonework. This programme will doubtless replace the shaped bronze bars which were inserted at an earlier date to support the fragile fifteenth century tracery. The nave contains many monuments and headstones but the principal one can be seen near the east end of the south aisle wall; the ogee-arched tomb of Bishop Robert de Cardeny (1398–1437). The effigy of the bishop, mitred and holding a pastoral staff, lies in a canopied niche, while underneath are carved four angels holding shields, upon which are defaced armorial bearings. The two eastern bays of the south aisle formed St Ninian's Chapel and the holes into which the screens fitted can still be seen in the pillars. Beyond the tomb are the remains of a piscina. In the north east corner is the badly weathered remnant of a memorial of about 1600.

On moving from the south aisle into the nave itself, the great blocked arch which led into the chancel can be seen. The triforium has round semi-circular apertures with simple but giant tracery. The great west window is a later insertion and now almost devoid of tracery.

The tracery of the north aisle windows is in a better state of preservation. There is no sign of vaulting and this aisle may have been simply roofed with timber. The base of vaulting shafts can be seen on the north wall. An altar dedicated to the Blessed Virgin Mary stood at the east end of the aisle; another to the Virgin was at the west end of the same aisle. The altars of St Martin and St Michael stood before the rood screen, and the altar of the Holy Cross on the screen itself. The other bays of the nave aisles had altars dedicated to St Nicholas, St Catherine, St John the Baptist, St Andrew, St Stephen, the Holy Innocents and All Saints, each of which was surrounded with screens of wood or iron. In many places the sockets for the screens still exist in the wall and pillars. A stone by the stair doorway in the south west corner commemorates Colonel Cleland, who commanded the Cameronians (the Lowland regiment) and was killed at the battle of Dunkeld in 1689.

Leaving the nave by way of the south porch and moving round to the west end, there is a sundial of 1701 on the south-west corner of the nave wall. Curiously, the ogee dripstone of the great west window has been twisted to one side to make room for a small wheel window. On the south side of the west gable is an octagonal stair turret with a decorated parapet at the top. The great square tower on the north side is 29.2m high and 7.3m square. A heraldic stone can be seen on the buttress. The lower storey of the tower, which was begun in 1469, is vaulted, and an arch from it opens into the north aisle. Access to the top of the tower, which is nearly 30.4m high, is by way of the south-west stair turret; a passage then crosses the great west window, from whence stairs proceed upwards again in a turret at the south east corner of the tower.

The ground stage of the tower was used as a consistory court and has early sixteenth century wall paintings of judgement scenes: those above the windows on the north and west walls portray the Judgement of Solomon and the Woman taken in Adultery. The others are fragmentary. Of the several memorial stones preserved here one is Celtic and another bears the early sixteenth century effigy of Canon Douglas.

The bishop's palace stood to the south-west of the cathedral and was protected by a castle erected about 1408. There is no remaining trace of either edifice; Castle Close marks the site. The bishops of Dunkeld also had residences at Loch Cluny and Cramond. Cramond Tower is now an ivy-covered ruin overlooking the Firth of Forth and seems to have been a favourite haunt of the bishops, far removed from the marauding clans round Dunkeld and within easy reach of the capital. Three bishops at least died in the tower and were buried in the abbey church on the island of Inchcolm which, like their own cathedral, was dedicated to St Columba.

Cluny Castle stands on an island in Loch Cluny and was built by Bishop Brown (1484–1515). From the time of the last pre-reformation bishop, Robert Crichton (1543–71 and 1584–5), it passed into the hands of his family and it was here that James Crichton (1560–85) spent his childhood. Crichton was a traveller, scholar and swordsman. He is said to have disputed on scientific questions in twelve languages, served in the French army, made a Latin address to the doge of Venice, disputed with university professors their interpretations of Aristotle and exposed their faulty mathematics. He was dubbed 'The Admirable Crichton' in John Johnston's *Heroes Scotici*, and portrayed as such by Sir Thomas Urquhart (1611–60) in *The Exquisite Jewel*. A novel by Harrison Ainsworth (in 1835), and a play by J. M. Barrie (in 1902), both entitled *The Admirable Crichton*, have perpetuated his memory.

Although in reasonable condition, the nave is still roofless and therefore subject to the continuing onslaught of the weather. When one observes the result of the magnificent restoration of the nave of Dunblane Cathedral in 1893, the state of the nave of Dunkeld is a cause of abiding sadness. Somehow one senses that the present state of the cathedral is the result of a series of mistaken decisions, lost opportunities and failures of nerve, all of which only add to the disappointment. Dunkeld has much to learn from Dunblane, and could still do so. 'The ruins still speak of the former grandeur of this old church-town, and perhaps a like-day may yet dawn for Dunkeld, as has been seen at Dunblane'.[9] The restoration of the nave and the opening up of the entire cathedral would be a major undertaking, but it only requires vision, commitment and funding; surely these things can be found. The nave of Dunkeld has been roofless for a century longer than the nave of Dunblane and time is running out.

As it stands today, the reputation of Dunkeld Cathedral rests more on the beautifully screening effect of its surroundings than on the structure itself. The immaculately-groomed setting is lovely – aquatic, arboreal, arcadian – and seems to promise an enchanting place, but close examination of the cathedral is a disappointing experience. The combination of a ruined and badly-weathered nave with a dull and lifelessly furnished chancel – a lifelessness more confirmed than lifted by Lorimer's woodwork – presents an altogether depressing sight. It seems that spirits can be raised only by the river, the woods and the hills which seem to envelop the building protectively as it were, shielding it from the scrutiny of those seeking a long-departed spirituality.

1 MacGibbon, D & Ross, T (1896): volume 3, p. 28.
2 Lewis, Samuel (1846): volume 1, p. 328.
3 ibid.
4 Walcott, Mackenzie E C (1874): volume 1, pp 190–191.
5 Lindsay, Ian Gordon (1926): p. 82.
6 Skrine, Henry (1813): p. 58.
7 Ditchfield, P H (1932): p. 503.
8 Southey, Robert (1929): p. 45.
9 Butler, Dugald (1901): p. 37.

Edinburgh

Edinburgh is the capital city of Scotland and the seat of Scotland's government, lying 630km north-west of London and 3.2km south of the Firth of Forth. The city is built on a group of hills, and that occupied by the severe and frowning castle shows evidence of occupation in the Bronze Age and the Iron Age. The site is naturally defensible and a fortress seems to have been maintained here in subsequent ages. The name 'Edinburgh' derives from 'Edwin's fort', a reference to a castle established here by Edwin, king of Northumbria in the seventh century. Edinburgh was of sufficient importance for King David I (1124–53) to transfer his capital here from Dunfermline in 1124. Four years later he founded an abbey at Holyrood and the city was granted a royal charter by King Robert I (1306–29) in 1329.

The Cathedral Church of St Giles
(Church of Scotland)

St Giles' Cathedral occupies a prominent site in Parliament Square on the historic Royal Mile between the castle and the palace of Holyroodhouse; but for all its prominence and history, it has only a slight claim to be included among the list of Scotland's cathedrals. Ecclesiologically, St Giles' was a cathedral church for only thirty-two years, from 1633 to 1638 and again from 1662 to 1689. The diocese of Edinburgh was a late addition to the dioceses of the Scottish church, being founded in 1633, and St Giles' Church, already collegiate and having been under the direct authority of the pope, was the most prominent church in the city and a natural choice to be the cathedral church of the new diocese.

The dedication to St Giles is curious. Many legends have been woven around the memory of this obscure saint, whose feast day is on 1 September. Although he is now mostly forgotten, Giles was one of the most popular saints of the Middle Ages. More than one hundred and sixty churches were dedicated in his name in England alone. He is venerated as the patron saint of the disabled, and of beggars and blacksmiths, but nothing certain is known about his life. Stories that he was a Greek, born in Athens in 640, who emigrated to France to live in a grotto near Nîmes to pursue a contemplative life, are now dismissed as legends. It is more likely that he was a Provençal by birth and abbot of a monastery on the Rhône. He may have lived in the eighth century but even this is uncertain. It has been suggested that he was chosen to be Edinburgh's patron saint because France was Scotland's oldest ally, but this is speculation and very few churches in Scotland are dedicated in the name of Giles.

The earliest record of a church on the site of the cathedral is found in the year 854; it would probably have been constructed of timber, but nothing is known of its appearance and nothing remains from that period. A new church was built during the first half of the thirteenth century and consecrated in 1243 by Bishop David de Bernham of St Andrews (1239–53). This fully cruciform church consisted of a five-bay nave, a four-bay chancel, north and south transepts, and a small tower without a crown. The church was burnt by King Richard II of England (1377–99) during the course of an English invasion in 1385, in revenge for a Scottish raid into England the year before. The church was almost totally destroyed with the exception of a very fine Romanesque doorway that survived until the late eighteenth century when, in an age less sympathetic to architectural conservation, it was taken down to save the cost of repairing it.

Notionally a late fourteenth century building, St Giles' Cathedral was so extensively altered and restored in the succeeding centuries that it is now difficult to distinguish medieval fabric from the work of later ages.

Rebuilding began almost immediately after the 1385 fire, and a series of chapels were added to the cathedral from the late fourteenth to early sixteenth centuries. Five chapels, entered by a central doorway, were added to the south aisle of the nave in 1387 at the request of the provost of the city; three of these remain today and form the Moray Aisle. The doorway has gone, but its stonework survives as the east doorway into the Thistle Chapel. A chapel of St John, later replaced by the north porch, was built off the north transept by 1395. Three chapels were added to the north side of the nave in the early fifteenth century, probably about 1410; one, constructed west of a Romanesque doorway, survives as the present Albany Aisle. Two chapels were added to the east of the door, and one survives as St Eloi's Chapel. The Romanesque doorway was demolished in 1797.

The Preston Aisle, on the south side of the chancel, was added in 1454 to house a relic – an arm bone – of St Giles. The relic was given to the church by William Preston of Gorton, who had acquired it in Europe with the help of the king of France. After his death, Preston was buried in the Lady Aisle, and the Preston Aisle was built in his memory to house the relic. The arms of Preston of Gorton can be seen on the capitals of the pillars in this aisle.

About 1454, and probably contemporary with the construction of the Preston Aisle, the chancel was extended by the addition of two bays at the east and the insertion of a clerestory by raising the roof. The work is thought to have been done at the direction of Mary of Gueldres, wife of King James II (1437–60).

Due principally to its increasing size and importance, St Giles' was granted collegiate status in 1467. It was removed from the jurisdiction of the bishop of St Andrews and placed under the direct authority of the pope; and governed much like a cathedral, with a chapter consisting of a provost and canons. The grant coincided with the rebuilding of the chancel and transepts and prompted the adding of yet more chapels. The tower, with its unusual 'crown', was completed in 1495. The Chepman Aisle, a small chapel on the south side of the Preston Aisle, was added in 1507–13. The Lauder Aisle and the Holy Blood Aisle, finished in 1518, were added to the five south chapels of 1387, but only a small portion of the Holy Blood Aisle remains.

The structural extension of St Giles' coincided with the darkening cloud of the sixteenth century reformation. In 1556, three images were stolen from the church. The theft was reported to the archbishop of St Andrews who, without any result, commissioned the town authorities to find the offenders. In 1557, the statue of St Giles was also stolen. The theft occurred shortly before St Giles' Day and, by long-established tradition, the statue was due to be carried through the streets of the city in solemn procession. The archbishop was again informed, and ordered the town council either to find the old statue, or produce a new one by the day itself. They did neither, and when the day came an image had to be borrowed from Greyfriars Church. To show her displeasure, and to prevent any attempt at a riot, Mary of Guise, queen regent of Scotland for her young daughter Mary, walked in the procession. The day passed without incident until the queen withdrew as the procession approached the church, at which stage a general riot occurred.

Remembering the theft of the statue, and in anticipation of a more serious assault on the cathedral, an inventory of the church furnishings was made, and most of them were given into private care until the troubles lessened. But the influence of the reformers was rapidly increasing and events were now beginning to move quickly. In 1559, the Lords of the Congregation (leaders of the protestant party) entered Edinburgh and, on the afternoon of their arrival, John Knox preached in St Giles' for the first time and was quickly appointed minister of the city. The first protestant occupation was brief; a short while later the church was reconsecrated by the bishop of Amiens and mass was again said. It was a brief respite of only five months before the protestant party was back in permanent control of St Giles'.

Before long, St Giles' suffered the same fate as St Kentigern's Cathedral in Glasgow. Such a large building was too reminiscent of Catholic days to survive intact. The new liturgy required not large single churches, where a large and mostly passive congregation could watch the beautiful but distant offering of the mass, but smaller auditoria where congregations could be harangued by fiery preachers. The western three bays of the nave were walled off to provide offices for the town council, and the area became known as the Outer Tolbooth. It was used as the town clerk's office, housed the town council, the Court of Session (until 1639) and a prison; even the town's guillotine was stored within the church for a time. The south-west part of the Outer Tolbooth was re-arranged as a preaching house towards the end of John Knox's life when his voice was no longer powerful enough to fill a larger area. The remainder of the nave became known as the Great Kirk, while a third church, known as the Little or East Kirk, was formed in the chancel in 1578. As the population of Edinburgh expanded, more parish churches were required, and so galleries were erected, and the cathedral was divided yet further. By the mid-seventeenth century, there were six parish churches within its walls.

Fynes Moryson visited St Giles' in 1598, and found it 'large and lightsome, but little stately for the building, and nothing at all for the beauty and ornament. In this Church the Kings seate is built upon some few staires high of wood, and leaning upon the pillar next to the Pulpit. And opposite to the same is another seat very like it, in which the incontinent used to stand and doe pennance; and some weeks past, a gentleman, being a stranger, and taking it for a place whereir men of better quality used to sit, boldly entered the same in sermon time, til he was driven away with the profuse laughter of the common sort, to the disturbance of the whole congregation'.[1]

St Giles' Church reached the zenith of its existence in the seventeenth century. King Charles I (1625–49) visited Edinburgh in 1633 and founded a new diocese of Edinburgh, which was formed from the archdeaconry of Lothian; and the bishop was given precedence between the archbishop of Glasgow and the bishop of Galloway. By royal charter, St Giles' Church was made the cathedral church of the new diocese and, for a while, it was again made to resemble the building that it was intended to be. The dividing wall between the Great and Little Kirks was taken down in 1634, and James Hanna, the dean of Edinburgh, was ordered 'to repair to Durham... to take a Draught of the Choir of the Cathedral Church in that City, in order to fit up and beautify the inside of the Choir of St Giles' after the same Manner'.[2] At least one of the congregations was ejected and given a home in Tron Church in High Street, built 1636–47.

The king appointed William Forbes as the first bishop of Edinburgh and was said to have remarked that Forbes was worthy to have a see erected for him. Forbes had enjoyed a distinguished career, including holding the appointment of professor of logic at Marischal College, Aberdeen. He was a strong High Churchman, keen on reconciliation with the Roman Catholic Church and a zealous believer in episcopal government. His eucharistic theology was based on a belief in the doctrine of the real presence, although he criticised the doctrine of transubstantiation. His episcopate, which might have been eminent, was unfortunately brief. Consecrated on 28 January 1634, he died less than three months later on 12 April, and was succeeded by David Lindsey (1634–8), formerly bishop of Brechin (1619–34).

Three years after Forbes' death, there occurred at St Giles' an incident which is imprinted on Scottish ecclesiastical folklore, but the details of which are unsubstantiated and mostly legendary. A new Scottish prayer book, prepared on the orders of King Charles I, was enforced on Scotland by William Laud, archbishop of Canterbury (1633–45). On 23 July 1637 the new prayer book was used in St Giles' for the first time. Bishop Lindsey entered the pulpit and the dean of the cathedral took the reader's place. After the service had begun some people began to murmur such things as 'false anti-Christian', 'beistlie belliegod', 'Judas', and other such comments. The bishop rose and managed to quieten the congregation, and then ordered the dean to read the collect for the day. At this point, a woman named Jenny Geddes, described as 'a low disreputable kail-wife',[3] is alleged to have said 'Deil colic the wame of thee; out, thou false thief! Dost thou say mass at my lug?' and then thrown her stool at the dean's head. The story is unproven, and there is no historical record of a woman of that name earlier than 1660, when her behaviour got out of hand at the time of the restoration of King Charles II. She was probably no more than a disruptive trouble-maker and rabble-rouser. But there was undoubtedly a riot in the cathedral in 1637, and the magistrates had to clear the building before the service could be continued. When the bishop went home he was pelted with stones, until rescued by the earl of Wemyss. That afternoon, a few extracts were read from the new book, and the bishop was again attacked on leaving the church, but the earl of Roxburghe took him home in his coach. After these scenes, the prayer book was not used again in the cathedral.

St Giles' first brief taste of episcopacy and cathedral status ended with the general expulsion of the bishops from their dioceses on 13 December 1638 by the Glasgow Assembly. Once again, presbyterianism imposed its mark on the ancient church. The partition walls, which had been taken down in 1634, were rebuilt and again the cathedral was converted into several preaching houses. During the years of the Commonwealth, Oliver Cromwell (Lord Protector 1653–58), came to Edinburgh and used the Little or East Kirk as a barracks.

The restoration of the monarchy in 1660 led to another period of episcopacy and cathedral status for St Giles'. In 1661 the marquess of Montrose (1612–50), a royalist general in the civil war, was buried with great pomp in the Chapel of St John the Evangelist (the Chepman Aisle). Montrose had been defeated, captured and hanged in 1650 after landing in Orkney with a small army. In 1662 George Wishart, formerly chaplain to the marquess, was consecrated bishop of Edinburgh in the renewed episcopate.

In 1685, King Charles II bestowed the dignity of chancellor of the university of Edinburgh on Bishop John Paterson (1679–87) and his successors ex officio. Paterson was translated to Glasgow as archbishop in 1687, and was succeeded by Alexander Rose. On 3 November 1688, the Scottish bishops commissioned Rose to go to London, with Bishop Andrew Bruce of Orkney (1688–99), to support the cause of King James VII (1685–9) and to confer with Archbishop William Sancroft of Canterbury (1678–90). The illness of Bishop Bruce delayed departure; eventually Rose went alone and arrived in London to find that King James had fled. Rose was a man of total integrity, but he was not enough of a politician to cope with a crisis. He was granted a famous and fateful interview with the new King William III (1689–1702), who said, 'I hope you will be kind to me and follow the example of England' (i.e. to recognise me as the lawful king in succession to the deposed King James VII). To which the bishop replied, 'Sir, I will follow you so far as law, reason, or conscience shall allow me'.[4] That honourable statement effectively sealed the fate of episcopacy within the established church. Rightly or wrongly, Rose had given a clear indication that the Scottish bishops regarded their oath of allegiance to the deposed and exiled King James VII as binding. As Rose recalled many years later, 'the prince, without saying any more, turned away from me and went back to his company'. The bishops were deprived of their dioceses on 22 July 1689, and presbyterianism was established on 7 June 1690. The Scottish bishops were not alone in refusing to abjure their oath of allegiance to King James. They were accompanied, among the English bishops, by Archbishop Sancroft and the bishops of Bath and Wells, Ely, Oxford, Gloucester and Peterborough; all were deprived of their sees on 1 February 1690.

After the restoration of the episcopate in 1662, and throughout the eighteenth century, the history of St Giles' was comparatively uneventful. No attempt was made to repeat the experiment of 1634–8 by reconstituting St Giles' as a single church. A visitor in 1669 described it as being divided into 'six sermon houses',[5] and it remained so until the nineteenth century. 'Famous ministers preached from the pulpits of the several churches, well known and less well known people nodded in the high pews, cobwebs gathered on the roofs, the Norman doorway was destroyed, Dr Johnson came and went with the remark, "Show me what was once a church", and for over a hundred years the beauties of St Giles' were forgotten'.[6]

By the beginning of the nineteenth century, there were four parish churches within the walls of the cathedral. The High Kirk met in the chancel; the Old Kirk occupied the south transept and part of the Moray Aisle; the Tolbooth Kirk, provided for John Knox in his last years, continued to exist in the south-west part of the nave. The Haddo Hole Kirk met in the north-west part of the nave – the curious name derives from the small priest's chamber opening off the church itself, and commemorating Sir John Gordon of Haddo, a distinguished royalist imprisoned there in 1644 before his execution. The Preston Aisle was used for meetings, including the General Assembly of the Church of Scotland. The Chepman Aisle was walled off and divided into three storeys. The lower floor was a coal cellar; the middle floor had a stove, and the upper floor had a fireplace. The town police station was housed in the crossing and part of the north nave aisle. The town clerk's office occupied what is now the Chambers Aisle.

By the early nineteenth century, the cathedral was a ramshackle structure in a deplorable condition. The Romanesque doorway had been demolished in 1797, as were two of the five chapels of 1387.

The first signs of renewed interest in the old cathedral came in 1807 and again in 1817, when the tolbooths (prisons) and luckenbooths (shops) which clustered around the cathedral between its buttresses were removed, revealing the medieval rubble walls of the cathedral for the first time in centuries. Further interest in restoring the old cathedral came with the visit of King George IV (1820–30) to Edinburgh in 1822.

With a government grant of £12,600, a destructive restoration took place in 1829–33 under William Burn. The architectural irregularity of the cathedral was quite shamelessly 'tidied up'. The virtues of medieval architecture were not yet fully appreciated and, despite their antiquity, the rubble stonework of the external walls was not universally admired. With the exception of the tower, the entire exterior of the cathedral was faced with ashlar to conceal the rough medieval walls. The Lauder Chapel, and most of the Holy Blood Aisle at the south-west of the nave, were demolished to make a wider entrance into Parliament Close. The roof of the nave was raised to allow the insertion of a clerestory to match the chancel; the construction of the clerestory involved the removal of the stone vault and the bell ringer's house above it, and its replacement by a plaster vault in the nave and transepts. Newer, thinner piers replaced the original piers.

Even with this work, St Giles' was still divided into three churches (the Haddo Hole Kirk and the Tolbooth Kirk were amalgamated), a meeting hall for the General Assembly of the Church of Scotland, and a spacious lobby. Henry Parry Liddon, later dean of St Paul's Cathedral in London, visited St Giles' in July 1851, and shuddered at the sight: 'St Giles' is now cut up into three meeting-houses of the Scotch Establishment … All are furnished with very capacious galleries, the whole arrangements centering towards the pulpit … We passed the tomb of Montrose: his aisle has been fitted up to make a comfortable vestry for the minister of the central church. Several Presbyterians went round with me; they seemed to think the whole affair a due blending of the beautiful and the useful. The men did not take off their hats, and seemed surprised at my doing so. I could not forget that in past ages the Shekinah [the visible glory of God] of the Catholic Church had rested beneath that roof. I left the church feeling a deep and unutterable aversion for a system whose outward manifestations are so hatefully repulsive. I thank God the Church of England *is very different from the Kirk of Scotland*'.[7]

Although much medieval work was lost irretrievably, some of the damage done during the Burn 'restoration' was undone in a more responsible restoration in 1871–83 by William Hay. The work was paid for by William Chambers, lord provost of Edinburgh, and a partner in the publishing company of W & R Chambers.

Without ignoring the generosity of Chambers, the work of 1871–83 will be referred to throughout as the 'Hay' restoration, following the practice of ascribing restorations to the name of the architect. Any visitor undertaking a detailed tour of St Giles' Cathedral will find the names 'Burn' and 'Hay' often used to describe the two great nineteenth century restorations of the building.

Hay's concept of restoration centred on recovering the medieval plan of St Giles' as a single church. The work began with a restoration of the chancel in 1871–3, and the removal of all its galleries and pews. In 1879, a second phase restored the Preston Aisle, revealing the groined roof and pillars which had been hidden under several layers of whitewash. Restoration of the nave began in 1881 and included the replacement of Burn's thin piers with more appropriately substantial ones, reflagging the floor and rebuilding the west door. The oak pews in the nave date from this time.

The fully restored cathedral was re-dedicated at a service of thanksgiving on 23 May 1883, the sermon being preached by the minister of the cathedral, James Cameron Lees, on the text 'What mean these stones?' (Joshua 4:21). The service was attended by a galaxy of the great and the good, headed by the lord high commissioner to the general assembly of the Church of Scotland. Forty-seven years later, that same lord high commissioner, the marquess of Aberdeen and Temair, and a descendant of Sir John Gordon of Haddo, well remembered the occasion: 'At last the work was completed, and from what had been for whole generations a confused and unordered collection of interior buildings a splendid edifice emerged, in every way worthy of its origin and sacred purpose… I had the special honour of being deputed by Queen Victoria to perform the opening ceremony on Her Majesty's behalf on the day before entering upon the duties of the Lord High Commissioner to the Church of Scotland, to which I had been appointed that year. And thus it came about that one was called upon as representing the Sovereign of the realm, to take the chief official part in the solemn and impressive ceremony of re-dedicating to its sacred use the very building from whence his ancestor had been dragged to a martyr's death'.[8] The event was overshadowed by one note of sadness. In recognition of what he had accomplished, William Chambers was offered a baronetcy, but he did not live to receive it. He died three days before the re-dedication service.

The last substantial building work at the cathedral was the construction of the Thistle Chapel in 1909–11 to a design by Sir Robert Lorimer (1864–1929). Construction was funded by Ronald Ruthven, eleventh earl of Leven and tenth earl of Melville, who had been appointed a Knight of the Thistle, Scotland's own Order of knighthood in 1903. The earl had hoped to restore the chapel royal at the Palace of Holyroodhouse, the original chapel of the Order. Unfortunately the walls proved to be unable to bear the weight of a new vaulted roof and a restoration would effectively have meant a rebuilding. 'Whatever sympathetic understanding of the spirit of the past might have been exercised, the result could hardly have been other than the destruction of a relic of high national and historic interest, and the substitution of a modern building in which, at best, some traces of its predecessor would have been incorporated. The dream therefore of a restored chapel of Holyrood had to be given up, though not without regrets'.[9] The scheme was abandoned and the disappointed earl died in 1906. The sum of £40,000, that he had provided for the work, reverted to his estate. However, the new earl and his brothers decided to fulfil their father's wish and made the money available again. King Edward VII (1901–10) asked the kirk session of St Giles' to consider making space available, and the result was the construction of the Thistle Chapel and its lobby in the angle at the south-east of the cathedral formed by the Preston Aisle and the south chancel aisle.

The biggest project undertaken in recent years was the provision of the Lower Aisle in 1981–2 at a cost of about £500,000. A new stone stair, by Bernard Fielden, Simpson and Brown, leads down from the east end of the south chancel aisle to a gallery of rooms, some of medieval origin, under the south side of the cathedral. Under the Thistle Chapel there is now a session room, used for meetings of the kirk session and open to the public on weekdays as a coffee room. At the same time the walls and ceiling of the south-east corner of the cathedral were resurfaced. In 1987, a plaque was placed on the east wall above the stairs to the Lower Aisle, in memory of Wellesley Bailey, an Edinburgh man who founded the Leprosy Mission.

The above summary of the structural evolution of St Giles' Cathedral should make it clear to the visitor, who sees it today, that it is a complex building. At the heart of it there lies the traditional plan of cruciformity (nave, chancel, crossing and transepts), but the cathedral has been subjected to so much addition and subtraction, and two major restorations, that the building is now virtually a rectangle, inside and outside. The interior of the cathedral has a slightly unbalanced feeling in that the chancel is longer than the nave.

The exterior, with the exception of the tower (which retains its fifteenth century appearance) was almost entirely refaced with ashlar during the Burn restoration of 1829–33 and now vaguely resembles a church of the Classical Revival. The distinctive crowned tower, mercifully untouched by Burn, was completed in 1495; the lower parts of the tower are earlier. The crown is not unique, though more elaborate than most in having eight flying buttresses, which meet to form a small spire. [The towers at Haddington and Linlithgow Churches formerly had crowns but both have been destroyed. The tower at King's College, Aberdeen has a four-ribbed crown as does the tower of Newcastle Cathedral.] The tower was restored in 1648 and again in 1980. It has been used as a prison, a fortress housing three brass cannons, and accommodation for weavers after the reformation in the sixteenth century. The gold weathercock is sixteenth century.

The large monument outside the west doorway is by Clark Stanton and commemorates the fifth duke of

Buccleuch (1806–84). The doorway itself dates from the Hay restoration, replacing a Burn doorway, and has an 1884 sculpture by John Rhind representing St Giles'. On the south side, past an oriel window that formed part of the vanished south porch, once stood the statue of John Knox cast in 1904 by Pittendrigh MacGillivray; formerly inside the north aisle it is now back inside the cathedral at the west end of the nave. Further on is the blocked window behind the organ and then, in the south part of Parliament Square, an equestrian statue of King Charles II (1660–85). The Thistle Chapel, at the south-east corner of the cathedral, has an external entrance which leads into the lobby between the chapel itself and the south chancel aisle. The entrance incorporates a fifteenth century round-headed arch from the old south porch which led into the nave. The octagonal structure at the north-east of the cathedral is a 1885 reproduction of the sixteenth century Old Mercat Cross.

The interior of the cathedral, although much altered, is impressive and retains a distinctly medieval appearance and atmosphere. It consists of a nave of five bays with aisles, a crossing, a chancel, also of five bays, and a variety of attached aisles and chapels of differing sizes. The nave arcades in their present form, with octagonal columns and moulded capitals, date from the Hay restoration of 1881–3, but the clerestory and the plaster quadripartite vault with central bosses, are the work of Burn. The Hay piers replaced Burn piers of the same height, which in turn replaced fourteenth century piers of a much lower height. The outer arcades with their clustered columns, and the aisle vaults, are original fifteenth century work.

The elaborate west door lobby with seats and canopies and the royal arms in the centre dates from 1873. It was originally designed, as part of the Hay restoration, to be a new royal pew to be placed against the partition built between the two easterly massive pillars at the crossing when the High Kirk was limited to the chancel. During the restoration the pew, then in hand, was modified to be a part of the west door porch. It bears the royal cypher VR (Queen Victoria) and the motto of the Order of the Thistle NEMO ME IMPUNE LACESSIT (No one provokes me with impunity). The great west window was dedicated on 30 June 1985 as a tribute to Robert Burns (1759–96). The design is by Leifur Breidford of Iceland. It replaced painted glass of 1886 on the theme of the Prophets by Daniel Cottier; this glass, currently stored in the cathedral crypt, was a memorial to Fanny Bruce who died in 1881 at the age of 24.

The cathedral has unfortunately become the 'Westminster Abbey' of Scotland (this was the declared aim of William Chambers), and the internal walls are covered with memorials to various distinguished Scots men and women. The banners in the outer south aisle are colours of eighteenth and nineteenth century Scottish regiments.

At the west end of the nave, on the north side, can be seen the statue of John Knox by Pittendrigh MacGillivray. This statue has experienced a somewhat peripatetic existence. Cast in 1904, it first stood in the north aisle. Then it was taken outside the cathedral, and stood on the south side. It was moved back into the cathedral to its present location in 1983. As one author has noted: 'Strange is it not, that the statues of Christ and the saints should be torn down and replaced by one of such a man?'[10] On a more sacramental note, opposite the statue of Knox stands an angel with shell font, carved in Caen stone by John Rhind in imitation of Bertel Thorvaldsen's font at Copenhagen Cathedral. Another copy of the font can be seen in Inverness Cathedral.

War memorials cover the west wall of the north aisle and its 1891 west window was designed by Edward Burne-Jones and made by William Morris & Co; it shows the people of Israel crossing the Jordan and various Old Testament heroines. There is a fine war memorial to the Royal Scots Greys, in the shape of an elaborate patterned Celtic Cross, and a memorial to the Queen's Own Cameron Highlanders.

The north-west corner of the north aisle is separated from the aisle itself, by a low iron screen, to form the Albany Aisle, which is now reserved for private prayer. The aisle, built 1401–10, was founded by the duke of Albany (d.1420) and the earl of Douglas (d.1424) in expiation of their crime of causing the death of David, duke of Rothesay (1378–1402), eldest son and heir to King Robert III (1390–1406). Legend says that the duke was starved to death in Falkland Palace, but it is more likely that he died of dysentery. The aisle consists of two bays divided by a clustered pillar upon the capital of which are carved the armorial bearings of Albany and Douglas. The vault is original early fifteenth century work. In the north wall is a heavily restored round-arched tomb recess containing a memorial to members of the congregation who died in the Second World War. The walls of the Albany Aisle are lined with war memorials, including one to the Scottish soldiers who died in France during the First World War; it was erected by Edinburgh's French community. The chief interest of the aisle lies in its modern furniture and decoration – the Cross with four texts in stone, the large sanctuary lamp ornamented with thistles, and the patterned marble floor with heraldic roundels. The aisle was refurnished in 1951 by Esmé Gordon as a war memorial, and the lamp was lit in that year by Admiral of the Fleet Viscount Cunningham of Hyndhope. The glass is by Francis Spear (1957), and

Ballantine (1876), showing the parables of the wise and foolish virgins and of the talents.

Leaving the Albany Aisle, and continuing along the north nave aisle, there are more war memorials; the first, to the Royal Scot Fusiliers, being in a recess which led to Haddo's Hole, a small chamber where Sir John Gordon was imprisoned in 1644. Haddo's Hole and the adjacent Romanesque 'Marriage Porch' were removed in 1797, their place being taken by the former session room, access to which is by means of a small doorway. An adjacent memorial to Sir John Gordon was erected in 1933 by his descendant, the first marquess of Aberdeen and Temair. Memorials follow to the Highland Light Infantry, the Black Watch and the 74th Highlanders. Then there is a piscina, above which is a memorial to the 72nd Duke of Albany's Own Highlanders, the Forth Royal Garrison Artillery and the King's Scottish Sharpshooters. A staircase then leads down to an office, followed by two further memorials to the 1st Battalion Seaforth Highlanders and the King's Own Scottish Borderers.

The next bay to the east is St Eloi's Chapel (also known as the Argyll Aisle), which formerly housed an altar of the guild of Hammermen. It is now a dark little place with an iron screen and an Irish marble and mosaic floor. The chapel houses an ornate nineteenth century memorial in seventh century style to the first marquess of Argyll (1607–61), who was executed for treason, and a frontal chest with fine ironwork. The glass (1895), by the Glass Stainers' Company of Glasgow, shows the arms of the leaders of the Covenanters. The stone Romanesque scallop capital was found in 1880 and built into the west wall for safe keeping, during the Hay restoration. Only springers and a carved boss remain of the original vault, the rest is a plaster vault by Hay.

Next to St Eloi's Chapel is the notional north transept, which was completely rebuilt by Burn to make a ceremonial entrance and now barely projects beyond St Eloi's Aisle and the Chambers Aisle, which flank it to the east and west. Entrance to the transept is blocked by the grey Gothic screen of Aberfeldy stone, added by Hay in 1881–3. The figures represent patron saints of the craft guilds which had altars in the church. The transept has a clerestory and a plaster tierceron vault like the nave. The transept walls are lined with memorials, but the area is now used as a store room and not normally open to the public. The glass is by Douglas Strachan (1922) and shows Christ walking on the water.

The crossing vault is medieval, and the large octagonal piers, no higher than those of the arcades, may encase Romanesque piers.

The north chancel aisle is five bays long. The three western bays are fourteenth century; the two eastern bays date from the sixteenth century extension. The vaulting, except in the two eastern bays, is similar to the nave but lower and with a later tierceron vault. The aisle begins on the east side of the north transept with the Chapel of Youth, formed in 1929 in a recess known as the Chambers Aisle, which is virtually all nineteenth century. The chapel was formed from a Burn restoration vestry, as a memorial to William Chambers, benefactor of the Hay restoration (by MacGibbon and Ross 1889–91). The banner belonged to Field Marshal Earl Haig. The oak screen and Nativity reredos are the work of Sir Robert Lorimer 1927–9. There is a Victorian carved seat with Flamboyant tracery and there is a memorial to Sir William Smith, founder of the Boys' Brigade in 1883. The glass is by James Ballantine (1892 and 1894) and shows scenes from the life of St John the Baptist, Solomon dedicating the Temple, and Zerubbabel rebuilding the Temple. The west window of the chapel is fourteenth century and was formerly the external window of St John's Chapel (1395) in the north transept. Outside the Chambers Aisle stands a 'music bell' of 1698 on a stand, and a 1942 bell from HMS *Howe*.

Leaving the Chambers Aisle, and moving along the north chancel aisle, on the left, in the third bay, is a door leading into the cathedral shop, formerly an office known as St Margaret's Room. The nineteenth century room was converted into a shop c.1984. Above is a memorial to Brigadier Francis Aylmer Maxwell, with very fine enamel representations of his VC, CSI and DSO insignia; beyond is a tomb recess. The nineteenth and twentieth century memorials on the north wall include those of the two women medical pioneers, Sophie Jex Blake (1840–1912) and Elsie Inglis (1864–1917), founder of the Scottish Women's Hospital during the First World War, and to Scottish nurses who died in that conflict. The Ballantine windows in this aisle portray scenes from the life of Christ. The two eastern bays now constitute a chapel (the Holy Cross Aisle) and have been enclosed by railings (1883) by Francis Skidmore, which formerly enclosed the Moray Aisle. The communion table (1910, and lengthened in 1953) is by Sir Robert Lorimer. On the east wall, the royal arms and the arms of the Company of Merchants commemorate the visit of Queen Elizabeth II in 1953 when she received the Honours of Scotland.

The chancel is original fifteenth century work throughout and reckoned to be the finest piece of late medieval parish church architecture in Scotland. The western three bays of c.1400 are very simple, but the eastern two, added c.1450, have heraldic carvings on the capitals of the ornate pillars and clustered responds. The so-called King's Pillar carries the arms of King James II (1437–60), Mary of Gueldres, France, and the duke of Rothesay, who became King James III (1460–88). The Town's Pillar bears the arms of John Halkerston of that Ilk, designer of the extension to the chancel; Bishop James Kennedy of St Andrews (1440–65), to whose diocese Edinburgh then belonged; Sir William Preston of Gorton, who bequeathed the relic of St Giles to the cathedral; and Provost Cranstoun of Edinburgh. The stained glass in the east window is by Ballantine and depicts the Crucifixion and the Ascension.

A marble platform at the crossing supports the present square altar. The four canopied wooden stalls on the north and south sides are those of the sovereign (dedicated in 1911), the duke of Edinburgh, the moderator of the Church of Scotland (dedicated in 1913), and of the dean of the Thistle and the dean of the Chapel Royal (dedicated in 1930). The ornate octagonal Caen stone pulpit (1883), at the north-east of the crossing, is by Sir George Gilbert Scott, the Acts of Mercy scenes (Matthew 25:35–40) being by John Rhind. The brass eagle lectern on the south side was presented in 1886 as a thank offering for a child recovered from a dangerous illness. The steps of cast iron were designed by Jacqueline Grueber-Steiger and given in 1991 by the Normandy Veterans Association. Above the western arch leading into the crossing can be seen the royal arms of 1736. During meetings of the general assembly of the Church of Scotland, the lord high commissioner occupies the royal pew, but neither the sovereign nor the lord high commissioner are in any sense head of the assembly or of the Church of Scotland.

The five-bay south chancel aisle was the Lady Chapel before the sixteenth century reformation. The windows are by Ballantine – first the Resurrection and then the Prodigal Son – and then a post-1913 window by Karl Parsons showing Scottish saints. On the east wall of the south chancel aisle is a war memorial to Church of Scotland army chaplains who died in the Second World War; on the south a Jacobean-style memorial to Lord Justice John Inglis (1810–91), and a bas-relief bronze bust by Pilkington Jackson to James Cameron Lees (1834–1913), dean of the Thistle 1888–1913. Above the flight of stairs leading down to the Lower Aisle is a memorial to Wellesley Bailey (1846–1937), founder of the Leprosy Mission. The stairs, and the Lower Aisle to which they lead, were formed partly by excavation in 1981–2. The Lower Aisle includes a meeting room for the kirk session and a restaurant.

A bas-relief bronze memorial to Andrew Williamson (1856–1926), dean of the Thistle 1913–26, is just past the wrought iron screen by Thomas Hadden, leading to the ante-chamber of the Thistle Chapel. The lobby has giant bosses on its vault and a roll of Knights of the Thistle from 1687 to 1908.

The ante-chamber is an indication to the visitor of what to expect in the Thistle Chapel itself. There is probably no other building in Scotland quite like the chapel of the Order of the Thistle. It is a very elaborate and very small Gothic Revival structure on which has been lavished far more decoration than its small size warrants; it measures only 11.2m long, 5.4m wide and 12.7m high. There is no doubting the magnificence of the craftsmanship, but one wonders quite why so much elaboration was given to such a small building. The interior feels cluttered and claustrophobic, and resembles nothing so much as an over-sized dolls house, and its decoration is 'quite alien to the sombre dignity of the rest of the cathedral'.[11] When thinking of the splendour of the other Order chapels – St George's, Windsor Castle (the Order of the Garter); St Patrick's Cathedral, Dublin (the Order of St Patrick); the Henry VII Chapel, Westminster Abbey (the Order of the Bath); and even the Chapel of the Order of St Michael and St George, and the Chapel of the Order of the British Empire, in St Paul's Cathedral in London – one cannot help but feel that the Thistle Chapel at St Giles' need not have been quite so small.

The chapel is built of Cullaloe stone from a Fife quarry and the stained glass of the east window, depicting St Andrew, is by Douglas Strachan. The fifteenth century style oak stalls were designed by Nathaniel Grieve & Co. and carved by W & A Clow. The handrests are carved with a variety of animals including a bear, a sheep, a dog, a lion, an otter, and a boar. The stall plates, the earliest ones by Phoebe Traquair, provide a record of the knights appointed since 1909. In the canopy above the sovereign's stall are figures of St Margaret, St Columba and St Kentigern. The little communion table, cross and hangings were dedicated by King George VI (1936–53) on 29 July 1943 as a memorial to King George V (1910–36). The royal arms set into the grey floor of Ailsa Craig and Iona marble is by Esmé Gordon (1962) and is inserted as a memorial to King George VI. The knights hold an annual service in the chapel on the Sunday closest to St Andrew's Day, but the sovereign only attends when a new knight is to be installed.

Next to the Thistle Chapel is the three bay tierceron-vaulted outer south chancel aisle, known as the Preston Aisle, furnished as a chapel with a fine Gothic oak communion table. Because of the limited space in the Thistle Chapel itself, the banners of the Knights of the Thistle are suspended from the capitals of the piers of this aisle. The chapel's designer, Sir Robert Lorimer (1861–1929), is commemorated on a tablet round the corner on the east wall of the Preston Aisle, and above it is another bronze bust, of Arthur Stanley (1815–81), dean of Westminster Abbey (1864–81). The east window of this aisle, on the theme of Pentecost, is by Ballantine and Gardiner (1895).

The Preston Aisle was founded in 1455 by the town council of Edinburgh in memory of Sir William Preston. Despite their undertaking to finish in seven years, work was still in progress in 1487. From 1643–1829 it was used as a separate church. An old stone carved with a triple-tower castle, the traditional emblem of Edinburgh, was discovered during the restoration of 1882–3 and is now set in the east wall. An empty tomb niche can be seen in the centre bay of the south wall.

The little chapel opening off the western bay of the Preston Aisle, and divided from it by a low iron screen, is the Chepman Aisle. The aisle is named after Walter Chepman (d.1532) who, with Andrew Millar, introduced printing to Scotland in 1507. Permission to build the chapel was granted in 1507 and it was consecrated in 1513, the year of the Battle of Flodden. The entrance to the chapel is a former window, extended downwards, of the Preston Aisle. The chapel was formerly dedicated to St John the Evangelist, and an eagle (the emblem of St John) can be seen carved on one of the roof bosses. The aisle houses a large canopied monument (1888) to the marquess of Montrose, who was executed 1650. His dismembered remains were gathered together and buried in the cathedral in 1661. The polychromatic tiled floor centres around a white plaque simply inscribed 'Montrose 1661'. A small but intricate brass by Francis Skidmore on the west wall commemorates Walter Chepman. The heraldic glass is by Ballantine (1888). A marble plaque on the south wall commemorates the work of William Hay (d.1888), architect of the 1871–83 restoration. The framed parchment outside the aisle is the original portion of the National Covenant of 1638 sent to Linlithgow for signatures.

Adjacent to the Chepman Aisle is the south transept which, like the north transept, does not project beyond its flanking chapels. The transept, once the Chapel of St Anthony, was mostly rebuilt by Burn and has a plaster tierceron vault. Much of the transept is now occupied by the organ, built by the Austrian firm of Rieger, and dedicated in May 1992. It was donated by Alastair Salvesen in memory of his father and mother. The previous Victorian organ was dismantled and parts of it were dispatched to churches throughout Scotland.

Beyond the south transept is the outer south aisle of the nave, known as the Moray Aisle, and dating from 1830; it was formed from the three easternmost bays of the five built in 1387; the other two were demolished by Burn in 1829. The Ballantine glass (1881) depicts the assassination, in 1570, of the earl of Moray, regent for the young King James VI (1567–1625). The little chapel immediately adjacent to the south transept was formed by Hay out of a heating chamber built by Burn. It occupies the site of the chapel completed in 1518 for the merchant confraternity of the Holy Blood and is sometimes called the Holy Blood Aisle. It had two bays, but the western bay was demolished by Burn. The chapel has a fourteenth century foliated tomb recess and an 1864 monument incorporating the original brass to the earl of Moray. A flight of steps goes down to a door in the east wall of the chapel that leads into the cathedral restaurant.

Outside the Holy Blood Aisle, along the south wall of the Moray Aisle, can be found memorials to Margaret Oliphant (1828–97), novelist, essayist, biographer and historian; Robert Fergusson [both in bronze by Pittendrigh MacGillvray]; John Blackie (1809–95), professor of Greek at the university of Aberdeen; Thomas Chalmers (1805–82), professor of theology at Edinburgh; William Hanner (1808–82) his biographer; and Dr John Brown (1810–82), physician and essayist [both portrayed by Jackson]. The large Art Nouveau bronze plaque on the west wall of the Moray Aisle, commemorating Robert Louis Stevenson (1850–94), is by Augustus Saint Gaudens (1902). Above the memorial is an oriel window containing heraldic glass by Ballantine (1883).

Below the arcade, connecting the Moray Aisle with the inner south nave aisles, can be seen a square grave-marker stone (formerly outside the cathedral) with the inscription IK 1572, and a stone inscribed JOHN KNOX 1559. These are the dates of Knox's last and first sermons at St Giles'. There is also a vesper bell with a Latin inscription which translates, 'O Mother of God, remember me, the year of God 1452.' Nearby is a bronze tablet to Jenny Geddes who, in legend, hurled her stool at the dean of Edinburgh in 1637 and, surprisingly, a bronze stool by Merilyn Geddes, dedicated in 1992 to the memory of Jenny Geddes, who is described here, bizarrely, as 'a brave Scotchwoman'. The truth of the Geddes story will never be known, but it could be described as an act of violence that should best be forgotten; the perpetuation of the myth by this stool is curious.

The two westernmost bays of the Moray Aisle are very shallow, barely more than recesses, containing military memorials; these are all that remain of the two bays demolished by Burn in 1829. The white marble bust at the west end of the main south aisle is of General Sir William Lockhart (1841–1900), by Sir George Frampton. The windows here are by Ballantine and Gardiner (1900–1), showing scenes from the life of

Joseph; and Kempe (post-1898), showing scenes from the life of Moses.

St Giles' Cathedral has a dark and brooding atmosphere; a soot-blackened cathedral in a soot-blackened city. But, albeit much restored, it still has a strong medieval atmosphere. Recent developments, including weekly celebrations of the eucharist and the central position of the altar from the 1980s, have done much to recall the cathedral's past and to introduce the changes of the late twentieth century liturgical movement.

1 Brown, P Hume (1891): pp 83–84.
2 Lindsay, Ian G (1926): p. 96.
3 Walcott, Mackenzie (1874): volume 1, p. 135.
4 Lindsay, Ian G (1926): p. 101.
5 Brown, P Hume (1891): p. 224.
6 Lindsay, Ian G (1926): p. 101.
7 Johnston, John Octavius (1904): p. 15.
8 Aberdeen and Temair (1929): pp 196–7.
9 Paul, Sir J & Warrack, J (1911): p. 28.
10 Lindsay, Ian G (1926): pp 105–6.
11 New, Anthony (1980): p. 136.

The Cathedral Church of St Mary

Diocese of Edinburgh

(Scottish Episcopal Church)

After the expulsion of the bishops from the Church of Scotland in 1689, and the loss of St Giles' Cathedral in Edinburgh, those in the city who remained loyal to Bishop Alexander Rose (1687–1720) moved to a chapel on the site of the church of St Paul and St George in York Place but, because of their Jacobite leanings, the episcopalians were subjected to severe penal laws until 1792. For most of the eighteenth century, worship took place in obscure meeting houses, apart from the 'qualified' chapels, i.e. those who were prepared to take the oath of allegiance to King George III (1760–1820). Bishop Rose, who died on 20 March 1720, was almost the last survivor of the bishops deprived in 1689; the only one to outlive him was Bishop John Gordon of Galloway (1688–1726), who left Scotland and ultimately became a Roman Catholic. Alexander Rose was succeeded as bishop of Edinburgh by John Fullarton (1720–7) and an unbroken succession of bishops of Edinburgh has been maintained since that date. A new church (St Paul and St George) was built in 1816–18 and served as the pro-cathedral of the diocese until the construction of the present cathedral.

Perhaps surprisingly, given the status of Edinburgh as the capital city of Scotland, the diocese of Edinburgh was the last of the seven dioceses of the Scottish Episcopal Church to be given its own purpose-built cathedral church. St Mary's Cathedral is prominent and splendid, but something of a textbook cathedral.

This impressively bulky cathedral stands between Manor Place and Palmerston Place in the western New Town district of Edinburgh. It was built in three stages between 1874 and 1917, substantially as the result of a bequest from two unmarried sisters, Barbara and Mary Walker. The Walker sisters had inherited the estates of their brother Sir Patrick Walker (d.1837). Walker had developed the lands of Easter Coates and his daughters bequeathed their fortune to the Scottish Episcopal Church on the condition that a cathedral, dedicated to St Mary the Virgin, should be built on the site adjacent to their home. The sisters lived at Old Coates House which still stands on the north side of the cathedral. Barbara Walker died on 3 March 1859 and Mary Walker on 4 March 1871. By the terms of her will, Mary Walker directed that plans should be submitted by four to six architects, and that the plan 'most suitable for the site, and the sum to be expended on its construction, shall be adopted after my trustees have maturely considered it'.[1] The Walker Trustees were formally established by Act of

Parliament in 1877, principally to exercise the ancient office of Usher of the White Rod which Patrick Walker had purchased in 1806.

The trustees invited three architects from England (George Gilbert Scott, George Edmund Street and William Burges) and three from Scotland (Lessels, Peddie & Kinnear, and Alexander Ross) to submit designs. The terms of reference required a cathedral to seat 1500 people, and a chapter house to seat 150. The budget was initially set at £45,000 and later increased to £65,000. The architects submitted their plans to the trustees in 1872. The trustees initially favoured the three-spired design of Alexander Ross (architect of the episcopal cathedral at Inverness), but the final decision went in favour of one of three designs submitted by Sir George Gilbert Scott (1811–78), whose design incorporated a large central tower and spire. The choice of Scott was said to have been governed by the fact that his design was 'the only one embodying features from ancient Scottish buildings'.[2]

Scott's intention was clear; he proposed to construct a very grand cathedral; and that is indeed what was built. 'The church must, both within and without, bear such unmistakeable credentials of high dignity, as to be obviously suited to its rank as the chief church of the diocese, and that which its chief pastor adopts as more especially his own'.[3]

The foundation stone was laid on 21 May 1874 by the duke of Buccleuch and the sum of £65,000 agreed by the Walker trustees in 1872 was soon left behind. By 1874 the budget had risen to £89,770 and it was to rise still higher. Later in the same year the trustees, seemingly having had second thoughts about their rejection of Ross's design, instructed Scott to add another bay to the nave, and two towers and spires to the west gable; for the time being the towers only were to be built, construction of the spires being postponed to a future date. The cost had now risen to £95,016.

The nave was opened on 25 January 1879, the central spire was capped on 6 June that year and the cathedral was consecrated by Bishop Henry Cotterill (1872–86) on 30 October, at a final cost of £110,000; there was still no chapter house and no west spires. Construction of the chapter house and the two western spires was abandoned at the time 'owing to a rise in wages'.[4] Scott's son, John Oldrid Scott, supervised the construction of the chapter house in 1890–1, when the £5,000 cost was met by John Rollo. The two west spires were completed in 1913–17 by Charles M Oldrid Scott; the cost, £13,200, was raised by the congregation.

The architectural style of the cathedral is thirteenth century, with features borrowed from Elgin Cathedral and Jedburgh Abbey (the west door), Dunblane Cathedral (the triforium) and Coldingham Priory (the chancel clerestory). The plan is cruciform, with a seven-bay aisled nave, a four-bay aisled chancel and a chapter house at the north-east. The cathedral is 84.6m long and 20.8m wide. The length is exceeded only by St Andrews Cathedral, St Kentigern's Cathedral (Glasgow) and Elgin Cathedral. The western towers are 63.6m high. The central tower and spire is 83.7m high, taller than any other in Scotland, and the weight is estimated at 6096 tonnes, the foundations being 18.3m deep. The tower is supported by conventional crossing-piers but strengthened by diagonal buttresses across the transept/aisle junctions. The tower is square at its lower stages and then develops into an octagonal ringing chamber, rising to a spire containing a peal of ten bells, the largest weighing two tons. The bells, cast by Taylor of Loughborough in 1878, charmingly bear the names of virtuous attributes: Humility (treble), Faith, Self-Control, Patience, Reverence, Piety, Hope, Peace, Joy, and Caritas (tenor). Humility, at 343.2kg, is the lightest bell; Caritas, at 2.1 tonnes, is the heaviest.

The two western towers and spires were thoughtfully named Barbara (south) and Mary (north) after the Walker sisters. Above the west doors, a variation of that at Holyrood Abbey, are the figures of Christ with St John the Baptist and St Peter. Much of the stone here was renewed in 1990, when three new statues – representing St William, St Philip and St Richard – were carved and placed in niches, previously vacant. The west wall is pierced by four tall lancets below a wheel window. The lancets contain glass depicting various texts from the bible.

The nave has alternate round and octagonal columns with foliage capitals, a triforium with two pairs of windows to each bay, a clerestory, and a surprisingly battered-looking floor. The open timber roof is a slightly pointed wagon roof with applied ribs. The rood at the crossing, very much the focal point of the cathedral, was designed by Sir Robert Lorimer as part of a war memorial; it was carved by Pilkington Jackson and erected in 1922. The figure of Christ is shown against a field of Flanders poppies. The octagonal Italianate pulpit is of Caen stone with Dumfriesshire stone panels and marble pillars, and was designed by John Oldrid Scott. The carved figures represent Christ and Saints Peter, John the Baptist, Matthew, Mark, Luke and John.

The vaulted north-west tower space forms the verger's vestry. In the north nave aisle there is a Madonna painting by Matteo Cerezo (1635–85), and a painting, entitled *Altarpiece I*, by Sir Robin Philipson, presented to the cathedral by the painter when he was President of the Royal Scottish Academy in 1973. There are two other paintings: one depicts the Virgin and Child, the other, the Virgin and Child with St John the Baptist.

In the north transept is the King Charles Chapel, commemorating King Charles I (1625–49) who founded the diocese of Edinburgh in 1633; the armorial bearings of the king can be seen on the brilliant altar frontal. The painting of the king and of William Forbes, first bishop of Edinburgh (January–April 1634), are contemporary work, in gouache on wood, by Mabel Dawson. The king is shown holding a crown of thorns, symbolising his martyrdom (he was beheaded in 1649). The wooden font is by Mary Syme Boyd (1959).

The rest of the north transept is obscured by the organ, a four-manual, sixty-stop Willis instrument of 1879, enlarged by Harrison of Durham in 1929 and again in 1959, and restored in 1979. The mahogany case was designed by John Oldrid Scott. Two tablets commemorate Dr Collinson and Dr Head who, between them, were organists of the cathedral 1879–1957.

The north chancel aisle has a blind triforium, triplets of lancets in the clerestory, and a stone vault; the architecture at this point is something of an optical illusion and makes the square east end of the aisle look like an apse. A white marble recumbent effigy under the first arch commemorates Dean James Montgomery, the first of the cathedral's presiding clergy. All his successors have used the more usual Scottish title of provost. Montgomery and his wife were both generous benefactors of the cathedral. Several years after their deaths, Bishop John Dowden paid tribute to the way in which they had helped to fund the costs of the cathedral. 'In Dean Montgomery's time the cathedral was not much troubled by… recurring deficits… It was the practice of Dean Montgomery… when a deficit was apparent, to take his cheque-book and write an order on his bank for £100, or £150, or £200 as the case required. People heard no more of the matter'.[5] The dean had paid for the peal of ten bells in the central tower out of his own income. After the death of Mrs Montgomery in 1902, it was noticed that the amount of money contributed to the cathedral collections fell noticeably!

In the north chancel aisle hangs a painting entitled *The Presence* by Captain A E Borthwick, with a plaque describing its chequered history. Shortly after it was finished in 1910, it was exhibited throughout the British Isles and then sent to Germany for reproductions to be made. Instead of being returned to its owner, it was sold to an American for £5,000. It came to light when a New York newspaper published a section of the painting as an illustration to an article entitled 'Is religion dead?' The paper was sued for £30,000 for breach of copyright. After the war, a special act of congress enabled the picture to be returned to Scotland rather than being sold as confiscated enemy property. During the Second World War it was kept in the vaults of the Royal Scottish Academy before being returned to the cathedral in 1944. Next to *The Presence* hangs a sixteenth century Italian picture of *Christ Healing the Dumb*, by Francesco Maria Mazzola (1503–40).

The septum, a low screen between the nave and crossing, is Italianate in style and constructed of Derbyshire alabaster with diamond inlays between red marble shafts. The choir is located at the crossing, west of the chancel, to ensure its proximity to the organ in the north transept. The bishop's throne is in the first bay of the chancel on the south side. The throne, sedilia and choir stalls, are carved from walnut, with ebonized colonettes, and display plant and animal motifs. They have elaborately arcaded desks and traditional but uncanopied seats. All were carved in 1878–9 by Farmer & Brindley to John Oldrid Scott's designs. The stalls are labelled as follows:

S. TRIDUANA	S. BAITHAN
S. BALDRED	KING DAVID
S. GILES	HENRY COTTERILL BP.
QUEEN MARGARET	S. BRIDGET
S. HELEN	S. EDWIN
S. KENTIGERN	S. EBBA
S. BOISIL	ROBERT FORBES BP.
DANIEL SANDFORD BP.	S. COLUMBA
JOHN DOWDEN BP.	S. CUTHBERT
S. ADRIAN	WILLIAM FORBES BP.
S. NINIAN	KING CHARLES I

Brasses in the chancel floor commemorate Bishop John Dowden (1886–1910), nearest the organ console on the north side, Bishop Henry Cotterill (1872–86) in the centre of the floor, and Bishop James Walker (1830–41) nearest the throne. The memorial to Bishop Walker, who died more than thirty years before the cathedral was built, was dedicated by his daughter. The chancel floor, of tiled diamonds and whorls, is laid with marble from Durham and edged with grey limestone. The main paving of Victorian encaustic tiles includes various Christian symbols.

The chancel is separated from the north aisle by a fanciful wrought iron screen of 1879, the work of Francis Skidmore of Coventry. The screens were painted shortly after the Second World War by Vice-Provost Norman Cockburn in colours derived from a medieval Book of Hours. The mensa of the high altar is a single marble slab 3m in length. The reredos, alabaster with marble shafts, is by John Oldrid Scott and presents a tableau of the final

The Cathedral Church of St Mary

moments of Christ before his last words *Father, into thy hands I commend my Spirit*. The central panel and the flanking figures of St Margaret and St Columba are the work of a local sculptress, Mary Grant of Kilgraston. To the north of the high altar are memorial brasses to Bishop Seymour Reid (1929–39) who died in 1943, and further east, Bishop George Walpole (1910–29) who died in office. The ambulatory behind the altar is used as a vestry. The east window, consisting of three tall lancets, is framed by black marble pilasters. The mahogany chair, inlaid with mother-of-pearl, was given to the cathedral by Henry Parry Liddon, a canon residentiary of St Paul's Cathedral in London. Liddon was elected bishop of Edinburgh in 1886 on the death of Bishop Henry Cotterill and received the news by telegram from the dean of Edinburgh at the Hotel Royal in Constantinople. 'I took twenty-four hours to think it over; but cannot say that I ever had any doubt about the right decision to give. The bishops of the Church of Scotland should be Scotchmen. So long as they are Englishmen that Church will always wear the appearance of an English importation in the eyes of the presbyterian majority… The freedom from State Courts (in Scotland) is a powerful attraction to me… And the Scottish Bishops are none the weaker for being without the unmeaning trappings of feudalism which still hang around our English sees. But I should not forgive myself if I were in my own person to aid an evil tradition of seeking bishops for Scotland south of the Tweed, which I have deplored ever since I have been able to think about these things seriously at all'.[6] Liddon had similarly declined the diocese of Brechin in 1876 and, although pressed to reconsider his decision on his return to London, he never doubted that his arguments were sound. He refused to accept the result of the election, graciously, and presented this chair to the cathedral in gratitude for the compliment that had been paid to him.

The south chancel aisle was formed into a Lady Chapel in 1897–8 by George Henderson. The Italian Romanesque altar and reredos are of jaspe marble, and the flanking narrow tapestries depict the Annunciation. On the south wall is a double piscina and an unusual brass with recumbent effigy of Sub-Dean Cazenove (d.1896).

The Chapel of the Resurrection in the south transept is entered by a screen similar to the north transept, but made for the chapel of The Hirsel, Berwickshire, in 1928 and moved here in 1959. The oak screen, the silver sanctuary lamp and the altar furniture are all memorial gifts. The chapel was dedicated on 19 February 1922 as a war memorial. The panels commemorate the dead of the two world wars, and a marble memorial cross of 1878 to the 1st Battalion Royal Scots 1857–78. An aumbry with brass door is set into the south wall. The carved granite cross forms part of the Scottish National War Memorial.

In recent years, this area has become a repository for contemporary religious art and the worth of each piece is a matter of personal taste. A sculpture made from 22.8m of sisal rope impregnated with polyester resin is entitled *Crown of Thorns* and is the work of Edith Simon. The acrylic *Ascension of Elijah* was painted in the cathedral in 1976 by a Viennese Roman Catholic, Ernst de Gasperi. There is also a long seat with sixteenth century carved panels, two carved seventeenth century tables, and a large eighteenth century cabinet. The little Madonna carving on the south west crossing pier was carved by Lesley Crowe from silver birch in 1971. On a pillar beside the Resurrection Chapel is a hanging produced with natural dyes on specially treated calico by the Edinburgh artist Marianna Lines. The design is derived from the Farr Stone, a ninth century Celtic Christian monument in Sutherland.

In the south nave aisle are many nineteenth and twentieth century brass memorials and, on the right, a brass pelican lectern with enamel inlay. Further on stands a plain smooth octagonal freestone font with an open-work iron cover. The work of Edith M B Hughes, it was given by the earl of Home (prime minister of the United Kingdom 1963–4) in 1959. Its Romanesque style predecessor was of alabaster and red marble.

The area to the south of the main west door was formerly a chapel dedicated to St Margaret. The chapel is entered through an iron screen designed by Edith M B Hughes in 1959, and now houses the cathedral library and the gift stall. On the west wall is the Dunmore Reredos, an early sixteenth or seventeenth century oak panel, possibly made in the Low Countries. Formerly in the chapel of Dunmore House, it was given to the cathedral by the earl of Dunmore in 1955.

The chapter house, not normally open to the public, has a vault supported by a central granite column, a display of the architect's competitions designs, and a painting (1976) *The Incarnation* by Brian Slack.

Easter Coates House, to the north of the cathedral, was built (1610–15) by John Byres as a small two-storey L-plan house. It wears something of the appearance of a hunting lodge; perhaps not surprisingly as it was once surrounded by the ancient forest of Drumsheugh; a few trees standing nearby are all that remain of the forest. The house has been much altered since the mid-eighteenth century. Restored and extended by Sir Patrick Walker in the 1830s, and restored again by Sir George Gilbert Scott, it formed part of the Walker bequest on the death of Mary Walker in 1871. It became the home of the first cathedral organist and housed the cathedral choir school from 1887, which became St Mary's Music School in 1971.

The Song School, further north, was built in 1885 by John Oldrid Scott as a rehearsal space for the cathedral choir. The colourful murals on the theme of the Benedicite were painted by Phoebe Traquair in 1889–92. Its organ is by Henry Willis and Sons, 1887. Walpole Hall, further north again, was built in 1933 to designs by Sir Robert Lorimer and J F Matthew; it is used for social functions and houses the offices of the diocese of Edinburgh.

The exterior of St Mary's Cathedral is a splendid addition to the townscape of Edinburgh. The east end dominates Melville Street and the west spires dominate Palmerston Place, leaving the observer in no doubt that here is a powerful building of massive strength and considerable importance. As the architect of the Albert Memorial and the Midland Grand Hotel at St Pancras Station, we should expect nothing less of Scott. But the interior of the cathedral is surprisingly unmoving and almost disappointing. Somehow it is an all too perfectly regimented attempt at mimicry of medieval Gothic, in a way that many other nineteenth century examples of Gothic Revival are not. This cathedral is a product of the nineteenth century Gothic Revival, not of the thirteenth century Gothic Original, and one would love to have seen something of the authentic distinctiveness of the nineteenth century Revival style, exemplified for example by the polychromatic work of Butterfield and Burges. It may be that Scott designed St Mary's Cathedral as the perfect composition of every aspect of thirteenth century ecclesiastical architecture that he loved; if so, then let it stand as the apotheosis of his dreams. It has, as he intended, 'unmistakable credentials of high dignity'.

1 *History of the Erection of the Cathedral Church of St Mary* (1879): p. 10.
2 *The Cathedral Church of St Mary, Edinburgh* (1934): p. 4.
3 *History of the Erection of the Cathedral Church of St Mary* (1879): p. 11.
4 *The Cathedral Church of St Mary, Edinburgh* (1934): p. 4.
5 Dowden, John (1909): p. 16.
6 Johnston, John Octavius (1904): pp 327–8.

The Cathedral Church of St Mary

Diocese of St Andrews and Edinburgh
(Roman Catholic Church)

After the sixteenth century reformation, Scotland's Roman Catholics were served mostly by visiting missionary priests from Europe. Native Roman Catholic priests had been exiled to Europe under pain of death should they ever return. The first sign of a new administrative organisation to replace the former hierarchy emerged in 1694 with the appointment of Thomas Nicholson as vicar apostolic for Scotland. Effectively, the whole of Scotland was placed under the jurisdiction of a single bishop. In 1727 the country was divided in two, for pastoral purposes, by the creation of the Highland District and the Lowland District.

The origin of Edinburgh's Roman Catholic cathedral begins with the ministry of George Hay (1729–1811) a native of the city and the son of episcopalian parents. He had served an apprenticeship to a surgeon and was caught tending wounded Jacobite soldiers after the Battle of Prestonpans during the Jacobite rising of 1745. Hay was captured, and imprisoned for two years in the Tower of London. After his release, he met Bishop Richard Challoner (1691–1781), coadjutor vicar apostolic of the London District and himself born of presbyterian parents. Challoner made a powerful impression on Hay and, after the latter was released in 1747, he returned to Edinburgh and was received into the Roman Catholic Church in 1748. After pursuing a career as a surgeon, Hay went to Rome in 1751 to study at the Scots College. He was ordained in 1758 and returned to Edinburgh in the following year. In 1769 he was appointed coadjutor vicar apostolic of the Lowland District and succeeded Bishop James Grant as vicar apostolic in 1778. Hay now had responsibility for more than seventy-five per cent of the geographical area of Scotland. It was a vast area, and much of it was not easily accessible in those days of primitive transportation.

Although most of his time was spent in Edinburgh, Bishop Hay was known to walk from Edinburgh to Aberdeen and even further north, to visit the far-flung parts of his jurisdiction. Shortly after his arrival in Edinburgh, he acquired a tenement building in Blackfriars Wynd for use as a priest's house. The dining room, sitting room and kitchen were then converted into a church, with a movable partition to allow the kitchen still to be used as such. The new church was used by Gaelic-speaking Catholics from the north-west of Scotland. At the end of the eighteenth century a floor was acquired in a building almost opposite, for English-speaking Catholics. In 1779 Hay purchased a building in

Chalmers Close near the top of Leith Street. The ground floor contained six cellars, some with fireplaces which could be used for dwellings. The first floor formed a hall, 10.3m long, 6.09m wide and 4.2m high. The second floor was the bishop's residence, and the third floor above was the garret.

The eighteenth century was not an easy time for Scotland's Roman Catholics. They had had to endure suspicion and hatred in the days before the repeal of the Penal Laws in 1792, and any overt signs of Roman Catholicism, especially a building where they were known to gather for worship, was likely to attract the hostility of sections of anti-Catholic opinion. In the year that it opened, the church in Chalmers Close was plundered and burned by a mob, incensed (and no doubt incited) by a government proposal to relax the penal laws; this was sufficient to inflame anti-Catholic sentiment. The Chalmers Close church was burnt on 2 February 1779. When the bishop arrived at the scene, he was told by one of the mob, 'We are burning down the Papist church, and looking for the Papist bishop to put on top of the blaze'.[1] The bishop prudently retreated to the safety of Edinburgh Castle, where he was welcomed by the governor and given refuge. On 3 February, the chapel in Blackfriars Wynd was also attacked and plundered, though it was not destroyed, and continued in use until the completion of the new chapel in 1814.

Bishop Hay appealed for compensation to the government who gave the sum of £1,600; a similar amount was given by the city. In 1801 he used the money to purchase, from the Heriot Trust, the site on which the present cathedral stands. Located in the First New Town, away from the centre of the city and, at that time, hidden from public view, the new site was a sensible choice. Hay did not live to see the new chapel; he resigned in 1806 and died in 1811 before negotiations were complete. Bishop Hay was buried within a ruined chapel on the banks of the Don, not far from Fetternear, Aberdeenshire. A new chapel was later erected on the site, and the bishop's grave is now covered by the south transept. It was left to Hay's successor Bishop Alexander Cameron (1806–25) to begin the building of St Mary's Chapel.

By 1812, the original site had been enlarged by the purchase of surrounding plots of ground and a building could be erected in front of the chapel to act as additional protection in case of any further riots. The new chapel (the word 'chapel' was commonly used instead of 'church' for Roman Catholic places of worship at that time), opened in 1814. The architect was James Gillespie Graham (1777–1855) who started the neo-Gothic Revival in Edinburgh. The most notable aspect of the building was the Gothic Revival west facade, which is still standing; the chapel behind was no more than a plain rectangle with an apse, and has mostly disappeared through successive fires and rebuildings. The chapel was furnished with a wooden altar with a painting of the *Deposition from the Cross* above it. The painting, long believed to have been the work of Van Dyck, was presented to the cathedral by the daughter of Sir George Chalmers, a contemporary portrait artist. King George IV (1820–30) is said to have offered £4,000 for the painting on his visit to Edinburgh in 1822. Seating was only provided around the walls of the church, the central space accommodating some 500 standing worshippers. The priest's house was located on the site of the sanctuary of the present cathedral.

Simple as it was, the building was praised, with appropriate and predictable restraint, in the local press: 'An elegant Roman Catholic Chapel is now built in the vicinity of Corries' Rooms...The doorway enters by way of a pointed arch, supported on columns, and the windows are also pointed above. Pinnacles, according to the antique, rise from the front which is to the east and produce a fine effect to those who admire the style adopted'.[2] Apart from the admired west front, little else remains of the 1812–14 chapel. Successive and severe fires and rebuildings have destroyed all but the west front of Graham's chapel.

The ornamentation of the interior of St Mary's Chapel continued under Bishop Cameron, who resigned through ill-health in 1825 and Bishop Alexander Paterson (1825–31). The first new structural addition to the simple chapel was the construction of a long 'cloister' (in reality a hall) on the north side in 1828, on the site of the present north aisle and Lady Chapel. The 'cloister' was the dream of an enthusiastic young priest named James Gillis, born in Montreal of Scottish parents. Gillis spent a year in France raising money for the construction of the 'cloister', which would be used for catechism classes and weekday services. Gillis was fluent in French and a powerful orator, and in 1831 he was invited to preach at Orleans at the celebration arranged to mark the four hundredth anniversary of the death of Joan of Arc.

Gillis was appointed coadjutor vicar apostolic of the Eastern District in 1837, to assist Bishop Carruthers, and in 1841 alterations were made to St Mary's to enhance its appearance: 'The sanctuary has been considerably enlarged, and is enclosed by a light perforated screen of oak, carved in the richest manner, and finished by lofty pedestals supporting lights... on the Epistle, or right side, the centre division of the screen rises in a pyramidical form, and sprouts a beautiful light-groined and carved oak canopy, with flying buttresses, under which, on a

The Cathedral Church of St Mary

raised platform, stands the bishop's seat. The old pulpit has been replaced by one in the light and florid Gothic style… The Gothic framework of the altar-piece is a fine imitation of the black and gold, and of the Rosso antico marbles. The candelabra pedestals are an imitation of malachite marble; and the panels of the altar table are of the same imitation surrounded by white and gold'.[3] Bishop Gillis regarded these attractive embellishments as only ancillary to his real aim – the construction of a completely new pro-cathedral on a different site. 'His dream was to erect a Cathedral that could vie in grandeur with the great medieval Cathedrals on the mainland of Europe'.[4] He purchased a stretch of meadow land on Strathearn Road in the developing suburb of Grange and engaged Augustus Pugin to design a cathedral and an adjoining seminary. The plans were duly drawn up and exhibited at Edinburgh in 1850, but the plan failed because the bishop's financial adviser was made bankrupt. The only relic of the plan is a chalice presented to Bishop Gillis in 1847 by Pope Pius IX in anticipation of the proposed new St Margaret's Cathedral.

Bishop Gillis died in 1864 and was succeeded by Bishop John Strain who was consecrated in Rome by the pope. On 13 January 1865, a few months after the new bishop had returned to Edinburgh, a fire destroyed the Theatre Royal adjacent to the chapel and for a while there was a danger that the chapel itself might be completely lost. As it was the damage was grievous enough. A large chimney fell through the roof of the cloister chapel, killing one fireman on the spot. The wall of the theatre then collapsed on to the chapel, destroying a third of its roof. In the subsequent restoration the cloister chapel was rebuilt, but to only two-thirds of its previous length, while the sanctuary of the cathedral was extended.

In 1878 Pope Pius IX formally re-established a full Roman Catholic hierarchy for Scotland. On the restoration of the hierarchy in 1878, St Mary's Chapel became the pro-cathedral for the diocese of St Andrews and Edinburgh, and Bishop Strain became the first archbishop of the new diocese and primate of the Roman Catholic Church in Scotland. In 1883, after the death of Archbishop Strain, William Smith, the cathedral administrator began work on enlarging the cathedral. Graham's west front was given a new central porch, in similar style, and the central gable above was given a new ornamental parapet surmounted by a cross, to replace one blown down twenty-five years earlier. The cloister chapel was extended to its original length, and an altar-piece depicting the *Assumption of the Blessed Virgin Mary*, was donated. A much-needed sacristy was built at the rear of the chapel. The total cost of the work was £1,500, and on 5 July 1886 St Mary's was raised to the status of a cathedral church.

On 28 December 1891, another fire, the cause of which was never discovered, destroyed the cloister chapel and spread to half the main body of the cathedral. The fire brigade saved the building from being gutted, but the destruction caused by the fire was used to rebuild and extend much of the cathedral over the next few years, to designs by John Biggar. The site of the former cloister was fully incorporated into the cathedral as an arcaded north aisle, and the south wall was turned into a matching arcade opening into a new south aisle; this work gave the cathedral its present very wide appearance. The cathedral was given a new entrance porch and an octagonal baptistery at the north-west. The baptistery was thought by some to be one of the best features of the cathedral. It contained an octagonal stone font covered by an ornate suspended canopy of oak with a brass flange, and a small altar with an oak frontispiece printed with a circular panel showing dove, sea and fish. Biggar also designed a new chancel and two west towers, but his plans were never implemented. The present three bay aisled chancel with quatrefoil piers, semi-octagonal apse and a low-pitch hammerbeam roof, was built in 1895 to designs by Buchanan and Bennett.

In 1932 Monsignor McGettigan (d.1947), the cathedral administrator, proposed an astonishing plan to Archbishop Andrew Macdonald – to raise the roof of the cathedral. It was ambitious or audacious according to view, but not purposeless. Biggar's north and south aisles had given the building great width, but without a corresponding increase of height. He had retained Graham's original roofline, intended for a much narrower building, leaving the cathedral with an extensive roof that seemed oppressively low. The concept of raising the roof was accepted and Reid & Forbes raised the height of the cathedral walls by about 6m as far as Graham's east front would allow. The raising of the walls allowed enough space in the nave arcades to introduce a new upper clerestory of circular windows and reduced Biggar's lower clerestory to the appearance of a glazed triforium. The roof of the nave was supported by seven steel trusses, lined with oak and following the contour of the chancel arch, to which was affixed a canvas painting depicting the *Annunciation*, by Louis Beyart of Bruges. One of the most distinctive and attractive features of the interior – the giant crowned painted wooden angels – were the product of the 1930s' alterations.

In the 1940s, the Theatre Royal was, for the last time, destroyed by fire. It remained as a roofless shell until 1956 when the site was put up for sale. It was prudently purchased by the diocese to safeguard the amenity of the cathedral and to provide space should it be needed in future. The purchase was put to good use in the alterations of 1976–8. Biggar's west porch and baptistery, the fabric of which had deteriorated, were removed and replaced by a new and spacious hexagonal porch into the side street so that the parishioners would not be endangered by the heavy line of traffic. The south wall, previously shared with the Theatre Royal, was faced with stone. A wide flight of steps was built up to the west front of the cathedral, and the original facade was revealed for the first time in the twentieth century. The architects were Thomas Haddow and Harley and the work was carried out in 1976–8. The brief was to retain the Gillespie Graham facade and to continue it along to the new porch on the Theatre Royal site. This concrete-framed brick-lined porch has its own altar with the painting of the *Deposition from the Cross* given to the cathedral in 1814. Long thought to be the work of Van Dyck, it is now accepted as a contemporary copy by an unknown artist, probably by a member of Van Dyck's studio, of a painting in the Kaiser Friedrich Museum, Berlin, which was destroyed with many other pictures in an air raid in 1945.

The work of 1976–8 also reordered the cathedral in accordance with the decrees of the Second Vatican Council. The marble high altar was dismantled and the blocks used to build a podium on which the tabernacle now stands, under the 1928 baldachino by Reginald Fairlie. The polished stone and marble baldachino, is relatively large to the size of the former sanctuary, and tended to cramp movement on major liturgical occasions. For the purposes of record, the old high altar was constructed of plain white marble blocks with a gradine of fine-grained peach-coloured marble. The 91cm high tabernacle was enclosed in oak with doors of brass. The former gradine remains in position with the traditional six candles. The new marble altar, panelled with Derbyshire and Whitehaven alabaster, was designed in 1878 by Rowland Anderson and generously given to the cathedral by the trustees of the nearby former Catholic Apostolic Church in East London Street. The trustees also donated the bishop's throne, two banks of choir stalls and the brass eagle lectern. The chapter stalls came from the chapel of St Margaret's Convent. The refurbished and reordered cathedral was dedicated on 18 April 1978.

The nave as reformed in 1932 is very wide and chiefly memorable for the giant and brightly-painted Art Deco crowned angels, bearing shields. They act as corbels, their golden wings clasping the ribs of the vaults and stretching up into broad arches. The angels were carved by Scott Morton and bear shields depicting the armorial bearings of St Andrew, St Cuthbert, St Margaret and St David, and then of successive vicars apostolic and archbishops. An upper row of angels bear scrolls inscribed with the words of the Agnus Dei. The lamp fittings are in the same Art Deco style.

Although the arcade walls were raised 6m in height in the 1930s alterations, the red sandstone piers and arches were left alone and consequently the arches now appear to be very low. Above is the unusual double clerestory, the upper row of windows (dating from the heightening of the walls in the 1930s) being circular and having ornamental wall plates both above and below. The lower row sometimes has one light and sometimes two lights over each arch. The 1932 painting by Louis Beyart over the chancel arch, depicts the coronation of the Blessed Virgin Mary by Christ, flanked by angel musicians. The aisle floors are mosaic, the rest of the floor is parquet.

The broad low north aisle has a Piéta in the second bay, and the remainder of the side wall is taken up with Stations of the Cross by Mayer of Munich, a 1919 war memorial. The stations are plaster models hand-painted in oils. The oak-panelled Lady Chapel at the east end of the north aisle was dedicated on 11 November 1905 in memory of Canon James Donleavy who served on the cathedral staff 1878–1903. The 1905 white marble altar is the work of Sir Robert Lorimer. The centre panel of the altar has a circular carving of lilies in relief and an Agnus Dei. The white and gold reredos, also the work of Lorimer, has a cornice worked with the lily design. The centre of the reredos forms a niche to hold the statue of the Blessed Virgin Mary and the Christ child. The tabernacle door is of beaten silver. The ceiling is panelled in oak. The floor is of Greek rippolino marble with bands of white. The stone font, under the last bay of the arcade is nineteenth century, circular and undistinguished, and came from a redundant presbyterian church.

The chancel has much taller clerestory windows of Perpendicular style. These, with the exception of some scattered thistles in the west windows, have the only pictorial glass in the cathedral. The central window glass, depicting the Crucifixion, is by Hardman of Birmingham; the rest of the glass in the sanctuary is thought to be by Mayer of Munich. The chancel has a hammer-beam roof, far too large and heavy for this confined space, which continues awkwardly round the apse. The stalls discreetly occupy the aisles, and the 1932 organ by Lawton of Aberdeen, stands at the north-east, behind the archbishop's throne. The central Italianate altar is fronted by a dark red marble communion rail. To the south is an ungainly canopied octagonal oak pulpit by Reid and Forbes.

The south aisle is walled with confessional boxes, and terminates in the Chapel of St Andrew (formerly the Chapel of the Sacred Heart). It has an oak-panelled sanctuary and a brown-veined onyx altar into which are set relics of Saint Andrew.

Within the vaults below the sanctuary are the remains of Bishops Alexander Cameron, Alexander Paterson and Andrew Carruthers, and Archbishops John Strain, William Smith, Angus Macdonald, James Smith and Andrew Joseph Macdonald. Plaques record Bishop George Hay, who is buried at Fetternear, and Bishop James Gillis whose remains are in the vaults of St Margaret's Convent. The partly refaced west and north fronts, the latter with new entrance on a piazza, are attractive. In 1990 plans were unveiled to replace the large traffic island in front of the cathedral with a new layout incorporating a much smaller island with tree-lined, landscaped pedestrian priority areas. The work is now complete and the cathedral stands as a focal point at the top of Leith Walk. Eduardo Paolozzi's sculptures are a matter of personal taste.

To the west of the cathedral, and used as its halls in the years 1935–78, was the former St James Place Relief Church of 1800, a stern seven-bay front with three deep archways in the pedimented centrepiece. Round and square-arched openings alternated curiously in its four storeys.

A stepped way leads around the east end of the cathedral and down a dingy cobbled alley called Cathedral Lane, but there is nothing of interest here.

Graham's 1812–14 facade betokens a modest building, more of a humble parish church than a cathedral church in the capital city; but this is because of the architectural history of the building and the way in which it gradually emerged from hiding, slowly developing in the years between 1814 and 1932. Passing through the west door and into the interior produces a quite different reaction. The spacious and expansive interior, with its acreage of chairs, slightly suggests a large airport departure lounge, although one that is pleasantly warm and welcoming. The greatest delight of St Mary's Cathedral is its wonderful collection of gaudy giant angels, and the building is worth a visit if only to see them.

1 Gray, Joseph Gordon, Cardinal (1990).
2 Donlevy, James (1890): p. 92.
3 ibid., pp 108–109.
4 Gray, Joseph Gordon, Cardinal (1990): p. 9.

Elgin

The Cathedral Church of the Holy Trinity

Elgin (population 18,000) is a town in the east of Scotland, 280km north of Edinburgh, 102km north-west of Dundee and 8km south of Lossiemouth at the beginning of the Moray Firth. The origin of the name 'Elgin' is obscure and there is no agreed translation; 'beautiful valley' from the Gaelic words *aille* (beautiful) and *gin* (little) is one possibility.

Elgin's past is as obscure as its name and it does not really emerge from the shadows until the end of the twelfth century. It was important enough to become a royal residence of the Scottish kings and it became a natural target at the time of the invasion by King Edward I of England (1272–1307) in 1296. In 1224 Elgin became the see town of the diocese of Moray and the remaining ruins of its cathedral indicate that it was one of the most beautiful in Scotland.

The diocese of Moray was probably founded about 1107 during the reign of King Alexander I (1107–24). The early history of the diocese is very uncertain and Bishop Brice de Douglas (1203–22) is the first bishop of Moray who is anything more than a name. The see of the diocese was first established at Birnie (until 1184), then at Kinnedar (1184–1208) and then at Spynie (1208–24). Then it was finally established at Elgin in 1224. The bishops of Moray continued to live at Spynie, 3.2km to the north of Elgin, where their great ruined palace-castle can still be seen. While at the Lateran Council in 1215, Bishop Brice had suggested to Pope Innocent III that Spynie was not an appropriate site for the cathedral church of the diocese: 'Spynie was a solitary place; it was not safe for residence; was far from the necessaries of life; and that divine service was much neglected',[1] and he sought the pope's permission to transfer the see to Elgin.

The site chosen for the new cathedral may have been occupied by an earlier church dedicated in the name of the Holy Trinity, but this is by no means certain. It seems more likely that Christianity at Elgin was based on the site of the parish church of St Giles' in the centre of the medieval burgh, and that the site of the present ruined cathedral was unoccupied.

After a fire in 1270 the cathedral was extensively rebuilt with full outer south aisles, a south porch, a much longer, aisled chancel and an octagonal chapter house. The great west door was also rebuilt on a more impressive scale.

Although the English invasions of 1296 and 1336 both reached Elgin, the cathedral, which could have been sacked and burned, was apparently left untouched. Bishop Alexander Bur (1362–97) wrote to Pope Urban V (1362–70) informing him that the cathedral was ruinous as the result of neglect and hostile invasion, but it is difficult to know quite what the state of the cathedral was at the time. If it was one of ruin and neglect, any restoration work was obliterated by a sudden, merciless and thorough conflagration at the end of the fourteenth century.

In 1390 Alexander Stewart, earl of Buchan and Ross, and son of King Robert II (1371–1406), was excommunicated by Bishop Bur. The earl, known as the 'Wolf of Badenoch', exacted a savage revenge for his excommunication. From his island stronghold in Lochindorb, he arrived at Elgin on 17 June 1390. With his 'wyld wykkyd hieland-men he burned the town of Forres, the Choir of the Church of St Laurence there also the Manse of the Archdeacon... and the whole town of Elgin, 18 noble and beautiful manses of canons and chaplains, and what was still more accursed and lamentable the noble and highly adored Church of Moray [the cathedral] with all the books, charters and other valuable things of the country therein kept'.[2]

Bishop Bur was heartbroken and appealed to the king for help. 'My church was the ornament of the realm, the glory of the kingdom, the delight of foreigners and stranger guests; an object of praise and glorification in foreign realms by reason of the multitude of those serving and the beauty of its ornament and in which we believe God was rightly worshipped; not to speak of its high belfries, its ancient furniture and its innumerable jewels'.[3] The destruction was so extensive that the work of restoration had hardly begun before the bishop's death in 1397. The progress was delayed again, in 1402, when the cathedral was raided by Alexander, a son of the Lord of the Isles, who came twice in the same year. Consequent repairs and renewals included the west front and part of the nave arcades, the chapter house and a completely new central tower. Restoration continued throughout the fifteenth century and the chapter house, which bears the arms of Bishop Andrew Stewart (1482–1501), was probably the last part of the cathedral to be restored.

Within seventy years of the restoration, the reformation of 1560 signalled the end of the cathedral's life. It was unfortunate for Elgin Cathedral that, like St Andrews, but unlike most other Scottish cathedrals, it was a monastic church and not a parish church. In the eyes of the reformers it was a monastery and therefore to be abandoned; no part of it was needed for worship. The reformers were bent on the destruction of 'popish

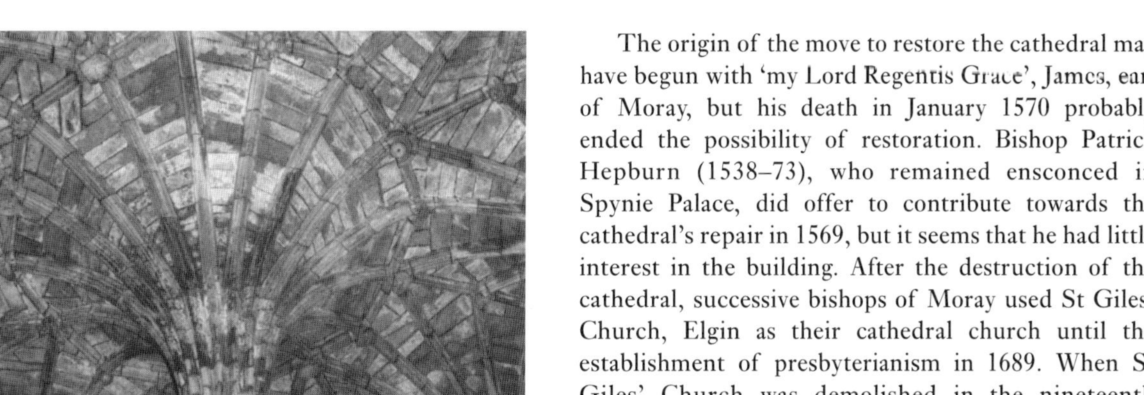

The chapter house of Elgin Cathedral

trappings' and the elaborate cathedral was bound to suffer. By order of the Privy Council the lead was removed from the roof in 1567 to be sold to pay the army and that sealed the fate of the cathedral. 'That seeing provisioun must be maid for the entertaining of the men of weir quhais service cannot be sparit quhile the rebellions and disobedient subjictis troublaris of the commonweil in all partis of this realm be reductit', the lead should be removed 'in Abirdene and Elgyne, and sauld and disposit upon for sustentation of the said men of war'.[4] It is said that in both cases the lead, which was to be sold in Holland, was lost at sea.

In 1569 the Privy Council, meeting at Aberdeen, changed its mind and ordered Elgin Cathedral to be re-roofed. 'Forasmekill as my Lord Regentis Grace, Patrik, Bischop of Murray, the Channonis of the Cathedrall Kirk of Murray, willing to repair the samyn, hes condescendit to satisfie, content, and pay ane ressonabill contributioun, for mending, theking, and reparaling of the Cathedrall Kirk of Murray, for the furth setting of Goddis glorie and decoriatioun of the Cuntre, my Lord Regentis with the avise of the Lordis of Secreit Counsale, ordainis lettres to be direct to the various Prelattis Channonis and beneficit men within the Diocie of Murray'.[5]

The origin of the move to restore the cathedral may have begun with 'my Lord Regentis Grace', James, earl of Moray, but his death in January 1570 probably ended the possibility of restoration. Bishop Patrick Hepburn (1538–73), who remained ensconced in Spynie Palace, did offer to contribute towards the cathedral's repair in 1569, but it seems that he had little interest in the building. After the destruction of the cathedral, successive bishops of Moray used St Giles' Church, Elgin as their cathedral church until the establishment of presbyterianism in 1689. When St Giles' Church was demolished in the nineteenth century, the episcopal monuments were moved to the chapter house of the old cathedral.

The north-east of Scotland remained a conservative area and a public mass was celebrated in the cathedral after the battle of Glenlivet in 1594. The battle had seen the defeat by the Roman Catholic earl of Huntly of the government forces led by the earl of Argyll. In his book, *Elgin, Past and Present*, Mackintosh dates the last public Catholic mass in the cathedral to the year 1594, though Roman Catholics were said to worship there secretly until 1714. If so, it is unlikely that this was done in any structured or organised way.[6] William Clark states that 'some of the rooms in the western towers and in the cloisters were so entire, and the paintings on their walls so perfect, that the Roman Catholics residing in Elgin used to retire to them to say their prayers, as places of greater sanctity that any other that could be found'.[7] Gradually the cathedral came to be regarded as 'a piece of Romish vanity, too expensive to repair'.[8] At one particularly grimly puritanical date, the kirk session declared the cathedral to be out of bounds. 'All profane pastyme... and specially futballing through the toun, snow balling, singing of carelles or other profane songis, guysing, pyping, violing and dansing... All women and lassis forbidden to haunt or resort in the Chanonrie Kirk or kirkyard thereof'.[9]

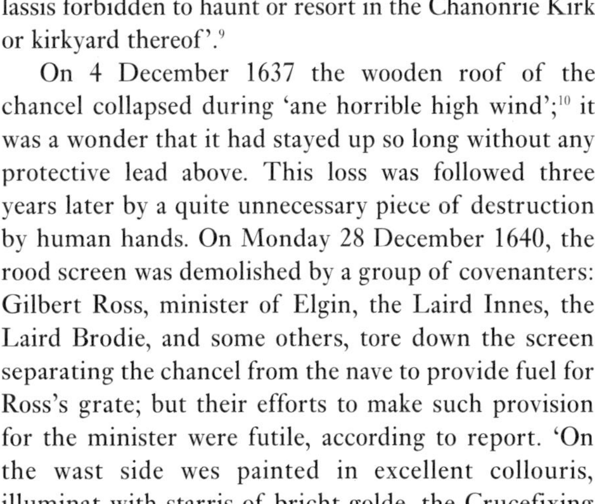

On 4 December 1637 the wooden roof of the chancel collapsed during 'ane horrible high wind';[10] it was a wonder that it had stayed up so long without any protective lead above. This loss was followed three years later by a quite unnecessary piece of destruction by human hands. On Monday 28 December 1640, the rood screen was demolished by a group of covenanters: Gilbert Ross, minister of Elgin, the Laird Innes, the Laird Brodie, and some others, tore down the screen separating the chancel from the nave to provide fuel for Ross's grate; but their efforts to make such provision for the minister were futile, according to report. 'On the wast side wes painted in excellent collouris, illuminat with starris of bricht golde, the Crucefixing

of our blessed Saeouer Jesus Christ. This peice was so excellentlie done, that the collouris nor starris never faidit nor evanishit bot keipit hails and sound as thay were at the beginning notwithstanding this college or channourie Kirk wantit the roof sen the refourmation, and no haill wyndo thairintill to saif the same from storme, snaw, sleit or weit, quhilk myself saw, and mervallous to consider. On the uther side of the wall, towardis the east wes drawin the day of judgement. Alwayes all is throwne doun to the ground. It wer said thair minister causit bring hame to his hous the tymber thairof, and burne for serving his ketching and vther uses; bot ilk nicht the fyre went out that it wes burnt, and could not be haldin in to kyndle the morning fyre as vse is; whairat ther servandis and vtheris mervaillit and thairupone the Minister left of and forboor to bring in or burne any more of that timber in his house. This was markit, spred throwe Elgin, and credible reportit to myself'.[11]

The destruction of the 1630s and the 1640s was followed in 1651 by the usual damage by Cromwellian troops who were said to have amused themselves by knocking tracery out of the windows. When Thomas Kirk visited Elgin in 1677 he was depressed by what he saw: 'Here is the ruins of a very good church, the model not unlike York Minster: it pitied us to see so fine a structure so demolished'.[12] But there was still more damage to be done. The greatest single disaster to befall the cathedral after its abandonment was the collapse of the central tower on Easter Day 1711. The tower fell to the north and west demolishing much of the nave and north transept. The surprising factor in this disaster is that no one was killed. 'Several children were playing, and idle people walking within the area of the church, and immediately as they removed to breakfast, the tower fell, and no one was hurt'.[13] For about a century thereafter the ruins were thought of only as a useful quarry. So Elgin Cathedral fell prey to 'deliberate robbery and frigid indifference'.[14] Other travellers to Elgin were saddened by the sight of its ruined cathedral. Robert Southey visited Elgin in 1819: 'The ruins of the cathedral 'made me again... groan over the brutal spirit of mob-reformation'.[15] Robert Billings in the mid-nineteenth century: 'Few places impress, in what remains, so deep a regret for what is gone'.[16]

The Cathedral Church of the Holy Trinity

The nineteenth century brought a new fascination, bordering on romanticism, for the Middle Ages. There came an appreciation of medieval architecture and a renewed interest in what remained, and gradually the state of Elgin Cathedral took a turn for the better. In 1807 the wall enclosing the ruined cathedral was built by the exertions of a Mr King, a local resident. In 1816, the town council, growing conscious of the poor state of a valuable piece of its heritage, petitioned the Barons of the Exchequer to take charge of the ruin. The Exchequer eventually made a grant of money in 1820 for preservation purposes and, in 1824, the council appointed a paid keeper to care for the ruins. John Shanks was 'a thin, lank, spider-looking being, and clad in obsolete costume, with a quiet earnest enthusiasm in his manner – a sort of Old Mortality, whose delight it was to labour among old ruins and tombs'.[17] His efforts on behalf of the cathedral are worthy of praise and commemoration by all except archaeologists. With the help of the Morayshire Farmers' Club, who loaned him horses and cart, he removed 2,866 barrowfuls of rubbish from the cathedral. 'All the accumulated debris was cleared away, and many forgotten tombstones brought to light. The actual level of the floor was reached, the towers where shaky were secured with iron bands, a new lead roof was put on the Chapter House, a neat lodge built for the keeper, and what had once been a scandal and disgrace alike to the nation and the town became the fame of the one and the ornament of the other'.[18] An inscription recording his efforts, was cut on a tablet in the cathedral ruins, but it was later removed, 'as it appeared to convey a reproach to the public officers, who had left

ELGIN: *The Cathedral Church of the Holy Trinity*

FORTROSE: *The Cathedral Church of St Peter and St Boniface*

GLASGOW: *The Cathedral Church of St Mary the Virgin*

the care of this fine ruin to the zeal of so humble an individual'.[19] The keeper's lodge, although indeed neat, was not liked by everyone, especially by Shanks himself. 'The good work of the Lords Commissioners of Her Majesty's Woods and Forests will not be completed... until they buy up and remove that disgrace to the pile, the contiguous brewery which they have hitherto tolerated, and raze to the ground that incongruous porter lodge, the erection of which they themselves inadvertently authorised'.[20]

Elgin Cathedral has been described as one of the most perfect churches in Scotland, 'which far surpasses all other ecclesiastical remains in Scotland in loftiness and extent, in impressive magnificence and elaborate decoration';[21] and by another as 'the finest building north of the Tweed... the loveliest and most majestic building in Scotland'.[22] Like St Andrews Cathedral, Elgin must have been a magnificent building in its functioning days, and what remains is still impressive. Unlike St Andrews Cathedral, now wrecked almost beyond imagination, it is not difficult to imagine the spectacular majesty of Elgin Cathedral, because so much of it is still standing. The missing details from the majestic west front can easily be filled in with a little imagination.

The cathedral had an aisled nave of six bays, twin western towers, a central tower and spire, transepts, an octagonal chapter house, and a choir of seven bays with aisles on the western five. The two thirteenth century west towers, probably built soon after 1224, are still about their original height and in a good state of preservation. Each tower originally carried a leaded spire. They flank a fine deeply-recessed double doorway of eight orders and west window, both reconstructed c.1395 after the attack of the Wolf of Badenoch; the window has a few remaining fragments of tracery. The vesica-shaped panel above, now blank, probably held a representation of the Holy Trinity.

Very little remains of the nave; little more than the bases of the clustered columns of both inner and outer nave arcades, which stand 30–60cm high towards the west end. The north and south arcades were probably crushed by the fall of the crossing tower in 1711. High on the south face of the north-west tower (as well as on the interior of both), areas of stone burnt in the 1390 fire can be detected. Also because of the collapse of the crossing tower in 1711, the crossing itself has all but disappeared. The tower, built in 1404–14, first collapsed in 1506 and, as rebuilt with a spire, stood 60.3m high. It was in ruins by 1668 before the final collapse in 1711. Nothing remains to be seen today, although one suspects that much of its stonework, and that of the cathedral in general, can be seen in the houses of the town.

The north transept, part of the original late twelfth century building, and formerly the Chapel of St Thomas a Becket, has the start of a spiral stair in the north-west corner, which led to a clerestory passage and then to the central tower. The north wall has mostly gone – probably another victim of the collapse of the crossing tower. The tablet of 1590 on the west wall and the two earlier damaged figures in recesses in the north wall commemorate Bishop Columba de Dunbar (1422–35) and Sir Alexander Dunbar (d.1498). There is an aumbry in the north-east corner.

The south transept is the oldest part of the cathedral and, being unaffected by the fall of the crossing tower, is comparatively well-preserved. It is built in the Transitional style between Romanesque and Early English, with lancet windows below and round-headed windows above on the clerestory level. Over the south doorway, a vesica-shaped window, with a deep reveal and stone seats beside it, indicates a now vanished upper floor. An aumbry and a piscina can be seen in the north-east corner. The two altar tombs in the south wall are of Bishop James Stewart (1460–2), to the west, and of an unknown knight. The effigy on the bishop's tomb is of Robert Innes of Innermarkye, who died about 1528. In the centre of the floor is a memorial to Colin Innes, inscribed, to his eternal credit, HERE LYES ANE HONEST MAN.

The chancel was probably built after the fire of 1270. It has a distinguished east gable containing two rows of five lancets and a large rose window at the summit. This is flanked on each side by octagonal turrets with arcades. The three great steps which led up to the high altar still remain. There is a granite monument to a seventeenth century Church of Scotland minister on the site of the high altar; either a gesture of contempt for the medieval liturgy, or of respect for the minister. In the north wall is a big canopied, cinquefoil-headed tomb, alleged to be that of Bishop Archibald (1253–98); on the south side is a weathered four-seat sedilia, once vaulted and with remaining traces of the springing. Among many floor slabs, the most interesting is a large one near the south arcade that formerly contained the Flemish brass of a bishop. The remains of Bishop Andrew de Moravia (1222–42), the founder of the cathedral, lie under a blue slab below the lowest step.

In the north chancel aisle traces of the springing of the vault can be seen on the tower wall. The north chancel aisle, also known as St Columba's Aisle, is divided from the chancel by a solid wall and only connected with it by a doorway. The east bay of the aisle still has its tierceron vault and the east window has slight remains of tracery. There is a piscina in the north-east corner. A small arch leads through into the chancel. The adjacent larger arch is thought to have formed a canopy for the tomb of Bishop John de Pilmor (1326–62).

A trefoil-headed doorway leads from the north chancel aisle to the chapter house vestibule, with a little stone-roofed sacristy with a stone basin where the priests would have washed their hands before mass. Then a thirteenth century doorway leads to the beautifully restored chapter house itself, the only one of its kind left in Scotland. After the destruction of 1390 the upper parts of the walls were thickened and the splendid stone vault was built, supported by an added central column. The chapter house was dedicated to the Passion of Christ, and symbols of the Passion can be seen on the roof bosses and corbels, column capital and frieze below the window sills, and in the arcading that runs around the walls forming canopies to the low stone seats. Five taller seats for dignitaries can be seen on the north wall. A stone reading desk is attached to the central column. The memorials around the walls commemorate the families of various bishops of Moray. Mostly dating from the period 1670–1812, they were brought here from St Giles' Church in the town centre when that church was demolished in 1826. In recent years, the chapter house has been re-roofed, the decayed window tracery renewed and the windows re-glazed and the structure is now in an excellent state of preservation.

The south chancel aisle, known as St Mary's Aisle, is well-preserved, partly due to its use as the burial place for members of the Gordon family. Its three eastern bays are still vaulted and the second one has its window tracery. The two free-standing tombs are of the first earl of Huntly (d.1470) (centre) and Sir William de la Hay (d.1422) (west). Huntly's effigy depicts him in civilian dress rather than the more usual armour and excavations revealed the base of an altar under this tomb. To the left of the remains of the altar is the well-preserved tomb of Bishop John Winchester (1435–60), with his effigy. Opposite is a piscina, then a monument to Henrietta, Duchess of Gordon, who died in 1760 at the age of seventy-eight. Many of the floor-slabs commemorate church dignitaries. The effigy under a canopy at the west end on the north wall is said to be the same Bishop John de Pilmor whose tomb was on the north side of the chancel.

Against the east wall of the south nave aisle, the centre headless figure is virtually all that remains of the tomb of Bishop John de Innes (1407–14). The other two were once in niches on the central tower: one is another representation of Bishop Innes and the other is a torso of an unknown knight. In the second bay of the aisle is a stone coffin; in the third are two aumbries and another window with tracery; in the fourth, a piscina; and at the end, doorways into the south porch and to the south-west tower the ground floor of which retains its original vaulting.

In the tower itself, the treads of the steep spiral stair have at some time been re-made from ledger stones. The stairwell ends in a vault which leads to a walkway that overlooks the nave and connects with the north-west tower where a collection of carved stones can be glimpsed through a doorway. The stair then ascends first to a wooden gallery on the second floor and then to a small railed enclosure at the top of the tower with a rewarding view.

Little is left of the late thirteenth century south porch but the inner doorway is complete and there are traces of a vault. Under the middle window of the aisle is a seventeenth century tablet with a trumpeting cherub. The churchyard contains an inexhaustible series of such memorials and bigger tombs, and two with moralising verses, are on the churchyard wall: to John Geddes (d.1687), due south-west of the tower, and James Young (d.1697), south of the east corner of the south transept, both glovers. One of 1627 has the following inscription:

This world is a cite
Full of streets and
Death is the mercat
That all men meets.

If lyfe were a thing
That money could
Buy, the poor could
Not live, and the rich
Would not die.

The cathedral and chapter houses were formerly surrounded by a great wall pierced by four ports or gates. The wall is almost entirely demolished, but the eastern gate called Panns Port still remains.

Near to the west end of the cathedral stands an L-shaped fifteenth century building which was long called the Bishop's House and was also known as Dunfermline House. Modern scholarship is of the opinion that the house was not grand enough to have been a bishop's palace, and was probably the residence of the precentor. After the sixteenth century reformation it was granted to Alexander Seton (later first earl of Dunfermline), who died in 1622. The fourth earl, who fought on the side of King James II and VII (1685–9), lost the estate to the Crown in 1690 through forfeiture. The estate was purchased by the duke of Gordon in 1730 and the house was complete until the end of the eighteenth century when the roof, floors and wainscoting were removed. The fifth duke of Gordon died in 1836 and the estate was purchased in 1838 by William Innes who afterwards sold it to the Seafield family. In 1851 the earl of Seafield remodelled the grounds and began to demolish the house. A public outcry halted the work and the finer portions of the house, including the square tower, the corbelled turret and the east gable, were saved. In December 1884 the house and grounds were presented to the town by the dowager countess of Seafield and have remained in public ownership since that time. The house today is mostly complete, although the south wing collapsed in 1891. It is a fine specimen of fifteenth century domestic architecture, but comparatively small, being only 23.9sq.m. When complete, it had three floors and an attic storey. On the ground floor was a vaulted kitchen, two cellars and two other rooms. The first floor had three rooms at the front and one in each wing. The principal room had been ornamented with fresco paintings, the remains of which were still visible at the beginning of the twentieth century.[23] Fragments of two other canons' houses lie beneath modern houses nearby.

After the abandoning of the Elgin Cathedral in 1560, the parish church of St Giles' in Elgin was used as the cathedral church of the diocese of Moray, but nothing remains of the structure from the cathedral period. The transepts were demolished in 1700, the chancel in 1800 and the nave and tower in 1826. The present Classical Revival church was designed by Archibald Simpson and built in 1827–8. The tower is partially modelled on the Choragic Monument of Lysicrates. The whole edifice is severe and uninviting, and glowers over the high street of Elgin. The church is usually locked and inaccessible. As the old church was being demolished it was proposed that the remaining part of the chancel of the old cathedral should be re-roofed and used until the new St Giles' was built. The proposal found no favour, and the last possibility of life for the old cathedral died.[24]

Kinnedar

Kinnedar was the see of the diocese of Moray 1184–1207. It is now little more than a churchyard. The site of the bishop's castle is north of and adjacent to the churchyard, but only a small section of original masonry survives, built into the modern churchyard wall. It was an hexagonal courtyard castle. A modern cairn allegedly marks its centre. In the churchyard is an old mercat cross. The church was adjacent to the cross. It fell into decay after the Reformation and, though ruinous in 1649, it continued to be used until 1679.

Spynie

Spynie was the see of the Moray Diocese 1207–24. Holy Trinity Cathedral probably stood on or adjacent to Spynie

The Cathedral Church of the Holy Trinity (early 20th century postcard)

Churchyard, about one and half miles from the bishop's great palace–castle. The decay and depopulation of Spynie led to demands for a new church to be constructed at a more central and populous part of the parish. This took place in 1735 with the construction of a new church at Quarrelwood (now Quarrywood) on the north slope of the central ridge of the parish, where there were not only a number of small tenants, but also the two sizeable villages of Dykeside and Quarrywood. The old church was abandoned and partly dismantled; the last remnant of it collapsed about 1850. 'All that remained of the old parish church was a gable in the Gothic style of architecture, which, not being kept in repair, fell about twenty years ago, and all trace is now lost of the building to which it apertained'.[25] The foundations were traceable above the grass of the churchyard until the end of the nineteenth century. They showed a small church of simple character, 22.5m long and 10.6m wide; the east door is marked by a cross erected in 1908. The head of the cross is medieval and was found among the ruins of the building; the shaft and the base are modern. The dressed stones which formed the doorways of its south and west walls were removed and built into the new church. On the lintel of the east doorway there is a date which appears to be 1691. It may indicate that the old church was either rebuilt or restored in that year. The belfry, which had been erected in 1723, was also removed from the old church and now bears the date 1735. It has a single bell inscribed as follows: 'This beal – for the Pearis of Spynie Me Fecit 1637, Soli Deo Gloria. Michael Bogertwys'. To the south of the site of the cathedral is a simple granite memorial to Ramsay Macdonald.

There are substantial remains of the fourteenth – sixteenth century Spynie Palace between Elgin and Lossiemouth. After the expulsion of the bishop in 1689, the palace reverted to the crown. By the end of the eighteenth century it was in ruins and had been sold to a private owner by 1836. It returned to state care in 1973.

1 Mackintosh, Herbert B (1914): p. 40.
2 Billings, Robert (1845-52): volume 2, p. 2.
3 Thorold, Henry (1993): p. 245.
4 Shanks, John (1866): p. 203.
5 Mackintosh, Herbert B (1914): p. 66.
6 ibid., p. 67.
7 Clark, William (1826): p. 2.
8 Mackintosh, Herbert B (1914): p. 66.
9 McKean, Charles (1987): pp 12–13.
10 Mackintosh, Herbert B (1914): p. 66.
11 ibid., p. 67.
12 Brown, P Hume, (ed.) (1892): p. 25.
13 Grant, John (1835): p. 6.
14 Botfield, Beriah (1830): p. 82.
15 Southey, Robert (1929): p. 90.
16 Billings, Robert (1845-52): volume 2, p. 2.
17 ibid.
18 Mackintosh, Herbert B (1914): p. 69.
19 Billings, Robert (1845-52): volume 2, p. 2.
20 Shanks, John (1866): p. 205.
21 Botfield, Beriah (1830): p. 82.
22 Walcott, Mackenzie (1874): volume 1, p. 140.
23 Mackintosh, Herbert B. (1914): 29.
24 Grant, John (1835): p. 8.
25 Young, Robert (1871): p. 135.

Fortrose

The Cathedral Church of St Peter and St Boniface

Fortrose is a small town with a population of about 1,000 on the misnamed Black Isle, 14.4km north-east of Inverness. The 'isle' is in fact a tapering promontory 25.7km long from Tore to Cromarty (with Fortrose, one of the two principal towns on the Isle), and up to 12.8km broad, jutting out to the north-east between Moray Firth on the south and Cromarty Firth on the north. The isle was the site of the historic see of the diocese of Ross; first at Rosemarkie and then, from the early thirteenth century, at Fortrose (*Fortrose* is translated as 'under the headland or promontory').

Rosemarkie, half a mile to the south-west of Fortrose and effectively adjacent to it, was once thought to have been the site of a monastic foundation of St Moluog (died c.572, feast day 25 June), but this is no longer accepted. Moluog, a Scot educated in Ireland, worked mainly in the Hebrides and especially with the island of Lismore, where his memory is preserved by the small truncated former cathedral of the diocese of Argyll. Although Moluog may have died at Rosemarkie, a shrine to his memory was erected at Mortlach [see Aberdeen – the Cathedral Church of St Mary and St Machar].

A more reliable tradition links Rosemarkie with the work of St Boniface Curitan (died c.660, feast day 14 March), whose name is perpetuated in the dedication of Fortrose Cathedral. Boniface was probably a Roman by birth, and, among others, he was instrumental in promoting and securing the acceptance of Roman discipline and observance in place of the usages of the Celtic church.

The subsequent history of Fortrose and the diocese of Ross is obscure. It is possible that the Irish-born St Duthac (died 1065, feast day 8 March) may have been a bishop here in the eleventh century, but the evidence is unreliable and he is associated more with Tain or Dornoch.

The diocese of Ross first emerges as a recognisable entity in the reign of King David I (1124–53), and the first diocesan bishop, named Macbeth, and styled 'of Rosemarkie', is mentioned in a royal charter of that king, dated between 1128 and 1131. The precise location of the cathedral at Rosemarkie is uncertain, but it would have been a building of modest dimensions. It most likely stood on the site of the present mid-eighteenth century parish church, which replaced a thirteenth century church, which probably replaced the cathedral. No structure in Rosemarkie today is earlier than the eighteenth century, although the Groam House Museum possesses an eighth century decorated cross slab which may be a relic of the vanished cathedral.

In 1239 Pope Gregory IX gave Bishop Robert (1214–49) permission to reform and enlarge the cathedral chapter, the change being confirmed twenty years later by Pope Alexander IV. The move to Fortrose was probably contemporary, the intention being the construction of a larger cathedral, but the name Rosemarkie appears to have lingered for a while. In 1388 Sir Andrew de Moravia, lord of Bothwell and Avoch, was buried in the 'Kyrk Cathedral of Rosmarkyne',[1] and the dedication of the cathedral at Rosemarkie, to Saint Peter, was incorporated into the dedication of the new cathedral at Fortrose. The two sites are quite close to each other, Fortrose Cathedral standing only about a mile to the west of the presumed site of its predecessor at Rosemarkie.

The diocese of Ross was never wealthy and Fortrose Cathedral was originally a simple rectangle 58.4m long by 8.2m wide. There was a bell tower at the north-west corner which seems not to have been very high, and a thirteenth century two-storeyed chapter house on the north side of the chancel. A south nave aisle of two and a half bays, with a more spacious chapel of two bays to the east, was added at the turn of the fourteenth and fifteenth centuries. The much altered chapter house and the south aisle are all that remain of the cathedral.

Fortrose Cathedral seems to have been spared the destructive violence of the sixteenth century reformers for a while, possibly because of its remote position. The appointment of Bishop Henry Sinclair (1558–65) was followed in 1561 when he was formally appointed by the pope. The first signs of trouble came in 1572 when Lord Ruthven was given, by order of the earl of Mar, regent for the infant King James VI (1567–1625), 'the hail leid wherein the Cathedral Kirk of Ross was theckit', the excuse being that the cathedral 'was nae paroch kirk, but ane monasterie to sustene idle bellies'.[2] The statement that Fortrose Cathedral was a monastic foundation was without authority; the cathedral was served by a chapter of secular canons, of whom there were perhaps nineteen or twenty; there is no evidence of any religious house at Fortrose. Lord Ruthven having been given the lead, there was some attempt to provide alternative covering, and Bishop Patrick Lindsey (1613–33) undertook some restoration in 1615, but by 1626 the cathedral was in a poor state of repair.

Tradition, which has been merciless to Oliver Cromwell on the subject of the care of cathedrals, alleges that he demolished the nave and chancel in 1652–3 to build his fort at Inverness, leaving only the south aisle of the cathedral and the chapter house still standing; but the extent of his demolition is not really clear and the tradition can be neither proved nor disproved. Despite an incident in 1662 when the earl of Seaforth accidentally set fire to the roof while shooting pigeons in the churchyard,[3] services seem to have been held in the building for several years after the restoration of the monarchy in 1660. But by the early eighteenth century whatever remained of the cathedral was increasingly unfit for worship. In 1720 the town council ordered it to be abandoned: 'Taking into consideration that ye kirk of this place is now ruinous and in danger of falling, so as ye same, specially in ye winter time, cannot be made use of', the congregation were ordered at 'ye sight and advice of ye Magistrates', to move their seats to the Council Room in the old chapter house, where divine worship was to be held'.[4] Decay gathered pace in the eighteenth century, and by 1750 there was little more than can be seen today, i.e. the south aisle of the nave, which was used as a burying place by the Mackenzies of Seaforth, and the chapter house, which was partly reconstructed in the eighteenth century as a council chamber.

What remains of the cathedral today is set in an attractive low-lying churchyard, surrounded by large yew trees, in the centre of the town, below a hill to the west. The churchyard is entered on the north side by a war memorial gate of 1921. Since the middle of the nineteenth century the site has been in government care, and repairs began in 1853. The enclosing wall and railings were erected in 1857. So complete was the obliteration of the nave and chancel by that date, and so fine was the condition of the remaining south aisle, that it was believed by earlier antiquarians that the aisle was the main body of the cathedral. The true extent of the cathedral was not fully realised until the area of the nave and chancel was excavated by the Commissioners of Woods and Forests in 1871, and the foundations were marked out in 1897.

The remains of the cathedral convey an almost domestic feeling of warmth and friendliness, unlike the pathetically wrecked ruin of St Andrews or the imposing grandeur of Elgin. Walcott thought it 'an architectural gem, and remarkable for finish and the exquisite beauty of its smallest mouldings'.[5] The red sandstone of which the cathedral is constructed is thought to have come from Arkerdeith or Suddie Quarry near Munlochy.[6] The total original length of the cathedral was 58.4m, and the width of the demolished nave and chancel was about 8.2m. The remaining south aisle measures 32.5m long; the section adjacent to the nave is 4.4m wide, and the section adjacent to the chancel is 6m wide. The aisle roof is unusually gabled instead of the more usual lean-to that would have been expected for an aisle.

Access to the aisle is now prevented by the railing that follows the arcade of clustered columns, the gate usually being kept locked; but the interior is easily seen through the wide arches. The two-bay chancel aisle to the east may be slightly later in date than the three-bay nave aisle to the west. The east gable has three windows, one above the other, all unaligned, but each in the centre of its own section of wall; a large five-light window below, lacking most of its tracery, and two small lancets above. The half-effigy under a slender arch has been assigned, without any definite evidence, to Bishop Robert Cairncross (1538–45) although, as the head wears a mitre, it certainly commemorates a bishop. The further tomb to the east, in the shape of a plain chest with a moulded canopy, is supposed to be that of Euphemia, countess of Ross (d.1394), who married firstly Walter de Leslie, earl of Ross and, after his death, Alexander Stewart, earl of Buchan, the notorious Wolf of Badenoch who destroyed Elgin Cathedral in 1390. After his death she joined the Cistercian abbey at Elcho, near Perth, and became its abbess; only one or two pieces of her effigy remain. The bosses on the western part of the vaulting bear the arms of Leslie and Bullock, an indication that construction was completed under the supervision of her son, Alexander Leslie, earl of Ross, during the episcopate of Bishop John Bulloch (1418–39).

The presence of an aumbry and a piscina at the east end of the aisle indicates that an altar stood close by, against the east wall. This area, on the south side of the chancel, would have been the traditional site of a Lady Chapel. The plain octagonal font, with a simple panel on each face, is probably fifteenth century and was brought from the west end of the aisle when that area was made into a burial ground; the base of the font dates from 1853. The font is in good condition and one of only two remaining ancient Scottish fonts, the other being at Whithorn.

On the south side, between the chancel and nave sections of the aisle, is the polished sandstone Renaissance monument to Sir Alexander Mackenzie, who died in 1706 at the age of fifty-five. The monument frames a little vaulted recess containing some seventeenth century memorials on the floor and walls; the Mackenzie family are buried below this point. There is a blocked window above the monument. The Mackenzie family is further commemorated by the collection of nineteenth century memorials in the railed-off western bay. In the bay opposite the Mackenzie tomb, stands the tomb of Bishop John Fraser (1497–1507), with a weathered effigy of the bishop wearing mitre and eucharistic vestments.

There are two features on the exterior of the south side of the aisle; the turret and the remains of the porch. The turret marks the division between the nave aisle and the chancel aisle. The turret is square at its base and then octagonal above the height of about 3m; the roof is modern. It contains the town clock and a recast bell of c.1460 dedicated to St Mary and St Boniface. On the now discredited belief that the aisle was the complete cathedral, the turret was occasionally referred to as the rood turret, as though it was designed to give access to the rood loft above the screen that would have divided the chancel from the nave. It is more probable that it was constructed to give access to an upper room. At the west end of the aisle is the foundation of the two-storeyed porch and the former main doorway which is the earliest part of the existing building and probably dates from the late twelfth century. The doorway has four orders and is in good condition; a Romanesque arch can be seen above. Of the porch itself only slight traces remain of the projecting walls and the lines of the roof.

The other remaining structure at the cathedral site is the chapter house on the north side of the chancel. The chapter house measures 13.6m in length and 3.5m wide. It is a simple structure and has later square-headed windows. Dating from the early thirteenth century, it was rebuilt in the seventeenth century and altered again in the eighteenth century; the incongruous chimney on the north gable presumably dates from this time. The undercroft, which adjoined the north side of the chancel and probably served as a sacristy, is vaulted and contains a small collection of carved stones. The vaulting divides it into six small bays; the eastern end has an aumbry in the north wall and the next three bays contain a stone bench under a niche. On the south side only two bays have the bench, the third being occupied by the door. At the west end is a deeply splayed window, from the sill of which a narrow stairway leads to the upper room. It was blocked at the top when the upper room was rebuilt with an external staircase in the eighteenth century. Carved above the door are the words: 'Decorated in the year 1780 by General Sir Hector Munro, KB, and MP.' For 'decorated', the visitor should probably read 'rebuilt'. The upper room was used as the meeting place of the town council until 1939 and the lower floor was used as the town prison until the early twentieth century. The council used a seal identical to that of the cathedral chapter. It bears the figures of St Peter with his keys and St Boniface wearing mitre and vestments and carrying a crosier in his right hand, and carries the inscription SIGILLUM SANCTORUM PETRIE ET BONIFACII DE ROSMARKIN.

The cathedral churchyard was surrounded on all four sides by the bishop's palace and the canon's houses; slight fragments remain. The bishop's palace stood at the south-west; destroyed by Cromwell, it was said to be 'inferior to few in splendour and magnificence'.[7] The dean's house stood to the east of the cathedral.

1 Beaton, Angus J (1885): p. 21.
2 Marshall, Elizabeth (1969): pp 2–3.
3 ibid., p. 3.
4 Fraser, Dorothy (1912): p. 68.
5 Walcott, Mackenzie (1874): volume 1, p. 156.
6 Beaton, Angus J (1885): p. 21.
7 Walcott, Mackenzie (1874): volume 1, p. 157.

Glasgow

Glasgow is the second city of Scotland, 70km to the west of Edinburgh, and the principal commercial and industrial centre of the kingdom. The city lies on the north and south banks of the River Clyde, formerly one of the chief commercial estuaries in the world. The name 'Glasgow' is thought to derive from *Glas-achadh*, meaning a green field or a dark glen. The ease with which the river could be forded at this point accounts for the long history of settlement at Glasgow. There is evidence that the site was occupied during the Bronze Age, but permanent occupation probably did not begin until c.4000BC. Glasgow has four cathedral churches.

The Cathedral Church of St Kentigern
(Church of Scotland)

The oldest and largest of Glasgow's cathedrals is the great medieval cathedral, dedicated to St Kentigern, in the Townhead district of the city, between Wishart Street and Castle Street.

By tradition, Christianity first entered the history of Glasgow in the fifth century with the blessing of a burial ground by St Ninian, who died c.432 (feast day, 26 August). Although there is no reason to dispute this received tradition, Ninian's main area of activity was at Whithorn, 157km to the south of Glasgow, and his connection with the city is slight and tenuous. A more reliable tradition claims that continuous missionary work in the area began a century later with St Kentigern. Although Kentigern (feast day, 13 January) remains the most outstanding figure in the history of Glasgow, everything concerning the history of his life should be treated with caution. The tradition of a man named Kentigern exercising some form of Christian ministry at a place now called Glasgow is generally accepted, but all other details are likely to be no more than pious embellishment. The earliest accounts of Kentigern's life were written in the twelfth century at the behest of Bishops Herbert (1147–64) and Jocelyn (1174–99), and appear to have relied on sources no earlier than the eleventh century, although those sources may themselves have embodied earlier traditions. That Kentigern was held in affection seems beyond doubt by the fact that he was accorded the nickname 'Mungo', meaning 'darling' or 'well-beloved'; he is sometimes referred to as St Mungo.

The stories about Kentigern say that he was of royal descent and was brought up in a monastery at Culross (in Fife) under the care of St Servan, sometimes styled the 'Apostle of West Fife'. Servan was an obscure saint of whom nothing reliable is known; all that survives is a collection of contradictory and extravagant legends. When Kentigern left Culross he travelled west and came to Carnock, where he was present at the death of a holy man named Fergus. Kentigern placed the body of Fergus on a cart drawn by two oxen, and prayed that they would stop at the place where God had decreed that Fergus should be buried. Somewhat conveniently they stopped at the cemetery consecrated by St Ninian. So Kentigern came to the kingdom of Strathclyde, to the place now known as Glasgow. Encouraged to stay by the people living in the area, he remained there for some time; but with the accession of a new and less sympathetic king, he moved south to Carlisle, and then to Wales where he is said to have stayed with St David at Menevia. Tradition also credits him with the foundation of a monastery at Llanelwy (St Asaph) in north Wales, but it is now thought that he only served a term as abbot. Eventually he returned to Glasgow, died in 603, and was buried probably near the place where his shrine stands today in the cathedral crypt.

Glasgow lapsed into obscurity after the sixth century until the emergence of a territorial diocese, founded by Earl David of Strathclyde (later King David I, 1124–53) in c.1115. Although a list of bishops appears from the mid-eleventh century, the first three were probably suffragans at York having no active connection with Glasgow, and nothing is known of any church building at Glasgow before the twelfth century. Construction of a stone cathedral began during the episcopate of Bishop John (1117–47), chaplain to King David I, and was consecrated in the presence of the king on 7 July 1136. A single painted voussoir survives from this earliest cathedral which was most probably a simple single-chamber structure. By 1181 Bishop Jocelyn was said to be 'gloriously enlarging' the building. The work was interrupted by a fire, but a new east end and crypt were consecrated on 6 July 1197.

The nave was planned by Bishop William Malveisin (1199–1202) and completed during the time of Bishop Walter de St Albans (1207–32), but only the nave walls up to the level of the window sills belong to this time. The chancel and the church below it were rebuilt in their present form, probably c.1240–55, during the episcopate of Bishop William de Bondington (1233–58); the transepts followed soon after. It is thought that construction of the now demolished north-west tower may have begun in the late thirteenth century, but this is uncertain since the demolition of the tower in the nineteenth century took place before detailed records had been made. The south-west tower, also demolished in the nineteenth century, was a fifteenth-sixteenth century addition.

The nave was rebuilt in the fourteenth century, using the existing wall from the ground to the level of the window sill. The rebuilding was done during the episcopate of Bishop Robert Wischard (1273–1316), a vigorous supporter of King Robert I (1306–29) and previously of William Wallace. The bishop was not untypical of his age in possessing a somewhat militaristic frame of mind, and was accused of making siege engines from timber provided for the cathedral. He absolved Robert Bruce (later King Robert I) of the murder of his rival John Comyn only five days after the event in 1306, and provided him with coronation robes from the cathedral sacristy. 'He went about preaching war against England as if it had been a crusade, and was taken prisoner in full armour at the taking of the Castle of Cupar in Angus'.[1] He died, blind, on 26 November 1316 after having been a prisoner in London for eight years. His body was returned to Glasgow and buried in the cathedral between the altars of St Peter and St Andrew.

Bishop Robert Wischard had succeeded his brother Bishop William Wischard in the see of Glasgow, William being elected in 1270 and translated to St Andrews in 1273. The following story gives an amusing illustration of clerical life at the time: 'There was a certain vicar, in the year 1272, well known for leading an indulgent life, who, though he had often suffered punishment for her sake, persisted in retaining a hearth-side companion whom he fondly loved. His bishop came round in the course of his visitation as ordinary, and in due course the unhappy man was put under suspension until he should be taken back into favour. Full of confusion and shame, he went home, and at the sight of his darling, his grief was redoubled with the addition of some reproaches to the lady. Naturally she enquired the cause of his vexation. "Alas", said he bitterly, "I must fain give you up." "Nay," she returned, "do nothing of the kind; I will confront the bishop and put him to rout." Next morning the bishop was on his road to church, when she came tipping in his way, laden with poultry, vegetable and eggs. "Whither are you going? Whence do you come?" said the bishop. "I am the vicar's leman, my lord," she answered; "I am going to visit the bishop's dearie, who has just had a baby, and I wish to be of any service that is in my power." Conscience spoke; away went the bishop to church; he sent for the vicar, and told him to make ready for celebration. "My lord," says he, "I am under suspension." "I absolve thee," replied the bishop, and put up his hand. As soon as the service was over he took himself off without another word, as if he had been dumb'.[2]

With the exception of the later additions of the Blacader Aisle and the south-west tower, the cathedral had been completed by the end of the thirteenth century, but extensive damage by lightning c.1406 caused another long period of rebuilding during the time of Bishop William de Lauder (1408–25), who erected the central tower and began the reconstruction of the north-east sacristy and chapter house. His successor, Bishop John Cameron (1426–46), finished the chapter house, and began the sacristy above, built the spire, the Lady Chapel and the great keep of his palace-castle. Bishop William Turnbull (1447–54) completed the chapter house.

The odd extension to the south transept was built about 1500 by Bishop Robert Blacader (1483–1508), first archbishop of Glasgow from 1492, and known ever since as Blacader's Aisle. It appears to have been the lower part of a projected extension to the south transept; the upper part, which may have been intended to provide a permanent place for St Kentigern's shrine, was never built. The archbishop also constructed the surviving beautiful stone pulpitum which divides the chancel from the nave. Archbishop Blacader died in 1508 while on a pilgrimage to the Holy Land.

The elevation of Glasgow to the status of an archbishopric in 1492 incurred some resentment from the archbishop of St Andrews, whose metropolitan jurisdiction was now reduced. Even members of the cathedral chapter at Glasgow feared the lessening of their authority as that of the archbishop increased.

By the beginning of the sixteenth century the cathedral had reached the zenith of its splendour. Glasgow was now an archiepiscopal see with metropolitan jurisdiction over the dioceses of Argyll, Galloway, Dunkeld and Dunblane. King James IV (1488–1513), who had always favoured the city and wished it to be equal to St Andrews, took pride in being a member of the cathedral chapter, which now numbered thirty-three, including twenty-six canons. After the king's death at Flodden in 1513, Archbishop James Beaton (1508–22) crowned King James V (1513–42) at Stirling and became chancellor of Scotland in 1514. He was translated to St Andrews in 1522. His successor, Archbishop Gavin Dunbar (1523–47), built a gatehouse for his castle and gave two bells to the cathedral.

Such a prominent building might have been a principal target for the destructive hatred of the reformers in the 1560s but, surprisingly, the cathedral was spared. Although stripped of its furnishings, and the lead removed from the roof in 1573, alone among the mainland Scottish cathedrals, Glasgow remained virtually intact. According to one (disputed) tradition, the tradesmen of Glasgow took up arms to defend the cathedral in 1578, against the orders of Andrew Melville, principal of the university of Glasgow, who had ordered the cathedral to be demolished. 'The magistrates of the city… had condescended to demolish the cathedral, and build with the materials thereof some little churches in other parts, for the ease of the citizens. Divers reasons were given for it, such as the resort of superstitious people to do their devotions in that place; the huge vastness of the church, and that the voice of a preacher could not be heard by the multitudes convened to sermon; the more commodious service of the people; and the remaining of that idolatrous monument… To do this work a number of quarries, masons and other workmen, were conduced, and the day assigned when it should take beginning. Information being given thereof, and the workmen by sound of drum, warned to go to their work, the crafts of the city in a tumult took arms, swearing with many oaths that he who would cast down the first stone should be buried under it, neither could they be pacified til the workmen were discharged by the magistrates'.[3]

If not destroyed, the cathedral was certainly neglected, and the city records describe the concern felt by the citizens of Glasgow at the time of the sixteenth century reformation. The 'greit monument,' it was noted, had 'cum to gret dekaye and ruyne throh taking away of the leid, sklait, and uther grayt [material] thairof, in the trublus tyme bygane, sua that sick ane greit monument will alluterlie fall down and dekay wt. [unless] it be remedit', and they accordingly, 'all in ane voce hes consentit to ane taxt and imposition of twa hundredth punds money to be taxt and payit be the townschip and fremen thairof, for helping to repair the said kirk, and haldyng of it watterfast'.[4] In 1609 the town council reminded King James VI (1567–1625) that, 'our Metropolitan Kirk, brig and river is nocht estemit the smallest… knawin to strangeris and forein nationals quha neirtofoir has vewit and sein the same'.[5]

By the middle of the seventeenth century, bearing in mind one of the reasons for the proposed demolition of the building – 'the huge vastness of the church, and that the voice of a preacher could not be heard by the multitudes convened to sermon' – the great cathedral had been structurally divided to provide churches for three separate congregations. The Inner Kirk congregation met in the chancel, which by 1636 had been divided from the rest of the cathedral. 'There is a great partition or wall 'twixt the body of the church and the chancel; there is no use of the body of the church, only divine service or sermon is used and performed in the quire or chancel, which is built and framed church wise; and under this quire there is also another church, which carries the same proportion under this, wherein also there is two sermons every Lord's Day'.[6] A second congregation, known as the Barony Kirk, was established in 1596 in the Lower Church below the chancel. A third congregation, known as the Outer Kirk, was established in the five western bays of the nave in about 1647, and a stone wall to divide the Inner and Outer Kirks was erected at about the same time. Patrick Gillespie, first minister of the Outer Kirk, was a supporter of Oliver Cromwell and a strong opponent of King Charles I (1625–49). He was an able, fluent and popular preacher, but also ambitious, domineering and extravagant, and it was said that no Scottish bishop ever lived as well as did Gillespie. He was deposed by the General Assembly of the Church in 1650 for protesting against its lawfulness and its proceedings. Called to London by Cromwell to discuss the affairs of the Scottish Church, he preached before the Protector and the sentence of deposition was annulled in 1655. He was indicted before Parliament on a charge of treason in 1661 and narrowly escaped execution. His death at Leith in 1675 was said to have been hastened by depression of spirit aggravated by intemperance. Such was the beginning of the Outer Kirk. Galleries were added to the aisles of the Outer Kirk in 1647, and to those of the Inner Kirk in 1657.

In 1638, the infamous General Assembly which abolished episcopal government in the Scottish church, was held in the nave of the cathedral. On 8 December the bishops, none of whom attended the assembly, were removed from office and, on 13 December, one by one, they were deposed and excommunicated. The deposition of the bishops was performed in an atmosphere charged with hysteria and hatred, and shiveringly similar to the witch trials at Salem, Massachusetts in 1692, and on grounds of unbelievable triviality. The bishop of Galloway was charged with Arminianism (a movement theologically opposed to the Calvinism then prevalent in Scotland), to have possessed a crucifix and to have conducted two fasts in his diocese. The archbishop of St Andrews was charged with profaning the Sabbath, 'carding and dicing' when he should have been in church, riding through the country the whole day, and 'tippling and drinking in taverns till midnight'. The bishop of Brechin was charged with 'most vile drunkenness' and 'using a massy crucifix in his chamber'; a woman and child were also produced 'that made his adultery very probable'. The bishop of Ross was charged with being 'a wearer of the cope and rochet, a deposer of godly ministers and an admitter of fornicators'; 'instead of going to thanksgiving on a communion day… he called for cards to play'. The bishop of Orkney was charged with being 'a curler of dice on the Sabbath day, a setter of tacks to his sons and good-sons… he oversaw adultery, slighted charming, neglected preaching, and doing any good there'.[7] There was no point in the archbishops and bishops being present at the Assembly, which had decided to employ any means to get rid of them. Archbishop Patrick Lindsay of Glasgow (1632–8) went to England and died there, destitute, in 1644.

In 1641, in the aftermath of these farcical trials, the kirk session of Glasgow ordered the destruction of the last surviving relic of pre-reformation worship from the wall of the cathedral, the inscription 'Sancte Quitegerne ora pro nobis [Saint Kentigern, pray for us]', at a time when some would have said that they most needed the prayers of the saint.

A succession of six further archbishops of Glasgow followed the restoration of the monarchy and the Scottish episcopate in 1661. In 1674, Thomas Kirk visited Archbishop Alexander Burnet (1664–9 and 1674–9) in his castle next to the cathedral, and found 'a comely, courteous gentleman about sixty years old. He likewise craved a blessing before we drank with him'.[8] Archbishop Robert Leighton (1671–4) did his best to unite episcopalians and presbyterians, but only gained the enmity of both parties. Eventually he gave up the unequal struggle, and resigned and retired to Sussex. His grave and the house in which he lived can still be seen in the village of Horsted Keynes. Archbishop John Paterson (1687–1708) was expelled in 1689, left Scotland and went abroad. In 1697 he asked to be allowed to return and was given permission to reside at or within four miles of Coupar Angus. Not finding anywhere suitable, he moved to Airth in Stirlingshire and later to Edgar in Clackmannanshire, where he died on 8 December 1708. He was buried at Holyrood.

For most of the eighteenth century, the cathedral continued as three separate and structurally neglected churches, but the oddest of the three was the Barony Kirk. A visitor in 1772 was struck by the peculiarity of the Barony Kirk, 'deep underground, where the congregation may truly say, *clamavi ex profundis* [out of the depths have I cried – Psalm 130, verse 1]. The roof of this is fine, of stone, and supported by pillars, but much hurt by the crowding of pews'.[9] Sir Walter Scott (1771–1832), witnessed a service in the Barony Kirk, and described it in *Rob Roy*: 'We entered a small low-arched door, secured by a wicket which a grave-looking person seemed on the point of closing, and descended steps, as if into the funeral vaults of the church… Conceive an extensive range of low-browed dark and twilight vaults, such as are used for sepulchres by other churches… In those waste regions of oblivion, dusty banners and tattered escutcheons… I found a numerous congregation engaged in the act of prayer'.[10] 'The pulpit stood near the south door, with a great pillar to interrupt what light the narrow windows might have given it. The elders were dimly seen on a raised platform… and great box pews stretched in the gloom from column to column'.[11]

Principally because of problems with damp, the Barony congregation left the Lower Church in 1798. The only surprise is why they did not move at an earlier date; one author attributed it to nothing more than downright meanness. 'The long retention of the gloomy Barony can only be attributed to the heritors or landowners of the parish being too parsimonious to assess themselves for the building of a proper and presentable edifice… When, by long experience, they had become convinced that their underground tabernacle was unsuitable and uncomfortable, they actually applied for unoccupied space between the choir and the division wall of the nave [the crossing], that they might fit it up as a church'.[12] The request was denied and the congregation moved to a new church which stood on what is now the open ground of Cathedral Square, on the east side of Castle Street. The church, built to a design by John Robertson in 1793–1800, was demolished c.1885 and replaced in 1886–9 by the Barony Church, designed by Burnett and Campbell, on the other side of Castle Street. That church was itself closed in September 1982; it was purchased from the Church of Scotland by the university of Strathclyde in 1986 and re-opened as the ceremonial hall of the university in 1991.

After their departure from the cathedral the Barony congregation continued to regard the Lower Church as their territory, but without any effort at maintenance. Its condition steadily deteriorated and its appearance grew steadily more frightening. The pews were removed in 1801 and the congregation, having moved out because of damp, determined to make it even damper by converting it into their own burial ground; it seems quite without any authority. 'The splendid architecture for which this part of the venerable pile was so remarkable, has, under the Vandal hands of these mutators, been entirely spoiled. The lower shafts of the columns have been buried five or six feet in earth, while the walls have been daubed over with the most disgusting emblems of grief'.[13]

As the years went by, it became an unhealthy and uninviting place and began to acquire the appearance of the set of a horror film. The following description was written in 1825. 'The pillars here… are exceedingly strong and massive and from their position and the smallness of the windows, which are no more than narrow apertures, the area is rendered dark and gloomy with the grave and solemn air peculiar to the Gothic architecture, [and] cannot fail to cast a temporary damp upon the most volatile spirit… To the east of this place and immediately below the altar, is situated the place of interment for the heritors of the Barony Parish; and wherein is still shown the monument of St Mungo, or Kentigern, as well as the reservoir wherein the priests formerly kept their holy water. A still more dismal gloom here prevails! The walls are black and hung round with shreds of Escutcheons. These shadowy emblems of human grandeur, while on every side lie skulls and coffins epithecs and worms. The Barony Church… being found very damp and inconvenient, it was shut up some time since'.[14] In 1833, Archibald McLellan gave an even more graphic description of the Lower Church, which now resembled a graveyard scene from a nightmare. 'They have marked the size of the lairs by rows of sharp pointed iron railings, of about four feet in height, which serve no purpose of protection, and confine the spectator to two narrow passages. The original level of the floor has been raised, by the introduction of fresh mould, covering up the bases of the columns and a portion of their shafts… The lanceted windows are all built up, excepting a very small space at the top, which gives the crypt… a gloomy and dismal appearance; the pillars… are, many of them… painted with soot or lamp black besmeared over clustered column, carved capital, and ornament of every description, and this black blazonry is liberally besprinkled with white tadpoles, representing tears, giving the place a most horrific appearance'.[15] A rising tide of opposition to the continued use of this gruesome place caused the government to intervene and forbid any further burials in the Lower Chuch.[16]

While the Lower Church was falling into decay, the chancel above (the Inner Kirk) was refurbished in 1805 by William Stark in a style quite unsympathetic to the architecture of the building, but typical of the time. New pews were installed and large galleries were erected on three sides of the chancel. 'Its original grandeur… is much injured by the area being filled with pews, which destroy the proportions of the main tier of arches; and the galleries which are suspended between its piers conceal from the view and block up the windows of the aisles'.[17] The pulpit was placed at the eastern end 'right opposite a rather prominent pew in front of the western gallery, which was set apart for the Magistrates, the Judges of the Justiciary Court, or other dignitaries of the land who might choose to attend'. 'Mr Stark, in the course of his work, made deep incisions upon the beautiful stone pillars, and into these he thrust the beams for the support of the galleries, without the slightest respect to architecture, or even to the safety of the structure, which at length actually became endangered from this rude alteration'.[18] In 1833, Archibald McLellan found the Inner Kirk, like the rest of the cathedral, to be in need of urgent repair. The retro-choir, which he described, wrongly, as the Lady Chapel, was in poor condition. 'The walls are encrusted with mildew, the carved capitals are encrusted with and choked up by dust, and in many places, in the eastern windows particularly, they are deeply corroded'.[19] The adjacent chapter house was virtually disused. 'The appearance of this chamber is much injured by the arches of the windows being blocked up with stone, and its area is deformed by mean and decaying fir benches; on one side stands a deal pulpit, from whence I believe the probationers of the district delivered their first discourses. As the application of the chapter house to this purpose has long been given up, I see no reason why these decayed sittings, which are so offensive to the eye, should not be immediately removed'.[20]

The early nineteenth century saw a renewed interest in medieval architecture and from the early 1830s concern about the structural stability of the cathedral, together with an appreciation of the worth of medieval architecture, led to calls for the total restoration of the building. In 1833 Archibald McLellan published a pamphlet pleading for action to restore the cathedral and to reintegrate the three divided sections. As the Barony Kirk had already vacated the Lower Church, he now urged the Outer Kirk in the nave to follow their example and leave, to allow the partition wall to be removed and the two principal sections of the cathedral to be re-integrated. The appearance of the nave was not as desperate as the Lower Church, but it was still in poor condition. The congregation turned their backs on the chancel by facing west, and a wall of masonry, blocking the great west door, provided a screen for the platform carrying the pulpit. McLellan noted that the external appearance of the nave was ruined by the accumulation of several feet of earth above the original layer of the soil, which only succeeded in contributing to the chronic problem of damp in the nave. 'The rank green mould which prevails over its columns and walls, as high up as the beams which support the galleries. The constant dampness, of which this is the sure indication, speedily destroys the pews and flooring… The present powerful furnace… whilst it almost calcines the sitters in its immediate neighbourhood… is so partial in its favour, that the great mass of the congregation are quite unsusceptible to its influence'.[21] McLellan's opinion of the unhealthiness of the Outer Kirk was supported by two physicians who, in 1835, declared the nave unfit for worship on sanitary grounds.[22] There was no more to be said. The congregation of the Outer Kirk moved to a new church, known as St Paul Outer High, built in Frederick Street in 1836 by the town council. That church was replaced by a new St Paul Outer High Church at the junction of John Street and Martha Street in 1907; it survived until June 1953 and was subsequently demolished. Through a series of subsequent closures of churches and amalgamations of congregations, the spiritual descendants of the Barony and Outer Kirk congregations, which once shared the cathedral church, are now united within the walls of another church.

With the departure of the Outer Kirk congregation, the wall between the nave and the chancel was removed, but there was little agreement in the succeeding years as to what else should be done. A contemporary guide book indicated the problems that beset the cathedral at the time. 'Nominally it was under the custody of the department of the Woods and Forests; but practically, it was in the keeping to a Church Officer, an humble official, who had neither the taste to appreciate its beauties, nor the means to arrest their decay, even had he understood them'.[23]

Suggestions were put forward, including a rebuilding of the west front and an attractive proposal to complete the Blacader Aisle. The completion of the aisle was never a serious consideration; it had problems of its own in the fact that its flat roof had been used as a garden by the warden of the churchyard, and the moisture from the garden was seeping through into the aisle 'destroying the archings beneath'.[24]

The proposal to rebuild the west front was adopted and caused an architectural scandal. It was argued that the west front lacked symmetry and looked untidy, and that the two medieval west towers should be demolished. The towers had few supporters. Billings felt it bad enough that the visitor to the cathedral had to pass through a line of sordid filthy streets, only then to be confronted with 'the unfortunate predominance of the north-western tower'.[25] Even McLellan, whose essay had done much to heighten public awareness of the state of the cathedral, had no time for the two towers. 'Placed in the most conspicuous situation, on approaching the cathedral they thrust their ungainly forms between it and the spectator: they have not even the merit of antiquity… their architecture marks no period, nor displays anything but the poor ambition which could be contented with creating even deformity'.[26] His judgement was severe but justified, although on the subject of the antiquity of the towers, he was inaccurate. Surviving prints show two lumpish towers with minimal ornamentation, bolted on to the west end of the cathedral, giving the appearance of fortification rather than decoration. 'The first was removed as an excrescence; and, as a consequence, the second followed it, because it looked odd; and in addition to this it was stated that the tower was not ornamental enough'.[27]

The south-west tower was squat and dumpy, measuring 10.3m from north to south, 9.7m from east to west and 36.5m in height, and resembled a baronial keep. The lower two storeys were thought to have been constructed during the episcopate of Bishop John Cameron (1425–46) and excavations in 1988 confirmed a fifteenth century date; the third storey, with crow-stepped gables, being added by Archbishop James Law (1615–32). Used first as a library and, by the seventeenth century, as a consistory court, it had fallen into disuse by the early nineteenth century. McLellan described it as 'a large high gabled tenement… the ground floor, where the consistory courts were held, is fitted up with benches, and on the western wall is some panelled woodwork, in the centre compartment of which is painted the royal arms, with the initials of Charles the second. These fittings up are all in a state of decay'.[28] A protest against the destruction of the tower was made to the town council, but it had few friends and was demolished in 1846; countless valuable documents were lost in the process. 'As no one seemed to care for them, they were allowed to disappear, having either been burned, or carried away by any one who took a fancy to a handful of what seemed a litter of manuscripts. Some of these documents which have been preserved, are exceedingly interesting, and throw curious light on the manners of a bygone age. It is most humiliating to admit that this work of spoliation and destruction has taken place within these last dozen years'.[29] Although what were deemed to be the most important documents were removed and saved, the destruction took place in the days before there was a full appreciation of the need to preserve public records, and references to the destruction of an early eighteenth century seal and papers relating to trade between Scotland and Norway indicate that much of value was indeed destroyed. There is no surviving record of what was lost. A witness to the destruction recorded his memories in a letter to the *Glasgow Herald* in 1850. 'I one evening met with a friend who, from his personal observation the previous day, told me that what were considered the valuable documents connected with the consistory court had been carried off, and that the rest were being condemned to the flames; but that many people were taking away numbers of them. Having a species of literary avidity to share in part of the spoil, I went next morning as early as seven o'clock to the consistory house, the whole of the lower part of the ground floor of which I found filled with a heavy, dark brown smoke, where certainly conflagration was making its away – little tufts of loose paper flaming here and there – but the great mass smouldering; for sorry indeed did the documents appear to wish to become defunct, even by the help of two stout labourers stirring them up with long sticks'.[30]

The north-west tower, 8.9m square and 43.8m high to the top of the spire, survived a little longer, but it soon followed the fate of the south-west tower, and was demolished in 1848. A petition appeared in the *Scottish Reformers Gazette* on 25 August 1848, signed by twenty citizens, including ten architects, but the fate of the north-west tower was sealed. It was thought to have been built during the episcopate of Bishop Robert Wischard (1271–1316), the upper part being restored during the time of Bishop William Lauder (1408–25). Used as an adjunct to the officials' court in the north aisle, it housed a clock and 'a very large bell no less than 12 feet 1 inch in circumference which acts as the curfew to the inhabitants at the hour of ten each night; and from its grave and sonorous note, is excellently adapted to the purpose'.[31]

A plan was drawn up by Kemp for the erection of two symmetrical towers, but this was never implemented, a result which caused relief in some quarters. 'The only comfort of the demolition of the towers is that the proposed new ones were not erected in their place'.[32] 'All who now see the grand old building, shorn of its cathedral features, and made like a large parish church, mock and laugh at the action of the local committee, saying, "These men had two towers, and they went and pulled them both down".' [33]

With the exceptions of the fourteenth century west doorway and the much restored fifteenth century window above, the rest of the west front dates from the 'restoration' of 1846–8 and is the work of Edward Blore. Blore's restoration was not entirely destructive. The Lower Church was cleared of an accumulation of rubbish, and repaved; the north transept was dismantled and rebuilt; new mullions were put in the great window of the south transept; and Blacader's Aisle was restored. More importantly, the ground around the cathedral was cleared of soil to a depth of about 2.1m. 'This displays the structure in its proper elevations, and has added greatly to the security and beauty of the building'.[34] Blore worked on behalf of the government, since it had come to be recognised that the Act of Annexation of 1587, and the abolition of episcopacy in 1689, had left the Crown in technical ownership of the cathedral. The cost of restoration was borne partly by the Commissioners of Woods and Forests, and partly by Glasgow Corporation. Proposals by the corporation to extend the transepts and complete Blacader's aisle did not find government approval and were dropped. The newly-restored cathedral was visited by Queen Victoria and Prince Albert on 14 August 1849, the first royal visit to the building in 250 years.

By the middle of the nineteenth century, the William Stark additions of 1805 had come to be despised and, in 1852–6, the galleries, pulpit and pews were removed from the chancel. The work was supervised by William Nixon and Robert Matheson.

When Robert Southey visited the cathedral in 1819 he noted that 'the window in one of these kirks had been made to imitate stained glass, by painting on the glass, and this of course had a paltry and smeary appearance'.[35] Wherever it was, it was swept away in the mid-nineteenth century when the windows of the cathedral were completely renewed. In 1856, Andrew Orr, Lord Provost of Glasgow, put forward a plan to fill the cathedral windows with stained glass. It was funded by voluntary subscriptions and completed in 1859–64. The glass was made at the Königliche Glasmalereianstalt – the Royal Bavarian Stained Glass Establishment – at Munich, founded in 1827 by King Ludwig I of Bavaria. The manufacture of the glass was supervised by Maximilian Ainmiller, the inspector of the establishment. The decision to give the commission to a continental manufacturer aroused protest from those who felt that the commission should have gone to Scottish glass painters, but the glass was not altogether condemned: 'The result is perhaps the most beautiful and harmonious grouping of modern stained glass to be found anywhere; but on the whole, the architectural features of the cathedral are somewhat obscured by the great darkening it has undergone. The crypt has especially suffered'.[36]

It was remarkable that any stained glass should be inserted in a presbyterian church in the middle of the nineteenth century. It was an intolerant age and there was still a lingering dislike of anything that savoured of Roman Catholicism. In a brief typical of its time, the manufacturers of the glass were given strict and detailed rules as to what they might depict: 'No nimbus or aureole is to be place around the head of any saintly person represented. Apostles must not be distinguished by keys, swords, pilgrim's staves, escallop shells, etc., nor are any to be clothed in the costume of the Roman hierarchy. No representation of God the Father, of the Holy Trinity, or of the Holy Ghost, or of the Virgin Mary as Mother of God'.[37]

The Munich glass had a comparatively short life in the cathedral windows. By the end of the century, the painted detail was rapidly decaying. 'In the nave, as well as in the choir, the colouring is in several instances brilliant to garishness, and we also note with deep regret that in many windows the features of saints and prophets are sadly defaced, even to obliteration. Texts are also faded out, and within the past five years there has been marked deterioration of beauty and effect. The atmosphere of the city, heavily charged with chemicals in this particular neighbourhood, has been blamed as the cause thereof, but one feels dubious as to the acceptance of such a statement in its entirety. So far as known, stained-glass windows in other manufacturing towns, with equally impure atmosphere, have not suffered to the same extent. The windows in the crypts do not show so much deterioration; the beauty and the perfect condition of medieval glass is patent to all; and the window that cannot show forth clear and good to its own jubilee, surely betokens bad workmanship'.[38]

Continuing deterioration of the Munich glass led to a decision in 1938 to replace it. The work was delayed until after the end of the Second World War and completed by 1960. The cost of the new glass was met mostly by the descendants of the donors of the Munich glass. The work of eleven artists is represented. During the same period, and up to 1967, extensive improvements and additions were also made to the furnishings and fittings under the guidance of Sir Albert Richardson, and to the structure of the cathedral under the Ministry of Public Building and Works. The only panels of the Munich glass still in place are in the east clerestory windows of the transepts, but the heraldic achievements from many of the nave windows have been reset in modern clear glass. In the main building, only the rose window over the south doorway retains its original Munich glass, although some survives in the sacristy. With the exception of three panels displayed in the Lower Church, the rest of the Munich glass has been carefully stored in racks in the triforium.

Some refurbishment of the chancel took place in 1890. The pulpit was moved to the side, away from its central position on the site of the altar, and the present floor of encaustic tiles and marbles was laid. The last major structural alteration to the cathedral was the replacement of most of the roof in 1909–12, and it was at this time that it acquired its external copper sheathing. The natural development of a protective verdigris has given the roof its present pale green colour.

The cathedral is an impressive building although, externally, its sloping site conveys a hint (but no more than a hint) of structural instability. The site of the cathedral may well be that of Ninian's burial ground, but there is nothing of beauty to commend it today. It is horribly overshadowed by the vast, ugly, infirmary to the north and the sinister looking necropolis to the east.

The plan is cruciform: a nave of eight bays with shallow non-projecting transepts, now absorbed at ground floor level by the aisles, a single-storey extension of the south transept, known as the Blacader Aisle, a chancel of five bays with an eastern ambulatory, and beyond that a row of four chapels. The sacristy and chapter house are at the south-east corner. Beneath the chancel is the Lower Church, which also has four eastern chapels to match those off the ambulatory above.

The cathedral is 86.8m long; the nave is 37.4m long and 19.1m wide, and the nave roof is 31m high. The interior has an impressive black grandeur; more than can be said for the exterior which is simply grimy. Sir John Betjeman spoke of the cathedral as being 'severer even than the severe Cistercian buildings of England. Moulding, proportion, construction, no flowing cornice, no fal-diddles – because of its thoughtful simplicity, I find Glasgow Cathedral the most satisfying medieval cathedral in these islands, its severe serenity alarming'.[39]

The eight-bay nave is fourteenth century, with clustered piers, and triforium and clerestory united and framed by a single tall arcade, two bays to one main bay. The open timber roof dates from 1909–12, but is of medieval design. The roof is undoubtedly sturdy and waterproof but, despite the cost involved, the nave would have been better served by a stone vault, or even a plaster vault imitating stone. The cross beams give the roof the air of a country barn and the westernmost beam obstructs the view of the rose window at the top of the west gable. The square Romanesque revival font under the north arcade dates from 1919. A large sixteenth century iron chest made in Holland can be seen by the second pier.

The west window, depicting the Creation, was designed by Francis Spear and given by the corporation of Glasgow in 1958; the fine ornamental clock below it is of the same date. The design of the window is a matter of taste, but the representations of Adam and Eve resemble armoured androids; and women may not care for the face of Eve. To the right of the west doorway is a war memorial cross commemorating the soldiers of the Highland Light Infantry who died on tour in India and Ceylon.

The bell, near the west end of the aisle, was given by Archbishop Gavin Dunbar (1523–47) to hang in the demolished north-west bell tower. It cracked in 1593 and was recast the following year. It cracked again in 1789 and was recast in 1790, being given a pompous and inaccurate inscription which ignored the original generosity of the archbishop: 'In the year of grace 1594 Marcus Knox, a merchant in Glasgow zealous for the interest of the reformed religion, caused me to be fabricated in Holland, for the use of his fellow citizens of Glasgow, and place me with solemnity in the tower of their cathedral. My sanction was announced by the impress on my bosom. Come that ye may learn holy doctrine. And I was taught to proclaim the hours of unheeded time. 195 years had I sounded these awful warnings, when I was broken by the hands of inconsiderate and unskilful men. In the year 1790 I was cast into the furnace, resounded at London, and returned to my sacred vocation. Reader, thou also shalt know a resurrection, may it be unto eternal life'. Cracked a third time it was replaced in 1896 by the present bell, with an equally inaccurate and equally pompous inscription, which hangs in the central tower. The inscription reads as follows: 'John Garroway, merchant, Glasgow, presented to the cathedral church of Glasgow, the new bell in place of the old one given AD 1594, cast first at Holland, and again at London in 1790, and freely dedicated it to the greater glory of God. 1896. When you hear me, come that you may learn holy doctrine'.

In the north nave aisle, most of the memorials are arranged with a soldier in the centre of each bay and a doctor or politician on either side. In the first bay, moving from the west end, are memorials to John Stirling (d.1829) on the west wall; in the first bay of the north wall: Sir William Alexander Smith (1854–1914), founder of the Boys' Brigade; Colonel Henry Cadogan (by David Hamilton and Sons c.1816–17), who was killed at the battle of Vittoria in 1813; and four soldiers killed in France in 1918. In the second bay: a bronze by Alfred Gilbert (better known for the Shaftesbury Memorial Fountain at Piccadilly Circus in London) to William Graham MP; Lieutenant Donald Campbell (1799–1833); and Dr Peter Lowe, founder of the Faculty of Physicians and Surgeons. In the third bay: a golden jubilee tablet commemorating the inauguration of the Glasgow Corporation Water Works by Queen Victoria in 1859, which was erected in 1909 by the survivors of the 400-strong guard of honour on the occasion; a war memorial to soldiers of the Third Sutherland Highlanders who fell in the Crimean War 1854–6; and one to Captain George Grierson who died of cholera at Lucknow in 1892. In the fourth bay: a memorial to James Mitchell, a local politician in Lanarkshire, who died in 1910 at the age of fifty-six; a fine bronze and marble memorial, with sword, helmet and gauntlets, to Lieutenant Robert Burn Anderson (1833–60), who was killed in the Second Opium War and is buried in the Russian cemetery in Peking (monument by Robert Jackson fl. 1840–78); and James Grahame (1765–1811), a poet. In the fifth bay: a memorial to two engineers who died in South Africa in 1901; a white marble memorial to Major William Middleton, who died in Malta in 1859 at the age of thirty-four on his way back from India; and Sir Thomas Anderson (1836–1908), Regius Professor of Medicine in the University of Glasgow. In the sixth bay: John Browne (1701–97) a former lord provost of Glasgow; and a memorial with a Latin inscription. In the seventh bay: James Hedderwick (1814–97); a sentimental group with standing soldiers and a boy, commemorating soldiers of the 71st Highland Light Infantry who died on the North West Frontier of India in 1863; and James Nicol, chamberlain of Glasgow 1882–1911. In the eighth bay: David Allison, who died in 1808 aged fifty-eight, and Robert Potter, who died in 1822 aged twenty-six.

The fourth stained glass window in the north nave aisle is the only example in the cathedral of the work of Douglas Strachan (1936); it illustrates incidents in the life of Moses. The window pre-dates the later programme of restoring the Munich glass, and was left intact.

In the south nave aisle are numerous monuments arranged similarly to those in the north aisle. Moving from west to east, in the first and second bays: the colours of the Cameronian Regiment (the Scottish Rifles) in a glass case, with memorials and roll of honour and three Cameronian commemorative windows: two by Harry Stammers (1954) and one by William Wilson (1958). The Cameronians originated in the zeal of Covenanting preachers and their followers; the regiment was disbanded in 1968. The entrance door occupies the third bay. In the fourth bay: soldiers of the 74th Highlanders who were killed in Egypt in 1882; William Watson (1837–80), killed by the accidental explosion of a shell; and a First World War memorial to members of the congregation. In the sixth bay: a seventeenth century stone wall tablet commemorating the Stewarts of Minto, containing one of the few surviving Scottish brasses, and depicting a knight in armour kneeling before the divine radiance. Several of the Stewarts served as lord provosts of Edinburgh. One of them, Sir Matthew Stewart was charged with escorting the newly-appointed Archbishop Robert Montgomery (1581–86) to the cathedral. When it was known that the archbishop intended to preach, the presbyterians installed John Howieson (one of their own number) in the pulpit. Sir Matthew, armed with a royal warrant, ordered Howieson to leave. Howieson unwisely refused, and was forcibly removed, losing some teeth in the process. Sir Matthew was consequently excommunicated, and the archbishop eventually resigned. The other memorials in the sixth bay commemorate John Orr, principal town clerk of Glasgow, who died in 1803 at the age of sixty-eight, and Dr Andrew Ure (1778–1857). In the seventh bay: a memorial to members of the Glasgow Police Force killed in 1914–19; Sir James Grierson (1859–1914); and members of the Glasgow University Royal Army Medical Corps, killed in 1914–18.

Just before the crossing, on the north side of the nave, is an octagonal wooden pulpit given in 1902 by the widow of William Granger, a former assistant minister at the cathedral. On the left is the stair to the former rood loft.

GLASGOW: *The Cathedral Church of St Kentigern*

GLASGOW: *The Cathedral Church of St Kentigern*

GLASGOW: *The Cathedral Church of St Kentigern*

GLASGOW: *Cathedral Church of St Mary the Virgin*

GLASGOW: *The Cathedral Church of St Andrew*

The upper opening, a fifteenth century doorway with clear glass, is still visible. The line of the rood loft is marked by studs in the floor. The vault above the crossing is nineteenth century.

The transepts, which are virtually incorporated into the aisles at ground floor level, are late fifteenth century, and different from the nave. The triforium and clerestory are separated, the former, three-arched under a larger semi-circular arch and the latter a triplet of lancets. Each transept is entered by a flight of stairs from the crossing. The glass in the north transept lancet windows is by William Wilson (1960) and commemorates twelve Scottish regiments in its upper lights and the Royal Navy, Merchant Navy and Royal Air Force in the lower lights. The south transept windows opposite, by Gordon Webster (1951–4), constitute a memorial to the dead of both world wars. The south transept has a large number of nineteenth century brass memorials. Stairways, once forming a one-way route (an 'in' and 'out' so to speak) for pilgrims to St Kentigern's Shrine, descend from each transept to the Lower Church.

The low and solid late fifteenth century stone pulpitum was remodelled by Archbishop Blacader in the early sixteenth century; it is the only surviving medieval pulpitum in a non-monastic church in Scotland. The gallery of figures in the screen on top may represent the Seven Deadly Sins (pride, wrath, envy, lust, gluttony, avarice and sloth) or the Seven Ages of Man (Shakespeare, *As You Like It*, II, vii). Altar platforms flanking the steps up to the archway still remain, with saints in niches along their sides. The north altar was dedicated to the Name of Jesus, and the south altar to Our Lady of Pity. There are eleven figures, each wearing a cassock and carrying a scroll. They may represent the eleven disciples, after the defection of Judas Iscariot, and the scrolls may have been carved with clauses from the Creed.

The gateway through the pulpitum and into the chancel has no gates, but looped-back curtains; no doubt effective at coping with draughts but resembling an Edwardian parlour, and incongruous in this setting. The east side of the screen is ornamented with angels holding various heraldic shields. On the chancel side, the pulpitum has a nineteenth century wooden addition. Beneath it are two framed colours of the Scots Guards dating from the Napoleonic Wars. Passing through the pulpitum brings the visitor into the chancel of the cathedral: 'The first impression on entering through the pulpitum is sublime. It is not a large building in European terms, but the sense of scale far outstrips its real dimensions. The greatest initial impact is made by the four enormously long lancets, which rise above the twin arcade arches opening into the ambulatory, and which extend through triforium and clerestory levels up to meet the soffit of the wagon ceiling'.[40] The height of the chancel is about 22.5m to the apex of the roof.

The chancel has three distinct storeys like the transepts, and clustered columns with foliage capitals. The oak boarded ceiling dates from the re-roofing of the cathedral in 1909–12 and has rows of carved and painted bosses. The sanctuary floor was paved with marble and tiles in 1890, and is now covered by an unnecessary and crudely-patterned red carpet. The western part of the chancel is laid with encaustic tiles, then a step of Levanto marble leads to the main floor with a mixture of marbles: Victoria Red, Black and Green from Ireland; Pavonezza and Siena from Italy; Iberian Agate and St Sylvester from Portugal; and light and dark Numidian from Africa. The pews were installed in 1851–6, and rearranged and remodelled in 1957. They were much criticised as early as 1889 as being unworthy of the architecture of the cathedral, and a disgrace to the city.[41] The judgement is harsh; of their kind, the pews are not bad, but the chancel of a cathedral church needs space, or at least a feeling of spaciousness, and should not be choked with pews in this way.

The four great east lancets contain glass by Francis Spear depicting the Evangelists; the glass was inserted in 1951 to replace Munich glass depicting the same subjects, given by Queen Victoria. The chancel pulpit with semi-circular headed panelling and an hour-glass, is late sixteenth century and was used by the Barony congregation in the Lower Church until 1801, when their first church building outside the cathedral was built about 91m south-west of the cathedral. This church was demolished c.1885 and the pulpit wandered from place to place before being returned to the cathedral in 1905. The ornate communion table, with a foliate cornice representing the Crown of Thorns, above a carving of the Last Supper, dates from 1890. The carved eagle lectern is seventeenth century French work and was given by Sir John Stirling-Maxwell. On the south side is a royal pew, with chairs for the Queen and the Duke of Edinburgh.

The chancel aisles, especially the north, were extensively reconstructed in the fifteenth century. At the west end of the north chancel aisle, the first window (1939) is by Herbert Hendrie on the theme of Christ and the world's work; below it can be seen traces of the old entrance to the demolished former sacristy; the second window (1951) is by Robert Armitage; the third (1946) is another by Hendrie on Christ and the World's Happiness; and the fourth, a grisaille by Robert Armitage (1953); the next is Christ and the world's beauty by Sadie McLellan (1955), and the last (St Andrew and St James) is another

Hendrie (1940). Through the doorway beyond is the sacristy, the upper floor of the chapter house. Lead bullets are embedded in its oak doors, which are the only original doors in the cathedral. The sacristy itself dates from c.1440 (the chapter house below is earlier) and has a central column and a vault. It contains a fireplace and the royal arms of King George III (1760–1820). In the fifteenth century it was one of the first meeting rooms of the University of Glasgow. It still retains its Munich glass of 1862. The chapter house/sacristy is an annexe to the cathedral. There may well have been a mid-thirteenth century structure on the site, but the present chapter house/sacristy is early fifteenth century. The upper floor is now used as the sacristy. This level was reconstructed during the episcopates of Bishop John Cameron of Lochiel (1426–46) and Bishop William Turnbull (1447–54). Above the fireplace is the original Assaye Colour presented to the 74th Highland Regiment by the East India Company in 1804. The stained glass (1862–5), by Henry Hughes, illustrates works of mercy and the Christian mission.

The ambulatory has carved bosses and formerly housed four chapels. The northernmost chapel is thought to have been dedicated to St Ninian, although doubt has been expressed about the existence of this chapel, since the location of an altar here would have been inconvenienced by the doorway giving access into the sacristy. The stained glass, by Marion Grant (1954), depicts St Ninian and St Columba. The next chapel was dedicated to St Martin and has glass depicting the Nativity and the Crucifixion by Francis Spear (1953). Moving southwards, the chapel of St James the Greater (known as the East Chapel) is in use and has a communion table with an eighteenth century Italian frontal and a brass eagle lectern with onyx and agate stones of 1890; the glass depicts the Resurrection and Ascension of Christ, also by Francis Spear (1953). The chapel of St Stephen and St Laurence has a piscina, the rinsings draining through a gargoyle in the east wall, and the large tomb of Archbishop James Law (1615–32), which almost completely conceals the windows; the glass depicts St Stephen and St Laurence by Gordon Webster (1975).

The first window in the south chancel aisle, at the side of the chapel of St Stephen and St Laurence, is by Christopher Webb (1958) and depicts Queen Margaret and King David I. The second window, by Robert Armitage (1957), depicts various emblems of freemasonry, a relic of a time when Christianity and freemasonry were thought to be compatible. The third, fourth and fifth windows show scenes from the life of St Kentigern, by Sadie McLellan (1951) and William Wilson (1954 and 1956) and the sixth window (1951) again by Wilson, commemorates the merchants of Glasgow. The last window, depicting St Nicholas, is by Marion Grant (1955).

Access to the Lower Church below the chancel is by way of stairs in the north and south transepts. The pierced stone balustrades in the north transept are nineteenth century. On the first landing, by way of the north transept, the elaborate white memorial tablet with a medallion and allegorical figure of Fame commemorates the Revd George Burns (1830–96). The door in the north wall was for the use of canons and vicars choral who lived nearby. At the bottom of the stairs, two early sixteenth century carved heraldic stones from the former bishop's palace can be seen in the third bay of the north aisle.

The Lower Church, often called the crypt, but wrongly so since it is not below ground level, was built by Bishop William de Bondington (1233–58) as part of the same building programme including the chancel above. Its purpose was to provide a resting place for the tomb of St Kentigern and the provision of additional chantry altars. The tomb itself stood in a space formed by four columns directly below the site of the altar above and designed to carry its weight.

The Lower Church is now a quiet and pleasant place, and quite different from its early nineteenth century days as a gloomy graveyard. It has ten bays, two to every one in the chancel above. Each has a quadripartite vault and central boss, except in the area around the shrine and altar of Our Lady. In the first bay is a modern door which leads to a vaulted room that was once the cathedral treasury with the medieval sacristy (long demolished) above. For a long time the treasury was known as the 'Dripping Aisle' because of the constant oozing of water from the roof.

The east end is at a lower level still, down a flight of eight steps that stretches across the whole width of the Lower Church, and has four chapels to match those in the ambulatory above. Each chapel is separated from its neighbours by a stone screen pierced by two arches. During the days of the Barony Kirk this area especially was the first to be filled with soil and used as a burial ground.

The chapel of St Nicholas was furnished and dedicated in 1969 as an area in which the cathedral Sunday School could worship. The communion table, designed by Schomberg Scott, carries symbols of St Nicholas. The bronze sculpture is the work of George Wylie. One wonders whether current theological and liturgical practice would favour children being placed as far away as possible from the principal area and act of worship. From this chapel a thirteenth century doorway, with fine capitals and a band of carving, leads into the fifteenth century chapter house. It still has the fifteenth century stone seat reserved for the dean, which has a canopy above it, bearing the inscription WILMS : FUDA : ISTU : CAPLM : DEI (William founded this chapter house of God). The gentleman in question was Bishop William Lauder (1408–25), whose armorial bearings can be seen in a shield on the canopy.

The chapel of Saint Peter and Saint Paul has a Te Deum window by Gordon Webster (1979). The two original thirteenth century arches between this chapel and that of St Andrew, were remodelled later in that century to form a single arch. Beneath the enlarged arch is an effigy believed to represent Bishop Robert Wischard (1271–1316).

The chapel of St Andrew was furnished by nursing organisations for use as a nurse's chapel in 1969 and later refurnished by the Royal College of Nursing. The colours of the St Andrew's Ambulance Nursing Corps were laid up here in 1979.

The chapel of St John the Evangelist shares a piscina with the chapel of St Andrew on the dividing wall. Here in the south wall is the holy well of St Kentigern on its window sill; above is a window by Clayton and Bell (1869) showing St Kentigern baptising the child of Rhydderch, king of Strathclyde. The chapel presently contains fragments of the shrine of St Kentigern, dating from the thirteenth century, and other fragments including some from the western towers. The piscina, on top of the north partition screen, passes through the wall and is discharged through a gargoyle on the outside. On the south side can be seen the bulky tomb of Lady Colquhoun (d.1595).

At the upper level, the piers vary in size from the massive type supporting those above, to the more graceful clustered version around the central altar, raised on a dais, which marks the place of St Kentigern's tomb. Another centre bay further east is distinguished by a lierne vault, below which was the altar of the Lady Chapel dedicated to St Mary in the Crypt. The four portrait-headed bosses in this vault are said to represent Bishop de Bondington the builder, Isabella de Valoniis a benefactress, King Alexander II (1214–49) and King Alexander III (1249–86) as a boy.

Near the west end of the centre aisle are two coffin lids, probably thirteenth century; another near the exit at the south-west corner has interlaced ornament around the edge and dates from about 1200.

Half-way up the steps to the south transept is the much-altered thirteenth century doorway into the fifteenth century Blacader's Aisle, or Fergus's Lower Church, which is said to occupy the site of St Ninian's fifth century burial ground. The doorway was originally an external entrance for pilgrims to the shrine of St Kentigern. The aisle, four bays long and two bays wide, is now unfortunately whitewashed, but nonetheless a quiet and beautiful place. The tierceron vault, with its collection of recently coloured bosses, is encountered at unexpectedly close quarters before one descends an alarmingly steep flight of steps. In a spandrel between the vault ribs springing from the column nearest the entrance is a crude painting relating to the legend of the founding of Glasgow by Kentigern: two oxen drawing a cart bearing the body of Fergus, with the words: 'this is ye ile of car Fergus'. It may indicate a belief that Fergus lies buried in the area covered by the aisle. The windows in the south wall contain four small panels of sixteenth and seventeenth century glass from private chapels or houses in Switzerland. The remaining windows are by Harry Stammers: on the east side Archbishop Blacader (1960), followed by the Annunciation to the Virgin and to the Shepherds (1956), the Nativity and the Epiphany (1956), and the Presentation and the Flight into Egypt (1956). On the west side are scenes of Christ's healing, preaching and prayer (1960).

Outside the cathedral, the south doorway is flanked by large nineteenth century tablets. There are hundreds of other memorial stones in the churchyard, many much older; many lying horizontally with now illegible inscriptions; many others are embedded in its perimeter wall. Some are of vast size and some are entrances to vaults.

The south view of the cathedral shows the stepped levels that are so marked internally, caused by the steeply sloping site. In fact the site has been used so carefully that virtually no part of the lower building is below ground. The tower is late thirteenth century, but its 68.5m spire was not completed till about 1420.

The Lower Church has a separate entrance on this side: a weathered doorway with a little vault above it. Against the north-east of the cathedral stands the sacristy-chapter house. The north side has an array of monuments and the barrel-vaulted thirteenth century former treasury, once topped by the west sacristy. A little east of the north transept is another low building which at one time was two storeys high, the two being connected by a stair in the thickness of the wall. This was the hall of the vicars' choral and the cathedral song school.

The Z-shaped archbishop's castle stood to the west of the cathedral, occupying much of the area covered by the present Cathedral Square. The castle was a thirteenth century structure (the first mention is 1258), extended and fortified in the fifteenth and sixteenth centuries. It was stormed six times between 1515 and 1568, and restored by Archbishop John Spottiswoode (1603–15) in 1611. Although used as a prison to house 300 Highland rebels in 1715, it was abandoned and fell into decay after the departure of the archbishop in 1689. It became used as a stone quarry for new buildings in the neighbourhood after 1715 and was in ruins by the 1730s. The ruins were still standing in 1789 when most of them were swept away to make way for the Infirmary. The remaining part of the curtain wall and a solitary tower (Beaton's Tower) were demolished in 1792. Little remains today beyond a few carved stones inserted in various buildings. The baronial-style St Mungo Museum of Religious Life and Art was built over the site of part of the outer wall of the castle and there is a good view of the cathedral from the second floor. The archbishops also had residences in Edinburgh, Partick, Lockwood, Carstairs and Ancrum, but the remains of these buildings are equally scanty. Sir William Brereton visited Glasgow Palace in 1636: 'It seems a stately structure, and promises much when you look upon the outside… Here I went to see the hall and palace, and going into the hall, which is a poor and mean place, the archbishop's daughter, an handsome and well-bred proper gentlewoman, entertained me with much civil respect, and would not suffer me to depart until I had drunk Scotch ale, which was the best I had tasted in Scotland'.[42] The archbishop in question was Patrick Lindsay (1633–8), but which of his three daughters entertained Sir William will never be known.

The cathedral graveyard was filled by the early nineteenth century, interments taking place by that date at a rate of 750 each year. Burials continued in the necropolis, opened in 1833, which covers a hill to the east of the cathedral. At the summit is a dominating statue of John Knox, designed in 1825 by Thomas Hamilton. Viewed from afar the necropolis is an eerie sight, strangely reminiscent of the hill of Calvary. Like so many of its kind, it has been subjected to the unwanted attentions of those with no respect for the last resting place of human remains.

1 Walcott, Mackenzie (1874): volume 1, p. 188.
2 ibid.
3 *Historical and descriptive account of the cathedral church of Glasgow* (1904): pp 17–18.
4 Pagan, James (1856): pp 37–8.
5 Durkan, John (1986): p. 1.
6 Brown, P Hume (1891): p. 151.
7 Pagan, James (1856): pp 49–51.
8 Brown, P Hume (ed.) (1892): p. 46.
9 Pennant, T (1776): volume 1, p. 153.
10 *Historical and descriptive account of the cathedral church of Glasgow* (1904): p. 25.
11 Gordon, J F S (1994): p. 133.
12 ibid., p. 118.
13 ibid.
14 *The history of the cathedral or high church of Glasgow* (1825): pp 10–11.
15 McLellan, Archibald (1833): pp 66–7.
16 Gordon, J F S (1994): p. 68.
17 McLellan, Archibald (1833): p. 55.
18 Pagan, James (1856): p. 96.
19 McLellan, Archibald (1833): p. 60.
20 ibid., p. 61.
21 ibid., pp 77–8.
22 Billings, Robert (1845-52): volume 3, p. 7.
23 Pagan, James (1856): p. v.
24 McLellan, Archibald (1833): p 69.
25 Billings, Robert (1845-52): volume 3, p. 1.
26 McLellan, Archibald (1833): p. 62.
27 Pagan, James (1856): p. 77.
28 McLellan, Archibald (1833): pp 62–3.
29 Lindsay, Ian G (1926): p. 154.
30 Eyre-Todd, George (1898): p. 284.
31 Butler, Dugald (1901): p. 31.
32 *The history of the cathedral or high church of Glasgow* (1825): p. 4.
33 Butler, Dugald (1901): p. 31.
34 Pagan, James (1856): p. 77.
35 Southey, Robert (1929): p. 255.
36 Ward and Lock (1889): p. 247.
37 Henderson, John (1925): p. 182.
38 Addis, M E Leicester (1901): p. 24.
39 Betjeman, Sir John (1952): pp 21–22.
40 Fawcett, Richard in Williamson, Riches & Higgs (1990): p. 127.
41 Ward and Lock (1889): p. 247.
42 Brown, P Howe (1891): p. 151.

The Cathedral Church of St Mary the Virgin

United Dioceses of Glasgow and Galloway (Scottish Episcopal Church)

After the expulsion of the bishops in 1689, and the ejection of episcopalians from the parish churches, those in Glasgow who remained loyal to Archbishop John Paterson (1687–1708) led the usual shadowy and furtive existence until the repeal of the Penal Laws in 1792. The congregation worshipped in a schoolroom in George Street. In 1825 they moved to a newly built church in Renfield Street. There they remained for more than forty years until the construction of the present cathedral, in the new residential area west of the crowded and unhealthy city centre. The Renfield Street church was abandoned, partly on the insistence of Bishop Walter Trower (1848–59), who disliked its architectural style, and partly due to the fact that weekday services were often disturbed by the rolling of barrels in the crypt, which had been let out as a warehouse. The area around the church was becoming less residential and more commercial. By 1871 the most fashionable homes were to be found on the Great Western Road, a turnpike road formed in 1836, and here, at a site numbered '82' (there was nothing between 46 and 146), was built the present cathedral on the corner of Great Western Road and Holyrood Crescent in the Woodside district of the city. The Renfield Street church was sold to the City of Glasgow Insurance Company and demolished in 1920.

St Mary's Cathedral was designed as a parish church, supposedly by Sir George Gilbert Scott (1811–78), architect of the Glasgow University buildings at Gilmorehill, the Albert Memorial in London, and the great Midland Grand Hotel above St Pancras Station in London. In fact it has been suggested that, because of his large portfolio of commissions, the cathedral is little more than a composition of elements of designs already used elsewhere. 'Moreover his powers were fading, and if St Mary's, Glasgow, has been described as similar to this or that church in England, it may be that almost all his later churches were identical in overall design but differed in minor details. In the case of St Mary's, the minor detail was a zigzag pattern on the West Front, copied from the ruins of Elgin Cathedral, a Scottish fig leaf to cover an otherwise nakedly English design. But even this was not entirely original; it also appeared on St Mary's, Edinburgh. It is not a success on either'.[1] The clerestory, lit by cusped circular windows linked under a blind arcade, had already been used by Scott at All Saints, Sherbourne, in Warwickshire, in 1862–4. The style of the tower is drawn from All Souls, Haley Hill, Halifax.

The cathedral was substantially built in 1871–4 by Thompson of Peterborough, the tower and spire being completed in 1892–3 at a cost of £2,000 to designs by his son John Oldrid Scott. The building was constructed, as a parish church only, during the episcopate of Bishop William Scott Wilson (1859–88) and there was no thought of it becoming a cathedral in his time. Wilson was described rather unflatteringly by the *Church Review*: 'He is simply a clergyman of the No-Church school, old-fashioned, narrow, prejudiced, not always particularly urbane, neither a scholar nor a preacher, nor an organiser; a tolerant good man of business, and capable of being moderately pleasant and kind when not crossed. He would have made a very indifferent rector of a large parish, and what induced our Scottish Episcopal brethren to elect so obviously unsuitable an occupant to the See of Glasgow, we cannot for the life of us imagine'.[2] St Mary's Church was eventually raised to cathedral status at a ceremony on 28 January 1908 that, remarkably, was attended by clergy from the Church of Scotland and the United Free Church. The vestries and hall along the north side were added in 1913. The dedication to St Mary, with a side chapel to St Anne, perpetuates the dedication of the late medieval church of the same name in the city, which was second only in importance to St Kentigern's Cathedral.

After a long period of decline and shrinking congregations, including the possible threat of demolition in the face of a road development scheme, the cathedral vestry took a courageous decision to restore the cathedral, and fund-raising began in 1987–8. The redecoration was opened to competition, and won by the American-born artist Gwyneth Leech. Trained at the Edinburgh School of Art and married to a Scot, she has worked on the cathedral since 1989.

The exterior facing of the cathedral is built of Giffnock stone, with Lanark stone in the courses, and the interior is of Bath stone. The architectural style is generally Early English Gothic, with some elements of Decorated. The octagonal spire, with tall lucarnes and spirelets at the base, is 62.7m high, surmounted by a cross of bell metal. In niches in the spirelets stand statues of St Andrew, St Kentigern, St Margaret and St George. The tower contains a peal of ten bells by Taylor of Loughborough, hung in 1901, the tenor bell weighing nearly 1.6 tonnes. For most of the twentieth century, however, the bells have been silent, partly due to the lack of people able and willing to ring them, and partly due to the complaints of those living in the vicinity of the cathedral. 'Ten bells performing complicated mathematical formulae over a period of hours may sound very well across the English countryside, but it is not the same thing when it shatters the repose of Scots some few yards away'.[3] In 1928 it was reported that they had not been used for many years and the pulleys were clogged up with soot falling from the spire.

At the base of the tower can be seen a number of statues, including one of Bishop William Turnbull (1447–54), founder of Glasgow University in 1451, Archbishop Robert Leighton (1671–4) and Bishop Walter Trower, who holds a model of St Mary's; weather and pollution have caused much erosion of detail. The west doorway, still with empty niches, leads into a tall five-bay aisled nave with clerestory, 30.4m long and 9.1m wide and bordered by arcades of alternating octagonal and clustered piers of Bath stone. The westernmost bays of the north and south nave aisles have now been partitioned to provide a bookshop on the south side and an office on the north side.

The open timber roof springs from corbelled colonnettes attached above the spandrels of the arcade. The heads of various British saints are carved at the joins of the vault springers. The clerestory windows are sexfoils with clear glass. The beams of the open timber roof form a now painted wooden groin vault at the crossing. The west window, showing Christ commissioning the Apostles, is by Clayton and Bell (1877), a firm favoured by Scott, and was donated by John Houldsworth, a Glasgow industrial magnate. The aisle windows form an integrated scheme from the studios of Hardman of Birmingham.

The first bay was formerly the baptistery and the theme of the sacrament can be seen in the stained glass. The marble plaque of St Francis of Assisi, a private commission by Evelyn Beale, was a memorial gift in 1945, and the rails were another memorial gift in 1962. A wall panel at the junction of the third and fourth bays further along the aisle, designed by Farmer and Brindley in 1899, was the central panel of the former stone reredos of the high altar, with an alabaster relief of Christ in Glory; it was placed here in 1920 as a First World War memorial. The Second World War memorial is further to the east at the junction of the fourth and fifth bays.

A temporary nave altar stands in the central space of the crossing on a wooden platform, which raises the floor to the level of the chancel. But the most interesting aspect of the crossing is the great painted ceiling which focuses attention on the altar below. The decorative scheme, including the murals which adorn the walls above the arches of the crossing, is the work of Gwyneth Leech and was carried out between April and December 1990. The centre of the scheme is the figure of the ascended Christ, echoing the early Christian and Byzantine tradition of Christ depicted as the Pantokrator in the dome or apse of every church. On either side are the symbols of the four evangelists. At either foot of the mural are miniatures of the Holy Family and the Crucifixion. Mural paintings occupy the space above the north and south arches of the crossing and depict various endangered species; sea creatures to the north, and land and air creatures to the south. All are portrayed in motion, joining in the offering of praise to Almighty God. At the foot of the murals on the south side is the Garden of Eden and the expulsion of Adam and Eve, set against a modern industrial landscape. On the north side is the story of the Flood – the few saved in the ark while others, including a representation of the artist and her assistants, perish in the waters, and the ark coming to rest on the mountains.

The ceiling of the crossing reflects the medieval tradition of the rood screen, with a representation of the vault of heaven, incorporating gilt stars, crescent moons and – introducing a contemporary note – a space rocket. The vivid blue of the ceiling emphasises the cathedral's dedication to the Blessed Virgin Mary, and this is taken up in the fleurs-de-lys, white lilies and the white roses of the stencilled decoration on the east wall of the chancel.

A slender wrought-iron screen of 1894 divides the crossing from the chancel. The screen, with its intricate tracery and cresting, was designed by John Oldrid Scott and decorated by Gwyneth Leech. The screen is surmounted by a large cross, with the Agnus Dei at its centre and the symbols of the four evangelists at its arms. The brass eagle lectern was given in 1883; the icon of the Virgin and Child is nineteenth century Greek work; and the celebrant's chair, together with two matching smaller chairs and faldstool, was carved by Lionel Gliori in 1986. The ungainly octagonal pulpit, of Caen stone on a granite pedestal with polished granite colonnettes, is typically late Victorian. It was designed by George Gilbert Scott and executed by John Mossman.

The area between the screen and the north wall of the north transept was formerly the chapel of the Resurrection. The screen itself came from the demolished mission church of St Saviour's, Port Dundas Road. The chapel has now been divided; the western part is an office and the eastern part is retained as a small memorial chapel. The doorway between leads through to the synod hall, beautifully restored in 1996. The north transept window (1875), depicting the prophets Jeremiah, John the Baptist and Jonah is by Ward and Hughes.

A wrought iron screen adjacent to the north transept leads into the chapel of St Anne in the north chancel aisle. The chapel is in poor condition and awaiting restoration. The chapel was furnished 1895–1904 to designs by John

Oldrid Scott. The reredos, showing the Deposition from the Cross, with flanking panels, dates from 1902; they were copied from renaissance works in the National Gallery, London, by a Miss Hale, a member of the cathedral congregation at the time. The centre panel is in poor condition. The saints depicted in the panels reflect the Christian names of those in whose memory the chapel was furnished. The Blessed Sacrament is reserved on the plain marble altar. An oak screen by Scott separates the chapel from the chancel.

The mural above the east window is by Gwyneth Leech and depicts the Annunciation; the cathedral appears in the scene. The east window itself is by Clayton and Bell (1871–2) and depicts the Ascension, flanked by the Nativity and the Resurrection. The high altar has a 1922 carved oak reredos by Sir Robert Lorimer, set in a frame with saints and foliage. The reredos was cleaned and regilded in 1990 and is now in excellent condition. The triptych, displaying scenes from the life of the Blessed Virgin Mary, including the three Marys at the Tomb, is the work of the nineteenth century artist Phoebe Traquair when she was in her late eighties. During an inexpert restoration in the 1960s and 1970s, much of the colour was lifted and a crude black line was drawn around the figures; the painting was then varnished. Although the triptych was carefully restored in the 1990s, much of Traquair's artistry had been irretrievably lost.

To the left of the altar is the simple bishop's throne, given in memory of Bishop Trower; to the right is an old chest and in the chancel floor is a brass commemorating Bishop Archibald Campbell (1904–21). The choir stalls are the work of Scott. The north and south chancel windows (1872) are by Ward and Hughes.

The organ occupies the south chancel aisle, which is directly below the tower. Built by William Hill in 1871, it was rebuilt by Harrison in 1909 and again by Hill, Norman and Beard in 1967. It was restored in 1990 at a cost of £140,000.

The south transept is now used as the baptistery and houses the octagonal white marble font with nine supporting polished granite colonnettes. Formerly standing at the west end of the north nave aisle, it was moved to its present position in 1994. It was designed by George Gilbert Scott and executed by John Mossman. It was raised on marble steps and provided with a Perpendicular-style pinnacled oak cover of 1903 to the designs of John Oldrid Scott. The font is now divorced from its theme window at the west end of the north nave aisle, which depicts the sacrament of baptism. The transept window (1873), depicting Isaiah, Moses and Ezekiel, is by Ward and Hughes. On the west wall of the transept is the war memorial from another of the cathedral's former mission churches, St Peter's at St George's Cross.

St Mary's Cathedral suffers from a style of Gothic Revival architecture that is distinctly tired and unimaginative; and this intrinsic weakness is compounded by the setting of the cathedral in an unfortunately drab site on the monotonous Great Western Road. That said, the as yet unfinished story of the on-going decoration of the interior since 1987 proves that there is not only life and hope, but also interest and imagination. Much has already been done to whet the visitor's appetite. When the internal decoration is completed in the years ahead, St Mary's Cathedral will be able to boast a coherent and exciting decorative scheme dating from the cusp of the millennium; and that claim will be unique among the cathedrals of Scotland.

1 White, Gavin (1995): p. 29.
2 Gordon, J F S (1894): pp 281–2.
3 White, Gavin (1995): pp 43–4.

The Cathedral Church of St Luke
Diocese of Thyateira and Great Britain
(Greek Orthodox Church)

Although the Cathedral Church of St Luke ranks as Scotland's newest cathedral, the building has a history which stretches back to the last quarter of the nineteenth century; and its story divides neatly into two periods. From 1877 to 1960 it was Belhaven United Presbyterian Church, but since 1960 it has been the Greek Orthodox Church of St Luke. In 1971 it joined the ranks of Scotland's cathedral churches for the Greek Orthodox Church in Scotland.

St Luke's Cathedral stands on a hillside site in the Dowanhill district of Glasgow, at the junction of Dundonald Road and Kensington Gate. Dowanhill is bounded by the Great Western Road to the north, Byres Road to the east, Hyndland Road to the west, and Highburgh Road to the south. In the second half of the nineteenth century the area centred on the hill was transformed into a desirable residential quarter, following a plan devised in 1850, and by 1900 the hill was covered with the elegant terraced villas which remain to this day.

St Luke's Cathedral was constructed in 1875–7 for a congregation of the United Presbyterian Church, a body formed in 1847 by an amalgamation of two splinter presbyterian sects: the United Secession Church (formed in 1822) and the Relief Church (formed in 1761). The United Presbyterian Church itself amalgamated with the Church of Scotland in 1929.

The idea of a church came from a group of people residing in the Great Western Road area, who decided to take advantage of the development of Dowanhill to acquire land on which to build a church. On 12 January 1875 they notified the local presbytery of their intention to construct a church. A sum of £2,000 had already been collected and, on 10 August 1875, twenty-three members were formed into a congregation which met initially in Hillhead Burgh Hall. The completed church was dedicated on 9 October 1877; the total cost of the structure was £12,000, and £2,000 was given to the collection taken at the opening service. The name 'Belhaven Church' was adopted to commemorate nearby Belhaven Terrace, where the decision to build a church had first been taken.

The first minister was William R Thomson; inducted on 11 May 1876, he died suddenly on 1 September 1878 after contracting a severe cold. The second minister, Robert Drummond (1879–98) was prominent enough to become moderator of the United Presbyterian Church in 1889. Drummond was followed by James Witherow (1898–1906); Alexander Hutton (1906–23), author of a number of devotional works; William Jardine (1924–39); and George Sutherland (1940–58). Then the life of Belhaven Church ended as it had begun, with an ephemeral incumbency. William Stevenson, the last minister, was inducted on 16 December 1959, and died prematurely on 13 March 1960, from a coronary thrombosis.

Belhaven Church never really flourished. Built to seat 950 people, its membership numbered only 341 in 1879. Official membership was reported to be over 600 in 1899, but that included more than 100 members of a mission church, and the number of active members was probably far fewer. The church lost a large number of its members in the First World War and never recovered. The merger of the United Presbyterian Church with the Church of Scotland in 1929 created a new united church which, understandably but unwisely, retained in active use all the church buildings of its previously separate constituent churches. The decline in church attendance had already started and the future was pointing clearly towards redundant buildings. As late as 1960, the nominal membership role of Belhaven was 1100, but the names were scattered far and wide and the church had only 150 active members.

With only a small congregation, the future of the church was clearly limited and the presbytery of Glasgow decided to merge the Belhaven congregation with that of Westbourne Church in nearby Westbourne Gardens. The two churches were formally united on 23 October 1960 under the name of Belhaven-Westbourne. There was a note of irony in the merger since the two churches had originally belonged to rival denominations (Westbourne was founded by the Free Church of Scotland in 1881), each intended to counteract the influence of the other. For a period of twelve months, Belhaven and Westbourne were used on alternate Sundays by the united congregation. Then a team of experts selected the Italian Renaissance Westbourne Church as the permanent home of the united congregation. Westbourne was numerically stronger, with a congregation numbering about 550 active members, and the maintenance costs were far less. The union lasted for only thirty years before Westbourne Church itself closed in 1990.

After its closure in 1961, Belhaven Church was bought by the restaurateur Argyros Stakis, and presented to the Greek community in Glasgow in memory of his parents Anastasios and Caterina Stakis. By decision of Archbishop Athenagoras II of Thyateira and Great Britain, the church was raised to the status of a cathedral for the Greek community in Scotland on 23 May 1971. The cathedral serves some five hundred Greek families in Glasgow with a further two hundred in the rest of Scotland.

The cathedral was designed in the style of Normandy Gothic by James Sellars of Campbell, Douglas and Sellars, and is held to be Sellars' best piece of work: 'A striking example of his versatility and talent before his powers were blunted by overwork in the eighties. Perhaps too, an example of his persuasiveness; for he built for a United Presbyterian congregation what in structure, if not furnishings, looks distinctly Episcopalian'.[1] *The Building News* remarked that 'it is decorated in a degree quite unusual in a presbyterian place of worship'.[2] The external walls are built of freestone from Netherwood quarry. 'It is somewhat rough in texture, but has excellent weather qualities'.[3] Sellars' design produced a flurry of correspondence in *The Building News* early in 1879. A correspondent flung a charge of plagiarism at Sellars, accusing him of copying R Norman Shaw's 1865 design for the English church at Lyons.[4] The complaint was immediately rebuffed by another correspondent who made the valid point that few, if any, architects could claim total originality. 'It is better to perpetuate a good thing than perpetrate a bad one… I have no doubt that Mr Shaw has in his time been indebted to old work for ideas and for the contour of his mouldings, not fearing to reproduce them in his new work because they were copies of the work of our glorious old monk architects'.[5] A third correspondent claimed that Sellars' design was very inferior to that of Shaw. A further correspondent criticised the design of the west front. 'The monster buttresses and heavy pinnacles, the three large lights crushed between them, the centre pillar carved down to the lowest string, have the unfortunate effect of making the front, as a whole, a very heavy-looming affair, altogether lacking not only the rich design, but the graceful proportions of the several details in Mr Shaw's design'.[6]

The cathedral is orientated north-south. On the main front, the buttress turrets, which finish in octagonal pinnacles, flank a rose window in the gable, and three tall lancets below, said to have been inspired by Dunblane Cathedral. Below the lancets are three pairs of pointed-arch windows with colonette mullions. To the right, a flight of steps leads to the main entrance door. Above the door rises a transept-like tower which houses the stair to the gallery. The entrance porch links the hall and vestry (to the right) with the cathedral (to the left).

The plan is an aisled nave of four bays, 36.5m long by 10.3m wide, and nearly 18.2m in height. The arcades resting on octagonal columns, with a clerestory of triple lancets in each bay above. The piers and arcades are a finer grained freestone from the Overwood quarries. The west gallery is supported by brackets and has a panelled front. The aisles are 22.8m long and 3.6m wide and retain their original lighting, but the nave is lit by brass electroliers installed in 1993. The cathedral was originally elaborately stencilled and traces can still be seen on the timber lined collar-beam roof. Contemporary descriptions record that it was mostly decorated in red and black with some gold; the panels contained symbols of the evangelists. The upper part of the clerestory wall was painted in buff and decorated with red, the lower part in green. The spandrels of the arcade and the aisle walls were painted red with a decorative scheme of red, black and buff. The organ is in the apse with, in front of it, a modern Byzantine iconostasis of five pendant arches incorporating part of the original screen as balustrading. The original organ of the church was removed at the time of the closure in 1960 and sold to Chipperfield Parish Church in Buckinghamshire; it was manufactured by Thomas Lewis and Co. of London for £1,150. The bishop's throne is on the south side of the nave. The original octagonal timber pulpit is still in position. The 1877 stained glass in the west window is by Stephen Adam of Adam and Small. Despite the colourful icons which now adorn the walls, the interior of St Luke's Cathedral still has a slight feeling of presbyterian simplicity and severity.

The Cathedral Church of St Luke

The architecture of the cathedral is unremarkable, although Sellars made good use of a difficult sloping site. More interesting is the way in which a presbyterian church has been readily adapted for the beautiful and colourful liturgy of the Orthodox Church. This Greek Orthodox cathedral hidden among the hillside terraces of Dowanhill is a rather surprising discovery in Glasgow.

1 Young & Doak (1965): illus. 94.
2 *The Building News*, 12 October 1877.
3 ibid., 27 December 1878.
4 ibid., 3 January 1879.
5 ibid., 10 January 1879.
6 ibid., 17 January 1879.

The Cathedral Church of St Andrew

Diocese of Glasgow
(Roman Catholic Church)

After the repeal of the Penal Laws in 1792, Roman Catholics were allowed to worship freely in Scotland and the first purpose-built Roman Catholic church in Glasgow was erected in Gallowgate in 1797; it was superseded by the present cathedral in 1816.

St Andrew's Cathedral is located in the Saltmarket and St Enoch district of the city. It stands on the north bank of the River Clyde at the junction of Clyde Street and Dunlop Street. The cathedral was built in 1814–17, due to the efforts of Fr Andrew Scott, who came to Glasgow in 1805 and worked throughout south-west Scotland. He was made a bishop in 1828 and died in 1835. The architect was James Gillespie Graham (1777–1855) who designed the contemporary Roman Catholic cathedral Edinburgh. In 1889 the church was raised to the status of a cathedral for the diocese of Glasgow, during the episcopate of Archbishop Charles Eyre, previously vicar apostolic of the Western District. Renovation work was carried out in 1889, 1892 and 1904.

The cathedral is a very early example of the Gothic Revival style that dominated nineteenth century ecclesiastical architecture. 'Graham introduced a new standard of archaeological correctness into Scottish church architecture, in both plan (a tall nave and lower aisles, like those of a medieval church) and detail'.[1] The west front is not unlike a smaller version of King's College Chapel, Cambridge, but with added aisles and, because of its early nineteenth century date, an inevitable hint of late Gothick. The central doorway, with five orders of shafts and capitals, bears the architect's name and date on its soffit. The west door is framed by tall octagonal buttresses, panelled with tracery, that culminate in turrets on either side of the gable. The gable itself is surmounted by a tabernacle housing an effigy of St Andrew and outlined with an open quatrefoil parapet. The turrets had tall pinnacles which were removed for safety reasons during restoration work in 1952–4. Embattled parapets and tall pinnacles surmount the aisle walls. The façade windows have curvilinear tracery, the doorway a series of thin shafts, and mouldings of naturalistic oakleaf and acorn capitals in the style of the chapter house at Southwell Cathedral.

The west door gives access to a narthex, formed by a low space beneath the organ gallery. The narthex has a tierceron plaster vault with central rosette and a patterned tiled floor. A screened off 'crying room' (for noisy children rather than those in distress) separates the narthex from the nave. On the north side of the narthex is a door leading to a stair which gives access to the west gallery. On the south side is the former baptistery, now a bookshop. Marble holy water stoups can be seen on the north and south sides of the narthex, each surmounted with a scroll bearing an inscription in Latin from Psalm 51, verse 7, *asperges me domine hyssopo et mundabor* (Purge me with hyssop and I shall be clean).

The plan of the cathedral is a wide aisled nave with a clerestory and a very shallow polygonal apse. The nave had galleries until 1904, but only the west (organ) gallery survives; the organ pipework flanks the large clear west window. The nave has a plaster lierne vault with foliage bosses. At present, the ribs, originally painted a stone colour, are white on a pale cream background. The quadripartite aisle vaults are also plaster. The vaulting shafts descend through the clerestory to join the large clustered piers which land heavily and clumsily in the midst of the pews. The piers themselves are decorative plaster work concealing a stone centre; their unusual capitals depict a fringe of hanging leaves sheltering randomly distributed flowers. The sanctuary arch and apse vault ribs are heavily painted and gilded, in contrast with the restraint of the rest of the cathedral roof. The aisles have windows with stained glass representations of the apostles in quatrefoil openings. The pews are pine and have carved leaf ends and the cross of St Andrew; their layout ignores the structural division of nave and aisles, and they sweep through the arcades, swirling around the large piers, and into the aisles. The aisle floors are paved with red and yellow tiles. The Stations of the Cross are painted polychrome with applied metalwork within stone frames.

The east end of the cathedral, with its alabaster wall-panelling raised and curved in the centre and a gently curved tester over the altar, is much the same as it was in 1817. The wide and spacious apse is floored with a pinkish-grey marble with brown veining, but now completely covered by an unnecessary green carpet. The centrepiece of the east window takes the form of a rood. The flanking windows contain the armorial bearings of former bishops and archbishops of the diocese. The windows on either side depict St Patrick and St Brigid (a statement about the Irish origins of many Scottish Roman Catholics), and St Andrew and St Margaret.

The original sanctuary furnishings were designed by Peter Paul Pugin, a scion of the Pugin architectural dynasty, whose most famous member was Augustus Welby Northmore Pugin. The chapter stalls are oak and a matching nave altar was installed during a preliminary re-ordering in the 1980s; it was carved in oak in a simple Gothic style by Joseph MacNally. The original high altar of 1893 had an alabaster front and a traceried reredos with figures of St Andrew and St Paul, and formerly supported a jewel-encrusted brass tabernacle. In 1997 the high altar was dismantled and parts of it were used to construct a new permanent nave altar. The tabernacle is currently in store and awaiting a new home. The pulpit is of pink and red marble with brown veined onyx.

The elaborately canopied and pinnacled side altars, also both by Peter Paul Pugin, date from 1892. The wooden dividing screens were added by Pugin in 1904. On the north side is the altar of the Sacred Heart; on the south, where the Blessed Sacrament is reserved, the Lady Altar. The altars are screened by low (presumably stone, but now painted) communion rails with caps of red marble and little brass gates. The Decorated-style cup font of 1867, with decorative red marble shafts, stands at the junction of the Sacred Heart chapel and the sanctuary.

The cathedral today looks much as it did when finished in 1817, although an aborted plan in the 1970s by Wagner Associates envisaged extending the cathedral to the south in a completely unsympathetic modern style.

Cathedral House at the north-east corner was built c.1986 of yellow concrete blocks. On the north side of the cathedral is a former factory, refaced and refurbished with much reflective glass in 1988 as the headquarters of the archdiocese of Glasgow.

This confident little building is more like a well-used small parish church than the cathedral church of a metropolitan see. But there is something attractive about this rectangular, stocky and symmetrical cathedral, on its riverside site, seemingly defiant of the powerful waters of the Clyde that pass within two hundred yards of its front door.

1 Williamson, Riches & Higgs (1990): p. 193.

Inverness

The Cathedral Church of St Andrew

United Dioceses of Moray, Ross and Caithness
(Scottish Episcopal Church)

Inverness, popularly called the 'capital of the Highlands', is a town of 40,000 people on the east cost of Scotland, 251km north-west of Edinburgh, and lies at the point where the River Ness and the Beauly Firth merge to become Moray Firth. This geographical feature is echoed in the name of the town, which means 'mouth of the Ness'.

Although there was a Dominican friary here by the reign of King Alexander II (1214–49), there is no record of the date of its foundation, nor of any ancient Celtic or Culdee settlement. St Adomnán, biographer of St Columba, says that the latter visited the Pictish king Brude c.565 at a castle 'near the Ness', but there is no evidence that he established any kind of religious house there. The castle may have been at Craig Phadrig, the site of an Iron and Dark Ages fort, 3.2km west of Inverness, or possibly an early predecessor of Macbeth's eleventh century stronghold on Auld Castle Hill, to the east of the present Castle Hill. A new castle was founded on the site of the present castle, either by King Malcolm III (1058–93) in 1057, or King David I (1124–53) in c.1140, and the town was significant enough for the latter king to grant it a charter as a royal burgh. The present castle, standing on a rocky outcrop above the east bank of the Ness, has nothing to do with those remote ages. In all its romantic prettiness, it is clearly a nineteenth-century castellar folly.

The River Ness bisects the city from north to south, the main part of the city, sheltered by the castle lying on the east bank. The episcopal cathedral stands on a beautiful site on the west bank, across the river from the castle. It is a handsome and rose-coloured nineteenth century building, serving the united dioceses of Moray, Ross and Caithness.

The construction of the cathedral was due to the vision and effort of Robert Eden, scion of a distinguished family from County Durham. Eden was the third son of Sir Frederick Morton Eden (1766–1808), author of a magisterial three-volume work entitled *The State of the Poor* published in 1797; he was also a grand-nephew of the 1st Lord Auckland (1784–1849), governor-general of India 1835–41 and a great-uncle of the 1st earl of Avon (1897–1977), better known as Sir Anthony Eden, prime minister of the United Kingdom 1955–7.

Eden was elected bishop of Moray and Ross in 1851. He was rector of Leigh-on-Sea in Essex at the time of his election by the clergy of this far-flung diocese. The title 'bishop of Moray, Ross and Caithness' sounds impressive enough, and evokes pictures of the entire north-east of Scotland, and memories of the three former cathedrals of Elgin, Fortrose and Dornoch. But at the time of Eden's election, the united dioceses of Moray and Ross were nothing if not a missionary region. In accepting the election and moving to Scotland, Eden exchanged an annual stipend of £500–600 for one of £150. His vast diocese had only ten churches, seven priests, two parsonages and five hundred members. But Eden was a missionary and a builder, and quite undaunted. During his episcopate, the number of clergy rose to twenty-three and the numbers of the laity from five hundred to thirteen hundred; and he quadrupled the income of the see. In 1854 he re-established episcopalian congregations at Wick and Thurso in the north-eastern county of Caithness, and from 1864 he was styled bishop of Moray, Ross and Caithness. He was elected primus of the Episcopal Church in 1862, retired in 1886 and died in 1888 after several years of ill-health.

Like most of his predecessors as bishops of Moray, Eden had begun his episcopate by residing at Elgin, the historic see of the diocese, and taking charge of a congregation there. But he decided that Inverness, the highland capital, would be a more appropriate centre for his highland diocese, and he went to live in the city in 1853. Eden's position at Inverness was sensitive and sometimes difficult. He had been elected bishop of the diocese by only five votes to two, and the two votes had been cast for the incumbent of St John's Church, Inverness, who steadfastly refused to recognise Eden's authority. The new bishop's election had divided the congregation of St John's, which was the largest in the diocese at the time, and Eden's supporters left St John's to provide the nucleus of a new congregation which grew rapidly in numbers. Mindful of the difficulties surrounding his own election as bishop, Eden argued at the General Synod of the church in 1862 for the inclusion of lay electors in the electoral process. The debate was heated, but Eden's arguments won the day.

In 1865 Bishop Eden decided that the time had come to provide his three dioceses with a focal point – a cathedral church. He had thought of building a cathedral at Inverness on his arrival there in 1853 and a design was prepared by the architect R C Carpenter; at this stage it was little more than a dream. He was new to the city; his arrival divided the only episcopalian congregation there; and he was faced with the hostility of the incumbent of St John's. The Episcopal Church was small and poor, and there was no immediate prospect of building a cathedral church in those early days. But the new bishop had a vision and was intent on implementing it, and he generated enthusiasm among his small flock. He began in 1853 with a small cottage, fitted up as a mission chapel, on the bank of the river. By 1866 he had raised £20,000 and the foundation stone of the cathedral was laid on 17 October that year by Charles Longley, archbishop of Canterbury.

Archbishop Longley was a close friend of Bishop Eden and his High Church leanings made him naturally sympathetic to the Scottish Episcopal Church; but his visit to Inverness was an historic milestone. Throughout the eighteenth and early nineteenth centuries, the Scottish Episcopal Church had endured an underground and furtive existence. Although the Penal Laws against episcopalians had been repealed in 1792, the Church of England, was for long wary of acknowledging the existence of its sister church in Scotland for fear of jeopardising relations with the Church of Scotland. The Scottish Episcopal Church could, after all, be construed to be the sister church of the Nonjuring Church in England (which had died out by the beginning of the nineteenth century) and therefore a 'rebel' church.

Longley's visit to Inverness was the first occasion on which a Primate of All England had, at least implicitly, recognised the Scottish Episcopal Church as the sister church of the Church of England in such a public way. The archbishop was inevitably criticised in certain quarters. At the banquet following the laying of the foundation stone, he publicly declared that the Scottish Episcopal Church was 'the only representative of the Church of England in Scotland'.[1] *The Times* pompously described the gesture as an insult to the majority of the Scottish nation and accused the archbishop of siding with a nonconformist church. 'An archbishop of Canterbury is the very pinnacle of Establishment in the most establised Church in the world; and Mr Spurgeon [a well known contemporary Baptist minister] in the character of an archbishop would not be a greater anomaly than the archbishop in the character of a dissenter'.[2] The *Scottish Guardian* obliquely invoked Queen Victoria in remarking that the archbishop's action was not kindly regarded in 'quarters higher than Printing House Square'. In fact the archbishop's visit was long overdue and it marked the point at which the English bishops at last began to recognise that they shared a common heritage with the consecrated successors of the Scottish bishops expelled from their sees in 1689.

The cathedral was dedicated on 1 September 1869, the inaugural sermons being preached by the bishops of Oxford and Rochester. It was tribute to Eden that both bishops were willing to travel so far to the north for such an occasion. In his sermon Bishop Wilberforce of Oxford paid tribute to Eden. 'His power of surmounting obstacles was just that of his ability at school to jump over anything that he could reach with his nose'.[3] Further acknowledgement of Eden's reputation came in 1870 when Archbishop Longley chose the new cathedral in Inverness for the consecration of Allan Becher Webb, second bishop of the South African diocese of Bloemfontein.

The cathedral was not inexpensive; without stained glass, organ or furnishings, the structure cost £15,106 0s 4¾d; and at its opening in 1869 there was a debt of £6,835. Not until it was free from debt did Bishop Eden solemnly consecrate his cathedral church, on 29 September 1874, and Inverness Cathedral became the first complete cathedral to be built on a new site in Britain since the sixteenth century reformation. In the morning, the sermon was preached by William Alexander, bishop of Derry and Raphoe, and in the evening by Henry Douglas, bishop of Bombay. The partly triumphalist and partly dismissive comments in Alexander's sermon were typical of their time. 'As we rejoice with exceeding great joy in the consecration of this fair cathedral… None of us wish to speak lightly or hardly of the form of the Christian religion prevalent around you… I supposed that the presbyterian establishment has done much for this land… But in the days of fierce trial which are plainly coming upon Christianity itself, our church seems to have the possibility at least of performing a function here, which she alone can adequately fulfil'.[4] His comments may owe something to the fact that Alexander was himself a bishop in a minority church (the Church of Ireland) which had been disestablished only three years earlier, in 1871.

Inverness Cathedral was built to the design of Alexander Ross (1834–1925), who had designed a number of episcopalian churches in Scotland and Skibo Castle for Andrew Carnegie. In 1872, he was runner-up to Sir George Gilbert Scott in the competition to design an episcopal cathedral for the diocese of Edinburgh.

The cathedral is built in the Decorated Gothic style of pink Conon sandstone with dressings of cream Covosea freestone and a roof of green Westmoreland slates. The nave roof formerly had cast iron ridges at the apex and a flêche above the crossing; these were taken down in 1963 for structural reasons. The ridge was replaced by green tiles and the flêche by a copper Celtic cross by William Glashan. Although the building looks and is complete, Ross's original design provided for a more ambitious east end with a chancel extending 16.4m beyond the end of the present chancel, a semi-circular apse with an ambulatory around it, and flying buttresses.

The cathedral is nominally cruciform, but the transepts barely project beyond the aisles and the building is essentially a rectangle with a polygonal apse, and an octagonal chapter house at the north-east corner. The cathedral measures 50.5m in external length, 21.9m wide at the west front, and 26.8m high to the ridge of the roof. The twin west towers are 30.4m high and were intended to be surmounted by 30.4m spires. The west front is dignified and slightly French in style. 'Perhaps a little like Notre Dame. Admittedly bijou… it is on a good site and is as complete as any other cathedral in its appurtenances'.[5] The main double west door, again reminiscent of Notre Dame, is deeply recessed and divided by a single polished granite pier. On either side are statues of St Andrew, St Peter, St Paul and St John the Baptist. The tympanum above the door, depicting Christ blessing the Apostles, was designed by Thomas Earp and added in 1875. The north tower houses a peal of ten bells and a service bell. Cast by John Warner and Sons of Cripplegate, London, they were restored and re-hung in 1973 as a memorial to Bishop Duncan Macinnes (1953–70).

The four-bay nave is tall, wide and rather dark and measures 27m long and 30m wide. The impressive crossing arches rise almost to the ridge of the boarded Gothic arched roof, which is marked out with black patterns intended for coloured stencilling. The arcades rest on polished pink Peterhead granite cylindrical piers with foliage capitals. The clerestory is formed of triplet windows above the apex of each arch. The carved heads of various nineteenth century worthies, including Queen Victoria, can be seen at the springing of the nave arcades. On the north side are Bishop Arthur Maclean (1904–43) and Alexander Ross, and on the south side, Bishop James Kelly (1886–1904) and Bishop Eden. At the west end, a three-bay stone arcade separates the entrance lobby and supports a west gallery. The floors of the nave and chancel are polychromatic tilework.

Most of the cathedral stained glass is by John Hardman of Birmingham and was installed between 1867 and 1910. The glass was restored by Hardman in 1989. The clerestory glass is by Powell of London.

At the west end of the north nave aisle, a bust and white marble tablet commemorate Bishop Eden. Further east is a group of five nineteenth century Russian icons, three of which are said to have been given to Eden by Tsar Alexander II during a visit to Russia in 1866. Bishop Eden went to Russia partly to confirm expatriates and partly to attempt to establish communion with the Russian Orthodox Church. There had been earlier signs that the Russian church might be willing to establish communion with the Scottish Episcopal Church, but the Russian Synod decided not to proceed for fear of jeopardising relations with the Church of England. The picture of the Virgin and the Holy Child, with Franciscan saints, is a photograph of a fifteenth century painting by Sano di Pietro.

The north transept houses the poorly furnished Lady Chapel and was set out as such in 1900. The picture of the Madonna and Child is a nineteenth century copy of an original by Raphael. There is a cartouche memorial to Bishop William Hay of Moray (1688–1707) on the north wall. Hay was a much respected figure who retired to Inverness after his expulsion from the living of St Giles', Elgin, the pro-cathedral of the diocese of Moray. Despite the removal of the bishops from the established church in 1689, Hay never ceased to think of himself as bishop of Moray and was so regarded by congregations who remained loyal to the episcopate. After the deaths of Bishop Andrew Wood of Caithness in 1694, Bishop James Ramsay of Ross in 1696 and Bishop Andrew Bruce of Orkney in 1699, Hay became the last remaining bishop in the north of Scotland, and exercised episcopal oversight of the vacant dioceses as well as his own. Men travelled from as far as Orkney down to Inverness to seek ordination at the hands of the aged bishop. As late as 1706 the moderator of the synod of Orkney was instructed to write to the presbytery of Forres and Elgin urging that 'the pretended bishop of Moray be represented to the assemblie for the licensing of many profane youths ever since the abolition of that order'.[6] The cartouche was erected in the Old High Kirk of Inverness by the bishop's son-in-law and was removed when that church was rebuilt in 1769–72. Put up for auction in 1887, it was purchased and erected here in the new cathedral church of the diocese of which Hay had been bishop. The transept also houses a modern bronze of the risen Christ. The Blessed Sacrament is reserved in an aumbry beyond. An iron grill behind the altar leads to the cathedral sacristy and from there to the chapter house, neither of which is open to the public.

The pulpit, carved by local craftsmen in 1869 and typical of its time, is of Caen stone with green Irish marble colonettes, on three pillars of pink Abriachan granite. It has panels depicting St John preaching in the wilderness, Christ as the Good Shepherd, and St Andrew preaching from his saltire cross.

The oak screen and rood across the western crossing arch divide the nave from the ritual choir, which incorporates the crossing. The screen is the work of Sir Robert Lorimer and was erected in 1923 as a memorial to members of the congregation who died in the First World War. The screen has heavy ogee arches carved with fruit resting on emaciated and fragile spiralled columns. The brass lectern on the south side was presented in 1869.

The canopied and richly carved choir stalls were designed by C Hodgson Fowler and Alexander Ross, carved from Austrian oak and installed in 1909 as a memorial to Bishop James Kelly (1886–1904), Bishop Eden's successor. The bishop's throne was made by Andrew Fraser in 1869 and has carved angels at the corners of the canopy. The stalls are arranged and labelled as follows:

	The Cathedra
S. Marnanus	S. Moluocus
Cancellarius	Registrarius
S. Fergus	S. Kentigernus
S. Dubthach	Auditor/S. Gilbertus
S. Donnanus	S. Gervadius
S. Aidanus	Canonicus/S. Malruba
Canonicus/S. Drostanus	Canonicus/S. Brigida
Clericus Synodi	Decanus
S. Finnbhar	S. Margareta Reg.
S. Patricius	S. Adamnus
Cantor	Praepositus
S. Ninianus	S. Columba

The apsidal chancel is 18m long. The altar rail and panelling in the apse are by J Alistair Ross (c.1945), son of the cathedral's architect. The altar (the gift of Bishop Eden) and the reredos date from 1869 and are made from Caen stone, Devonshire marble and alabaster. The front of the altar has panels depicting the Agnus Dei and the Pelican in her piety, but these are usually concealed by a frontal. The three deep set panels of the reredos depict the Agony in the Garden, the Crucifixion and the Resurrection. The wood panelling on either side of the altar and reredos was installed in 1951 in memory of Bishop Arthur Maclean. The floor is covered with Minton tiles and includes representations of the sacrifice of Abel and the Passover; the standard candlesticks were presented in 1931. The stained glass in the apse windows depicts, from left to right (in a rather confused chronology), the Agony in the Garden and Pilate presenting Christ to the crowd; the Crucifixion and Christ carrying the Cross; and the Scourging and Trial. The triple sedilia on the south wall, with pillars of Cawdor granite, dates from 1871. An aumbry is set into the north wall. The boarded ceilings of the chancel and crossing have original but now faded stencilled patterns.

The south transept is largely occupied by the organ, a Hill instrument of 1869 with three manuals and thirty stops; it was rebuilt in 1928 but needs further restoration work. Finance has never allowed the erection of a suitable organ case, despite various plans for one. Behind the organ is a vestry, not open to the public. At the east end of the south nave aisle, in front of the organ, is the chapel of St Andrew. The white ensign, that hangs in the aisle, was formerly on the Cenotaph in Whitehall, London. It was given to the cathedral by the trustees of the Imperial War Museum in 1963.

The west window, reputed to be one of the largest in Scotland, depicts Christ in glory at the last judgement, and forms the diocese's memorial to Bishop Eden. The ground floor of the south tower forms the baptistery and the stained glass follows that theme: the work of St John the Baptist, Christ at the well of Samaria, and Christ blessing the children. The white marble angel and shell font is an 1871 copy, by Frank Redfern, of Bertel Thorvaldsen's font in Copenhagen Cathedral; the angel's face is a portrait of Mrs Learmonth of Dean, whose husband paid for the work. Bishop Eden had seen the original font on his journey to Russia in 1866. Another copy of Thorvaldsen's font can be seen in St Giles' Cathedral in Edinburgh. Redfern carved the statues on the west front of Salisbury Cathedral.

Along the north side of the cathedral is a pleasant walk along the bank of the Ness. The corbels over the Lady Chapel window commemorate the pony and pulley wheel used for lifting the stone to build the cathedral. At the north-east corner of the cathedral is the diminutive octagonal chapter house, modelled on the chapter house at Elgin Cathedral.

'Whatever else one may say about Ross's design at Inverness it is that of a cathedral, while the existing episcopal seat in Aberdeen could easily be mistaken for just one more of the Gothic revival kirks with which the 'Granite City' is plentifully supplied'.[7] The judgement is trivial and hardly worth repeating, because, despite the exquisite decoration of its interior, poor Aberdeen simply does not have the fine location of Inverness. Inverness Cathedral sails rhythmically along the tree-shrouded west bank of the Ness. Here is a charming and peaceful sight that evokes a sense of solidity and tranquillity at the same time. Bishop Eden must have been well pleased.

1 Carpenter, Edward (1971): p. 323.
2 ibid.
3 Lochhead, M (1966): p. 139.
4 Alexander, W & Douglas, H (1874): p. 10.
5 Fenwick, Hubert (1978): p. 262.
6 Craven, J B (19121): p. 5.
7 Fenwick, Hubert (1978): p. 262.

Iona

The Cathedral Church of St Mary
(Church of Scotland)

Iona is an austere, bare and windswept island 4.8km long and 2.4km wide, lying 2km south-west of the Isle of Mull off the west coast of Scotland, on the very edge of the Atlantic Ocean. Access is by ferry from Oban to Craignure, then a drive across Mull to Fionnphort, then a further ferry across the one mile wide Sound of Iona to the island itself. The cathedral and the monastery stand are within easy walking distance, on the east coast of the island overlooking the Sound.

From evidence found on the site of the small hill fort at Dùn Cùl Bhuig, on the west coast of the island, Iona was occupied during the Iron Age, but the settlement was only in use from the first century BC to the third century AD, and Iona was probably uninhabited when St Columba (521–97) arrived on the island about the year 564. Columba is said to have landed on 12 May that year at Port-na-Churaich at the southern end of the island, with twelve companions. He is supposed to have settled on Iona because it was the first island from which he could not see his homeland of Ireland.

The name 'Iona' has a complicated etymology. The Gaelic name for the island is *I Chaluim Cille* (I of Colum Cille). The name *I* derives from an ancient Celtic word for 'yew tree', and *Colum Cille* (Columba of the churches) commemorates the reputation of the saint as the founder of churches. Columba's biographer, St Adomnán, used the Latin form *Ioua insula*, 'the yewy island'. Iona is a medieval mistranslation of Ioua.

Although Irish by birth, Columba is the most famous of the saints of Scotland and the monastery that he founded on Iona acquired an international reputation. His missionary journeys extended throughout the whole of the north of Scotland and even during his lifetime the island's aura of holiness attracted pilgrims. Columba died on 9 June 597 and his remains were at first buried in the Reilig Odhráin (see below). Later they were exhumed and kept in a shrine, at first on Iona but then, about 850, taken to Dunkeld for fear of Viking attacks, and then to Ireland and reburied at Downpatrick.

The details of Columba's life are known from the biography written about 700 by one of his successors, St Adomnán, who became abbot of Iona in 679. Adomnán's description of Columba is famous: 'He had the face of an angel; he was of excellent nature, polished in speech, holy in deed, great in counsel… loving unto all'. Adomnán was concerned only to demonstrate Columba's depth of spirituality and was not greatly interested in the chronological facts of his life, and all subsequent biographies are worthless pieces of hagiography. But there is no doubt that Columba's life and work established Iona's reputation as a centre of piety and scholarship. His feast day is kept on 9 June, the day of his death.

Columba's monastery covered a much larger area than the present abbey precincts. The monastic enclosure measured 335m by 152m and the remains of the perimeter earthwork can still be seen, running north to just west of the road, then turning east across the field to the north of the abbey. The buildings of the monastery were constructed mostly of timber and turf and were frequently rebuilt during the two centuries following Columba's time.

The life of the monastery was drastically changed by the Viking raids, which began at the end of the eighth century, in the time of Abbot Bressal (c.770–801). Peaceful monastic settlements were often treasure houses and easy prey for the predatory Norsemen. A settled monastic life became impossible and the community left Iona in 804 and settled at Kells in Ireland. A small community either remained or returned to the island, but the Viking threat continued and the rebuilt monastery was probably not large. Little is known of Iona in the succeeding four centuries of the Dark Ages. The island was not completely abandoned, and tradition claims that St Margaret, wife of King Malcolm III (1058–93) contributed to the rebuilding of the monastery. There is no evidence for this and there is no trace of any building on the island dating from the time of the queen. The story was probably born of a desire to connect a holy woman with a holy island.

In 1098 Iona (with the rest of the diocese of the Isles) passed under Norwegian rule and, ecclesiastically, into the archdiocese of Trondheim, where it remained until 1266. The abbey was refounded as a Benedictine house in about 1203 by Reginald, Lord of Argyll. It was a small monastery, but the Columban foundation ensured its pre-eminence. Iona was highly regarded in the annals of Scotland and many minor chiefs and nobles from the surrounding islands were buried on Iona at the cemetery of Reilig Odhráin: King Macbeth (1040–57), whose fame is largely Shakespearean, was one of the last. In 1247, Pope Innocent IV granted the abbot of Iona the right to wear a mitre and ring, and other episcopal privileges, because of the distance from Norway. In 1289 Pope Nicholas IV confirmed that the abbot of Iona was free of the jurisdiction of the bishop of the Isles and subject only to the authority of the papacy.

The history of Iona in the fifteenth century is not very edifying. Such was the status and reputation of the island, that members of the monastic community were drawn increasingly from the aristocratic families of Mull and the Isles. The monastery appears to have gone to ruin during the time of Abbot Fingon Mackinnon (1358–c.1408), who was more interested in the secular politics of the Isles than in the life of his own abbey. By 1403 the abbey had collapsed and the buildings were still in ruins in 1428. For many years the abbey appears to have been little more than a private estate of the Mackinnon family. Both Abbot John Macallister (c.1408–21) and Abbot Dominic Mackenzie (1421–65) had considerable difficulty first in reducing and then eradicating the influence of the Mackinnons. In 1428 Abbot Dominic turned his attention to the work of restoring the fabric of the monastery. A major restoration of the abbey church was carried out, and the building as it stands today, disregarding the twentieth century restoration, is much as he left it.

The ecclesiastical status of Iona mirrored the changing political status of the region. Geographically, it lay within the diocese of the Isles, which in turn was subject to the Norwegian archdiocese of Trondheim. Norwegian control of the Isle of Man ended about 1265 and from then until about 1330 control of the island alternated between England and Scotland. English rule was permanently established in about 1330 and the bishops of the Isles became suffragans to the archbishops of York. A separate line of Scottish bishops of the Isles appeared from 1331 when the clergy of Skye elected a bishop to rule the Scottish part of the diocese of the Isles. The Great Schism of the papacy from 1378 institutionalised separate lines of Scottish bishops of the Isles ruling from St Columba's Island in the River Snizort at Skeabost on the Isle of Skye, and English bishops of the Isles ruling from Peel on the Isle of Man.

Skeabost is a remote and lonely place, although of Columban foundation, and the abbot of Iona had more lands, prestige and influence than the bishop of the Isles. In 1493, the Macdonald lordship of the Isles was forfeited and the abbey lost its principal protector against interference from the bishop. In 1498, the earl of Argyll petitioned Pope Alexander VI to establish the abbey church as the cathedral church for the diocese, 'quil his princpall kirk in the Ile of Man be recoverit fra Inglismen'.[1] The petition was not granted, but when the abbacy fell vacant in 1499, Bishop John Campbell of the Isles (1487–1510) was appointed commendator of Iona, with the right to enjoy the revenues of the abbey, but with no obligation to take Benedictine vows. From about 1506, at least until 1561, the abbey church was the cathedral church of the diocese.

Despite its fame, Iona was not spared from the destructive tendency of the sixteenth century reformation. Much of beauty and value was destroyed, including the fine library. The monastic community seems to have withered away and the last monk died in 1600. For much of the sixteenth century, Iona was subject to rivalry between the Campbells of Argyll and the Macleans of Duart, the latter gaining possession of the abbey lands in 1580. Although an intermittent succession of bishops of the Isles, many of them Campbells, continued until 1638, the abbey and cathedral were allowed to decay. The eastern parts of the cathedral were repaired in 1635–8 by order of King Charles I, with a grant of £600, but it was only a temporary respite, and there are hardly any remaining traces of the work that was done in those years. The King ordered the Maclean of Duart to contribute £400 towards the restoration; and Bishop John Leslie (1628–33) was ordered to return the two bells that he had removed from the bell tower at Iona on his translation to the diocese of Raphoe in Ireland. The expulsion of Bishop Neil Campbell (1633–8), and the beginning of the civil war, ended any further restoration work. Local attempts to maintain the cathedral as the parish church of the island fared no better. There were four further bishops of the Isles, from 1662 to 1689, but whatever their authority in and over the island of Iona, nothing was done to arrest the decay of the cathedral and the abbey, which continued steadily throughout the eighteenth century and early nineteenth centuries.

Iona remained in the ownership of the Macleans of Duart until 1691. The Macleans weakened their position by remaining loyal to the deposed King James VII (1685–9). The Campbell earl of Argyll seized the island in 1691 and Iona remained in the possession of the Campbells until 1979. From the mid-eighteenth century successive dukes of Argyll came to appreciate the significance of their island possession. In 1757, the third duke ordered his tenants to construct a wall around the precincts of the abbey to prevent their cattle from sheltering in the ruins; and refused to renew their leases until they did so. In 1797 the fifth duke ordered his tenants to cease using the abbey and cathedral as a stone quarry.

The first signs of interest in Iona came with a steady stream of visitors from the late eighteenth century onwards. Dr Samuel Johnson and James Boswell visited Iona in 1773 and were shocked to find the nunnery church full of dung and used as a cow house, and the cathedral 'so incumbered with mud and rubbish, that we could make no discoveries of curious inscriptions'.[2]

Some early visitors to Iona have left descriptions of what was long thought to be the mensa of the high altar. It was made from white marble veined with grey, and measured 1.8m by 1.2m. Sacheverell saw it in 1688 and described it as 'one of the finest pieces of white marble I ever saw… curiously veined and polished, it is all entire, except one corner'.[3] It acquired the reputation of possessing a charm against shipwreck and was gradually chipped away until there was nothing left. John Campbell, visiting Iona in 1749, found it 'much broke at one corner by the Country People, who imagine it to be a relict of St Colm and conclude it an antidote for any disease in man or beast, and especially the flux'.[4] When Pennant visited the island in 1772 he found that 'a very small portion is now left; and even that we contributed to diminish'.[5] In 1773 Dr Johnson spoke of it as 'destroyed'; by 1846 it had 'totally disappeared'.[6] The sole remaining known fragment, formerly in St Andrew's Episcopal Church in Glasgow,[7] is now (since 1975) in St James' Episcopal Church, Springburn, Glasgow. Although of Iona marble, the surface is now too worn to indicate anything else. There is no certainty that the original slab was the mensa of the high altar; its proportions would have been too small for that purpose. It may have been used for one of the smaller side altars, or it may have been part of a composite mensa.

With the nineteenth century renewal of interest in medieval architecture, various voices were raised in warning about the deteriorating state of the monastic complex. Allan Maclean, the island's longest serving schoolmaster (1796–1836), also acted as a guide to the ruins and made some efforts to clear the debris and look after the monuments, much like John Shanks, his contemporary at Elgin Cathedral. In 1854 a call was made for the cathedral tower to be re-roofed and for the nunnery church and St Oran's Church to be stabilised. The same author warned of 'the occasional depredations of specimen collectors or relique-hunters'.[8] In 1874–6 some repair work, under the supervision of Sir Rowland Anderson, was carried out to the cathedral and the nunnery church on the instructions of the duke of Argyll. The work included the clearing of the interiors of the churches and the excavation of the foundations of the abbey ruins, which were little more than green mounds.

In 1893 the duke granted land to the Scottish Episcopal Church for a retreat house. In 1888, and again

The Cathedral Church of St Mary (from the west)

in 1897 – the one thousand four hundredth anniversary of the death of St Columba – the eighth duke of Argyll allowed Roman Catholic pilgrimages to celebrate mass in the cathedral ruins. Also in 1897, the General Assembly of the Church of Scotland celebrated the anniversary of Columba in the cathedral. 'A canvas roof was stretched over the Cathedral, the rank grass was cut, and chairs for over three hundred worshippers were placed on Nature's carpet of soft turf... In the opening services, Gaelic was used by those dignitaries of the Scottish Church who are familiar with the Celtic tongue'.[9] The celebrations began with a preparatory service at 7pm on 8 June, followed by a service in Gaelic on the morning of 9 June, the principal service, in English, at noon and a concluding service on the evening of the same day.

The duke was a sensitive custodian of Iona; in 1870 and in 1889 he published highly romanticised, poetic and mystical accounts of the Columban history of the island, and in 1899 he gave the site 'to be used for public worship, under the trusteeship of a moderator, clerks of Assemblies, the ministers of Glasgow and St Giles' Cathedrals, and others, with the proviso that, at times the Cathedral might be granted to other religious communities for services of worship'.[10] The body was to be known as the Iona Cathedral Trust and was charged with re-roofing the cathedral church and re-using it for worship.

The chancel and transepts of the cathedral were restored in 1902–5, followed by the nave in 1909–10, to a design by John Honeyman (who had restored Brechin Cathedral in 1900–2), Thomas Ross and P Macgregor Chalmers. Regular summer services began again in the cathedral on 16 July 1905 and a special service on 16 June 1910 marked the completion of the restoration. From 1910 until 1939, whilst their own church was being renovated, the cathedral was used by the island's Church of Scotland congregation.

A second and significant phase began in 1938 with the restoration of the remainder of the abbey under the supervision of Ian Lindsay and the newly-established Iona Community. The community was the result of the vision of George Macleod, minister of a Church of Scotland parish in the Govan district of Glasgow. Macleod resigned from his parish and went to Iona with twelve young men; half were craftsmen and half were new ministers who had just finished their theological training. 'His plan was that, before young ministers went out into urban parishes, they should work alongside craftsmen on the physical renewal of what had once been the living quarters of Iona's religious community. The task would symbolise the need for spiritual renewal, for bridging the gap between church and daily life'.[11] Macleod believed that the way to new life in the church would be found by people, ministers and industrial workers living and working together. Macleod retired from the leadership of the community in 1967 and was granted a life peerage in the same year, taking the title of Baron Macleod of Fuinary. He died in 1991 at the age of 96.

Why was the rebuilding of the abbey on the island of Iona chosen for this semi-monastic experiment? Firstly, because it was felt to be a task that would appeal both to the clergy and to the craftsmen, and it was a task that could be carried out within a reasonable time, working only in the summer months. Secondly, 'it was a shame to many that this place of Columba's landing... should preserve sacred memories in ruins except for the Abbey Church, used at that time only for Sunday services in the summer'. Thirdly, 'there was a very practical reason: perhaps the very reasons why Columba chose Iona and other Celtic saints chose other islands. It is much easier to build up a new community life in a place that is fairly inaccessible and offers few distractions'.[12]

In the summer of 1938 the new Iona Community lived, ate and slept in one hut which had already been erected, while they spent their time laying the foundations and then erecting the huts which were to be the home of the community for eighteen years, until the east range of the monastic buildings had been finished in 1956. The chapter house, with the little library above its vault, was completed in 1940, the intention being that something complete should stand during the war years as a memorial to a dream.[13] Work did in fact continue slowly during the war years, although there was a fear that each summer would be the last. The community was only a token one for the duration of the war, and in one year, it consisted of Macleod, one other minister, and one mason. It was not altogether well received in more traditional presbyterian circles because it *was* so untraditional, as well as being a 'community' with echoes of monasticism. In 1951, after several years of considerable argument, the General Assembly of the Church of Scotland resolved 'to bring the Iona Community within the organisation and jurisdiction of the Church and to integrate it with the life of the Church'.[14]

The cathedral and the abbey are now owned by the Iona Cathedral Trust. The island itself remained in the possession of the dukes of Argyll until 1979 when it was sold to pay death duties incurred by the death of the eleventh duke in 1973. The island was purchased by Sir Hugh Fraser who presented it to the National Trust for Scotland in memory of his father, Lord Fraser of Allander (1903–66).

The Nunnery Church

The roofless Nunnery Church was built in the first quarter of the thirteenth century, but the cloister and conventual buildings to the south are late medieval additions. The convent was established as a house of Augustinian canonesses by Reginald, Lord of the Isles, in 1203. Very little is known of its history from the thirteenth to the sixteenth centuries. Prioress Anna Maclean died in 1543 and was succeeded in 1548 by Marion or Mary Maclean who held it through the reformation, secured confirmation of her position from the Crown in 1567 and finally surrendered the temporalities to Hector Maclean of Duart in 1574. The buildings had been reduced to their present state by the 1760s, except for the east vault and chancel which collapsed in 1830. In 1874 the eighth duke of Argyll began a programme of clearing the site and in 1899 he transferred the buildings to the Iona Cathedral Trust. Plans for a full restoration were prepared by P Macgregor Chalmers in 1917 but, sadly, the scheme was abandoned beyond repairs to the north chapel in 1922 and the laying out of the cloister garden.

The church measures 17.6m by 6m and is built partly of red granite and partly of dark grey rubble. It comprises a nave, with an aisle, adjoining which is the Lady Chapel still with some of its vaulting. The three Romanesque arcades dividing the nave from the aisle were filled in at an early date, and the springing of the aisle vaults can still be seen. To the south of the church are the remains of the cloister court, chapter house and refectory.

The church was described by Thomas Pennant in 1772: 'The roof of the east end is entire... a pretty vault made of very thin stones... The floor is covered some feet thick with cow-dung; this place being at present the common shelter for the cattle; and the islanders are too lazy to remove this fine manure, the collection of a century, to enrich their grounds. With much difficulty, by virtue of fair words, and a bribe, prevale of one of these listless fellows to remove a great quantity of the dung-hill; and by that means once more expose to light the tomb of the last prioress. Her figure is cut on the face of the stone; and angel on each side supports her head; and above them is a little plate and a comb'.[15] This was the tombstone of Prioress Anna Maclean; it can be seen in the Abbey Museum housed in the Church of St Ronan.

The Church and Cemetery of St Ronan

The thirteenth century Church of St Ronan, to the north of the Nunnery Church and within the same enclosure, has been re-roofed and now serves as a museum to house the many carved stones once scattered around the island. St Ronan's Church was the medieval

The Cathedral Church of St Mary (from the south-east)

parish church of Iona and was probably abandoned at the time of the partial restoration of the cathedral in the 1630s. There are a number of tombs of nuns and priests, including that of Prioress Anna Maclean. Her effigy in hood and cloak occupies one half of the slab, the remainder being broken away. When the church was visited in the late 1840s, the roof of the east end of the nunnery church had just fallen in, 'breaking off the lower half of this stone, which has either been taken away, or is lost in the rubbish'.[16] St Ronan's Church was restored as a museum of carved stones in 1923, and was reorganised in 1993.

Maclean's Cross

This late fifteenth-century high cross stands close to the former junction of three medieval streets. It is 3.3m high and the western face has a representation of the Crucifixion; the eastern side is covered with an intricate Celtic design.

The Parish Church and Manse

The parish church and manse were designed by Thomas Telford, built in 1828 and re-ordered in 1938. There appears to have been no parish church on the island, after the abandonment of St Ronan's Church, until 1828, and the present buildings were constructed in accordance with an act of parliament of 1824 which provided funds for new churches and manses to be built in the highlands. The interior of the church is exceptionally dull and of no interest, and much the same opinion was held in the nineteenth century. 'Scarcely one tourist ever thinks of taking a peep inside, and no photographer would waste time upon such an abortion... Pulpit and pews have never been painted, the exception being the minister's seat, having a little table in the centre painted the complexion of an orange'.[17] John Campbell, minister of the church in 1881, was subject to allegations that even he treated the church with a distinct lack of respect. It was charged that he had at one time used the church as a pigsty, at another as an enclosure for cattle, and every winter as a barn. On one Sunday in January, the lobby of the church was found to be full of straw and corn.[18]

The adjacent manse was single-storey until the central block was raised in the early twentieth century. The manse was converted into the Iona Heritage Centre in 1985.

The Church and Cemetery of St Oran

Oran (Otteran or Odhráin) was an Irish abbot of Meath, who crossed over to Scotland with Columba (they were said to be cousins) and was the first to die at Iona. He is the principal patron saint of Waterford in Ireland (feast day, 27 October).

St Oran's cemetery (Reilig Odhráin) is the oldest Christian burial place in Scotland and continues to be the graveyard of the island. In 1549 Donald Munro, later archdeacon of the Isles, claimed that in three tombs were buried the bones of forty-eight Scottish, eight Norwegian, four Irish and two French kings, but this is impossible to verify, and almost certainly a piece of fiction designed to enhance the status of the island. The list of mostly fanciful names stretches from the fifth to the fifteenth centuries. The Lords of Isles were also buried here from the thirteenth to the fifteenth centuries. The last Scottish kings to be buried here were Duncan I (1034–40), and his murderer and successor Macbeth (1040–57). Only one of the existing red slabs (a plain red stone with a Celtic cross) may be one of these kings. The many other carved slabs, fifteenth century and later, are mainly those of island chieftains, and they were only arranged in their present ridges in 1868. In 1772 the cemetery was 'so overgrown with weeds, especially with the common butter-bur, that very few are at present to be seen'.[19] The remains of John Smith, Leader of the United Kingdom Labour Party 1992–4, were interred in a modern extension to the churchyard in May 1994. A massive empty socket-stone is all that remains of St Oran's Cross, which was in fragments by the nineteenth century.

St Oran's Chapel is a small restored Romanesque chamber thought to have been erected as a family burial chamber by Somerled, the usurper Lord of the Isles (1158–64), or his son, Reginald, in the mid-twelfth century. The low deeply recessed doorway, with chevron mouldings, is typical of the period. The trefoiled canopied recess in the south wall may have been erected by John, fourth and last Lord of the Isles, who was deposed in 1493. Dr Johnson came here in 1772. 'Within, beneath a recess formed with three neat pointed arches, is a tombstone with a ship and several ornaments. I forget whether the sails were furled: in that case the deceased was descended from the antient kings of Man of the Norwegian race'.[20] By the mid-nineteenth century the church was described as being in a 'tottering condition, which is not likely to allow its existence to be of long duration. The walls and the gable are perfect, but the roof has been destroyed'.[21] The church was re-roofed and restored in 1957.

The Street of the Dead

In front of the cathedral is preserved a section of the Street of the Dead, a cobbled roadway of well-worn granite boulders, perhaps laid out in the thirteenth century, and uncovered in 1962–3. There is nothing

sinister in its name; the 'street' is merely a pathway connecting the cathedral and the cemetery, and once formed part of a series of streets linking the cathedral with the nunnery.

St Martin's Cross

Opposite the west front of the cathedral stands the eighth century St Martin's Cross, a single 4.2m high piece of epidiarite with jewel-like carving facing the cathedral, and a Virgin and Child and Old Testament scenes, such as Daniel in the lions' den, and David playing the harp, on the west face.

St John's Cross

To the left of St Martin's Cross is a concrete replica of the tenth century St John's Cross. The original cross was restored from fragments in 1926 but subsequently twice blown down. After substantial restoration it was returned to Iona in 1990 and is now displayed in the museum.

St Matthew's Cross

The remains of this late ninth or early tenth century cross, formerly standing close to the round tower in front of the cathedral, can now be seen in the Abbey Museum. The Cross is now little more than a broken shaft.

The Cathedral

The cathedral is a simple and solid, but not particularly striking, cruciform structure built of red Mull granite. It measures 48.7m long, 21.3m wide at the transepts, with a 22.8m high central tower. The interior has a number of elements of architectural interest, but the cathedral was probably never highly elaborate and, in the words of another author, 'not much is left to requite the pilgrimage of the mere architectural curiosity'.[22]

Before the west door stands the foundations of a round tower. Because of the rain water which collected at the base the remains were long thought to be a well.

The tiny structure at the north-west angle of the nave, known as St Columba's Shrine, seats just four people. Only its foundations survived before it was restored as a chapel in 1962. It has no particular connection with Columba. Tor Abb, a mound just west of the cathedral, has the remains of a cell which may have been that of the saint.

The west door is large and has continuous mouldings round the arch and jambs. It leads straight into the aisleless nave with a plain stone floor and a simple flat twentieth century roof. The north and west walls are largely twelfth century, but the west was refaced and the south side extended outwards in the fifteenth century when the tower was also built. The west and south walls were about the height of the west door, but the north was level with the ground in some places; everything above is early twentieth century work. The chancel, transepts and tower were roofed in 1905. The 1908 font, carved with Celtic emblems, is supported by a central pier of green-veined white marble guarded by four green marble colonettes; it was designed by P Macgregor Chalmers. It stands on the highest position in the church for, in an odd reversal of the norm, the cathedral floor gradually descends by steps towards the chancel, which is at the lowest level.

The north transept is substantially early thirteenth century work and separated from the crossing by a wooden screen donated by Queen Elizabeth II in 1956. Above the present arch can be seen an older arch. The doorway in its west wall goes through to the cloister, and the stair in the north wall to the rebuilt dormitory of 1954. The rose window dates from 1905. The thick east wall with its two window recesses contains a wall passage of obscure purpose above the windows. The niche between the windows contained a statue, the feet of which survive. The crucifixion painting over the altar between the windows is by Roy le Maistre.

The crossing is mostly fifteenth century, but the north arch of the earlier thirteenth century crossing can be seen above its successor. The south-east pier of the crossing bears a damaged inscription recording the name of Donald Ò Brolchán, the mason responsible for the fifteenth century rebuilding. The tower is reached by a spiral stair at the south-west corner of the crossing. The tower contains a single bell, cast by John Taylor of Loughborough in 1931.

The four-bay chancel with a three-bay south aisle dates from the rebuilding of 1450, although traces of the thirteenth century chancel can be seen on the north side. On the north side is the sacristy, divided from the chancel by a double arcade standing on a wall 1.8m high and connected to it by an elaborate doorway. The two easternmost windows contain glass depicting St Patrick (north) and St Brigid (south). The capitals of the piers are carved with a variety of scenes: strange beasts wandering through forests of foliage; the expulsion of Adam and Eve from the garden of Eden; the crucifixion; Peter cutting off the ear of Malchus; an angel weighing souls while the scales are being pressed down by a devil; two men stealing a cow, the owner approaching with a cudgel, and his wife at the rear, her arms raised in supplication.

The chancel floor was originally at the level of the piano loft with its two thirteenth century arches, and there was a crypt beneath. The floor of the crypt would have been a few feet below the floor of the present chancel, and the floor of the old chancel would have been level with the wall upon which the sacristy pillars rest. The loft was meant as the start of a north chancel aisle. By the time the sacristy was formed on that north side in the fifteenth century (the aisle above it being removed and the arches blocked) the chancel floor had been lowered; but its trefoil-headed doorway is probably fifteenth century, though copied from thirteenth century types. The glass in the north clerestory is by Douglas Strachan (1939). On the outer side the arcade and aisles are fifteenth century. The thirteenth century foundations of a large transept – which was never completed – project southwards from the south aisle. The transept, intended to incorporate an eastern aisle of three vaulted bays, would have superseded a two-level south aisle similar to that which exists on the north side of the chancel.

The two banks of stalls are twentieth century and in the centre of the floor is a fragmentary grave slab. The large altar is of Iona marble, quarried at the south end of the island, standing on a pavement of medieval sandstone slabs, and was designed (c.1912) by P Macgregor Chalmers. The quarry was first used in 1693 and the last period of activity was 1907–14. Behind the altar is a cross by Omar Ramsden. On the north side of the chancel is the effigy resting on four lions (one is medieval) of Abbot John MacKinnon. The abbot's mitre indicates the privilege granted by the pope in 1247. On the death of Abbot Mackinnon, Bishop John Campbell of the Isles (1487–1511) became administrator of the abbey, and his successors continued so until the dissolution of the monasteries.

Opposite Abbot Mackinnon is the earlier figure of Abbot Dominic (1421–c.1465). Behind are a piscina and the fifteenth century triple sedilia; on the centre seat of the sedilia is a large rounded stone, known as St Columba's Pillow, with an Irish cross incised upon it. In the floor is the matrix of a large Flemish brass, said to have been of a Maclean.

The south chancel aisle is entered by a triple arcade. A piscina is set into a window shelf on the south wall. The internal low flying buttresses are the result of placing the clerestory windows above the piers rather than above the arches. The tracery of the east window is modern.

The south transept is virtually occupied by a monument to George, eighth duke of Argyll (1823–1900) and the tomb of his third wife Ina (d.1925), a difficult and pretentious woman. The white marble recumbent effigies are by Sir George Frampton. Carved in the east wall is a circular consecration cross. The duke gave the abbey to the Church of Scotland, expressing the hope that it might be rebuilt and that any denomination might use it as a place of worship. In front of the rail is a showcase with a facsimile of the Book of Kells.

The Monastery

The monastic buildings were, unusually, on the north side of the church, because of the supply of running water there. They can be reached through a door in the north wall of the nave. The complex was in a very ruinous condition in the early nineteenth century to the point where it was difficult to determine the arrangement of some of the buildings. 'It is hard to distinguish the foundations of some of the walls among the masses of rubbish and overthrown buildings, and this is an almost impracticable task in summer, when the ruins are overgrown with rank weeds'.[23] This depressing picture is now history; the buildings have been fully restored, and in some cases completely rebuilt.

The cloister has been rebuilt since 1960 on its original base. Some original shafts remain but most are reproductions in yellow sandstone. The capitals of the inner shafts have been carved by different sculptors to their own designs. Those of the east walk are leaves and flowers. The timber roof of the cloisters was a gift from Vancouver. The cloister is now lined with tomb slabs dated AD 1300–1500 from Reilig Odhráin. The 1960 sculpture in the centre of the garth is the Descent of the Spirit by Jacob Lipschitz. It bears the inscription 'I, a Jew faithful to the Faith of my Fathers, have made this Virgin for goodwill among men, that the Spirit may reign'.

The chapter house, restored in 1940, is on the east side of the cloister, and was the first of the buildings to be restored. A century earlier it was a most uninviting place. 'A gloomy vaulted chamber… The roof is still entire, and overgrown with grass and wild juniper'.[24] In the mid-nineteenth century Iona was visited by an archbishop of Canterbury who asked to be shown the chapter house. He was taken there by the chamberlain to the duke of Argyll. 'The first thing they found was six inches of cow dung in the bottom of it. On asking the cause, it turned out that the innkeeper had the pasture of the field in which the ruins were. The ruins were divided from the innkeeper's ground by a low dry stone wall, and he was in the habit every year of pulling down a portion of this wall, and letting his cattle graze among the ruins'.[25]

The further half of the building with seat recesses, separated by two thirteenth century arches, is the chapter house proper and now has a library above; the upper floor of this east range was the dormitory, and now has fifteen bedrooms in the roof space. The timber in the east range was a gift from New Zealand. Beside the chapter house was the calefactory, the only place in the monastery provided with the luxury of a fire.

The doorway near the west end led to the refectory, along the north side of the cloister range, on the upper floor; this range was rebuilt in 1948–9. All the timber was a gift from Norway. The west range, rebuilt in 1965 and considerably larger than its medieval predecessor, contains kitchens. This range contained the storerooms for the cellarer, the monk responsible for the provisions of the monastery. Towards the end of its arcade are a bay and a half of original stonework, incorporated in the modern rebuilding. The first bay of the south walk also contains thirteenth century stones; the new part has birds carved in the capitals. To the west are the foundations of an oblong building now laid out as a garden. Excavations in 1966–8 revealed it to have been the medieval bakehouse and brewhouse.

The south wall of the nave is notable for its great pink blocks of stone, and the south transept with its main window tracery flanked by modern carvings of a girl and a boy. The clock face on this side of the tower replaces a medieval one. To the south of the south chapel, a depression and piece of foundation wall indicate the transept that was begun in the thirteenth century but never built.

On the north side are the sacristy and the other transept, the east wall of which, like the adjoining north wall of the chancel, dates from c.1200. Then comes the chapter house. The nearer detached building is the infirmary chapel, probably twelfth or thirteenth century, though restored in 1959 from its foundations and now called the Michael Chapel. The elliptical curved roof and the simple dark furnishings are made from the utile wood of Ghana. The further detached building, standing north of the Michael Chapel, was the infirmary. It was restored in 1964 through the generosity of the Carnegie trustees and is now used as a museum. It contains a great number of local carved stones of the seventh to sixteenth centuries including the original St John's Cross, placed here in 1990.

The small part of the main block projecting over the drainage channel was the reredorter (restored in 1943–4), and that round the corner the caretaker's house (built in 1950), preserving a gable of the old abbot's house. In their rebuilt form these are staff quarters.

In a field south of the abbey can be seen the fragments of St Mary's Chapel. Clearance work in 1874 revealed that it was about 18m long and had a north doorway. Nothing is known of its history or purpose.

To the north of the abbey is a fragment of the bishop's house, possibly erected by Bishop Neil Campbell (1633–8) when the cathedral was restored as the cathedral church of the diocese of the Isles. In his visit in 1773, Dr Johnson noted that the house was one of the two buildings on Iona to possess a chimney.

Sir Walter Scott visited Iona early in the nineteenth century and found it 'desolate and miserable'. He was followed by John Keats in 1818, Felix Mendelssohn (who travelled on an early steamboat excursion and bequeathed the overture *Fingal's Cave* as the enduring memorial of his visit) and William Wordsworth in 1835, who wrote four sonnets there. Even the formidable Dr Johnson was moved by his visit to Iona. 'The man is little to be envied whose patriotism would not gain force upon the plains of Marathon, or whose piety would not grow warmer among the ruins of Iona'. Boswell was a little less than impressed with the islanders: 'The inhabitants are remarkably gross, and remarkably neglected. I know not if they are visited by any minister. The island, which was once the metropolis of learning and piety, has now no school for education, nor temple for worship, only two inhabitants that can speak English, and not one that can write or read'. Yet he also was inspired by the atmosphere of the place: 'I left him (Dr Johnson)... and stole back again to the cathedral, to indulge in solitude and devout meditation... I hoped, that, ever after having been in this holy place, I should maintain an exemplary conduct'.[26]

Iona today is something of a disappointment. The restored abbey and cathedral represent a remarkable achievement, but the scenery is flat and uninteresting, and the reputation of the island is based largely on the piety of a long-departed monastic community and the uncertain legends that surround the memory of St Columba. The work of the Iona Community, founded by the late Lord Macleod of Fuinary, has done a little to restore some sense of spirituality to the cathedral, but this is effectively obliterated during the day by the mass invasion of tourists.

Perhaps the final comment should be allowed to Botfield, who visited the ruins in 1829: 'He who visits Iona in search of the sublime or beautiful will return as much disappointed and chagrined as the Cockney did from Staffa, after finding that it did not stand upon pillars in the same manner as a card table stands upon its feet. The interest and expression of the island must depend entirely on the mind which surveys it; for the ruins themselves, with all their ornaments, are surpassed in dignity and grandeur by many others, which many travellers would pass without emotion. It is to their antiquity and remoteness, and the piety of their ancient inhabitants, that the ruins of Iona owe that celebrity which have so long distinguished them from all others; for it is impossible to contemplate their venerable

fragments, and muse upon their history, without an emotion of melancholy and holiness which few other spots in the world can inspire'.[27]

1 Macquarrie, A & Macarthur, E M (1992).
2 Chapman, R W (ed.) (1924): pp 135–6.
3 RCAHMS (1982): p. 140.
4 ibid., pp 140–1.
5 Pennant, T (1776): volume 1, p. 290.
6 Lewis, Samuel (1846): volume 1, p. 582.
7 Carrick, J C (1905): p.32.
8 Laing, D (1854): p. 4.
9 Addis, M E Leicester (1901): p. 5.
10 Carrick, J C (1905): pp 30–31.
11 Macquarrie, A & Macarthur, E M (1992): pp 28–9.
12 Morton, T Ralph (1957b): pp 5–6.
13 Morton, T Ralph (1957a): p. 51.
14 Morton, T Ralph (1957b): p. 6.
15 Pennant, T (1776): volume 1, p. 283.
16 Graham, H D: (1850): p. 25.
17 Gordon, J F S (1885): p. v.
18 ibid., p. xv.
19 Pennant, T (1776): volume 1, p. 286.
20 Chapman, R W (ed.) (1924): p. 138.
21 Buckler, J C & Buckler, C A (1866): p.75.
22 Robertson, Joseph (1891): p. 78.
23 Graham, H D (1850): p. 18.
24 ibid., p. 21.
25 McCorry, J Stewart (1871): p. 32.
26 Chapman, R W (ed.) (1924).
27 Botfield, Beriah (1830): pp. 287–8.

Kirkwall

The Cathedral Church of St Magnus
(Church of Scotland)

At their closest point, the Orkney islands are separated from the Scottish mainland by 9.6km of the Pentland Firth. They can be reached either by a short passenger ferry from John o' Groats in Caithness, or by a longer car ferry from Aberdeen.

Orkney numbers about 70 islands and islets, of which eighteen are inhabited, with a total population of 19,000. The largest of the islands is known as Mainland, and its principal town is Kirkwall (population 6,700). The first sight of the town fully explains why the word 'kirk' is embedded in its name. Kirkwall (526km north of Edinburgh) is dominated by the striking Romanesque cathedral church of St Magnus, and the most northerly cathedral in Britain.

St Magnus' Cathedral is described by one author as 'next to Trondheim Cathedral the oldest monument of the whole of ancient Norway… Here, to, is a confirmation of what may generally be said of the Viking expeditions: namely, that although in themselves wild and barbaric, they always contained the germ of a new, rich cultural development, that stirred as soon as the warlike spirit sank to rest and left room for the play of the intellectual strength and civilising power that also dwelt in the Vikings. St Magnus' Cathedral is the living expression of this thought'.[1]

The bishopric of Orkney was founded by Thorfinn II, known as 'Thorfinn the Mighty' (1009–1056/65?) jarl (earl) of Caithness and Orkney. Thorfinn built Christ Church at Birsay and established it as the cathedral church of the diocese of Orkney. On his death the earldom was divided between his two sons, Erlend (d.1099) and Paul (d.1099), and they ruled jointly and harmoniously. Their shares of the earldom were inherited by their sons Magnus (c.1076–c.1116) and Haakon. Haakon was not content to rule jointly with his cousin and, in the ensuing dispute, Magnus was killed and buried at Birsay.

Haakon was left in sole possession of the earldom and, on his death, was succeeded by his son Paul. Rognvald, the son of the sister of Magnus attempted to claim his uncle's portion, but failed in his first attempt. Returning to Norway, he sought the advice of his father who instructed him to vow that, if he were successful, he would build a great stone minster in honour of his uncle Magnus. In a further attempt he was successful and, in 1137, he began work on the construction of the cathedral church of St Magnus at Kirkwall, the bishop's seat being moved from Birsay. The cathedral was usable by 1155, and the remains of Magnus were duly interred in the building. Earl Rognvald, murdered by rebels, was himself buried there in 1158. Construction started and stopped throughout the Middle Ages, and the west front of the nave may not have been completed until the late fifteenth or early sixteenth century.

Although Magnus and Rognvald were both murdered for political reasons, they have always been venerated as martyrs. Magnus' feast day is 16 April and he is depicted as richly robed, or in armour, and carrying an axe or a club. The cult of Magnus spread far beyond Orkney, and churches were dedicated in his name in Faroe and Iceland. Even the city of London boasts a church dedicated to St Magnus the Martyr. The feast day of Rognvald (sometimes anglicised as Ronald) is 20 August.

The first bishop of Orkney, William the Old, held the see for sixty-six years (1102–68). The suffix appears to have been bestowed to distinguish him from his successor, Bishop William II (1168–88). During his long episcopate Bishop William the Old may have constructed the first bishop's palace at Kirkwall, although he often lived on the island of Egilsay, where a ruined church dedicated to St Magnus can still be seen. The foundations, and some lower courses of masonry in the present ruined bishop's palace in Kirkwall, have been dated as twelfth century. In 1848, a stone cist was discovered on the north side of the chancel of St Magnus' Cathedral. Within was a skeleton, part of an ivory staff, and a lead plate upon which was inscribed: HIC REQUIESCIT WILLIALMUS SENEX FELICIS MEMORIAE (Here lies William the Old, of blessed memory), and on the other side: PRIMUS EPISCOPUS (first bishop).

At the time of the construction of the cathedral and the inauguration of Kirkwall as the see of the diocese, Orkney, Shetland and part of northern Scotland was ruled from Norway, and the diocese of Orkney was declared to be part of the jurisdiction of the archbishop of Nidaros (Trondheim), by Pope Anastasius IV, on 1 December 1154. Orkney remained part of the Norwegian church until 17 August 1472, when Pope Sixtus IV transferred it to the jurisdiction of the archbishop of St Andrews. Orkney had been pledged to King James III (1460–88) as a security for the dowry of his queen, a daughter of Christian I, King of Norway (1450–81), Sweden (1457–64) and Denmark (1448–81). As the dowry was not paid, Scotland took possession of the islands.

In 1263 King Haakon IV of Norway (1217–63) returned to Orkney after an unsuccessful expedition down the west coast of Scotland, and died there in December after lying ill in the bishop's palace. He was interred in the cathedral before the shrine of St Magnus, before his body was returned to Norway in the following year. To commemorate the seventh centenary of his death, a marble slab – inscribed in Latin bearing the date of the king's death – was donated by the Norwegian government and inserted in the floor of the chancel.

Bishop Robert Maxwell (1526–40) gave the cathedral bells in 1528, and it was said that 'the sound of the old great bourdon could be heard in Caithness, booming across the stormy strait'.[2] Bishop Robert Reid (1541–58) was one of the most notable and learned bishops of Orkney. Abbot of Kinloss and a Senator (and founder member) of the College of Justice from 1532, he was Lord President of the college from 1549 until his death. He rebuilt the bishop's palace at Kirkwall and added the round tower which still stands.

Bishop Adam Bothwell (1559–1611) officiated at the marriage of Queen Mary and the earl of Bothwell in 1567, in the chapel royal at Holyrood, and later in the same year he anointed and crowned the infant King James VI (1567–1625) at the High Kirk in Stirling. Bothwell appears to have accepted and co-operated with the reformation, but he surrendered the lands and revenues of the bishopric in 1568 to Lord Robert Stewart in exchange for land at Holyrood. He moved south and, although remaining bishop of Orkney and retaining a degree of spiritual authority, his work in the islands was ended.

The reformation of the church in Orkney was carried out with a degree of moderation, and the cathedral was spared the destructive frenzy of the sixteenth century reformers. Botfield commented that Kirkwall was 'remarkable as the only cathedral except that of Glasgow, which remained unscathed by the tumultuous violence of Knox and his fanatical canaille'.[3] Inevitably, the furnishings were destroyed, and services did become confined to the chancel, the nave being insufficiently maintained, but Kirkwall escaped the destruction that befell Elgin and St Andrews.

In 1614 the earl of Caithness decided to demolish the cathedral on the ground that the tower had for some time been occupied by rebels. With great difficulty, he was prevented from doing so by Bishop James Law (1611–15), but he may have started, as the western bays of the nave and its aisles were long unroofed and used as the town graveyard. The chancel was given galleries and divided from the crossing by a wooden screen in 1630, and there is much evidence of patching and mending throughout the seventeenth century. In 1642, the cathedral records note payment 'for mending and tarring the steeple head';[4] in the same year, David Sinclair was paid 'for 28 days work upon the kirk roof… glass for

The Cathedral Church of St Magnus

three windows in the kirk';[5] four years later in 1646, the same David Sinclair was paid 'for 67 days work upon the kirk'.[6] The same records note a grimmer side to the form of Christianity practised in the cathedral at the time. In 1640 was purchased 'five ell of harden to be a gown for adulterers';[7] and in 1646 'harden cloth to be sackgowns for penitents'.[8]

In 1671 the spire was struck by lightning: 'Quhilk day ther happened ane fearful and sad accident in this place to the great astonishment and terrification of all the beholders, by thunder and lightning which fell upon the steeple heid of the Cathedral Kirk of Orknay, called St Magnus Kirk of Kirkwall, and fyred the samen, which burnt downwards until the steeple heid, three loftings and all the timber work pertaining to the bells and the knock house were consumed to ashes'.[9] The timber work of the tower was burned and the wooden spire destroyed. The bells fell to the floor of the crossing, but the townspeople had tried to save them by bringing in earth and other material to soften the fall. The spire was replaced by the short pyramid which remained until it was itself replaced by the present spire in the twentieth century, 'although it is thought a mistake by many of the inhabitants'.[10] When Thomas Kirk visited Kirkwall in 1677 he found a cathedral church well regarded by the people of the town. 'Here is a church built in the form of a cross, with a steeple in the middle, which they value much, esteeming it one of the largest churches in Scotland; but we did not think it so; it is but a narrow church and very dark; it was made use of as a citadel to beat down the castle; the steeple has had a spire upon it, but it was burnt down with lightning'.[11]

There was a complaint in 1701 that 'the most unchristian and more than barbarous practice of the Town Guard of Kirkwall, at the time of the Lambas Fair, their keeping guard within the Church, shooting of guns, burning of great fires on the graves of the dead, drinking, fiddling, piping, swearing and cursing night and day within the Church, by which means religion is scandalised and the Presbytery most miserably abused: particularly when they are at exercise in the said Church, neither can the preacher open his mouth, nor the hearers conveniently attend for smoke'.[12]

In 1780 the cathedral was in a bad state of repair. The walled-off chancel formed the parish church, its walls receiving an occasional coat of whitewash, and the congregation were accommodated in a collection of pews and galleries garishly painted in red, blue and yellow. The nave was used only as a burial place; its pillars green with moss, and about three quarters of its windows blocked up. 'It would seem by the darkness into which this and some other old churches have been reformed, that the first Apostles of Protestantism in Scotland were much afraid of outward light, considering it no doubt a great enemy to inward light'.[13] A comment by Elizabeth, countess of Sutherland would seem to indicate that some restoration work may have been undertaken by 1805, although she may have referred only to the parish church chancel. 'The appearance of this church is handsome… and it is kept in perfect repair'.[14]

The state of the cathedral was no better by 1822 when a petition was presented to the presbytery, urging that something be done. 'The whole of the ground area in St Magnus Church which is occupied as a place of worship is considerably under the level of the ground… The rain water enters the roof, and at the top of the walls from the bartizans, notwithstanding every effort to prevent it, so that even the pulpit cannot be kept free from droppings… From the nature of the ground around the Cathedral – from the thickness of and constant moisture in the walls – from the massiveness of the pillars and the smallness of the windows, which admit little air and no sunshine into the body of the Kirk – it is in fact as damp, cold and unwholesome as any cellar or icehouse, and is altogether unfit to be occupied as a place of worship'.[15]

The cathedral was duly vacated by the congregation for ten years, from 1846–56, while the building was 'restored'. Worship took place at another (now demolished) building in the town. Ownership of the cathedral was granted to the town by King James III in 1486. In the 1840s ownership was claimed by a government department on behalf of the Crown and a restoration was undertaken in 1847–50 by William Nixon at a cost of £3,000. The walls were stripped of plaster and the galleries were removed from the chancel, the cathedral was re-roofed, the parapets renewed, and pinnacles added. No sooner was the work finished than the town council re-asserted its claim to ownership of the cathedral in 1851 and the crown gave way. Unfortunately the council embarked on a destructive tidying-up restoration in 1855–7, 'and accordingly set about making the building hideous again. The galleries were replaced and whitewash put on with a liberal hand'.[16] The antiquarian, Sir Henry Dryden, described the new furnishings as 'most barbarous outrages'. Although the despised whitewash was removed later in the nineteenth century, what remained was still fiercely condemned as an intrusion into a building of noble beauty. 'In spite of the appalling vulgarity that dominates the whole of the modern decoration, the view of the choir is imposing in its effect. Even the hideous galleries, squeezed in between the pillars, and the walling-up of the triforium arches, cannot entirely destroy the feeling that must have filled the building when the high altar with its shrine and sacred vessels of precious metal shone in the light of the candles… How gladly would we put in a word in favour of the removal of the disturbing additions, so that justice might be done to the original structure'.[17]

In 1913–30 more scholarly repairs were done under the supervision of George Mackie Watson, funded by a bequest of £60,000 from the late George Thoms, Sheriff of Caithness, Orkney and Shetland 1890–9, who had expressed a wish to see the cathedral restored. A sum of £9,000 was invested for the upkeep of the fabric and towards meeting the cost of heating and cleaning; the rest was spent on renovation and refurnishing. The nineteenth century pews and galleries, and the screens which enclosed the chancel, were all removed. The nave vaulting was renovated, and the wooden floor of the chancel removed, revealing the steps which had led to the high altar. The nave was furnished with chairs and stained glass by Oscar Paterson was inserted in most of the windows. The present pulpit, communion table and choir stalls date from this restoration. A pipe organ, by Henry Willis of London, was installed. A taller spire, cased in copper, replaced the short seventeenth century stone spire.

In 1937 the cathedral celebrated the eight hundredth anniversary of its foundation with a service of thanksgiving on 29 July (St Olaf's day) 1937. The obvious date of 16 April (St Magnus' day) was rejected in favour of a date in the summer holiday period. Among the distinguished guests present was the Moderator of the Church of Scotland, and invitations were issued to the Roman Catholic and Scottish Episcopal bishops of Aberdeen and Orkney, the bishop of Sodor and Man, and the rector of the church of St Magnus the Martyr in the City of London. The sermon was preached by the archbishop of Nidaros from Norway.

Urgent structural repairs took place in the years 1972–4. Cracks had appeared in the walls adjacent to the west gable and in the vaulting in that area, while the vaulting itself was being pushed outwards at the top. It became clear that the west end of the cathedral was in danger of collapse. Work included the grouting of the pillars, the placing of steel girders above the nave ceiling and the clerestory passage ways, the rebuilding of some of the stone vaulting, and the insertion of fibreglass shells in the interstices of the roof. The structural weakness of this part of the cathedral, of which an obvious memorial remains in the dramatic lean of one or two piers, is thought to originate with mistakes in the construction of the west gable and vault, rather than subsidence.

St Magnus' Cathedral is a cruciform structure built of grey flagstone and patterned red and yellow sandstone. The red sandstone was quarried not far from Kirkwall at Head of Holland; the yellow sandstone may have come from the island of Eday. The work was supervised by Earl Rognvald's father Kol, a chieftain from Norway who, it is generally agreed, employed masons trained at Durham.

The cathedral has a nave, with triforium and clerestory, of eight bays, transepts with eastern chapels, a chancel of six bays, and a central tower. The cathedral is 68.8m long, 17m wide, and 21.6m high to the vault; the tower is 40.5m high. Access to the tower is gained by means of a narrow winding stair in each of the four corners, but only one leads from the belfry up to the foot of the spire.

Although essentially Romanesque, the cathedral wears something of a Scandinavian air, especially in the narrowness of its nave in relation to the height and length. Initially it was shorter at both ends; the extra bays were begun in the thirteenth century but the two west bays at least were not finished until the fifteenth century. Unusually, they were completed in the Romanesque style, the architect presumably appreciating the worth of the style of the building. The small original chancel may have finished in an apse. The pillars of the chancel extension, although supporting the same rounded Romanesque arches, are more graceful than the rough massive piers of the nave. The crossing arches were rebuilt c.1190 in the Transitional style and the two transept chapels added at the same time. In each of these chapels, the windows are Gothic in style. The height of the tower was raised in the fourteenth century.

The nave is quite narrow and the narrowness is emphasised by the powerfully massive round piers, thought to be the work of Durham masons, which accord an air of mystery to this ancient building. The triforium has bronze guard rails and houses a relic of the punishment of former days in the hangman's double ladder (in the south triforium of the nave); the triforium also holds a pulpit of 1689. The small clerestory above the triforium, with single small lancets, is thirteenth century and wholly within the height of the vault. The difference in construction periods can be seen in the clerestory windows in the chancel, where earlier round-headed Romanesque windows replace the lancets of the nave. The ribbed quadripartite vault is mostly stone, though panels at the west end were replaced by sections of glass-reinforced plastic in the restoration of 1972–4.

A special feature of the interior is the decorative use of red and white sandstone which gives the cathedral something of a striped appearance. The crudely carved grave slabs which can be seen along the walls of the north and south aisles are mostly seventeenth century.

There is one to Lord Adam Stewart (d.1575), one of the seven illegitimate sons of King James V (1513–42), and another to an officer of the Spanish Armada, who died in 1597.

The west window is by Crear McCartney and depicts Christ with the emblems of St Magnus, St Luke and St John; it was unveiled by Queen Elizabeth II in 1987. At the west end of the nave can be seen the unusual 1883 wooden font with angels forming corners to a round bowl. Near the west end of the north nave aisle is a large monument to John Cuthbert (d.1650) flanked by Corinthian columns, with the symbols of mortality carved above. The doorway in the third bay, one of many dating from the Watson restoration, partly hides a thirteenth century arch. Changes, including interlaced wall arcading and shafted windows, appear in the fourth bay, indicating that the first three bays are of a different date. The aisle vault is thought to be fifteenth century. In the fifth bay, one panel of the vault retains its original red and black painted decoration. Close by, on the nave column, hangs the so-called Mort Brod or Death Board, a memorial to Robert Nicholson and his wife Jean Davidson (c.1685). The board, like a village inn sign, is gruesomely decorated with a shrouded skeleton and angels sticking arrows into a heart on one side, and a crude verse commemorating Nicholson, on the other.

The north transept, entered beneath a Gothic arch rebuilt c.1200 with the crossing arches, is tall and narrow, with four storeys of openings in its north gable wall, including a rose at the top. It has a timber wagon roof. The wall arcading and the triforium both continue around the transept. An early twentieth century screen encloses the vaulted late twelfth century former chapel, now a vestry, on the east side of the transept. Beside this stands the old Market Cross of Kirkwall, dated 1621, that formerly stood in Kirk Green. It was brought inside the cathedral in 1954 for preservation reasons, and replaced by a replica.

Another screen leads into the north chancel aisle, where the stone floor is replaced by tiles. At this point the Romanesque work ends and the Gothic begins. There is no wall arcade but the pointed window arches have chevron ornament and the wall pilasters are capped by portrait heads. In the first bay is an eighteenth century monument to the Traill family. In the second bay is a memorial to the men of HMS *Royal Oak*, sunk in Scapa Bay on 14 October 1947. In the third bay is a particularly large stone monument to David Monroe (d.1684). In the fourth bay is a thirteenth century coffin lid; the statue of St Olaf opposite was copied from an old one in Trondheim Cathedral and presented to the cathedral in 1937 by the archbishop of Nidaros, to commemorate the octocentenary of its foundation. Also in the fourth bay is a memorial to the distinguished Scottish jurist Lord Birsay, KT (1905–82), Chairman of the Scottish Land Court 1965–78. At the end of the aisle is the cenotaph of William Balfour Baikie (1825–64), the naturalist, philologist and surgeon. Settling in Africa towards the end of his life, he compiled vocabularies of fifty native dialects and translated parts of the Bible into Hausa, one of the three principal languages of Nigeria.

The three eastern bays replaced the Romanesque apse in the thirteenth century. Though the main arches are round-headed Romanesque in style, they are moulded and their clustered piers have foliage capitals. The triforium arcade is also still Romanesque in style, but the clerestory is Gothic.

The area at the east end of the chancel, beyond the screen, was designated the chapel of St Rognvald in 1965. New furnishings were dedicated in the following year, incorporating old carved panels from the sixteenth and seventeenth centuries. The pulpit, communion table and lectern were designed by Stanley Cursiter, a native of Kirkwall, and the Queen's Limner and Painter in Scotland, and executed by Reynold Eunson, a local craftsman in 1965. Eunson also carved, to Cursiter's design, the figures of Kol (father of Rognvald), St Rognvald and Bishop William the Old, which are attached to the blind arcade beneath the east window. The model of a Viking longboat on the table was made by Stanley Cursiter. The east window glass is a memorial to Sheriff Thoms, benefactor of the 1913–30 restoration.

In the east bay of the south chancel aisle is the free-standing tomb of the Arctic explorer John Rae (1813–93) who mapped some 2250km of the Canadian Arctic coast (1846–64) and proved King William's Land to be an island. The monument, sculpted by Joseph Whithead, depicts his exhausted figure lying on a rock. Nearby are six brass tablets to eminent local residents: Edwin Muir (1887–1959), poet and critic; Stanley Cursiter (1887–1976), painter; Robert Rendall (1898–1967), poet and conchologist; John Mooney (1881–1965), philologist; J Stores Clouston (1870–1944), historian; and Eric Linklater (1899–1974), novelist. Many sixteenth and seventeenth century slabs line the walls of the aisle. In the sixth bay is a tapestry presented in 1987 to mark the eight hundred and fiftieth anniversary of the foundation of the cathedral, and an opening into a dungeon between the south wall of the chancel and the south transept chapel. Known as Marwick's Hole, it was used as a prison until the late eighteenth century.

The design of the south transept repeats the design of the north, except for the later rose window in place of the two round-headed ones. As with the north

The Cathedral Church of St Magnus (early 20th century postcard)

transept, the little late twelfth century chapel on the east side is now a vestry.

The architecture of the chancel is similar to the nave. The vault is thirteenth century, but its shafts stop above the triforium, on corbels with groups of portrait heads. This part of the chancel (which could be described as the choir) could be as impressive as the nave, but the furnishing of the area has been badly mismanaged, presumably in an attempt to insert a traditional 'cathedral choir' into an area which is simply not capacious enough to allow it, and the result is a severely cramped central aisle. The stalls are fine pieces of work; they were designed by George Mackie Watson and carved from Scottish oak in the 1920s, but they have clearly been wedged into an area that was never designed to hold them.

The third bay is followed by two blank walls. Here stands the communion table, with a lace-like screen behind it concealing Henry Willis's oppressively dominating organ of 1925. It was restored by Henry Willis IV in 1971, but would be better moved out of sight to a transept. Beyond the organ was the Romanesque apse. Plaques on the large rectangular piers on each side of the chancel mark the resting places of the bones of St Magnus and St Rognvald, the former including a cleft skull, just as described in the ancient *Orkneyinga Saga*. The remains of St Magnus are in the south pier and were discovered in 1919. Those of St Rognvald are in the north pier and were discovered c.1820 and re-examined in 1925. The octagonal wooden pulpit with its high canopy stands against the north east pier of the crossing, and dates from the Watson restoration. At the crossing, the 1991 oak communion table is inlaid with marquetry patterns of interlocking rings, and stands on a 1994 dais. The font is a red sandstone bowl set within a belt of white and coloured marble. It rests on a central sandstone pier and eight slender white marble colonettes.

There is no remaining ancient woodwork in the cathedral, although the bishop's throne and Earl Patrick's pew survived at least until 1848. Apparently a few parts have been preserved and placed in the rood screen of St Olaf's Episcopal Church. This church also contains the remains of several interesting fragments from the pre-reformation parish church of Kirkwall, also dedicated to St Olaf.

The south nave aisle is also lined with mostly seventeenth century inscribed slabs. There is a piscina in the first bay, and a fourteenth century arched tomb recess of the Paplay family in the second bay, indicated as such by their armorial bearings. Wall-arcading, matching that in the north nave aisle, reappears in the third, fourth and fifth bays. The fourth bay has a memorial to Captain

Peter Winchester (d.1674) and his 'vertous' wife Jeane Bakie, with Ionic columns garlanded with vine. Further on is a rustic monument to Mary Young (d.1750), with a ghostly floating effigy, a skull, crossed bones and hour glass, and Ionic columns. In the words of the inscription, 'She lived regarded and dyed regreted'. Past the Romanesque south doorway is an almost identical memorial to Elizabeth Cuthbert (d.1685). Her effigy is roofed by a representation of the vault of heaven, a flowering rose, and a hand emerging from a cloud, offering her a crown, presumably a reference to Revelation 2:10, 'Be faithful unto death and I will give you a crown of life'.

The west front has three shafted doorways and four chimney-like pinnacles. The lower part of the front was built in the thirteenth century, in anticipation of a westward extension to the cathedral. The plan took generations to come to fruition and the doorways apparently stood for about two centuries as an isolated screen, waiting for the cathedral to join them in the fifteenth century. Although very badly weathered, they are the finest examples in Britain of the use of coloured stone. Red and yellow sandstone alternate on the arches and in layers on the buttresses between the doors. On the gable above the central doorway are the arms of Sir George Hay of Kinfauns, who held the bishopric lands at the beginning of the seventeenth century.

The doorway in the south aisle of the nave has a three-sided arch with the arms of Bishop Robert Reid (1541–58) above; it was inserted during his episcopate in place of the former Romanesque doorway, traces of which can be seen in the wall around. The triangular head of a doorway in the third bay is the result of a sixteenth century alteration and formerly led to a cloister. Next to the transept are traces of a second cloister doorway. In the south transept the weathered doorway is mostly thirteenth century but the rose window in the gable has been renewed.

To the north of the cathedral, a pink granite gateway, constructed as a war memorial in 1923, gives access to the churchyard which contains a fine but deteriorating collection of cast-iron grave enclosures. From the upper end of the churchyard a good view can be had of the tall early twentieth century copper spire added by Watson to the fourteenth century tower. The tower itself contains three inscribed bells given by Bishop Robert Maxwell (1526–41) in 1528. The inscription on the great bell reads as follows: 'Made by Master Robbert Maxvell. Bischop of Orkney the year of God MDXXVIII the year of the reign of King James V., Robert Borthwick made me in the Castel of Edinburgh'; a further medallion on the same bell records: 'Taken et brought againe heir by Alexander Geddus merchant in Kirkwa and recasten at Amsterdam Jully 1682 years by Claudius Fremy city bell caster. It weighs 1450P'. This was the bell broken in 1671 when the tower was struck by lightning. Robert Borthwick, its original maker, was master gunner to King James IV (1488–1513). The two smaller bells have similar inscriptions saying much the same, but have remained unbroken. The fourth bell has neither inscription nor date and is not hung.

On the north side of the cathedral the north aisle doorway of c.1190 has an unusual pointed gable.

To the south of the cathedral, on the other side of the road, stand the ruins of the earl's palace and the bishop's palace. In the seventeenth century, both became the inevitable stone quarries, 'until the fall of a stone out of a clumsy workman's hands upon a fellow's head put a stop to the abominable practice'.[18]

The bishop's palace is almost entirely a sixteenth century reconstruction on top of the original twelfth-thirteenth century building, of which only some ground floor masonry remains. Construction was probably first begun after the removal of the see to Birsay in 1137, but in 1320 it was reported to be mostly ruined due to neglect and alienation of the diocesan revenues. The palace was extensively reconstructed by Bishop Robert Reid (1541–58). The most conspicuous part is the great Round Tower (square within). It bears a small statue, possibly of St Olaf, but possibly representing Bishop Reid. The south extension was added c.1600 by Patrick Stewart, earl of Orkney from 1593, whose grandiose plan to join this palace to his own was ended by his downfall and execution in 1615. After his death the palace reverted to the bishops of Orkney, but during the period of presbyterian government 1638–60, the palace was described as being 'ruinated by the weather'. Later occupied by the marquess of Montrose and then by the earl of Morton, it was again occupied by the bishops from 1671 until the expulsion of the episcopate in 1689. Unused, the palace fell into its present ruined state during the eighteenth century.

The earl's palace was built by forced labour for Earl Patrick between 1600 and 1607. This was built at the time when castellation was beginning to be used more for ornamentation than defence. The palace consists of two long ranges set at right angles to each other with attractive oriel windows.

To the west of the cathedral stands Tankerness House, a well-restored example of a sixteenth-eighteenth century Orkney merchant laird's home with courtyard and garden. Earlier, the north and south wings were the home of cathedral clergy.

Entering St Magnus' Cathedral for the first time is an

INVERNESS: *The Cathedral Church of St Andrew*

KIRKWALL: *The Cathedral Church of St Magnus*

KIRKWALL: *The Cathedral Church of St Magnus*

OBAN: *The Cathedral Church of St John the Divine*

OBAN: *The Cathedral Church of St John the Divine*

unforgettable experience. 'It is small in comparison with other and better known cathedrals, but from the inside appears to be much bigger than it is; and this impression of magnitude is the consequence of the comparatively great height of the nave and choir, and the admirable proportions of the whole. From the west door one enters, as it seems, a tall magnificence of great strength – the seven columns of each side of the nave are round and massive – and a severity that is curiously tempered by the rose-red colour of the stone, for the walls and the columns recede in a rose-tawny gloom, and soar to lighter hues and the sky's illumination of the clerestory. The arches of the arcade are semi-circular, as are the arches of the triforium, but above them the arches of the clerestory are pointed; and if, from midway in the nave, you look up, that ponderous elevation of stone takes on, or is seen to possess, a quality of spiritual elevation that is strangely congruous with the earth-bound solidity of the round sandstone piers on which it is based. For this happiness of design we must be grateful to the art of English masons; and yet it is a very native church, for the old rock of Orkney has been shaped with an extraordinary strength and grace to proclaim the glory of God and yet not lose its persistent kinship with the island cliffs'.[19]

There is no other cathedral quite like it in Britain or Ireland, and it is not difficult to be captivated by the rough and powerful beauty of its architecture. Those who come to Britain's most northerly cathedral looking for marble or alabaster or polychromatic tilework or polished, intricate and sophisticated architecture, should not undertake the long journey to Orkney. The determined traveller and connoisseur of Britain's cathedrals must arrive at Kirkwall with an open mind and make no comparisons with anything that might already have been seen anywhere from Caithness to Cornwall. This is the cathedral of the Viking longboats, of North Sea gales, of storms and tempests, of jealousy and murder, of an age when faith and strife were familiar companions, when life could be brutal, when violence was endemic and political defeat ended in death. All this has somehow contributed to the architecture and atmosphere of St Magnus' Cathedral, but not in a way which has vitiated the prime purpose of its existence. For all the violence that washed around its walls in the early Middle Ages, there is still today something about St Magnus' Cathedral that is powerfully and deeply silent, holy and prayerful.

1 Dietrichson, Lorentz H S (1906): pp 45–6.
2 Walcott, Mackenzie (1874): volume 1, p. 173.
3 Botfield, Beriah (1830): p.129.
4 Mooney, Harald (1981): p. 69.
5 ibid., p. 70.
6 ibid.
7 ibid.
8 ibid.
9 Lindsay, Ian Gordon (1926): pp 187–8.
10 ibid., p. 188.
11 Brown, P Hume (1892): p. 30.
12 Lindsay, Ian Gordon (1926): pp 187–8.
13 ibid., p. 191.
14 Sutherland, Elizabeth, Countess of (1807): p. 12.
15 Cant, H W M & Firth, H N (1989): p. 86.
16 Lindsay, Ian Gordon (1926): p. 191.
17 Dietrichson, Lorentz H S (1906): pp 47–8.
18 Walcott, Mackenzie (1874): volume 1, p.174.
19 Linklater, Eric (1965): p. 111.

Lismore

The Cathedral Church of St Moluog
(Church of Scotland)

Lismore is a limestone island 16km long by 1.6km wide in Loch Linnhe off the west coast of Scotland, 9.6km north of the resort town of Oban. It has a population of about 150 people, and many more sheep. In the early nineteenth century it enjoyed a reputation for being the haunt of smugglers and the smuggling of whisky,[1] but the island today is beautiful, peaceful, undisturbed and mostly unvisited; its name derives from the Gaelic *Lios-mor*, meaning 'great garden'.

The island lies parallel with the Great Glen and can be reached by passenger ferry from Port Appin to Point or by car ferry from Oban to Achnacroish. From the high points of the island there are spectacular views to be seen of mountains, islands and the sea. To the east lie the Benderloch Hills and beyond them Ben Cruachan dominates the skyline. To the south the Paps of Jura can sometimes be seen and to the south-west is the island of Mull. To the north Ben Nevis can be seen on a reasonably clear day. The island is fertile and, in the early nineteenth century, it was 'accounted the granary of the western isles, from the crops which its surface yields to its proprietors'.[2] Today, Lismore is probably only surpassed by Skeabost, in being the least visited and least known of the cathedral sites of Scotland. Each day in the summer months, hundreds of visitors will cross by ferry from Oban to Mull and then on to Iona and Fingal's Cave. Lismore has no outstanding architectural or natural sites to attract visitors, nor does it have any public transport, and the island is usually ignored by the great majority of visitors to Oban.

The history of the island of Lismore begins in the sixth century with the work of St Moluog (also Maluogh, Molluog, Moluag, Moloc, Murlach or Lugaidh), who died c.572. A Scot educated in Ireland, Moluog returned to his native land as a missionary and his main work as a bishop was the evangelisation of the Hebrides. He was thought to have been buried at the cathedral church of St Peter at Rosemarkie, which became the cathedral of the diocese of Ross, but there is no evidence for this claim, and nothing remains of that cathedral. A shrine to the memory of Moluog was erected at Mortlach near Aberdeen and he may have been buried there; his feast day is 25 June.

The diocese of Argyll, of which Lismore became the see, was carved out of the diocese of Dunkeld c.1185. A charming story relates that Bishop John Scot of Dunkeld (1183–1203) petitioned that the western part of his diocese might be detached and formed into a new diocese, because he could not speak the Gaelic language of the people; and he asked that Harald, his chaplain, might be made bishop. The real reason was probably more political than pastoral (see Dunkeld), but the origin of the diocese of Argyll is certainly obscure. Even the date of the establishment of the see at Lismore is uncertain, though it may have taken place between 1183 and 1189. A theory that the first see of the diocese was at Muckairn, on the south side of Loch Etive, is conjectural and based on the interpretation of a place-name. There is no other evidence and the theory is now untenable. In 1236 the diocese was in the care of the bishop of the Isles and said to be in a state of poverty. In 1250 Pope Innocent IV authorised the bishops of Glasgow and Dunkeld to transfer the see from the island of Lismore to a safer and more convenient place, but this was never done.[3]

The first resident bishop at Lismore was William (1238–41), Bishop Harald's successor. Bishop William was unfortunate in choosing an island for the site of his new cathedral because in 1241 he was drowned at sea. Few of the succeeding bishops are of note. Bishop Finlay de Albany (1420–5) died in exile in Ireland in 1426 to where he fled after being implicated in the rebellion of the duke of Albany against King James I (1406–37). Sir James MacGregor, dean of Lismore, collected Gaelic ballads c.1530. They can be seen in a volume entitled *The Dean of Lismore's Book*. The cathedral was rebuilt in the fourteenth and fifteenth centuries, but the cathedral establishment gradually lapsed and before the sixteenth century reformation it was already merely parochial. In 1512 King James IV (1488–1513), wrote to Pope Julius II claiming that the cathedral was ruinous and deserted and had seen no capitular life for centuries, and recommended the transfer of the see to the former Cistercian house at Sadell on the east coast of Kintyre. Nothing came of this plan, which was probably forgotten in the aftermath of the devastating battle of Flodden in 1513, in which the king was killed.

It is uncertain whether the little cathedral attracted the hatred of the sixteenth century reformers, but it is said to have been burned,[4] and was certainly roofless in 1679. The nave was presumably abandoned and allowed to go to ruin and decay. In 1749 the floor of the chancel was raised by 0.6m, the walls were reduced by 2.7m, and the cathedral was given a new roof.

A further drastic remodelling in 1900 reversed the orientation of the cathedral. The altar was moved to the west end, in front of the chancel arch, and a small vestry was built on the other side of the arch on the site of the demolished nave. The main entrance to the cathedral was changed to the east end and the visitor now walks through an entrance porch on to the site of the high altar. The re-orientation of the church was a disastrous step which has left the building with the slightly peculiar feeling that it has today; everything seeming to be the wrong way round. A much more thoughtful piece of restoration occurred in 1956 when modern plaster was removed from the chancel arch, the sedilia, the piscina and other medieval features.

At first sight, this little wayside church, with its harled walls and slated roof, hardly warrants more than a cursory glance. The crenellated entrance porch, which is really only a narrow passage, might be better appreciated as part of a garden folly than incongruously attached to the remains of the cathedral church of the diocese of Argyll. In the late nineteenth century Joseph Robertson described the church as 'a small rude fane',[5] and so it is on first sight. Without time and careful instruction, a visitor would be hard-pressed to accept that this decidedly eighteenth century looking little country church with its bellcote atop the east gable comprises the remains of a cathedral church, but so it is.

The church consists of the much altered aisleless chancel of the medieval cathedral. It measures 15.6m long by 7.2m wide. The internal length of the vanished nave was 20.7m. The complete cathedral was 38m long and 7.2m wide. The height of the walls was reduced by between 1.8m and 3.1m during the alterations of 1749. The nave, which had a square tower at the west end, fell into disrepair after the sixteenth century reformation, and both have long since been demolished, but the foundations can still be detected to the west of the church.

The cathedral was built of local limestone and whinstone rubble with dressings of sandstone from the Ardtornish quarries. The excavated footings of the nave walls incorporate substantial slabs of slate. Two buttresses support the east wall. The south wall is divided into three bays by four buttresses; the upper parts were probably truncated and altered during the work in 1749. Their sandstone plinths are concealed by the higher turf-level of the churchyard. Each bay contains a round-headed eighteenth century window.

In the centre bay of the south wall is a round-headed blocked doorway of two chamfered orders, with a filleted hood-mould terminating in worn and crudely carved human faces; the face on the west side has a female head-dress. This was the main entrance to the church until the construction of the east porch in 1900.

The present entrance lies through the narrow passage-porch of 1900, which was formed from an

The Cathedral Church of St Moluog

annexe of 1749. The visitor enters the church by walking across the site of the high altar, beneath the 1900 gallery, which is supported by two iron columns japanned in black with gilt stencil decoration. The church is covered with a hammer-beam roof, also of 1900. On the left is a thirteenth century piscina within a pointed niche, which has another small cusped niche with a trefoil head in its back wall and mason's mark on the left shaft; then a triple sedilia with rounded arches and sloped-back jambs. Above the sedilia is a white marble memorial tablet to William Torne (minister of the church 1886–1911). The low level of these features was caused by the raising of the floor level in 1749. On the right is a fourteenth century doorway that led to a sacristy or chapel of which no trace remains. The mitred head on the left jamb is conjectured to be that of Bishop Martin de Ergaill (1342–82) who completed the cathedral. The west wall, including the rough semi-circular arch, is the medieval pulpitum, which led through to the demolished nave. The communion table, the round window above the arch and the small lean-to vestry beyond all date from 1900.

Under the gallery stair three medieval slabs with interlaced ornament are preserved. One of the stones is in memory of Duncan Stewart of Appin, who was murdered at Duart Castle in the sixteenth century. The east window glass, best seen from the gallery, was inserted in 1926 and depicts St Moluog and St Columba. Of the six windows in the north and south walls, four have stained glass. Two on the south wall, nearest the communion table, date from 1911 and depict Christ (as the Good Shepherd) and Dorcas (a woman briefly mentioned in the Acts of the Apostles who was 'full of good works and acts of charity'). The other window is modern and illustrates the command of Christ, 'Follow me'. The central window on the north wall is also modern and depicts the parable of the sower.

Turning right outside the porch, the first gate leads to a burial area, with a wall tablet to James MacGregor (d.1759), who is alleged to have fathered twenty-two children. The second gate leads round to the west end of the church, where the nave foundation can be seen over the field wall outside the vestry (the square ruin is a later burial enclosure). On the north side there is no way out, but two more medieval slabs are embedded in the grass.

The overgrown foundations of the nave and west tower, and possibly a south-west porch, are accessible from the lane through the glebe field to the north (now largely occupied by a new additional burial ground), and are easily traceable; they were revealed by excavations in the 1950s. The foundations of another building can be seen to the north in the same field. From here it can be seen that the dry stone wall and burial enclosure have, unfortunately, been built across the site of the nave.

Eight kilometres to the south of the cathedral, on a ridge overlooking the sea, is the ruin of Achinduin Castle. The castle is reached by a road to Achinduin Farm and then by a mile-long walk along a track through fields to where the remains of the castle stand on its rocky eminence. The first reference to this site is the grant of the land to Bishop William in 1240. This thirteenth century castle was the palace of the bishops of Argyll, probably until the construction of Sadell Castle by Bishop David Hamilton c.1508–12. A local tradition describes Bishop Hector MacLean (1680–7) living in the castle prior to the expulsion of the bishops in 1689, but this may refer to the seventeenth century dry stone building in the courtyard. The castle fell into disuse after the sixteenth century reformation and no part of the original structure was habitable in the late seventeenth century. Much of the castle is limestone with yellow sandstone dressings; the walls have been harled internally and externally. The fabric of the castle has continued to deteriorate and, since about 1890, much of the south-west curtain wall has collapsed. The castle is now in poor condition, but the foundations and inner walls are still visible. A mason's mark has been found in the castle identical with one on the left shaft of the piscina in the cathedral. The castle was excavated in 1970–3.

Lismore is a peaceful little island and worth a visit, though there is no public transport, and the visitor must be prepared to cycle or walk. The church is a long walk from the ferry; the castle is much further from the ferry and in the opposite direction from the church. Even with a bicycle, the visitor may have to choose between one or the other, or be prepared to return to Oban by a later ferry. The church is hardly worth attention at first glance; the nave and tower have gone, and the chancel has been altered almost beyond recognition. But beneath its coating, it still remains a substantially medieval building and the former cathedral church of the diocese of Argyll. The removal of rendering from the external walls and plaster from the internal walls; the lowering of the nave floor and the removal of the gallery; the reversal of the damaging re-orientation of 1900; the careful rebuilding of the nave and tower walls with the remaining stonework; all these things would do much to restore a medieval identity and atmosphere to the building, and reveal a more historic sight than that which first meets the eye.

1 Keddie, William (1850): p. 20.
2 Botfield, Beriah (1830): p. 225.
3 Easson, D E (1957): p. 171.
4 Fairweather, Barbara (1976): p. 2.
5 Robertson, Joseph (1891): p. 78.

Motherwell

The Cathedral Church of Our Lady of Good Aid

Diocese of Motherwell
(Roman Catholic Church)

Motherwell is situated 6.6km south-east of Glasgow and 3.2km north-east of Hamilton; its name derives from an ancient well dedicated to the Blessed Virgin Mary. The origin of the Roman Catholic cathedral at Motherwell lies in the Industrial Revolution. Coal, iron, steel and the arrival of the railways transformed a small rustic village of 300 people in 1800 into a grimy industrial town of 30,000 people in 1901. Here was the opportunity for work, and here, as in so many other parts of south-west Scotland, came great waves of immigration, not least from Ireland.

At the time of the Roman Catholic Relief Act of 1829 (Catholic Emancipation), a handful of Roman Catholics in Lanarkshire were served by a single priest resident in Glasgow. Motherwell's rapidly increasing Catholic population was later served from St Mary's Church, Hamilton and after 1873 from St Ignatius' Church, Wishaw. By 1873, the Catholic population of the town had risen to 400 and on 26 May that year a meeting, led by the parish priest at Wishaw, resolved to raise funds for the erection of a small, wooden, metal-roofed chapel in Coursington Road, adjacent to the site of the present cathedral church. The tide of immigration continued to swell the numbers of the Catholics, who quickly outgrew their wooden chapel, and on 26 September 1875, a new and larger dual purpose school-church was opened. Two months later, Motherwell became a separate mission with its own parish priest. The title of the new mission was derived from the name of the town – Our Lady of Good Aid.

Still the tide of immigration continued: the 400 Catholics of 1875 multiplied to 4,000 by 1883. The continuing rapid growth in the district's Catholic population caused the initiation of plans for building a much larger church in 1881 and an ambitious design was

The Cathedral Church of Our Lady of Good Aid

The Cathedral Church of Our Lady of Good Aid

prepared by Peter Paul Pugin. A new brick church was constructed adjacent to the school-church and opened in May 1884. This was probably only a temporary structure pending the raising of funds to construct the present cathedral, which is more modest than Pugin's 1881 design, but it is still by Pugin. The new plans were approved on 16 January 1899, the foundation stone was laid on 9 September 1899 and the completed church was opened on 9 December 1900. The total cost was approximately £11,000–12,000. Newly painted and decorated, and all the construction debts at last cleared, the church was consecrated on 14 December 1929.

The Catholic population of the Glasgow area continued to increase in the first decades of the early twentieth century, and there was a growing feeling that the large and populous diocese of Glasgow would be more manageable if it was split into three new dioceses. The division of the Glasgow diocese had first been considered in the 1920s during the episcopate of Archbishop Donald Mackintosh (1922–43), but high levels of unemployment, and then the outbreak of the Second World War, delayed implementation. In the years immediately following the war, new housing estates and a rapidly increasing population led the Vatican to believe that the vast diocese of Glasgow would be better run as a province with two suffragan sees. On 25 May 1947, by the Papal Constitution *Maxime Interest*, Pope Pius XII decreed the division of the diocese by the creation of two new dioceses of Motherwell and Paisley; the bull was implemented on 4 April 1948 when the parish church of Our Lady of Good Aid became the cathedral church of the new diocese of Motherwell.

The cathedral was reordered, on a temporary basis, in the 1970s in accordance with the requirements of the Second Vatican Council. Extensive alteration, redecoration and cleaning took place in 1984 when the cathedral was closed for four months. The temporary work was consolidated and made permanent, and the cathedral was re-opened on 9 December 1984.

Externally, the cathedral is an unexceptional Perpendicular Gothic Revival six bay rectangle of red stone. The west gable has an 8.5m high five-light window with simple tracery. The main west door leads into a spacious narthex. At the south end is the charming heptagonal baptistery. From the 1970s until the re-ordering of 1984, the baptistery was disused and the plain stone font was housed in the Lady Chapel at the east end of the south aisle. In a rare reversal of the re-orderings, caused by the decrees of the Second Vatican Council, the baptistery was brought back into use in 1984 and the font restored to its original position. The narthex is separated from the nave by a screen of leaded panes within a yellow border.

The cathedral is 39.6m long internally, 18.8m wide, and 18.5m high. The lean-to aisles are divided from the nave by arcades resting on cylindrical piers of pinkish sandstone with octagonal capitals. The clerestory lightens a low-pitched timber roof with varnished trusses and light blue paint on the panels between. The words of the *Magnificat* can be seen stencilled on the wall above the clerestory. The windows throughout are late Perpendicular, almost Tudor in shape. Those in the north aisle, with the exception of the westernmost, are squatter than those in the south aisle; this is to allow access to the Ogilvie shrine and the three confessionals.

At the west end of the north aisle, a staircase leads up to the gallery. The first recess off the north aisle contains a 1987 shrine to the Scottish Jesuit priest St John Ogilvie by Neil Finlayson. John Ogilvie is honoured as the first martyr of the Roman Catholic Church in Scotland after the sixteenth century reformation. Born in Banffshire and raised as a Calvinist, he was received into the Roman Catholic Church at Louvain in 1596. He joined the Society of Jesus (the Jesuits) in 1599 and worked in Austria and France until 1613. Returning to Scotland, he began to make converts until he was betrayed and imprisoned. He was deprived of sleep for eight days and nights in an effort to force him to reveal the names of other Catholics. He refused to speak and was hanged at Glasgow in 1615. Ogilvie was beatified in 1929 and canonised on 17 October 1976; his feast day is 10 March. The saint is shown ascending the steps of the scaffold at Glasgow Cross.

The Stations of the Cross are oil paintings on canvas within Gothic-style wooden frames. The aisles have mosaic floors. The north aisle leads to the Sacred Heart altar of white Carrara marble with colonettes of green marble. The statue is flanked by panels of coloured ceramic and mosaic. An adjacent doorway in the north wall leads to a series of vestries which surround the apse.

For the purposes of record, the pre-1984 arrangements are described here. A stone screen separated the polygonal sanctuary from the nave. The communion rail and the pulpit were of red and green marbles. A heavy green marble altar on two pillars stood in the centre of the sanctuary which had been extended and raised in the alterations of the 1970s. The pointed arched baldachino against the east wall was installed in the 1970s. It sheltered the tabernacle set on a wooden pedestal above which hung a large crucifix, all against a long curtain. The walls on either side were panelled to the height of the capitals of the nave piers and then curtained above almost to the sills of the three apse windows, each filled with stained glass. The windows were sited high above floor level to allow the vestries to be built against the east wall at ground floor level.

The present arrangement, introduced in 1984, is as follows: the tabernacle is now positioned prominently at the north-east of the sanctuary on a stone plinth above an unusual curved walnut balustrade whose inset carvings represent eucharistic themes. The matching balustrade on the south side depicts the Parable of the Sower and the proclamation of the Word, and leads up to the ambo. The inset marble in the stone pillars, surrounded by the balustrades, and the new altar, was fashioned from the former communion rails and pulpit. As a backdrop to the sanctuary, a new reredos in yellowish sandstone has been constructed, within which has been set the statue of Our Lady of Good Aid. This was done to highlight the dedication of both the diocese and the cathedral to its patron. Set below, and flanked by the stalls of the cathedral chapter, is the bishop's throne. On either side of the statue are the armorial bearings of the diocese (on the north) and those of Pope John Paul II (on the south). The alterations to stone and marble were undertaken by Thomas McMillan, and the sanctuary woodwork by Joseph McNally (who also carved the former central altar in St Andrew's Roman Catholic Cathedral in Glasgow). The words of the *Hail Mary* in Latin are painted around the wall of the apse just below the roof line.

Other changes included the refurbishment of the nave and aisles seating, the installation of a new lighting and sound system, the remodelling of the confessionals, the reinstatement of the font in the baptistery, and the cleaning of the woodwork. A strikingly new feature is to be seen in the arcades, which have been treated to give the impression of a continuous line in stone from their supporting pillars.

Above the timber and glass framework of the west gallery is the cathedral's finest feature, the great Jesse Tree window by Dunstan Powell of Hardman of Birmingham.

The interior of the cathedral is generally decorated in a sandy cream colour and the woodwork throughout is an attractive golden honey colour which gives the cathedral a sense of great warmth and light.

Francis Thompson (1917–87), Bishop of Motherwell 1965–83, is buried in the garden at the rear of the cathedral.

Hidden away in a back street, Motherwell Cathedral is difficult to find, and doesn't possess the external architectural grandeur popularly associated with the word 'cathedral'. But the present authorities of the diocese of Motherwell are probably quietly thankful that their predecessors did not embark on the planning and construction of what might have been a ruinously expensive purpose-built cathedral on a more prominent site. The Cathedral Church of Our Lady of Good Aid is not, and was never intended to be, a monument to ecclesiological triumphalism; instead, by promotion, it has become like its fellow cathedral at Ayr, the delightful epitome of a 'parish church cathedral'.

Oban

Oban (population 7,000), a coastal town on the Firth of Lorn, 137km north-west of Glasgow, is a popular tourist resort and a centre of cruises and ferries to the islands of the Inner Hebrides. Its origins lie in 'the establishment of a storehouse in 1713, by a company of merchants from Renfrew, attracted by the convenience of its position for trade, and the safe and extensive accommodations of its bay'.[1] The name of the town derives from the Gaelic for 'little bay'.

At the beginning of the nineteenth century, Oban began to expand from a small fishing village into a thriving commercial town. A population of 500 in 1800 had doubled to 1,000 by 1832 when the town was made a parliamentary burgh. By 1860 the population had risen to 2,000, by 1880 to 4,000, and by 1900 to 5,500. Sir Walter Scott's poem 'Lord of the Isles' had created interest in this part of Scotland, but the real expansion of Oban as a tourist resort began in the second half of the nineteenth century, especially with the arrival of the railway in 1880. At the end of the nineteenth century Oban had become known as the Charing Cross of the highlands.

Oban boasts two cathedrals – St Columba's Cathedral for the Roman Catholic diocese of Argyll and the Isles, and St John's Cathedral, for the Scottish Episcopal diocese of the same name. St Columba's Cathedral is complete and architecturally quite straightforward; St John's Cathedral is very incomplete and rather complex.

The Cathedral Church of St John the Divine

United Dioceses of Argyll and the Isles

(Scottish Episcopal Church)

In 1846 the dioceses of Argyll and the Isles were separated from the vast area of the united dioceses of Moray, Ross and Caithness, and Alexander Ewing was consecrated the first bishop of the new diocese. Bishop Ewing visited Oban in the spring of 1848. It was a quiet fishing village but already beginning to acquire a reputation as a resort for 'small reading parties, with tutors, from the English Universities, and of their assistance Bishop Ewing gladly availed himself'.[2] Services were first held in a house in Cawdor Place, then in the Caledonian Hotel and then in the Masonic Hall in Argyll Square. There are no surviving registers or records from these early days, but there was no permanent episcopal church in Oban until the construction of the earliest part of the present cathedral in 1864 at the junction of George Street and William Street. At the end of the 1850s, an appeal was launched for the sum of £2,000 to build a new church, supported by the efforts of two local lairds, Macdougall of Dunollie and Campbell of Dunstaffnage, and Robert MacGeorge, parish priest of Oban from 1859. Their argument centred on the lamentable lack of a proper church in a town of increasing importance: 'It is a very central point in the lately revived and united diocese of Argyll and the Isles. It is in the immediate vicinity of Lismore and Iona, the ancient cathedral seats of the two venerable sees from which the new diocese has been constituted. It is much frequented by members of the Church of England, and especially of the universities, who, coming to visit their northern sister, naturally expect some supply of their spiritual wants'.[3]

The chosen architect, Charles Wilson, died before the plans were finalised and the church was designed by his partner, David Thomson. The foundation stone was laid on 4 July 1863 and the church was consecrated on 22 September 1864. It was a small building, consisting of an aisleless nave, a small chancel with a tiny vestry attached, and a small porch at the north-east. A tower and spire were intended but never built. In 1872 the *Oban Times* described it as a 'pretty little place of worship'. At this time the town was fast expanding as a popular holiday resort and during the summer months the church was so crowded that there was not even standing room. Bishop Ewing died on Ascension Day 1873 and was succeeded by Bishop George Mackarness (1874–83), who commissioned the Inverness architects Ross and Mackintosh to submit plans for a new and larger church, reproducing the features of the ancient cathedral at Iona. The bishop's choice of Ross and Mackintosh was probably governed by the work of Alexander Ross in designing the recently completed (1869) cathedral at Inverness for the diocese of Moray, Ross and Caithness. In 1876, Mackarness had consecrated the little church on Cumbrae as the cathedral for the diocese of the Isles, and as a temporary pro-cathedral for the diocese of Argyll. The planned new church in Oban would now serve as the cathedral for the Argyll diocese. Because of sharply fluctuating attendance, according to the season of the year, a church was needed that could be arranged to seat 800–1,000 people in the summer and 250–300 people in the winter. The plan was abandoned, probably on the grounds of cost, before any work had begun, but the problem of insufficient space remained.

In 1882, a modest south aisle, designed by Thomson and Turnbull, was added to the 1864 church at a cost of £1,000. This church, as extended in 1882, now forms the rear of the present cathedral.

New plans for the erection of a larger church were commissioned by Bishop Alexander Chinnery-Haldane (1883–1906) before his premature death in 1906, and the designs of James Chalmers of Glasgow were chosen in 1908. Astonishingly, the first part of the work was completed in the short period of six months. The new structure was intended to be a memorial to Bishop Chinnery-Haldane and was mostly funded by members of his family. The late bishop had a good deal of money of his own and his wife had inherited a considerable fortune. The foundation stone of the new structure was laid by the bishop's three-year old grandson, Alexander Chinnery-Haldane, on 2 February 1910, and the church was ready for use on 17 August of the same year. The laying of the foundation stone was delayed until Alexander was three and, despite his youth, he could recall the occasion into his old age. He died in 1994 at the age of eighty-six.

Chalmers' plan involved turning the axis of the church through ninety degrees, and on the north side of the existing church he built a shallow sanctuary, a crossing, a south transept, one bay of a projected nave, a side chapel and a sacristy, with halls underneath. Chalmers favoured a mixture of styles and his work incorporates Romanesque, Transitional, Early English and Decorated. Although his plan envisaged an aisled nave of five bays, a lantern tower above the crossing, and a bell tower at the south-west, funds were exhausted by August 1910 and no more work was done.

In 1919, when there was still every prospect that the cathedral would be completed according to Chalmers' design, Bishop Kenneth Mackenzie (1907–42) took the decision to make St John's Church the cathedral church for the united dioceses of Argyll and the Isles, and so it was inaugurated on St Columba's Day 1920. The bishop had at first intended that St John's should replace the small cathedral on Cumbrae, but the legal constitution of the latter cathedral prevented it from being downgraded, and the two buildings have enjoyed co-cathedral status ever since.

Several attempts to complete St John's Cathedral, to different designs by different architects, have been considered at different dates since 1910, but with little result. In 1928 Harold Tarbolton of Edinburgh prepared a completely new design, incorporating a high tower at the south-east of the cathedral. The financing of the work was to have been supervised by the Oban Cathedral Appeal Fund based on Staten Island, New York, and led by Mary Alice Cisco; the Wall Street crash of 1929 ended the plan.

In 1958, Ian Gordon Lindsay of Edinburgh, himself the author of a book on Scottish cathedrals, was invited to examine the cathedral and submit plans for its completion. His scheme envisaged the demolition of the 1864 church with its 1882 aisle, to make way for the completion of the nave envisaged by Chalmers. A central altar with a lantern tower above was proposed for the area where the choir stalls now stand. The intention was to complete the crossing-tower with a much lighter construction than in Chalmers' scheme (owing to foundation problems), to place the high altar beneath it and to move the bishop's throne and stalls into what was the sanctuary. Under this scheme the cathedral would have taken the shape of a Greek cross. The nave would have been completed and displaced the original parish church. A similar system of screens would have allowed for the seasonal variations in sizes of congregation. The total cost of the work was estimated at £100,000. Another appeal was launched, led by two Highland chiefs – Cameron of Lochiel and Maclean of Duart – but this was eventually abandoned, again on the ground of expense. The last substantial alterations to the cathedral were made to a design by Ian Lindsay in 1968. The floor level of the nave was raised to its intended level, and a glass screen with sliding doors erected in place of an arcade.

The idea of completing the cathedral was kept alive until the late 1980s but has now been abandoned. Although nothing is visible, substantial work to stabilise the cathedral was undertaken in 1988, financed by a large residuary bequest from a couple who came to Oban on their honeymoon in 1910, and thought it a shame then that construction had stopped. The cathedral has recently had to sell a piece of land in order to spend £250,000 on making permanent the temporary roof of the 1910 structure.

The cathedral that is seen today is a complicated muddle, an awkward union of three separate building phases of 1864, 1882 and 1910. The comment made by Ian Gordon Lindsay in his *Cathedrals of Scotland*, published in 1926, still holds good: 'The whole presents a most incongruous appearance, for the parts of the two churches are at right angles to one another…When completed it ought to prove the most pleasing, though by no means the largest, of the cathedrals of Scotland'.[4] Although it is sad that his 1958 plans were never implemented, St John's Cathedral is a fascinating building to explore.

The main entrance is through the porch on George Street. This was built in 1882 allowing access from what had become the main street of the town. The doorway on the right leads to the (1864) base of the intended tower. The present vestibule, doubling as a baptistery, with its arch-braced roof, is the south aisle constructed in 1882. It now contains the octagonal white and pink marble font of 1904 given by the Macdougalls of Dunollie. A staircase at the far end of the vestibule descends to the choir vestry below. The internal window in the narthex, which leads down to the choir vestry, replaced one arch of the original arcade demolished in 1968. This was intended to be a doorway into a new organ and choir gallery in the cathedral, but was never completed.

The glazed screen divides the 1882 south aisle from the 1864 nave. It was installed in 1972, on the site of a stone arcade demolished in 1968, to allow the floor to be raised. Through the screen is the 1864 nave, with the old east window on the right. The window, by Wailes of Newcastle, was given in 1864 by Sir Donald Campbell of Dunstaffnage, in memory of his brother Sir Angus Campbell; it depicts episodes in the life of St John. To the right one jamb of the old sanctuary arch can still be seen.

Only parts of the nineteenth century roof are visible at the west end; most of what can be seen is modern and flat. The two west lancets in the 1864 section were hand-painted by Sarah Campbell of Dunstaffnage in the early 1990s; the left-hand window depicts the dream of Jacob at Bethel; the right-hand window depicts the vision of St John the Divine in which the elders cast their crowns on to a sea of glass. A round window can be seen above.

From here there comes a sharp contrast between the rubble walls of the 1864 parish church and the smooth ashlar of 1910. Here is one bay of the nave with its clerestory, the neo-Romanesque transept arches – although only one of the transepts was built – and then the sanctuary; and above, the high roof with sky lights, clearly intended to be temporary. Before any of these things are reached, the great diagonal steel shores, supporting the 1910 building, are very apparent. The shores go through the floor and deep into the earth below the undercroft which is the floor below the cathedral floor. The obvious incompleteness of the cathedral may seem quite peculiar and cause the cathedral to resemble a half-restored bomb site, but there is something quite endearing about this building, which invites curiosity and exploration.

Before the crossing, at the east end of the nave, is the semi-circular 1910 pulpit, constructed of St Bee's stone with marble and Mexican onyx embellishments. It has Romanesque arches and an uncomfortable-looking yellow sandstone angel. The pulpit has carvings of bishop's heads and other faces, emblems of the four evangelists, St Columba, St Mungo and the Hand of God. The 1881 brass eagle lectern to the right may have been intended to stand on the adjacent marble plinth.

The choir occupies the partially complete crossing and is entered through a granite septum with a yellow marble cap. The chancel and sanctuary steps are of green Iona marble; the chancel floor is composite. The timber roof here was framed up in 1958 but left with temporary, but now permanent, skylight glazing. This is where Ian Lindsay proposed a great lantern tower in 1958; it was to have had a viewing platform from which all Oban could have been seen.

The oak stalls have disproportionately large and ungainly carved ends, intended to represent tall roundheaded carved stones in a Celtic graveyard; the bishop's stall on the north wall is indistinguishable from the surrounding canon's stalls, apart from the canopy above. Placed in the midst of the cathedral chapter, the bishop's stall resembles a domestic throne rather than the full cathedra in the sanctuary. Above the throne, on the blocked north transept arch, is a splendid metal eagle representing St John the Evangelist; it was carved by George Wyllie in 1969. The chapter stalls are labelled as follows:

Chancellor	Synod Canon
Bishop	Bishop's Canon's Stall
Dean	Cumbrae Stall
Synod Clerk	Bishop's Second Canon's Stall
Chapter Clerk	Assistant Priest
Precentor	Provost

The stalls of the provost and the precentor are turned through a forty-five degree angle towards the altar. The provost's stall is heavily decorated with thistles; the precentor's stall is plainer.

The small cross incised above the base of the left-hand pier at the entrance to the sanctuary is the foundation stone laid by Alexander Chinnery-Haldane in 1910. The Gothic reredos is more than 12m high and contains an Ascension painting flanked by niches with statues. The reredos and high altar were given in memory of Bishop Chinnery-Haldane by his widow; the bishop is depicted as St Columba in the right-hand statue. The left-hand statue is a representation of St John. The central painting of the Ascension, and the outer paintings of the Annunciation on either side, and the Pieta below, are by the Glasgow artist Norman MacDougall; they were cleaned in 1989. The painting of the Ascension is charmingly set in the west Scottish Highlands, and the faces of the disciples are those of members of the congregation in 1910. A piscina and triple sedilia can be seen in the south wall of the sanctuary. On the north wall is the cathedra of the bishop.

The organ gallery, cantilevered over the stalls and resting gingerly on a three bay arcade leading into the south transept, is painted and grained in a light wood texture. The former pipe organ, by Blackett and Howden of Newcastle, was a poor hybrid instrument formed from two separate organs. It was removed in 1994 and replaced by a new electronic organ by J W Wood of Bradford in association with the Bradford Computing Organ Society.

The complete south transept houses the Lady Chapel with an altar of Siena marble framed by a Romanesque arch supported by responds with scalloped capital. A number of modern brass tablets can be seen on the wall. The altar is in memory of Charles Pressley-Smith, the first provost of the cathedral (1895–1920) and dean of the diocese (1897–1930), who lived at what is now the King's Knoll Hotel.

In the south aisle is a wooden pulpit of 1895 with gilt decoration; some preachers might find it a tight fit. It was transferred to the cathedral from St Columba's Church, in Portree on the Isle of Skye.

The best view of the exterior of the cathedral is obtained from crossing George Street and looking back towards the main entrance door; this is the porch that enters the 1882 south aisle. To the right of the porch is the east window of the 1864 church, then two windows of the 1910 nave, then the three lancets of the 1910 south transept. The roof above the 1864 east window and the 1910 nave has been altered to reflect the envisaged post-1910 arrangements. From George Street, a walk down William Street, along the side of the 1882 south aisle, reveals the beginning of the warren of underground rooms below the cathedral. At the end of the aisle, turn right into a rather dingy alley, and here the network of troglodyte dwellings below the cathedral becomes more apparent. Above ground one sees first the west window and gable of the 1882 south aisle, then the west gable and twin lancets of the 1864 church, and then the full pathos of this starkly unfinished cathedral. The large round-headed blocked arch of the intended north transept, in rendered cement, sharply distinguishes it from the mud-red colour of the rest of the cathedral; on the right side a scalloped capital pathetically and plaintively emerges from the cement as an indicator of what lies on the other side of the wall – the ambitious plans of 1910. To the left of the arch is a more evocative sight – the ghostly concave shadow of the half-completed cylindrical turret that would have carried the spiral stair up to the great central lantern tower. Everything here looks very unfinished, and there is no concealing the fact. Sadly, unless something is done, the cathedral from this point resembles nothing more than a derelict warehouse. Leaving all this behind by walking across the site of the north transept and turning right into Nursery Lane, the height of the cathedral floor above the road way becomes even more apparent. Because of the abutment of houses, there is no east window, and the one piece of ornamentation is a blocked rose window at the top of the gable – now probably blocked for ever.

It may be a pipe dream to hope for the completion of the cathedral in accordance with the plans of 1910 but, as it stands, the building is an odd, interesting and entertaining muddle and well worth seeing.

1 Lewis, Samuel (1846): volume 2, pp 325–6.
2 Craven, J B (1907): p. 375.
3 ibid., p. 377.
4 Lindsay, Ian Gordon (1926): p. 245.

The Cathedral Church of St Columba

Diocese of Argyll and the Isles
(Roman Catholic Church)

In 1843, the Roman Catholic community in Oban numbered only fifteen people, and this small group met in private houses. Before many years had passed, their numbers had increased to such an extent that Oban was made the see town of the diocese of Argyll and the Isles and, in 1886, a cathedral was built of prefabricated sheets of corrugated iron and lavishly decorated at the expense of the marquess of Bute; it became known as the 'tin cathedral'.

John Patrick Crichton-Stuart (1847–1900), third marquess of Bute, caused a major stir among his contemporaries when, in December 1868, five months after his twenty-first birthday, he was received into the Roman Catholic Church. Bute was a serious and scholarly individual and his decision to seek admission to the Roman Catholic Church was only made after much study and thought and travel in the Holy Land. Much to the surprise of his contemporaries, nobody actually 'influenced' him; the decision was his alone. Bute was a zealous supporter of the church of his conversion, and the pro-cathedral at Oban was only one example of his generosity. While staying in Oban, the baronet and Benedictine monk, Sir David Hunter Blair (1853–1939), remembered Bute's contribution towards the liturgy of the pro-cathedral: 'I preached every Sunday at the pro-cathedral, and enjoyed the daily singing of the office and high mass, due to the generosity of Lord Bute, who supported a choir of boys and men entirely out of his own expense'.[1] Bute was also an enthusiastic antiquary and contributed a good deal towards the restoration of the remains of the cathedrals at St Andrews and Whithorn.

The 'tin cathedral' at Oban was still in use in the mid-1920s, when Ian Gordon Lindsay observed: 'This is made of iron, and is quite as ugly as could be. However, it is only temporary, and the bishop is collecting money wherewith to build a new one, which will probably be better than any of its sister cathedrals'.[2] It was at first hoped that the 'tin cathedral' would before long be superseded by a permanent structure, and then dismantled and used elsewhere. In fact it remained in position for fifty years. Despite its nickname, the cathedral was as well furnished as it could be; it was equipped with stalls to the east of a tall screen with rood above; and the high altar had a baldachino.

The first design for a permanent cathedral was drawn up in 1913 by a London architect, Alfred Johnston. It was mainly in a Romanesque idiom with zigzagged and chevroned decoration to the piers, and a tower not unlike that proposed earlier in James Chalmers' design for St John's Cathedral, Oban. Johnston's plans were not implemented, nor was the plan for a permanent cathedral until the arrival, in 1919, of Donald Martin, bishop of Argyll and the Isles. As the diocese had very limited funds, the bishop's plans for a permanent cathedral were nothing short of visionary. He travelled as far as the United States to appeal to exiled Roman Catholic highlanders for support. The response was initially encouraging, but the financial collapse of 1929, and the ensuing depression, delayed construction.

The cathedral was designed by Sir Giles Gilbert Scott, architect of the Anglican cathedral at Liverpool, and the foundation stone was laid on 14 September 1932. Construction was undertaken by a local firm, Macdougall of Oban. By October 1934, the eastern part of the cathedral was nearing completion, and the rising structure was praised by *The Builder*: 'It is not difficult, even from this section, to realise the noble proportions, the symmetrical arrangement and the rugged simplicity which will be displayed to their fullest when the cathedral is finished… The walls and pillars are left in their rough-hewn granite, but one cannot omit to notice in the former that each block is differently shaped, thus maintaining the medieval character of the cathedral. This is also shown in the beams of the roof, the timbers being adze-cut and not sawn'.[3]

Work was stopped by the outbreak of the Second World War in 1939, and not resumed until 1945. The large west tower and the interior of the cathedral were not finished until 1953. Two bells, named Kenneth and Brendan, were blessed by Bishop Kenneth Grant and installed in the tower in 1959.

St Columba's Cathedral occupies a prominent position on the edge of the harbour, at the junction of Corran Brae and Corran Esplanade. Its sea front site, and its rough-hewn granite surfaces, give the building a somewhat tough and rugged appearance. The proportions are generally good, though the tower is over-large and dwarfs the low lean-to aisles with their stepped gables.

The style is generally Gothic, but Scott has not designed a slavish copy or stylish interpretation of one of its three principal phases. Instead, he has produced a rough and simple Gothic building constructed of pink Aberdeen granite – the hardest of stones – and consequently with minimal decoration and no attempt at sophistication.

The main entrance to the cathedral is through the south-west door which leads into the south aisle. Above the internal door can be seen a picture of St Columba on his boat, with pagan druids on the shore calling down curses on his head.

The first impression is of a simple, open and spacious building. The walls are mostly blue Kentallen granite;

The Cathedral Church of St Columba

the dado, window frames, arcades and piers are pink Aberdeen granite. The tall, rough arcades with no moulding – uncertain of whether to be Romanesque or Gothic – are supported by cylindrical piers laid in irregular-sized drums, with octagonal bases and simple, indistinct capitals. Quadruple lancets in each bay of the aisles lighten the interior, but the absence of a clerestory and the high open timber roof give the interior a heavy atmosphere. The aisle roof trusses rest on stone brackets on the outer faces of the columns. The wrought iron lamp brackets continue the general theme of simplicity.

The lofty baptistery beneath the tower is entered by a very tall, wide arch and the open timber ceiling is almost as high as the apex of the nave roof. The area is lit by three tall lancets within a Romanesque frame. The saucer-bowled font, set on a splayed pedestal, has a copper cover.

The internal north-west doorway, leading into the north-west porch, has a distinctive 'dropped ogee' head, and the door, like its counterpart at the south-west, has an adzed finish, which imparts a slightly medieval feel to the building. The Stations of the Cross along the north and south aisle walls are crisply carved wood parcel gilt.

At the east end of the north aisle is the Lady Chapel which has a modern Gothic reredos by Peter Watts of Bath, representing the Assumption of the Blessed Virgin Mary. Another carved and painted Madonna and Child on the north wall is probably nineteenth century Italian. The altar is composed of funnel-shaped blocks of sandstone and granite. The area beyond the chapel, seen through the range of eight lancets above the altar, is intended for a bigger organ than the cathedral so far possesses.

The extension of the raised chancel floor into what was the east bay of the nave has been subtly done; there is no chancel arch or rood. The communion rail is a low granite wall with wooden capping, and the adjoining pulpit on the south side is also granite. The high altar is made from Horton sandstone topped with a mensa of Italian marble. The oak reredos, set within a sandstone frame, is the work of Donald Gilbert of Sussex and depicts scenes from the life of Columba: his meeting with King Brude of the Picts at Inverness, and his meeting with St Kentigern of Glasgow. The two saints are exchanging their croziers as a sign of friendship and reconciliation between the Celts of Dalriada and the British people of Strathclyde. The vine, a symbol of Christ, is carved in stone around the panels. There is a wooden canopy above, carved with stylised thistles. The hanging sanctuary lamp is suspended from a gilt brass representation of the 'Galley of Lorne' of the Campbell clan.

The Gothic style stalls are of pale oak. The bishop's throne, formerly behind the altar, is now on the north side and marked out by its triangular-headed back. It was made for Bishop Roderick Wright and is modelled on the armorial bearings of the city of Glasgow. A piscina can be seen on the south wall.

The Sacred Heart Chapel on the south side of the chancel has an altar of Horton sandstone with a simple dorsal curtain and tester and dove. Matching the Lady Chapel is a range of eight lancets above the altar. There is also a heavy oak Gothic confessional.

The internal 'Tudor' frames to the lancet windows disappear on the outside where the windows become what they are – individual lancets more resistant to the battering of the wind and the rain. On the north sides of the cathedral and up the hill are the domestic buildings; from here the organ chamber masquerades as a mostly windowless transept.

The cathedral has suffered much with water penetration, and water stains can be seen almost everywhere on the internal walls. The white lime stains can be seen in many places, especially above the nave arcades, on the south wall of the sanctuary, and in the baptistery. But then this is a sea front cathedral for a sea-girt diocese – Argyll and the Isles – and one could imagine a congregation of seafarers wearing dripping oilskins. This is a tough building which exudes strength and nobility by the simplicity and roughness of its architecture. There is a refreshing absence of acres of Caen stone, Italian marble and statues, and sophisticated carving and polished finish. This is a rough and rugged cathedral whose clear intention is to resist the onslaught of the rain, the sea and the battering of a force nine gale.

1 Hunter Blair, David (1919): p. 209.
2 Lindsay, Ian Gordon (1926): p. 248.
3 *The Builder*, Volume CXLVII, 5 October 1934, p. 573.

Paisley

The Cathedral Church of St Mirin

Diocese of Paisley
(Roman Catholic Church)

Paisley (population 85,000) is a large industrial town, 6km west of Glasgow, and now virtually a suburb of the city. The derivation of the name is very uncertain, but may originate with the Gaelic *Bas-leac*, meaning 'a flat stone shoal', perhaps an allusion to the ridge of rocks across the River Cart near the town.

The only historic building is the twelfth–fifteenth century Paisley Abbey, of which the nave of the church is now a presbyterian parish church. The priory (of Pasletum) was founded by Walter Fitzalan in 1163, who installed thirteen Cluniac monks from Wenlock in Shropshire. The relics of St Mirin (or Merryn or Meadhran or Merinus), whose cell had stood here in the seventh century, were transferred to the new priory and it quickly became a centre of pilgrimage. The priory grew in wealth and importance and was raised to the status of an abbey in 1219. Of Mirin himself very little reliable information is known, beyond the fact that he is generally accepted to have been the first to preach Christianity at Paisley, and came from Ireland. He was a disciple of St Comgall at Bangor and a contemporary of St Columba. He is thought to have arrived in Scotland about c.585 and died about c.620; his feast day is kept on 15 September. The abbey has a late fifteenth century chapel dedicated to St Mirren, at the point of the south transept, with a series of twelfth century panels depicting episodes of doubtful authenticity from the life of the saint.

St Mirin's position as the founder of Paisley, as much as his Irish origin, made him the obvious choice to be the patron saint of Paisley's first Roman Catholic church since the sixteenth century reformation. The church, which stood in East Buchanan Street, was built in 1808–9 and was notable as the first large Roman Catholic Church to be built in Scotland, and the first in the west of Scotland, since the reformation. The new church was the work of Fr. William Rattray, the first resident priest, and was constructed to meet the needs of the increasing numbers of Roman Catholics in the town; an increase caused mainly by the growth in the weaving industry in Paisley at the beginning of the nineteenth century. The expanding industry brought an influx of mostly Irish Roman Catholics, with some Highlanders. Constructing the church was a bold venture at a time when bigotry and prejudice were still the norm among the non-Catholic population. Determined efforts were made to prevent the erection of the church, and it was not uncommon to have pulled down in the night what had been put up during the day. Against all difficulties, the new church was ready for use in October 1809 and could seat 600–700 people.

The church continued in use for more than 120 years until it was replaced by the present cathedral church in 1932. The old church had become structurally unsound by 1924, and a succession of appeals by the archbishop of Glasgow resulted in the construction of the present cathedral. Construction began in March 1930; the first bricks were put in place by the parish clergy on 14 June that year, and the foundation stone was laid by the archbishop on 28 September 1930. The new church was designed by Thomas Baird of Glasgow and stands at the junction of Glasgow Road and Incle Street.

The new St Mirin's Church continued as a parish church until 25 May 1947 when the diocese of Paisley was created, and the church was raised to the status of the cathedral church for the new diocese. The division of the large archdiocese of Glasgow, and the creation of the new dioceses of Paisley and Motherwell, had first been considered in the 1920s during the episcopate of Archbishop Donald Mackintosh (1922–43). Difficulties, including the high level of unemployment and then the outbreak of the Second World War, delayed implementation. In the post-war years, new housing estates and a rapidly increasing population led Rome itself to believe that the vast archdiocese of Glasgow would be better run as a province with two suffragan sees, and Pope Pius XII decreed the formation of two new dioceses (Paisley and Motherwell) on 25 May 1947 by the Papal Constitution *Maxime Interest*; the bull was implemented on 4 April 1948. The new cathedral church was solemnly consecrated on 27 November 1957.

Paisley Cathedral is built of white freestone in an attractive Romanesque style; Gothic was a spent force by 1930. The cathedral is rectangular; the nave measures 33.2m in length and 14.7m (between the arcades) in width; the sanctuary is 8.9m wide by 7m in depth and takes the form of a polygonal apse.

The west doors lead into a narthex, the two west windows of which have stained glass recording the names of the parish priests and administrators of the cathedral since 1808; there is also a shrine to St John Ogilvie (1579–1615), Scotland's post-reformation Catholic saint. The main body of the cathedral is virtually a single chamber with a shallow polygonal apse. Decorated in various shades of cream and yellow, the interior is bright and welcoming. The pews are pale oak

The Cathedral Church of St Mirin

and the doors are quarter cut oak. The Stations of the Cross are glazed ceramic tiles. The Romanesque arcades with scalloped capitals lead into corridor aisles, and support plain moulded arches. A wide barrel-vaulted plaster ceiling gives a tunnel effect to the interior, broken into by little transverse vaults to form the tall clerestory of twin openings.

Confessionals line the aisles. Although entered through doors in the aisles themselves, and seeming to be incorporated within the structure of the building, they project outwards from the aisle walls; this can be seen by walking around the exterior of the building. The chancel arch is slender and delicate and looks lost in an expansive wall. The last clerestory windows before the arch suggest a kind of transept effect by extending just a little higher than all the other windows of the clerestory.

The only stained glass is in the fifteen small windows of the apse. The windows are set high up, the lower walls being hugged externally by the vestries (rather like Motherwell Cathedral). The white marble font with a pierced brass cover now stands at the east end of the south aisle. The carved stone pulpit with wooden canopy is wrapped round a nearby column of the south arcade, and roofed by a gilt and wood tester which seems to cling precariously to the arch above. The chancel, extended forward with a white marble floor, has a communion rail with dark green marble cap and base, white marble colonettes and brass gates, and an unusual octagonal baldachino with an upper stylised temple cantilevered from gilded pilasters and square columns. The tall domed gilt brass tabernacle stands on a marble plinth. The apse is walled with a mixture of pink, dark green, grey and white marbles.

On the south side of the sanctuary is the marble-walled chapel housing the Lady Altar. On the north side is the similarly marble-walled chapel of the Sacred Heart Altar. Both chapels are domestic in size and entered by moulded Romanesque arches that are dwarfed by the immense size of the chancel arch. Iron screens divide the chapels from the sanctuary. On the pier to the south of the altar is a plaque commemorating James Black, first bishop of Paisley, 1948–68. From the east end of the cathedral can be seen the organ on its very plain gallery.

At first sight, the cathedral resembles a superior,

PAISLEY: *The Cathedral Church of St Mirin*

OBAN: *The Cathedral Church of St Columba*

SKEABOST: *The remains of the Cathedral Church of St Columba*

decorative and well-appointed folly, and the absence of a plinth gives it the appearance of being even more squat than it is. The narthex, entered by three round-headed west doors below a crenellated parapet – over which one might almost expect to see a row of cannon – and flanked by two squat little battlemented towers at the north and the south, creates an image of a well-defended little fort. The towers and the narthex provide a 'west front' that seem to be bolted on to the cathedral and designed to offer some protection against passing marauders. Paisley Cathedral is a tough, sturdy, attractive and rare example of Romanesque revival.

Perth

The Cathedral Church of St Ninian

United Dioceses of St Andrews, Dunkeld and Dunblane (Scottish Episcopal Church)

Perth has a population of 42,000, and lies 71km north of Edinburgh and 98km north-east of Glasgow, on the west bank of the River Tay. Its name may derive from *Bhar Tatha*, meaning 'height of the Tay'.

Although there may have been a Roman settlement here, this is uncertain and disputed; but the site was of sufficient importance and prominence for King Kenneth I of the Scots (834–58) to establish the first capital of a united kingdom of Picts and Scots at nearby Scone in 846. King William the Lion (1165–1214) founded a royal burgh at Perth in 1210, and the town remained the capital city of Scotland until c.1452. The importance of Perth in the Middle Ages was reflected by the number of religious orders that established houses there: the Dominicans, the Franciscans, the Carmelites, the Carthusians and the Augustinians. Due to the work of John Knox in 1559, and the ferocity with which he promoted the less wholesome principles of the reformation, there is no surviving trace of any of these great houses in Perth today.

Despite its civil and religious importance in the Middle Ages, Perth was never the cathedral city of a diocese. It lies roughly at the junction of the three ancient dioceses of St Andrews, Dunkeld and Dunblane. In the arrangement of the Scottish Episcopal Church, these three dioceses have been held together under the jurisdiction of a single bishop since 1837. As the most important town in the united dioceses, Perth was the natural choice for the location of a new cathedral in place of the former cathedral at Dunblane, the partly-ruined cathedral at Dunkeld, and the wrecked cathedral at St Andrews.

The establishment of a cathedral at Perth was due to the approval, though not the active participation, of Bishop Patrick Torry. Then parish priest at Peterhead, Torry was elected bishop of Dunkeld in 1808; Dunblane was added to his jurisdiction in 1835, and St Andrews in 1837. An episcopal chapel had existed in Perth, although for forty years, until the mid-nineteenth century, it was ruled by Henry Skete (d.1846), an eccentric priest who insisted on using the *Book of Common Prayer* of the Church of England and refused to acknowledge the jurisdiction of the Scottish bishop. The schism ended on 25 January 1849 and a new St John's Church was built at the same time as the cathedral. Given Skete's non-co-operation, Bishop Torry took the view that the Episcopal Church should be properly represented in so important a town and appointed a priest to reside in the city. The said priest, John C Chambers, held his first service in an upper room in Atholl Street on St Andrew's Day (also Advent Sunday) 1846. Chambers had no illusions about the task that lay ahead of him: 'The notices of the Services having first been published in the journals and posted in the town, I commenced the exercise of my functions without any hope of having more than six persons as members'.[1] His expectations were surpassed. 'By Christmas, about thirty communicants enrolled themselves, to the great gratification as well as astonishment of the bishop'.[2] The mission was a rapid success and, at his own instigation, Lord Forbes drew up a scheme to provide a cathedral, a collegiate residence for the bishop, and sufficient endowments for the bishop and the chapter. The church was built almost simultaneously with the little church and college Millport on the Isle of Cumbrae, built at the instigation of Forbes' contemporary, George Boyle. In August 1847, Bishop Torry wrote to Forbes giving his blessing to the plan: 'It is in my estimation, a noble scheme... When contemplated, even in prospect only, it excites joyful feelings. Were it the will of God, it would gladden my heart in the evening of my days to witness even the commencement of it, and its partial execution by the erection of the chancel to serve as an interim church. The entire completion of the scheme I dare not hope to see, for I am in my 84th year and the oldest prelate in the island of Great Britain, with the exception of the archbishop of York [Archbishop Vernon Harcourt was in his ninetieth year and died in 1847]. It appears that your lordship is the originator of this noble scheme, and that you have shewn your liberality by contributing a considerable sum of money towards its accomplishment. For this your lordship deserves the hearty thanks of the Church generally, and particularly of myself for the interest you have shewn in the welfare of the diocese'.[3]

A planning committee – including J C Chambers, Lord Forbes, George Boyle (sixth earl of Glasgow from 1869), Viscount Camden, and W E Gladstone, among others – had soon raised £6,000 and the church started to become reality. The building committee began its report with a nostalgic and wistful look to the past: 'We should have preferred the restoration of one of the ancient cathedrals; but it is enough for us to know that they are shut out from us for the present. And we know no reason why we should remain inactive, with folded arms, merely because we cannot have everything as we should like'.[4]

The names of the members of the building committee provide the clue to the troubles that lay ahead. All of them were in the tradition of the Oxford Movement and Boyle (at Christ Church) in particular was inspired by the work of John Henry Newman, the leading figure of the movement at Oxford. Forbes and Boyle took a leading role in the creation and funding of the cathedral, and both men were wealthy.

William Butterfield (1814–1900), architect of the church and college at Millport, was chosen to design the new cathedral. Butterfield was among the most prominent of architects in the Victorian age and completely in sympathy with the rising Anglo-Catholic movement in the Church of England. Bishop Torry was delighted with Butterfield's proposed design. In December 1848 he wrote: 'The plans for the new cathedral in Perth reached me two days ago, the designs of which I think extremely beautiful and admirably adapted for its high and holy purpose'.[5]

The foundation stone was laid on 15 September 1849, the eve of St Ninian's Day, and by December 1850 the chancel, transepts and one bay of the nave had been completed; enough for a congregation of 350, and enough, it was judged, for the structure to be consecrated. Because of Bishop Torry's age and infirmity, the cathedral was consecrated by Alexander Penrose Forbes, bishop of Brechin, and the sermon was delivered by John Mason Neale, one of the principal figures in the ecclesiological movement that wished to introduce a medieval orthodoxy into the architecture of nineteenth century churches.

The office of dean of the cathedral had first been offered to a Mr Kenrick, who declined, and then to John Mason Neale in August 1850. Neale had been pressed to accept the deanery by his friend Joseph Haskoll, one of the first three canons of the cathedral appointed by Bishop Torry [the others were J C Chambers and Henry Humble]. 'Of all things which I can think of, there is none which I should like better personally, and, still further, there is nothing which I believe would be better for the Church in Scotland, than for you to come here. You have no idea of the capabilities of Perth, but we want a Neale to set them going'.[6] This informal pressure was followed by a formal offer from the aged Bishop Torry. 'You would, in my opinion, be a valuable acquisition to our Perth Cathedral; but I scarcely dare indulge the hope of your becoming one of the staff of clergy of that institution which, although designed for the noblest and most holy of purposes, my eyes shall never be blessed with a sight of; being now more than half through my eighty-seventh year... It would, however, cheer the evening of my days were you to accept the office proposed to you'.[7]

The Cathedral Church of St Ninian

Neale was touched by the many letters that he received exhorting him to accept the office, but he declined, for three reasons. Firstly, he felt that he could do more good by remaining where he was in the Church of England; secondly, he would want to come as a missionary with a licence to preach and teach everywhere in Scotland, and that, he was sure, would kill him within a year; thirdly, despite his interest in music, he felt that he was not competent enough in the subject to be dean of a cathedral.[8] With Neale's refusal, the deanery was left vacant until 1851, and only the three residentiary canons were installed at the opening ceremony in December 1850.

Despite his refusals of the deanery, Neale felt it his duty to accept Bishop Torry's invitation to preach at the opening of the cathedral. The consecration date had originally been set for 16 September (St Ninian's Day), but work was not complete, and even as Neale arrived in Perth at sunset in December, the work was still going on. 'That night I shall ever remember as one of the strangest of my life. Many of the most necessary arrangements had been driven to the very last: the carpenter's hammer and the mason's chisel were still to be heard; a crowd of workmen were yet engaged in putting the finishing touches to their respective departments; the frescoes were still incomplete, and, in the later hours of the evening, the choir was practising the chants and hymns for the next day… Perfect silence settled down over the city, but still, as we visited the cathedral at twelve, at two, at four and, at six, the workmen were still engaged in their various occupations, nor was it till the late morning of a Scottish December day had fairly broken that everything was prepared for the approaching solemnity'.[9]

Perth Cathedral was the first new cathedral to be started in Scotland since the sixteenth century reformation [although Inverness was the first to be completed], and it remains the enduring memorial to Bishop Torry who, to the end of his life, retained a fondness for the building. 'My heart is in the spiritual prosperity of St Ninian's Cathedral. For every testimony, therefore, in its favour I feel grateful, because I heartily wish it God speed! I shall, however, never see it, because of my extreme old age, being now in my 88th year, and my locomotive powers being almost entirely gone. But I will not cease to pray for its welfare while I live and retain my

The Cathedral Church of St Ninian

senses'.[10] This letter was written by the bishop to J M Neale in 1851. On 14 August 1852 Bishop Torry was able to write a few brief words on the back of an envelope. 'Unable to take any concern in the future matters of the church'.[11] He died two months later at the age of eighty-nine.

Despite the evident pleasure of Bishop Torry, the first signs of trouble were already brewing in the diocese. The cathedral was the bishop's pride and joy and he loved it dearly; others were not so enamoured with the edifice. There were those in the diocese who maintained that the bishop should not have permitted the construction of the cathedral on his sole authority; others thought it inexpedient to embark on the construction of such a building when the church had other needs; others opposed the cathedral because of its distinctly 'high church' origins and associations; and others felt that the financial risks of the project were too great. Opposition had surfaced by the beginning of 1848 – before Butterfield had even produced the final plan – as the bishop indicated in a letter to Lord Forbes. 'I am sorry, and feel not a little mortified, that your lordship's wishes and great efforts in behalf of the church, have been but coldly received, if not thwarted by many influential persons, of whom better things might reasonably have been, and actually were expected'.[12] Even after the consecration Bishop Torry was still coming under attack from various quarters. The diocesan synod resented the fact that it had not been consulted; not until after Torry's death did it formally accept the building as the cathedral church of the united dioceses of St Andrews, Dunkeld and Dunblane. The 'low church' Church Society predictably fulminated against this 'high church' place of worship. Even Torry's colleagues on the bench of bishops expressed their concern about this unprecedented building; none of the other bishops of the Scottish Episcopal Church had a cathedral church in his diocese.

Whatever he may have felt about these objections, Bishop Torry was delighted by his cathedral church, and it was only right that he should be buried within its walls (on the north side of the chancel), but he bequeathed a divided diocese to his successor; divided between those who ardently supported the cathedral and everything that went on in it, and those who did not; and the worst was still to come.

The cathedral was incomplete at Bishop Torry's death, and it remained that way for more than thirty years because of almost constant wrangling between his successor, Bishop Charles Wordsworth (1853–92), and the cathedral chapter. There being no other Scottish cathedral to provide precedent or example, the constitution that governed Perth Cathedral was modelled by its founders on the those governing the English cathedrals. The general principle of cathedral governance in England is that the chapter, headed by the dean or provost, is supreme. Although the bishop of the diocese has his cathedra (throne) in the building, and he might wield a greater or lesser degree of moral authority, he is powerless to overrule or discipline the chapter as a corporate body, or any of its individual members.

This was the heart of the problem at Perth: the total independence of the cathedral chapter. There was no difficulty while Bishop Torry was alive, but when Bishop Charles Wordsworth arrived in 1853, the battle lines were quickly drawn. He had been elected diocesan bishop by his own casting vote, a decision which had caused much trouble at the time, and there was much more trouble to come. Wordsworth viewed this high church conventicle with deep suspicion, regarding its nature as fundamentally alien to the Scottish Episcopal Church. He admitted as much in his memoirs, together with a degree of resentment that, much as he disapproved of the ways of the cathedral, he was virtually powerless to wrest control from the hands of its lay patrons: 'It was from Oxford that Lord Forbes and

Mr Boyle derived their inspiration; it was to the leaders of the movement there, rather than to the Diocesan... that they looked for guidance; that is, they looked for it to those who had no responsibility, who were living far away, and whose experience was of another and different country, and of another and, in all temporal respects, very different Church... The clergy who were first appointed to offices at St Ninian's [Chambers, Haskoll and Humble]... were all English. I did what I could to correct the evil when Mr Chambers and Mr Haskoll resigned. The original impulse had gone too far to admit of guidance or control in the opposite direction; and meanwhile the financial support came almost entirely from those who, living at a distance, had prescribed and desired to sustain that impulse'.[13]

The members of the cathedral chapter were firmly in the high church tradition of the Oxford Movement and the provisions of the cathedral constitution ensured that they should be so; one of the rules, for example, required that its members should be celibate for the duration of their appointment (following the practice of Boyle's church and college on Cumbrae). In 1851, E B K Fortescue was elected first dean of the cathedral. He was described as 'a man of refinement but of no great learning, ignorant of Scottish traditions, impractical and deficient in some of the stronger qualities of character. He was donnish and reserved in manner, although when it pleased him, and in a select circle, freely to unbend, he was full of mirth'.[14] Fortescue had been rector of Wilmcote near Stratford-upon-Avon and was elected dean by the three residentiary canons. He was very interested in ritual, but knew little about the Scottish church, and was probably not the best appointment to make at that particular time. He resigned in 1871, married a Miss Robbins from the congregation, and soon afterwards in Belgium was received into the Roman Catholic Church. Of the three canons, the most prominent was Henry Humble, the precentor. His surname proved to be a complete misnomer. Humble was a strong-willed, aggressive and combative ex-journalist, who preferred a fight to a compromise and, until his premature death in 1876, he was undoubtedly a vexing irritant to the bishop. But he was much loved by those who knew him. 'Canon Humble was friendly, frank and open. His kindness and courtesy saved him, but perhaps only just saved him, from a tendency to brusquerie... He was a born warrior. He smelt the battle afar off. One thing that especially made him gird on his armour was anything that seemed to him like oppression, or the taking of unfair advantage of the weaker by the stronger'.[15]

The liturgy of the cathedral was far ahead of its time, and included such practices as the celebrant facing east during the eucharist, the mixing of water and wine, candles on the altar, incense, vestments and Gregorian chant. Bishop Wordsworth, son of the master of Trinity College, Cambridge, soon indicated his intention to curb the waywardness of the cathedral, and its powerful backers: 'Lord Forbes did not once appear upon the scene; nor had I even the honour of making his acquaintance... Being, I believe, of a weakly constitution, he shrank from the fatigue of the long journey to Scotland; and so the whole management of the cathedral scheme devolved upon young Mr G F Boyle, also non-resident in the diocese. A more unfortunate condition of things... it is scarcely possible to imagine... It seems never to have occurred to Bishop Torry, that a cathedral... must be diocesan: that as an exotic it could never flourish, and would tend to produce confusion, rather than concord and harmony, in a diocese'.[16] Wordsworth was determined to bring the cathedral into line, and he was not afraid of a fight. 'Not since the death of Bishop Rattray, one hundred and ten years previously, had so strong a personality presided over the see'.[17] The bishop declared that he would not be enthroned in the cathedral until its debt of £3,000 had been cleared; until the diocesan synod had given its formal approval to the existence of a cathedral church; and a new constitution for the cathedral had been agreed, reducing the power of the chapter and increasing the power of the bishop. George Boyle quickly paid off the cathedral debt from his own funds; the provisional approval of the diocesan synod was secured on 6 April 1853; and a concordat between the bishop and the chapter was agreed in September 1853, including a reduction in certain parts of the cathedral ceremonial. Fortescue agreed to renounce the title of dean (to avoid confusion with the dean of the diocese) and adopt that of provost instead. With all Bishop Wordsworth's conditions having been met, he was enthroned on 21 September 1853. Everything was set for a fair course and for three years peace reigned.

Then, in 1856, Bishop Wordsworth took up residence in Perth and, in a somewhat high-handed and autocratic way, decreed further changes to the cathedral's liturgy. Provost Fortescue and Canon Humble, believing that they had gone as far as their consciences would allow, refused to obey and stood their ground on the fact that they had a duty to submit to the bishop's canonical jurisdiction, but not to his personal requests. Had the bishop and the chapter been of a more gentle and pacific character and temperament, a different course might have ensued; and despite Wordsworth's comments in his memoirs, the fault was not entirely with the chapter. Bishop Wordsworth was idealistic enough to hope and work for a union between episcopalians and presbyterians, and he would not brook

anything which stood in the way of this cherished ideal. In turn, Provost Fortescue and Canon Humble regarded the bishop as 'unsound' and refused absolutely to comply with any of his requests or suggestions. 'It was not a tranquil or tolerant age; party feeling was intense and the spirit of individuals was fiery. There was a constant fear of Rome, because of the surge of conversions or submissions, and especially after the Restoration of the Roman Catholic hierarchy in 1878. There were two forms of Roman fever, a feverish hostility and an excess of admiration. The latter afflicted the cathedral clergy, the Bishop suffered intermittently from the former; and both suffered from bad temper'.[18] For nearly thirty years Bishop Wordsworth looked at his cathedral church with a mixture of irritation, exasperation, resignation and desperation, and so began the local legend of the Thirty Years' War.

Although its role had been modified by the concordat of 1853, power still lay with the chapter and, though the bishop was now a member, he was constantly outvoted by the other canons. At one particularly heated point, in May 1859, the exasperated bishop withdrew from the cathedral and attended St John's Church in Princes Street, and went to the cathedral only for confirmations and ordinations. At the same time, the five non-resident canons resigned in a gesture of support for the bishop, but it made no difference to Provost Fortescue and Canon Humble, who defiantly stood their ground.

With the departure of Provost Fortescue in 1871, Bishop Wordsworth entertained some hopes of peace. He filled the vacant canonries and began attending the cathedral again. But the new provost, John Burton, proved to be influenced more by Canon Humble than by the bishop, and periodic skirmishing, if not outright fighting, was renewed: 'These, and many other similar troubles, the outcome of the futile attempt to coerce the action of the cathedral body – to obey the imperious will – producing at one time, fierce and angry strife, at another the stupor of suspended animation',[19] earned St Ninian's the dubious distinction of being known as the battleground of the Scottish Church. After five years Bishop Wordsworth finally decided that he had had enough of the cathedral and in 1876 moved his residence to St Andrew's Church. Provost Burton and Canon Humble had the backing of George Boyle, now earl of Glasgow, who effectively funded the cathedral, as much as he did the cathedral at Cumbrae; and the two clergy were financially, as well as constitutionally, well protected against episcopal displeasure.

Canon Humble died of consumption in February 1876 at the age of fifty-seven, and again, it appeared as though peace might be possible; however, it was not to last for long. He was succeeded in 1878 by Canon Donald Mackey who quickly proved to be as obdurate as his predecessor. Not until 1885 did lasting peace become a real possibility. Provost Burton died on 8 July that year, and Lord Glasgow went bankrupt in the collapse of the fraudulent City of Glasgow Bank. With the appointment of Provost Vincent Lewis Rorison and the resignation of Canon Mackey, both in the same year, there arrived a third opportunity of making a fresh start. Bishop Wordsworth, now eighty-one years old, and mellower in temperament, withdrew the demands he had made of Provosts Fortescue and Burton and, at last, peace came to Perth.

After thirty years, the war was over, the cathedral could once again become the mother church of the diocese and there was now no reason for it to remain unfinished. In October 1886 the Diocesan Council resolved that the cathedral should be completed. The original design had provided for twin western towers and spires, but this was deemed to be too expensive, and William Butterfield, who was still alive, was asked to produce a revised plan for the western end of the cathedral. In 1887, he duly proposed a single western tower. This was started, and reached to just above the nave roof, when the foundations were discovered to be sinking, and it had to be dismantled. A further design for a tower on the south side of the nave was never implemented. Construction of the nave and a temporary west end began in 1889, and the nave was consecrated on 7 August 1890 by Bishop Wordsworth, by then eighty-six years old. The join between the first stage of the cathedral and the extensions of 1889–90 is apparent on the south side in the first bay of the clerestory; where one light is replaced by two lights in every bay thereafter.

Bishop Wordsworth died on 5 December 1892, and was succeeded by George Howard Wilkinson, formerly bishop of Truro (1883–91). Wilkinson was no stranger to cathedral building; much of the construction work of Truro Cathedral took place during his episcopate in Cornwall. Wilkinson arrived at Perth in 1893, and remained bishop of the diocese until his death in 1908. He added another [east] bay to the chancel, the chancel aisles, the organ chamber, the Lady Chapel, and the 'cloister' with its chapter house and vestries. The additions were designed by Frank Loughborough Pearson, built in 1899–1901 and consecrated in July 1901; the sermon at the consecration service was preached by Archbishop Frederick Temple of Canterbury. It would appear that initiative came entirely from Wilkinson, who raised much of the cost of the work: 'I was interested by the bishop's statement that he had now about £3,000… It has all come in quietly'.[20] The money continued to come in quietly, reaching the £14,000 required. The temporary west end of the nave, constructed in 1889–90, was replaced by the present lofty baptistery in 1910–11 and the basic structure of the cathedral has remained unaltered since that period.

Perth Cathedral suffers the disadvantage of being badly sited, 'being on a double corner plot, which the main road to Inverness cuts round in two right-angles, giving the cathedral prominence without displaying its architecture to advantage'.[21] The cathedral is basically cruciform with an aisled nave and chancel, but the transepts are very shallow and barely emerge beyond the aisles. The principal entrance to the cathedral is through the porch in North Methven Street which leads into a long arched passage. This 'cloister', together with the adjacent hall, was added in 1939 and designed by Tarbolton and Ochterlony. It joins, at right angles, Pearson's main 'cloister', which in reality is only another long passage, 3m wide. Doorways off the east side of Pearson's cloister lead into the chapter house, also serving as a library, built in memory of Bishop Charles Wordsworth (1853–93) in 1899–1901, and other vestries of the same date. The doorway at the end of the passage leads into the south nave aisle of the cathedral.

The completed cathedral is 61m long. The nave (21.3m high and 15.2m wide) has high and wide arcades, the apex of each arch reaching almost to the level of the sills of the clerestory windows. The roof framing begins immediately above the clerestory and rises vertically before a steep slope takes it up to the apex of the roof.

Two successive screens have occupied the space at the top of the chancel steps. Butterfield's screen of 1850 lasted until 1924 when it was removed to St Devenick's Church, Bieldside. The *Ecclesiologist*, always an admirer of Butterfield's work, praised the effect: 'It was the architect's desire to combine a complete separation of choir and nave, with a degree of lightness and pervisibleness (if we may coin a word), and in this he has most completely succeeded'. Butterfield had used gas lighting to illuminate the cathedral, with a mixture of standards, hanging coronae and concealed lighting behind the screen, to create, said the *Ecclesiologist*, 'an effect almost magical'.[22] Butterfield's screen was replaced in 1924 by a three-arched stone screen with blue and gold cresting and a rood above. Designed by Sir Ninian Comper as a war memorial, it was removed in the late 1980s and a movable wooden altar can now be seen on a dais before the chancel steps. Comper also designed vestments, plate and banners for the cathedral.

At the west end of the nave is the very tall arch giving access to the baptistery. On the north side of the baptistery is a brass memorial to Provost Fortescue (who died in 1877) erected by Blanche, countess of Kinnoull. The octagonal font of 1853 has a towering pinnacled Gothic oak cover designed by Pearson and presented c.1920 in memory of Ian Macgregor who had been killed in the First World War. The baptistery is very lofty and suggests a feeling of the tower that was partially constructed and then abandoned in 1887. The west window glass dates from 1890. Below the window is a blind arcade with polished granite pilasters and some polychromatic tilework.

The baptistery has very shallow transepts. The small empty area to the south of the baptistery was formerly the Chapel of the Resurrection. It contains a 1931 statue of the risen Christ and a tablet, both commemorating Robert Pullar (1892–1930). The canopy across the arch, above where the altar formerly stood, is by Comper. A change in funeral practices, followed by the discovery of dry rot, led to the abandonment of the chapel in c.1985. From the chapel a doorway leads to a stairway giving access to a room above the baptistery.

The easternmost window in the north aisle depicts St Ninian wearing a mitre and eucharistic vestments and holding a model of the cathedral as it was intended to be completed. The window was inserted in 1891 as a memorial to Walter, nineteenth Lord Forbes (1798–1868) and George, sixth earl of Glasgow (1825–90). The large round pulpit with carved scenes in niches dates from 1901. The north transept, from which one can look

The Cathedral Church of St Ninian (postcard c.1899)

across to the organ (rebuilt in 1963 and again in 1996) in the south transept, and to the rose window which is off-centre to the transept arch. The transepts themselves are very slight, merely continuations of the north and south aisles with only increased height and the off-centre rose windows to indicate any difference. The crossing itself is also confused by the extension of the ritual choir westwards to form a long chancel.

On the south wall of the chancel is the crozier of Bishop Patrick Torry. His tomb and bronze effigy can be seen set into the grey Aberfeldy stone wall arcading on the south side of the chancel. The white marble cross that marks the site of his tomb on the north side, formerly occupied the centre of the old reredos, erected about 1882 and dismantled during the alterations of 1910–11.

The choir stalls occupy the area of the crossing, and the canopied chapter stalls beyond, unusually, do not bear the titles of prebends or dignitaries, although some have memorial brass plates. There are six prebendal stalls, four on the north and two on the south. The dean's stall is on the north side, the canopy above being a memorial to Provost Rorison, and the provost's stall is on the south side. The baldachino was erected in memory of Bishop George Howard Wilkinson (1893–1907) in 1910–11, also grey but of Cornish granite and inlaid with gold and other mosaic. The arcading of Aberfeldy stone with sedilia at intervals, dates from the same time. There is a piscina in the south east corner. The wine-coloured, carpet-tiled floor enhances the greys of the stone as well as the browns of the pinnacled stalls and the canopied bishop's throne on the south side. The east window, with a tiny quatrefoil window above, contains glass inserted in 1876 commemorating Canon Humble. On the south side of the sanctuary, opening into the Lady Chapel behind, is the tomb canopy of Bishop George Wilkinson with his kneeling bronze figure by Sir George Frampton.

The apsidal wooden vaulted Lady Chapel by Pearson, is entered through an iron screen of 1931. The screen was erected in memory of Charles Plumb, bishop of St Andrews, Dunkeld and Dunblane (1908–31) and provost of the cathedral (1906–11). The Blessed Sacrament is reserved here, and a piscina can be seen on the south wall. The chapel was sealed by glazing in 1980.

Perth Cathedral is not one of William Butterfield's best pieces of architecture, but the vision that created it proved resilient enough to enable it to survive three decades of strife. The story of the public rows that constituted the Thirty Years War at Perth, is an extraordinary episode in the history of the Scottish Episcopal Church, and one that that communion might wish had never happened. But although it was caused and continued by intemperate behaviour on all sides, never, in all those years of fierce argument, was there any hint of scandal or impropriety on either side. From those long-forgotten disputes, all that emerges is a record of proudly held and staunchly defended principles, all focused on the worship of God in the one silent survivor of the battles – the cathedral church of St Ninian at Perth.

1 Farquhar, G T S (1927): p. 20.
2 Mackey, Donald J (1888): p. 234.
3 Farquhar, G T S (1894): p. 283.
4 Neale, John Mason (1856): p. 315.
5 Farquhar, G T S (1927): p. 21.
6 Towle, Eleanor A (1906): p. 182.
7 ibid., pp 182–3.
8 ibid., pp 184–5.
9 ibid., pp 186–7.
10 Neale, John Mason (1856): p. 375.
11 ibid., p. 381.
12 Bishop Torry to Lord Forbes, 8 January 1848. In Neale, J M (1856): p. 344.
13 Wordsworth, Charles (1893): pp 62–3.
14 Lochhead, Marion (1966): p. 145.
15 Wordsworth, John (1899): p. 49.
16 Wordsworth, Charles (1893): pp 156–7.
17 Farquhar, G T S (1894): p. 330.
18 Lochhead, Marion (1966): p. 147.
19 Mackey, Donald J (1888): p. 237.
20 Mason, Arthur James (1909): volume 2, p. 243.
21 Fenwick, Hubert (1978): p. 266.
22 *Ecclesiologist*, Number 12, 1851, p. 26.

Skeabost

The Cathedral Church of St Columba

The history of the remains of the cathedral church on St Columba's Island, at Skeabost on the Isle of Skye, is very obscure, as is the place of Skeabost among the cathedrals of Scotland. The etymology of the name 'Skeabost' is equally obscure and open to wide interpretation, but the constituent parts of the word are of Norse origin. The suffix *bost* means a farm or homestead or dwelling, but there is no agreed origin of the prefix *skea*; suggestions include *sgiath*, a portion of land projecting into the sea; *sjar*, sea; *skjar*, possibly meaning a window; *sgiach*, representing a hawthorn; *skeif-r*, skew or oblique; and even *Skidhi*, a proper name. There is no doubt that the name is Norse, and that it indicates some form of dwelling, but anything beyond that is a matter of speculation.

The history of the diocese of the Isles and its bishops is complicated and requires explanation. The church of St German, at Peel on the Isle of Man, was certainly in existence by 1231 when it was mentioned in a bull of Pope Gregory IX to Bishop Simon of Sodor,[1] and was the cathedral church of the diocese of the Isles, covering Man and the Hebrides. There is no reason to presume the existence of a cathedral church at Skeabost before the political upheaval of the early fourteenth century, which saw the Isle of Man fall alternately under English and Scottish rule. English rule was finally and firmly established over Man in c.1330. While this island and the cathedral church was now under English control, the rest of the diocese, the Hebrides to the north, remained part of the kingdom of Scotland and of the Scottish Church. This effective division of the diocese of the Isles is the origin of the cathedral church on this remote islet at Skeabost.

Although a bishop named Wimund was resident on Skye c.1109–34, and he may have had successors, no other named bishop is known and there is no evidence for the existence of a territorial diocese based around a cathedral church on Skye until the division of the diocese of the Isles in the fourteenth century.

In 1331, a separate line of Scottish bishops of the Isles appeared when the clergy of Skye met at Skeabost and elected a bishop to rule the Scottish part of the diocese of the Isles. The Great Schism in the papacy from 1378 institutionalised the schism in the diocese of the Isles, with separate lines of Scottish bishops of the Isles ruling from Skeabost and English bishops of the Isles ruling from Peel on the Isle of Man. Scotland had declared for the popes ruling from Avignon in France, while England declared for the popes ruling from Rome. Although the Hebridean islands effectively ceased to be part of the diocese after 1331, the bishop of Sodor and Man still maintains the use of the Norse word Sodor (*Sudr-eyjar* – southern isles) in his official title which is, officially and confusingly, 'bishop of the Isle of Man, of Sodor, of Sodor and Man, and of Sodor of Man'.

Despite its Columban origins, Skeabost was always overshadowed by the great Columban monastery on Iona, and probably so too was the bishop of the Isles by the abbot of Iona. At the end of the fifteenth century, Iona displaced Skeabost as the see and cathedral church of the diocese, and the little islet on Skye seems to have been forgotten by the 1540s. Only in the twentieth century was the importance of Skeabost rediscovered, and St Columba's Island rescued from neglect. Recent research in the Vatican archives in Rome has confirmed that the island was indeed the site of the cathedral church of the Isles. In 1433, Bishop Angus Macdonald petitioned the pope for permission to move the cathedral from Skeabost to a more appropriate place within the diocese. In 1498 the earl of Argyll petitioned that the abbey church of Iona become the see of the bishop of the Isles 'quhil his principall kirk in the Ile of Man be recoverit fra Inglishmen'. It would seem from this statement that the history of the island cathedral in the River Snizort was deliberately ignored or suppressed. Perhaps Skeabost was only ever seen as a temporary pro-cathedral until the true cathedral church on the Isle of Man was 'recoverit fra Inglishmen'.

St Columba's Island takes its name from the Irish saint who is said to have visited Skye in the late sixth century. The story goes that Columba and a group of his followers arrived at a site close to the island, and saw a party of armed warriors approaching them. They were accompanied by their chieftain, a very old man carried on a litter. The chieftain explained that he had heard much of Christianity and had seen in a dream that he should not die until Skye was visited by a holy man who would baptise him. He now wished to be baptised as he was very old and tired. Columba granted the old man's wish, but as the water touched his forehead, the chieftain collapsed and died. His death came as no surprise to his followers who had been warned to expect it. The body of the old chieftain was carried to the little island in the River Snizort and there he was given a Christian burial.

The island can be reached by crossing to the Isle of Skye from the Scottish mainland, by the Skye Bridge, and taking the main road from Portree to Dunvegan. The small island is 8.8km north-west of Portree and can be seen in the River Snizort at the village of Skeabost, at the point where the road crosses the river. It was formerly only accessible by boat, but access is now quite effortless, with the construction of a wooden footbridge in 1990 by the Officers' Training Corps of Edinburgh and Heriot-Watt Universities. The island (islet would be a better description) is believed to have been the site of the cathedral church of the diocese of the Isles from about 1331 to about 1506 when it was displaced by Iona during the episcopate of Bishop John Campbell (1487–1510).

The island is undoubtedly rich in history and tradition, but it is now little more than a derelict burial ground containing the fragmentary remains of five buildings, of which the most prominent is the so-called Nicolson Aisle, a mortuary chapel of the Nicolson family. The chapel belonged to Clan MacNeacail, the Nicolsons of Sgoirebreac, and stands at the north end of the island. The 'Aisle' is a single chamber church with one square-headed lancet remaining, and tradition claims that twenty-eight clan chiefs are buried in or around it. The story is reminiscent of the more extravagant claims made for Reilig Odhráin on Iona. One of the walls of the church contains an effigy dating to the fifteenth century, which is believed to be that of a MacSween. There is also a sixteenth century effigy of a MacNeacail, represented as an armoured knight bearing a sword. South of the Nicolson Aisle are the tumbled remains of two small buildings, perhaps oratories.

The centre of the island rises to a mound, and here can be detected the grassed-over remains of the walls of a large two-chamber rectangular building that was probably the cathedral church. Its external measurements are 24m long and 8.1m wide, but there are no remaining distinctive features to be seen. A broken stone font or stoup, 40.6cm long, 38.1cm wide and 27.9cm in depth, was seen in 1892 and, lying on the grassy mound of the western wall of the church, in 1914; it had disappeared by 1928.[2]

At the south end of the island is another single-chamber building, now housing a collection of carved stones, believed to date from the thirteenth century. Scattered stones are everywhere on St Columba's Island, including a flat slab showing a weathered recumbent effigy of a knight.

The island, like so many ruined holy places, became used as a burial ground and most of the surviving graves appear to date from the nineteenth and twentieth centuries; the most recent interment, of the postmaster of Skeabost, took place in 1966. Also to be found are the graves of the nineteenth century evangelists Angus Munro, Donald Munro and Murdoch Macdonald. Donald Munro (1773–1830) was a strange fanatic who came to believe that the only way to achieve eternal salvation was to renounce the evils of music. Although he had previously loved music and was a talented fiddler, he ordered his flock to gather together all the bagpipes and fiddles in their possession and, on a designated day, he cast them into a great bonfire at the head of Loch Snizort.

In their magisterial work on the ecclesiastical architecture of Scotland, published towards the end of the nineteenth century, MacGibbon and Ross noted the existence of this remote little island on Skye: 'In an islet in the River Snizort there is an open burying ground containing a group of five or six chapels, the shell of two pretty entire, the others reduced nearly to the ground. Of the former, the one least perfect is a featureless building, externally 82 feet [24.9m] in length; the other... is externally 21 feet [6.3m] in length, and has a flat-headed window... in the east end. In the larger building there is a basin of a baptismal font, square, with rounded corners. On making the shore one is immediately struck with the intensely ecclesiastical character of the spot. From end to end the islet is covered with the remains of chapels'.[3] The authors would have had no information that this place was once the site of the cathedral church of the diocese of the Isles, but they noted a significant and obvious piece of evidence – a large church surrounded by a constellation of smaller churches.

There is little more to be said at present, because the island remains to be properly excavated, though as a burial ground, this may cause difficulties; but the task would be well worth the effort. Hopefully some archaeological excavation can be undertaken if only to clarify the history and development of this island. This is a secret, hidden and forgotten little place, and a full-scale investigation would probably remove much of its charm; but it would shed light on a place that is believed to have been the site of the cathedral church of the diocese of the Isles for 175 years.

1 Easson, D E (1957): p. 198.
2 RCAHMS (1928): p. 192.
3 MacGibbon, D & Ross, T (1896): volume 1, pp 68-9.

St Andrews

The Cathedral Church of St Andrew

The coastal town of St Andrews, with a population of more than 11,000, is one of the most historic towns of Scotland, but not because of its internationally-renowned golf course. The status of St Andrews is due partly to its association with relics of the apostle Saint Andrew, but primarily to its status as the titular primatial see of the Scottish Church.

The legendary story of the foundation of St Andrews by a Greek monk named Rule or Regulus (died c.260), who was in charge of the relics of Saint Andrew after the crucifixion of the apostle at Patras, is quite untrustworthy. A more reliable story relates that a certain Bishop Acca (c.660–742), who was banished from Hexham, brought some of the relics of Saint Andrew to Scotland some time between 736 and 761, and founded a church dedicated in his name. There was certainly a Culdee community at St Andrews, and some tenth and eleventh century bishops, without territorial designation were, in the fifteenth century, believed to have been based at St Andrews, but the evidence is confused and the first named bishop of St Andrews was Maelduin (c.1028–55).

During the twelfth century reformation of the Scottish church by Earl David of Strathclyde, later King David I (1124–53), the Augustinian Order gradually displaced the Culdee community at St Andrews, as it did elsewhere in Scotland, and St Rule's Church, much of which is still standing, was enlarged to serve as the cathedral church of a new territorial diocese. The first bishop of the new regime was Turgot (1107–15), who had been prior of Durham, and was therefore consecrated by the archbishop of York. The claims of successive archbishops of York to metropolitan jurisdiction over the Scottish bishops caused much trouble between England and Scotland until, in 1192, Scotland was recognised as an independent province, though without an archbishop, directly responsible to the pope. There were two exceptions to this new arrangement – the diocese of Orkney was subject to the Norwegian church until the fifteenth century, and the diocese of Galloway remained subject to York until the Great Schism in the papacy at the end of the fourteenth century. Not until 1472 were Galloway and Orkney formally incorporated into the Scottish church, and the bishopric of St Andrews was raised to the status of an archbishopric.

With the arrival of the Augustinians at St Andrews in the twelfth century, there came a new priory church, which in turn became the new cathedral church of the diocese of St Andrews. The old cathedral church of St Rule was replaced by the great new cathedral church which stood adjacent to it, and of which only pathetic fragments remain today. Construction of the new cathedral began during the brief episcopate of Bishop Arnold (1160–2), and continued for more than a century and a half. When completed, the cathedral of St Andrews was the largest church in Scotland and at one time the second longest cathedral in Britain after Norwich. The chancel was completed in 1238, and the cathedral was consecrated in 1318 by Bishop William de Lamberton (1297–1328) in the presence of King Robert I (1306–29).

A serious fire in 1380, during the episcopate of Bishop William de Laundels (1342–85), was caused by the carelessness of a workman. The most urgent work of restoration took seven years, but the work drifted on for decades and was compounded by the partial collapse of the south transept in 1409. The cathedral was not fully repaired until 1440 during the time of Bishop Henry de Wardlaw (1403–40). De Wardlaw is remembered as the founder of the University of St Andrews in 1411, and the bishop responsible for building the bridge over the Eden at Guardbridge.

The reiterated claims of the archbishop of York to metropolitan jurisdiction over Scotland caused Bishop Patrick Graham (1465–78) to go to Rome and seek a final adjudication from the pope. Pope Sixtus IV decided in favour of the Scottish church and raised St Andrews to the status of an archbishopric in 1472. Bishop Graham was ill-treated for securing such a prize. On his return, the new archbishop found himself the victim of false charges laid by William Scheves, a canon of the cathedral. After bitter struggles, he was committed to prison and died in a dungeon in Lochleven Castle; Scheves succeeded him as archbishop (1478–97). Many of his successors fared little better and the story of the archiepiscopate in the late fifteenth and sixteenth centuries is not edifying. Archbishop Alexander Stewart, the illegitimate son of King James IV (1488–1513), was appointed in 1504 at the age of eleven or twelve and was killed with his father at the Battle of Flodden in 1513, at the age of only twenty or twenty-one. Cardinal David Beaton succeeded his uncle as archbishop in 1537. Beaton was typical of the ecclesiastical politician of his day and made a bid to secure the regency of the kingdom on the death of King James V in 1542. He is chiefly, and unfairly, remembered as the archbishop who presided at the trial of George Wishart, the reformer and friend of John Knox. Wishart was condemned to death and burnt at St Andrews on 1 March 1546. Partly in revenge, Beaton was himself murdered – on 29 May, three months later – in his castle at St Andrews.

The Cathedral Church of St Andrew

The deaths of Wishart and Beaton were symptomatic of the savagery with which the sixteenth century reformation took hold in Scotland; and the death of Beaton was followed, before many years had passed, by the death of his great cathedral church. Like so many other Scottish cathedrals, St Andrews fell prey to the destructive hatred of the reformers; but the primatial cathedral was to suffer a far worse fate than most, as evinced by the fact that so little of the building survives. Like the great cathedral at Elgin, St Andrews was a monastic church, served by the Augustinian Order; it had no parish and therefore it was simply not required for public worship. On 14 June 1559, the reformers broke into the cathedral and subjected it to the usual desecration, pillage and destruction and, like Elgin, the cathedral never recovered. Beaton was succeeded by John Hamilton (1547–71), the natural son of the earl of Arran. Hamilton had been appointed abbot of Paisley at the age of fourteen and became primate of Scotland at the age of thirty-six. He was an influential opponent of the reformers, and a faithful and loyal supporter of Queen Mary (1542–67). After the queen's fateful flight to England, Hamilton was pronounced a traitor and eventually captured at Dumbarton Castle where he had sought refuge. Three days later, wearing his pontifical vestments, he was hanged at Stirling.

Archbishop Patrick Adamson (1575–92) was a preacher of great oratory, but used his gifts to discredit presbyterianism and was excommunicated by the General Assembly of the Scottish church. Archbishop John Spottiswoode (1615–38) crowned King Charles I (1625–49) as king of Scotland in 1633 but, in the general abolition of episcopacy in 1638, he was deposed on a series of unproven allegations, including adultery, incest and sacrilege. He died in the following year and was buried in Westminster Abbey. Archbishop James Sharp (1661–79) aroused the bitter resentment of his opponents by the severe measures he took to abolish presbyterianism. He survived an assassination attempt by James Mitchell in 1668 but, when Mitchell was executed in 1678, hatred against the archbishop increased. In the following year, he was dragged out of his coach and murdered by a party of Fife lairds and farmers.

In spite of this continued succession of resident archbishops of St Andrews, the great ruined building on the cliff was never again used as the cathedral church of the diocese. Archbishop Hamilton's successors used the parish church of Holy Trinity, South Street, as the cathedral of the diocese. Of that church, only the fifteenth century tower and a few other fragments remain; the rest was demolished and rebuilt in 1907–9.

St Andrews Cathedral was a magnificent building in its day. Jean de Beaugue, who visited it in 1548–9, described it as 'a very large and beautiful structure'.[1] But it suffered the fate of many monastic ruins and was being used as a quarry by 1577, when the crown ordered 'the priour of Sanctandrois and all uthiris demolesaris of the cathederall kirk thairof to desist and ceis for all forder douncasting thairof'.[2] Lord James Stewart, appointed lay administrator of the priory, lived in part of the canons' cloister for some years after the reformation, but by 1597 the priory was unoccupied and decaying. There was some thought of reconstructing the cathedral in 1634, but the deposition of the archbishop in 1638 ended the hope, and the process of quarrying began again after 1649 and continued for many years. As early as 1680 all that remained of the cathedral were the fragments that can be seen today. In 1773, Dr Samuel Johnson visited St Andrews and, according to his biographer, James Boswell, was much moved by the sight of the ruins. Upon dinner being mentioned he said, 'Ay, ay; amidst all these sorrowful scenes, I have no objection to dinner'. He mentioned that 'till very lately' the ruins had been 'so much neglected that every man carried away the stones who fancied that he wanted them'.

The cathedral ruins were taken over by the Barons of the Exchequer in 1826. The priory buildings were excavated and partly repaired on the instructions of the marquess of Bute in 1894, under the superintendence of the architect, J Kinross. John Patrick Crichton-Stuart, third marquess of Bute (1847–1900), had been received into the Roman Catholic Church in 1868, shortly after his twenty-first birthday (see St Columba's Cathedral, Oban), and one of his great pleasures was the excavation of antiquities. The marquess had 'a passion for the excavation and exploration of ancient buildings; and I think some of his happiest hours were spent standing by, wrapped in his long cloak and smoking innumerable cigarettes, while a band of workmen dug out the foundations of a medieval lady chapel or broke through a nineteenth century wall in search of a thirteenth century doorway'.[3] In 1892 he was elected rector of the university of St Andrews, and purchased a modern house, called the Priory, adjoining the monastic ruins, and soon began carefully to explore them. Bute was something of a romantic visionary and he soon dreamt of a scheme much more ambitious than the stabilisation of ruins. 'It was during his second term of office that Bute conceived the project – which would probably have occurred to no one but himself – of restoring the vast ruined cathedral of St Andrews, or a portion of it, for the purposes of a university church. The plan might, he thought, be realised if every member of the Scottish peerage could be induced to subscribe a thousand pounds towards it. But there were at least three reasons which militated against the success of the proposal. In the first place, the pedigrees of the peers of Scotland were in most cases a great deal longer than their purses; in the second, few of them were probably much interested in university education in general, or in St Andrews in particular; in the third, the majority of them were members of the Episcopalian body, not of the Established Church, to which the university church would as a matter of course be aggregated. It is curious that the only promise of substantial support received by the Catholic rector towards a scheme which must, it is to be feared, be pronounced fantastic, came from a wealthy nobleman who was not a member of either the Episcopalian or the Established Church, but a devoted and almost fanatical Free Churchman'.[4]

The cathedral itself was beyond help except for the stabilisation of the remaining fragments, but Bute's restoration of the monastic buildings at St Andrews Cathedral, and his work at Whithorn Cathedral, is a credit to his memory. The priory buildings at St Andrews were given to the Ministry of Works in 1946 by his grandson, Michael Crichton-Stuart (1915–81).

The cathedral stands near the top of a cliff overlooking the sea. Once the greatest and longest church in Scotland, it is today only a fragmentary ruin. Because of its primatial status, and the beauty of what little remains, the cathedral was sometimes thought to have been larger than it is really is, but this belief owes more to imagination and reputation than to fact. Some seventeenth and eighteenth century writers thought it longer and wider than the St Peter's Basilica in Rome, but its length is only a little more than half that of St Peter's; its external length is about 113m, whereas that of St Peter's is about 213m.

St Andrews Cathedral consisted of an aisled nave of twelve bays, 60.9m long by 18.8m wide; a five bay aisled chancel, 29.8m long by 10m wide; a presbytery without aisles, 14m long; three-bay transepts, and a large chapter house. But of most of this building, no more than the foundations remain. The best view of what remains of the cathedral is from the north. On the left is the east gable and, to the right, close to the road, is the west front. In between stands the whole south nave aisle wall, which is only intact because the proprietor of the adjoining land found that it was a convenient protection for his property; behind the wall were the monastic buildings.

Following storm damage, the west front of the cathedral was rebuilt two bays inwards by Bishop William Wischard (1271–9), reducing the length of the nave by 10.3m. This was probably with the dual purpose of avoiding the damaged walls of the two westernmost bays, and to allow those walls to be used for the construction of a new porch or narthex. Parts of the porch side walls and vault corbels are still visible. The porch survived until the fire of 1380, when it was removed, and the upper part of the west front, including the wall-arcading, was rebuilt.

There is nothing left of the nave beyond the column bases, but the twelfth century south aisle wall, including its windows, is fairly complete. The windows change from round-arched late twelfth century to two-light thirteenth century, indicating only a later rebuilding and not separate periods of construction. Except for the two west bays, rebuilt in the late thirteenth century, the wall is entirely twelfth century. Further east in the nave is a deep well, believed to have been originally put in for the use of masons working on the cathedral. Of the crossing, only the lower courses of the western piers remain.

Of the north transept, not much more than the foundations can be seen, but the transept had three eastern chapels which can be identified. The twelfth century west wall of the south transept is almost complete, and has intersecting wall-arcading. Much of the remainder of the transept, again with three eastern chapels, is early fifteenth century, and was probably built during the reconstruction after the collapse of the transept gable in 1409. In its south-west corner is the night stair that led down from the monks' dormitory. Among the tombstones, one has been identified as being that of Canon Robert Cathall (d.1380).

In the chancel, the bases of clustered late twelfth century piers remain. Tomb slabs here include one of Tournai marble set up on medieval stone coffins at the top of the sanctuary steps, roughly where the high altar once stood. Here, at the easternmost end of the cathedral is the clearest evidence of departed magnificence of St Andrews – the twelfth century 18.2m high east wall. Given the state of the rest of the cathedral, the wall is surprisingly complete, apart from the gable which has gone. The great upper window, with the tusks of its Decorated tracery hanging from the arch, was a curiously unnecessary insertion during the time of Prior Haldenston (1419–43), replacing two rows of three round-headed windows that probably matched those surviving at the lowest level; traces of the earlier windows can still be seen. The window was probably inserted to give more light to the chancel, but it has destroyed what must have been an attractive repetitive rhythm of triplet windows. Around the window are remains of the vault which extended over the chancel. The ends of the north and south sanctuary walls show the openings of the triforium and clerestory passages.

The chapter house lies to the south-east of the south transept. The original structure, built in the mid-thirteenth century, was nearly square and had its roof supported by four small pillars; a triple doorway led into the cloister. Bishop Lamberton built a large addition to the east between 1313 and 1321, and the original chapter house then became a vestibule. Lamberton's chapter house, like its predecessor, had benching and a blind arcade around the walls, but only a part of the south wall remains. Two stone coffins were found in the earlier chapter house. They are thought to be those of Prior John de Hadyngton (1304) and Prior John Machane (1313). In Lamberton's chapter house were found five stone coffins and fragments of two others. Prior John of Forfar (1321) was the first to be buried there, to be followed by John of Gowry (1340), William of Lothian (1354), Robert of Montrose (1393) and James Bisset (1416).

The cloister, adjacent to the south aisle, has mostly gone, but the thirteenth century doorway at the north-west, and the twelfth century doorway at the north-east, can still be seen. On the east walk is a collection of carved memorial stones, many being of the eighth, ninth and tenth centuries, as well as some medieval fragments. The monks cemetery lay to the east of the cloister. The well in the south side was the well of the lavatorium, where the monks washed before entering the refectory. The south range, the undercroft of the refectory, is largely a reconstruction of 1894 on the orders of Lord Bute. The west range was used for storage.

The dilapidated barrel-vaulted cellars are of late date and little importance. The bulbous projection in the south wall was the support for the refectory pulpit. A doorway at the end leads back into the cloister, and beyond is a projecting wing, the end of the dormitory range with the restored vaulted calefactory in its undercroft. Six bays long and two bays broad, the calefactory is now the museum. The room with a single standing column was the reredorter which projected eastwards from the dormitory. The foundations of its vaulted basement remain with the bases of two of the central vaulting piers. Running along the south side is the monastic drain.

On the left of the road is another building called the Prior's House. It is a later restored building, now used as a museum for post-reformation tombstones.

St Rule's Church

The twelfth century Church of St Rule stands to the east of the chapter house. Most of it has been demolished; all that remains is the small chancel and the remarkable 5.8m square and 32.9m high tower. The church was probably built in the period 1127–44; its resemblance to the twelfth century church at Wharram-le-Street, in Yorkshire, is so striking that it is suggested that the same school of Yorkshire masons was employed on both churches. There are also close similarities with the church at Aubazine near Limoges in France. The roofless walls east of the tower represent the chancel; beyond that was the sanctuary, which has disappeared except for the toothings on the side walls of the east face of the chancel. The vanished nave, west of the tower, was long thought to be a later twelfth century addition. It is now believed that the nave and tower are nearly contemporary. It is possible that the addition of the nave may have been merely a change of plan during construction. The staircase was constructed in 1789.

The Precinct Wall

The precinct of the cathedral and priory is enclosed by a fourteenth century wall, heightened and strengthened about 1516 by Prior Patrick Hepburn, later bishop of Moray. The wall is 6.7m high, 1.2m thick, and was 1.6km long; about three-quarters of it survives. The wall begins with the fourteenth century main gatehouse called the Pends, south-west of the cathedral; only the outer shell of the building remains. The wall was fortified by a mixture of round and square towers. The towers are still standing and embellished with niches for figures and the armorial bearings of their founders. The road passes through the wall, and then roughly bisects the former precinct. Leaving the cathedral on the left, it leads down the hill to the harbour gate, called Mill Port or Sea Gate. By turning left beyond that, a path can be followed just outside the wall, leading along the cliff top, past the foundations of the cruciform twelfth century Church of St Mary of the Rock. The church was demolished in 1559 and forgotten until 1860 when the foundations were excavated and exposed.

St Andrews Castle

The castle, which stands on a rock jutting out into the sea to the north of the cathedral, was the official residence of the bishops and archbishops. There was a castle here from the end of the twelfth century, but the present building is the result of a substantial rebuilding at the end of the fourteenth century and some later sixteenth century additions. The castle is substantially ruined, but enough remains to show that it was very large. It is entered by a bridge over a moat and through the gateway built by Archbishop John Hamilton (1547–71). The most interesting remaining features are the bottle dungeon in the late fourteenth century Sea Tower, and the subterranean mine and counter-mine. The bottle dungeon is cut out of solid rock and shaped like an ordinary bottle, 7.3m deep, with a narrow neck, down through which the prisoner was lowered. The mine below the Fore Tower is a fine example of sixteenth century siege engineering, a spacious underground corridor dug in an attempt to force an entry into the castle at the time of the siege of 1546–7.

The castle was severely damaged in the siege although repair work was undertaken. By the end of the sixteenth century, it was occupied by a succession of constables on behalf of the archbishop. In 1612 the castle was returned to Archbishop Gordon Gledstanes (1604–15), who carried out some repairs. With the expulsion of Archbishop Arthur Rose in 1689, the castle was abandoned and fell rapidly into ruin.

The destruction of the cathedral in the years after the reformation has left a pathetically tragic sight. 'The nearer we approach, the fragments become more ghastly, the scene more desolate',[5] wrote Robert Billings in the mid-nineteenth century. Dr Johnson was moved when he saw the town in the late eighteenth century: St Andrews, 'when it had lost its archiepiscopal pre-eminence, gradually decayed. One of its streets is now lost, and, of

The Cathedral Church of St Andrew (early 20th century postcard)

those that remain, there is the silence and solitude of inactive indigenve and gloomy depopulation'.[6] Ruskin was more poetic, and described the ruin of the cathedral as 'those rent skeletons of pierced wall through which our sea winds moan and murmur'.[7] Botfield penned an even more evocative sketch: 'Seen through the mist of last night, St Andrews indeed appeared like the ghost of a fine city; nor did the dawn of the wet gloomy day… tend to dissipate the illusion. The town is still and lifeless, smitten as it were with the curse of eternal silence – tower and spire, pinnacle and battlement, rise in hoary magnificence over the waves of the bay, which again lave its cliffs in mournful cadence, as if they sighed over the glory that hath departed, while the towers themselves echo only the monotonous cries of the birds which haunt them'.[8]

To see the wrecked glory of a building that was once the primatial cathedral of the Scottish church, is a deeply depressing experience. Of all the ruined cathedrals in Scotland, the wreckage of St Andrews is the clearest evidence of the most shameful part of the sixteenth century reformation – its vindictive hatred of the pre-reformation church and its philistine behaviour towards anything of beauty.

1 Brown, P Hume (1891)
2 Gifford, John (1988): p. 362.
3 Hunter Blair, David (1919): p. 191.
4 Hunter Blair, David (1921): p. 207.
5 Billings, Robert (1845-52): volume 4, 'Cathedral of St Andrews', p. 4.
6 Botfield, Beriah (1830): p. 32.
7 Pride, Glen L (1980): p. 119.
8 Botfield, Beriah (1830): p. 32.

Whithorn

The Cathedral Church of St Martin of Tours

Whithorn lies 157km south of Glasgow, on a promontory that extends into the Solway Firth. Its name derives partly from the horned shape of the promontory, and partly from the 'white' church that was built there fourteen hundred years ago.

The origin of Whithorn lies in the middle of the fifth century with the ministry of St Ninian, one of the greatest saints of Celtic Scotland. Ninian evangelised the northern Britons and the Picts, and is credited with bringing Christianity to Scotland. What little is known about him comes from the mid-eighth century writings of St Bede the Venerable, some three hundred years after his death.

Ninian is said to have been born c.368 of allegedly Christian parents. He was named Ringan, but is more usually called Ninian. He went to Rome at an early age and remained there for some years. Before his departure he is said to have been made a bishop by the pope, but as he would only have been about eighteen or nineteen years of age, this is unlikely, though not impossible. Ninian left Rome and travelled home to Scotland by way of Tours in France, where he made the acquaintance of the famous St Martin (c.316–97), bishop of Tours. Martin allowed Ninian to take with him some stonemasons to construct a church when he returned to Scotland. When St Martin died in 397, the church was still in the process of construction and, on hearing of his friend's death, Ninian ordered the new church to be dedicated to Martin. To build in stone at that early date was unusual, and the church, covered with white plaster, became known in Latin as the *Candida Casa*, or White House, when compared with the dark wattles of the peasant huts. The title Candida Casa was in general use to denote the pre-reformation diocese of Galloway and is still used today in official documents for the Roman Catholic diocese of the same name.

The precise location of Ninian's 'White House' is uncertain, but there is no reason to doubt that it was on the site of the surviving cathedral church at Whithorn, and buried fragments of the early Christian church at the east end of the chancel vaults support this view. The theory that it may have been on the Isle of Whithorn, about 5km south-east of Whithorn itself, is untenable. The island, which is joined to the mainland by a causeway, is the location of a small chapel, measuring 9.5m by 5m dating about 1300. Excavations have revealed evidence of an older chapel, of which this may be the replacement, but the building was probably more a convenient spiritual reception area for pilgrims arriving by sea. Of more interest is St Ninian's Cave, about 5km south-west of Whithorn. Following the discovery of an incised cross in 1871, excavations in 1884 revealed crosses dating back to the eighth century and earlier. The presence of so many crosses indicates that the cave was a very early site of pilgrimage, and there is no reason to doubt its connection with Ninian, who may well have used this remote place for silent retreat.

Bede wrote of Ninian as follows: 'The Southern Picts who dwelt on this side of those mountains had long before, as is reported, forsaken the errors of idolatry and embraced the truth by the preaching of Nynias, a most reverend bishop and holy man of the British nation who had been regularly instructed at Rome in the faith and mysteries of the truth; whose Episcopal see, named after St Martin, the bishop, and famous for a stately church (wherein he and many other saints rest in body) is still existent among the English nation. The place belongs to the province of the Bernicians, and is generally called Candida Casa, because he there built a church of stone, which was not usual among the Britons'. Ninian spent his life preaching to the Picts and died c.432 and is thought to have been buried in his own cathedral. His feast day is 26 August and he is shown dressed as a bishop, with heavy chains about him or hanging from his arm.

There are unreliable and unsubstantiated records of a succession of bishops following Ninian, but bishops or not, in the three hundred years after Ninian's death, Whithorn became famous as a centre of learning, attracting Irish scholars among others, and dispatching missionaries to other parts of Scotland.

Ninian's Celtic monastery survived until a Northumbrian invasion early in the eighth century. The Northumbrians established a bishopric c.731, and enthusiastically propagated the cult of Ninian. Excavations in 1990, in the area between the cathedral and the town, revealed the foundations of an eighth–ninth century Northumbrian-style church. The church was built of timber and dismantled in the mid-ninth century, but the surviving foundations show it to have been a nave and chancel church. To the east of the church stood a burial chapel constructed of clay on stone foundations. The distinctly Anglo–Saxon names of five Northumbrian bishops are known – Pechthelm (?731–c.735), Frithowald (735–763 or 764), Pehtwine (763 or 764–776 or 777), Aethelberht (777–89) and Heathored (791–803). Northumbrian power ended with the Viking conquest of York in 867 and the excavations have proved that the Northumbrian settlement at Whithorn was already in an advanced state of decay by that time. Bishop Pechthelm was friend of Bede, and probably supplied much of the information about Ninian that Bede used in his history.

The ecclesiastical status of Whithorn during Viking rule is uncertain and there are no surviving names of bishops after Heathored until the end of Viking rule, probably at the beginning of the twelfth century. The diocese of Whithorn came to life again in 1128, when Gilla-Aldan was consecrated by Archbishop Thurstan of York as the first bishop of a new episcopal line, and the diocese began to emerge as a territorial entity. A new Romanesque cathedral was built in the mid-twelfth century by the secular canons who served the church. It was cruciform, with a nave about 11m long and 7.3m wide, and small transepts. Part of the north wall of the existing nave is among the surviving fragments of this building. The cathedral was initially staffed by secular canons until Bishop Christian (1154–86) refounded Whithorn as a Premonstratensian priory c.1160. The priory church was the cathedral church for the diocese of Whithorn – or Candida Casa, as it was correctly known – but the bishops were always popularly styled 'of Galloway'. After a fire in the thirteenth century it was rebuilt on a much larger scale, with a nine-bay nave, aisled transepts, each with an east chapel, an aisled chancel of five bays with a sixth bay beyond the high altar, constituting a shrine to St Ninian, and a cloister to the north of the nave.

Hardly anything is known of the diocese of Whithorn from its establishment until the early fourteenth century but, difficult as it was to reach it, the shrine to the memory of Ninian ensured its lasting fame. King Robert I (1306–29) created the town a royal burgh and visited it in 1329, seeking a cure from the leprosy from which he died three months later. King James III (1460–88) and King James V (1513–42) came on pilgrimage to Whithorn. King James IV (1488–1513) was especially fond of the shrine, and came at least once – and often twice – every year during his reign. The priory soon grew to be one of the richest in the country and an important site of pilgrimage in medieval Scotland. In its earlier years, the diocese of Galloway was reckoned to be one of the poorest in Scotland, but from 1504 King James IV made its bishop ex-officio dean of the Chapel Royal of Stirling, and from 1531 the bishops of Galloway received the revenues of the Premonstratensian abbey of Tongland in Kirkcudbright. By the time of the sixteenth century reformation, the annual income of the diocese was about £1,200, with quantities of barley, meal, malt and salmon worth an additional £300. After 1504 the bishops were officially styled *episcopus Candide Case et capelle regie Strivilingensis.*

The diocese comprised most of the border counties of Wigton and Kirkcudbright, and came within the jurisdiction of the archbishop of York. Successive archbishops strove to claim primacy over the entire Scottish church. In 1192 the pope declared the Scottish bishops, with the exception of Galloway, to be subject to Rome alone and not to any archbishop. The claim of York was rarely acknowledged beyond the diocese of Galloway which, although in the kingdom of Scotland, remained part of the York archdiocese. Many of the bishops of Galloway were consecrated at Westminster Abbey, York Minster, or the church of St Mary 'de Suthwerke'. The invasions of King Edward I of England (1272–1307) at the end of the thirteenth century began to cause difficulty, and any form of divided allegiance became impossible to maintain in the struggle to assert the independence of Scotland. Bishop Thomas de Kirkcudbright (1294–1324) was the last bishop of Galloway to act as a suffragan in England. His successor, Bishop Simon de Wedale (1326–55), tried to establish the direct relationship with the pope enjoyed by the other Scottish bishops (there was no Scottish archbishop until 1472). Bishop Michael de Malconhalgh (1355–9) was the last bishop of Galloway to make a profession of obedience to the archbishop of York.

The Great Schism in the papacy after 1378, with separate popes at Rome and Avignon, was reflected in the diocese of Galloway. Bishop Oswald (1378–9) was recognised by the archbishop of York, and followed the English line of acknowledging Pope Urban VI at Rome; but was unable, except at the risk of his life, to set foot in his diocese. Bishop Thomas de Rossy (1379–97) followed the Scottish line of obedience to the Anti-Pope Clement VII at Avignon, and gained possession of the see. Oswald retained his title of bishop of Galloway until his death in 1417, but could only exercise his ministry in England. Bishop Thomas wrote a treatise in defence of Anti-Pope Clement VII, and concluded by challenging any English bishop who disagreed with him to decide the matter in personal combat. That was the end of the archbishop's claim to include Galloway in his province. In 1430, King

The Cathedral Church of St Martin of Tours

James I (1406–37) declared the see to have the same standing as the other Scottish dioceses in their relationship to the pope. Papal recognition of the severance between York and Galloway came in 1472 when the see of St Andrews was raised to the status of an archbishopric and given metropolitan powers. When the see of Glasgow was raised to an archbishopric in 1492, Whithorn was transferred to its metropolitan jurisdiction.

A shaft of light on the history of the cathedral is recorded in the year 1408, when the twelve canons of the cathedral were ordered to pay half of their revenues for ten years to help repair the cathedral and the bishop's palace. A report that year described the structure of the cathedral as 'unsound, mean and old, more than is fitting for such a church'. Records report the construction of a new chapel in 1424, paid for by Princess Margaret, countess of Douglas, and a new Lady Chapel at the south-east, c.1430. Further construction or repair was in progress in 1491 and 1502, and in 1560, on the very eve of the Scottish reformation, Bishop Alexander Gordon acknowledged the receipt of 500 merks for the 'reparation and bigging of his kirk'.

Monastic foundations were usually a target for the hatred of the sixteenth century reformers, and the cathedral and priory were ransacked in 1560. In fact, Bishop Alexander Gordon (1559–75) welcomed the reformation, promoted the cause of reform in his diocese and persuaded many of his clergy to accept the principles of the reformed church. He was supported by at least seven of the eleven Premonstratensian canons who acted as ministers or readers in the new regime. The last canon died shortly after 1590. The church was still in use in 1573, but by the end of the century the nave was derelict. In 1600 the nave was repaired and brought back into use as a parish church, and a tower was added at the west end. The chancel and crossing were abandoned and later almost entirely demolished. Further remodelling in 1635 saw the construction of a platform at the east end of the nave, to raise the altar.

Although a succession of resident bishops continued until 1689, with two intermissions, and Whithorn remained the cathedral church of the diocese, it was never so important again as it had been in the pre-reformation church. The priory buildings were allowed to fall into disuse and ruin, although there is evidence that some of them may have been used as a school for some time in the seventeenth century. Bishop John Gordon, nominated to the see of Galloway in December 1687 and consecrated February 1688, died in 1726. He was the last survivor of the bishops deprived of their sees in 1689, although he was received into the Roman Catholic Church before his death.

The west tower collapsed at the end of the seventeenth century, destroying the west gable and parts of the adjoining walls. A new west gable was built about 1700, together with internal galleries, but the cathedral was abandoned in 1822 when a new parish church was built on the site of the monastic dormitory. The cathedral then entered on its final, ruined stage. The nave walls and the chancel vaults were repaired in 1895 by the architect William Galloway at the direction of the marquess of Bute, but the nave has remained a ruin. John Patrick Crichton-Stuart, third marquess of Bute (1847–1900), was a learned and scholarly individual who had been received into the Roman Catholic Church in 1868, shortly after his twenty-first birthday (see St Andrews, and St Columba's, Oban). One of his great pleasures was the excavation of old buildings. 'He would stand by, wrapped in his cloak and smoking innumerable cigarettes, while a band of workmen dug out the foundations of a medieval lady chapel'.[1] Bute was responsible for similar reconstructive work on the cathedral at St Andrews.

Whithorn Cathedral lies on a small hill west of the main street of the town. The approach is by a narrow lane known as The Pend, which passes under the arch of the fifteenth century priory gatehouse. The only really old features of the arch are the two shafts and a panel above containing the armorial bearings of the kings of Scotland. Of the incongruously domestic-looking windows on either side of the royal arms, no more need be said.

The most substantial and obvious remaining part of the cathedral above ground is the much-reconstructed nave. There are slight remains of the crossing and transepts, but this area is now mostly a graveyard. A collection of vaults and crypts, usually inaccessible, can be seen under the area of the demolished chancel.

The aisleless nave, 22.5m long by 11.5m wide, is roofless but otherwise well preserved. It is impossible to assign a single date because it has been rebuilt on several occasions. The main entrance to the nave is through an eighteenth century doorway set in the seventeenth century east wall, which stands on the base of the medieval pulpitum, the remains of which can be seen projecting from the external wall face. The present grass floor of the nave is about 0.6m above the level of the original, as can be seen from the two empty fourteenth century cinquefoil-headed tomb recesses on the north wall, which stand on the level of the medieval floor. Another, twelfth century, recess was mostly destroyed when the door at the east end of the south wall was inserted. A fourth is near the centre of the north wall. It dates from the early seventeenth century and was probably intended as the burial place of a bishop.

The eastern part of the north and south walls is mostly thirteenth century, with some twelfth century masonry visible on the external south wall. The western part represents a thirteenth century extension which doubled the length of the cathedral. The prominent west gable itself is an eighteenth century rebuilding, east of its original position, following the collapse of the early seventeenth century west tower. The foundations of the tower can still be seen outside the west wall. The high lancet window with sandstone dressings was designed to give light to the gallery at this end of the nave as well as to the ground floor itself.

The older part of the north wall has no windows, because the cloister lay on this side. The corbels carrying the roof of the south cloister walk can still be seen. Above this roof was a range of small lancet windows destroyed when the wall was cut down in the seventeenth century; the sills of two lancets can still be seen. The three large windows on the south wall are fifteenth century, though the arched heads date from a seventeenth century rebuilding. The moulded window is sixteenth century. At the eastern end of the south wall is an inserted composite doorway; the inner arch is thirteenth century, but the outer arch is c.1500. The hood mould bears a shield carrying the arms of Bishop George Vaus (1492–1508). The door was inserted by Bishop Thomas Sydserf (1635–8) to provide access to the east end of the cathedral.

The south-west Romanesque doorway has some unusual carvings on the capitals and arch and is not in its original position. It may have been reset here when the cathedral was repaired in the early seventeenth century. It has a dripstone supported by two angels holding shields bearing the arms of Bishop Alexander Vaus (1422–48). Above the arch is another shield depicting the lion rampant of Scotland.

Situated under what was the east end of the demolished chancel are four vaults dating from c.1200. The largest, a long low barrel-vaulted chamber, projects southwards, and may have been the crypt of a south-east chapel or transept. The smallest, which is to the north of the others, seems to have been a larder, because of quantities of feathers found there during excavations, and the vaults may have been used for domestic rather than ecclesiastical purposes. The terrace and reconstructed low wall represent the east end of the cathedral, and date from the Bute restoration of 1895. Under the terrace is another crypt and beyond that a small re-roofed fourteenth century building, which may have been a sacristy for the cathedral, or part of the monastery. The Norman font is preserved nearby, and was used until the early twentieth century for pounding stucco.

The area immediately outside the east end of the church was also cleared during the Bute restoration. The low walls were erected by Bute and mark old stonework below ground, none of which is now visible. The site was excavated in 1949 and again in 1965 and revealed the walls of an Early Christian structure. Because this stands near the heart of the Celtic monastery, and because a light-coloured plaster was found on the walls during excavation, it has been conjectured that this is the site of the White House of Bede's description, although it is more likely that the walls represent the remains of a seventh century church that succeeded Ninian's building. The 1965 excavation also uncovered a series of associated graves that might date from the time of Ninian.

The cathedral continued to be used until 1822 when the nearby parish church was constructed. The church is a three-bay box of no interest beyond the fact that the east wall incorporates masonry from the dormitory of the priory. The prominent rubble-walled three stage tower was added to the south wall of the church in the mid-nineteenth century.

Whithorn Cathedral today is only a truncated remnant of the nave; and that remnant has been so mutilated by repeated alteration, that the structure is a poor reduced shadow of the departed cathedral. The abandonment and ruin of the priory was to be expected, and the almost total destruction of the crossing, transepts and chancel of the cathedral is not altogether surprising. But the saddest part of the architectural history of the cathedral is the way in which the nave was steadily, and almost systematically, reduced to the size of a little parish church, and then discarded when its usefulness was ended. The memory of Ninian deserved something better than this.

1 Bence-Jones, Mark (1992): p. 234.

Bibliography

Aberdeen and Temair, The marquess and marchioness of, *More cracks with 'we twa'* (London, 1929).

Adams, David, *Celtic and medieval religious houses in Angus* (Brechin, 1984).

Addis, M E Leicester, *Scotland's cathedrals and abbeys* (London, 1901).

Alexander, J H, *Index to occasional papers 1–12.* Friends of St Machar's Cathedral (Aberdeen, 1989).

Alexander, J H, and others, *The restoration of St Machar's Cathedral* (Aberdeen, 1981).

Alexander, William, and Douglas, Henry, *Two sermons preached on the festival of St Michael and All Angels, 1874, on the occasion of the consecration of the cathedral of St Andrew, Inverness. By the lord bishop of Derry and the lord bishop of Bombay* (Inverness, 1874).

Allchin, A M, *Alexander Penrose Forbes.* Oxford Prophets, number 9 (London, 1983).

Alstead, Stanley, *Dunblane Cathedral. The Flentrop Organ* (Glasgow, 1990).

Anderson, William, and Hicks, Clive, *Cathedrals in Britain and Ireland. From early times to the reign of Henry VIII* (London, 1978).

Anson, Peter, *Fashions in church furnishing 1840–1940* (London, 1960).

Anson, Peter, *Building up the waste places* (Leighton Buzzard, 1973).

Ball, Thomas Isaac, *A pastoral bishop. A memoir of Alexander Chinnery-Haldane DD. Sometime bishop of Argyll and the Isles* (London, 1907).

Barrow, G W S, *King David I and the church of Glasgow* (Glasgow, 1996).

Beaton, Angus J, *Illustrated guide to Fortrose and vicinity, with an appendix on the antiquaries of the Black Isle* (Inverness,1885).

Beaton, Elizabeth, *Ross and Cromarty. An illustrated architectural guide* (Edinburgh, 1992).

Beaton, Elizabeth, *Sutherland. An illustrated architectural guide* (Edinburgh, 1995).

Bence-Jones, Mark, *The Catholic families* (London, 1992).

Bentinck, Charles D, *Dornoch Cathedral and Parish* (Inverness, 1926).

Betjeman, Sir John, *First and last loves* (London, 1952).

Billings, Robert William, *The baronial and ecclesiastical antiquities of Scotland.* 4 volumes (Edinburgh, 1845–52).

Black, David Dakers, *The history of Brechin to 1864* (Edinburgh, 1867).

Botfield, Beriah, *Journal of a tour through the Highlands of Scotland in the summer of 1829* (Norton Hall, 1830).

Boyle, George, *Primary constitution and statutes of the church and college of the Holy Spirit* (Glasgow, 1851).

Brogden, W A, *Aberdeen. An illustrated architectural guide* (Edinburgh, 1986).

Brooks, J A, *Welcome to Iona* (Norwich, 1987).

Brown, P Hume (ed.), *Early travellers in Scotland* (Edinburgh, 1891).

Brown, P Hume (ed.), *Tours in Scotland 1677 and 1681 by Thomas Kirk and Ralph Thoresby* (Edinburgh, 1892).

Buckler, John Chessell and Buckler, Charles Alban, *The cathedral, or abbey church of Iona* (London, 1866).

Butler, Dugald, *Scottish cathedrals and abbeys* (London, 1901).

Campbell, George (Duke of Argyll), *Iona* (Edinburgh, 1889).

Canby, Courtlandt, *A guide to the archaeological sites of the British Isles* (Oxford, 1988).

Cant, H W M, and Firth, H M, *Light in the north. St Magnus Cathedral through the centuries* (Kirkwall, 1989).

Cant, Ronald G, *Historic Elgin and its cathedral* (Elgin, 1974).

Cant, Ronald G, *The building of St Machar's cathedral, Aberdeen.* Friends of St Machar's Cathedral, Occasional Papers, No. 4 (Aberdeen, 1976).

Cant, Ronald G, *The parish church of the Holy Trinity St Andrews. A short account of its history and architecture* (St Andrews, 1992).

Carpenter, Edward, *Cantuar. The archbishops in their office* (London, 1971).

Carrick, J C, *The ancient cathedrals of Scotland* (London, 1905).

The Cathedral Church of St Mary Edinburgh. A handbook for pilgrims (London, 1934).

Cathedral Church of Saint Paul Dundee (c. 1965).

Cathedral of St Mary of the Assumption 1860–1985. Souvenir Brochure.

Cathedral of the Isles and the College of the Holy Spirit (Cumbrae, 1982).

Chalmers, P Macgregor, *The cathedral church of Glasgow. A description of its history and a brief history of the archi-episcopal see* (London, 1914).

Chambers, William, *Story of St Giles' Church Edinburgh* (Edinburgh, 1879).

Chapman, R W (ed.), *Johnson's journey to the western isles of Scotland and Boswell's journal of a tour of the Hebrides with Samuel Johnson, LLD* (Oxford, 1924).

Clark, William, *A series of views of the venerable and magnificent ruins of Elgin Cathedral, engraved from very accurate drawings taken on the spot* (London, 1826).

Close, Rob, *Ayrshire and Arran. An illustrated architectural guide* (Edinburgh, 1992).

Cockburn, James Hutchison, *The Celtic church in Dunblane* (Edinburgh, 1954).

Cockburn, James Hutchison, *The medieval bishops of Dunblane and their church* (Edinburgh, 1959).

Collie, J, *Plans, elevations, sections, details and views of the cathedral of Glasgow* (London, 1835).

Cowan, Ian B, *St Machar's cathedral in the early middle ages.* Friends of St Machar's Cathedral, Occasional Papers, No. 6 (Aberdeen, 1980).

Cramond, W, *The church of Birnie* (Elgin, 1903).

Craven, J B, *Records of the dioceses of Argyll and the Isles 1560–1860* (Kirkwall, 1907).

Craven, J B, *A history of the episcopal church in the diocese of Caithness* (Kirkwall, 1908).

Craven, J B, *History of the episcopal church in Orkney 1688–1912* (Kirkwall, 1912).

Crawford, Barbara E (ed.), *St Magnus Cathedral and Orkney's twelfth-century renaissance* (Aberdeen, 1988).

Cruden, Stewart, *St Andrews cathedral* (Edinburgh, 1986).

Cruickshanks, James, *Spynie Kirk 1736–1986* (Lossiemouth, 1986).

The Cumbrae College Calendar (Edinburgh, 1869–1878).

Dietrichson, Lorentz Henrik Segelcke, *Monumenta Orcadia. The Norsemen in the Orkneys and the monuments they have left* (Kristiania, 1906).

Ditchfield, P H, *The cathedrals of Great Britain. Their history and architecture.* 5th edition (London, 1932).

Donlevy, James, *Historical account of St Mary's cathedral and its place in the ecclesiastical history of Scotland* (Edinburgh,1890).

Dowden, John, *Observations on the legal constitution and statutes of the cathedral church of St Mary, Edinburgh* (Edinburgh, 1909).

Dryden, Sir Henry, *Description of the church dedicated to St Magnus and the bishop's palace at Kirkwall* (Kirkwall, 1878).

Dunbar, John G, and Fisher, Ian, *Iona. A guide to the monuments.* 2nd edition (Edinburgh, 1995).

Durkan, John, *The precinct of Glasgow cathedral* (Glasgow,1986).

Easson, D E, *Medieval religious houses. Scotland. With an appendix on the houses in the Isle of Man* (London, 1957).

Eyre-Todd, George, *The book of Glasgow Cathedral. A history and description* (Glasgow, 1898).

Fairweather, Barbara, *Lismore, Duor and Strath of Appin. A short history* (Fort William, 1976).

Farquhar, George T S, *The episcopal history of Perth 1689–1894* (Perth, 1894).

Farquhar, George T S, *Our ancient Scottish cathedrals: An historical sketch and a constitutional explanation* (Perth, 1928).

Farquhar, George T S, *A short history of St Ninian's Cathedral, Perth to 1926 AD* (Edinburgh, 1927).

Fawcett, Richard, *Beauly Priory and Fortrose Cathedral* (Edinburgh, 1987).

Fawcett, Richard, *Dunkeld Cathedral. A short history and guide* (Dunkeld, 1990).

Fawcett, Richard, 'Glasgow Cathedral': In Williamson, E, Riches, A & Higgs, M (1990).

Fawcett, Richard, *Elgin Cathedral* (Edinburgh, 1991).

Fawcett, Richard, *St Andrews Castle* (Edinburgh, 1992).

Fawcett, Richard, *St Andrews Cathedral* (Edinburgh, 1993).

Fawcett, Richard, *Scottish Cathedrals* (London, 1997).

Fawcett, Richard, with Bunney, Herrick, and Macmillan, Gilleasbuig, *St Giles' Cathedral* (Andover, 1991).

Fenwick, Hubert, *Scotland's abbeys and cathedrals* (London, 1978).

Findlay, W H, *Heritage of Perth* (Perth, 1984).

Fraser, Dorothy, *Fortrose: a garden city by the sea* (Glasgow, 1912).

Fryde, E B, Greenaway, D E, Porter, S, and Roy, I, *Handbook of British chronology.* 3rd edition (London, 1986).

Galbraith, J D, *St Machar's cathedral: the Celtic antecedents.* Friends of St Machar's Cathedral, Occasional Papers, No. 8, (Aberdeen, 1982).

Gifford, John, *The buildings of Scotland: Fife* (London, 1988).

Gifford, John, *The buildings of Scotland: Highlands and Islands* (London, 1992).

Gifford, John, *The buildings of Scotland: Dumfries and Galloway* (London, 1996).

Gifford, John, with McWilliam, Colin, and Walker, David, *The buildings of Scotland: Edinburgh* (London, 1991).

Gordon, Fiona, *Brechin Cathedral.* Walk around guide (Brechin, 1992).

Gordon, George, *A new cathedral for Aberdeen: considered in a letter to the Right Rev. Thomas George, Lord Bishop of Aberdeen* (London, 1861).

Gordon, James Frederick Skinner, *Iona* (Glasgow, 1885).

Gordon, James Frederick Skinner, *A vade mecum to and through the cathedral of St Kentigern, Glasgow* (Glasgow, 1894).

Graham, H D, *Antiquities of Iona* (London, 1850).

Grant, John, *Grant's views of Elgin Cathedral* (London, 1835).

Grant, Malcolm, *The cathedral church of Saint Andrew at Inverness* (Inverness, 1994).

Gray, Cardinal Joseph Gordon, *St Mary's cathedral Edinburgh. One hundred and seventy-five years 1814–1989* (Edinburgh, 1990).

Guide to the ruins of Elgin Cathedral (Elgin, 1913).

Gunnis, Rupert, *Dictionary of British sculptors 1660–1851* (London, 1951).

Henderson, John, *Glasgow Cathedral. Dr Burns' ministry and labours in the High Church parish 1865–1896* (Glasgow, 1901).

Henderson, John, *Glasgow Cathedral. Dr M'Adam Muir's ministry in the High Church parish 1896–1915* (Glasgow, 1925).

Hill, Peter, *Excavations at Whithorn Priory 1990–91* (Whithorn, 1991).

Hill, Peter, *Whithorn and St Ninian. The excavation of a monastic town 1984–91,* (Stroud, 1997).

Hill, Peter and Pollock, Dave, *The Whithorn dig* (Newton Stewart, 1992).

Historical and descriptive account of the cathedral church of Glasgow, necropolis, etc. (Glasgow, 1904).

The history of the cathedral or high church of Glasgow (Falkirk, 1825).

History of the erection of the cathedral church of St Mary, Edinburgh (Edinburgh, 1879).

Honeyman, John, *The age of Glasgow Cathedral and of the effigy in the crypt* (Glasgow, 1854).

Houghton, Leighton, *A guide to the British cathedrals* (London, 1973).

Howard, Donald, *The cathedral church of St Andrew at Aberdeen* (Aberdeen, 1987).

Hunter, Charles, *Oban – past and present* (Oban, 1993).

Hunter, J R, *Rescue excavations on the brough of Birsay 1974–82.* Society of Antiquaries of Scotland Monograph Series Number 4 (Edinburgh, 1986).
Hunter Blair, David, *A medley of memories. Fifty years' recollections of a Benedictine monk* (London, 1919).
Hunter Blair, David, *John Patrick, third marquis of Bute, KT (1847–1900): A memoir* (London, 1921).
Hunter Blair, David, *A new medley of memories* (London,1922).

Iona Abbey. A short tour. (n.d.)

Johnson, Paul, *Cathedrals of England, Scotland and Wales* (London, 1990).
Johnston, John Octavius, *Life and letters of Henry Parry Liddon* (London, 1904)

Keddie, William, *Staffa and Iona described and illustrated* (Glasgow, 1850).
Keillar, Ian, *Cathedrals, abbeys and priories in Moray* (Moray, 1982).
Kennedy, William, *Annals of Aberdeen, from the reign of King William the Lion, to the end of the year 1818; with an account of the city, cathedral and university of Old Aberdeen.* 2 volumes (London, 1818).
Kirk, James, *Archbishop Spottiswoode and the see of Glasgow* (Glasgow, 1988).

Laing, D, *On the present state of the ruins of Iona, and their preservation: in a letter to the Honourable Lord Murray* (Edinburgh, 1854).
Lewis, Samuel, *A topographical dictionary of Scotland.* 2 volumes (London, 1846).
Lindsay, Ian Gordon, *The cathedrals of Scotland* (London & Edinburgh, 1926).
Lindsay-Dougall, Katherine and Abott, Nigel, *Guide to the cathedral church of St John the Divine Oban* (n.d.).
Linklater, Eric, *Orkney and Shetland* (London, 1965).
Lochhead, Marion, *Episcopal Scotland in the nineteenth century* (London, 1966).
Look at St Andrew's cathedral Glasgow (Doncaster, 1989).

McCall, Peter, *Some history and St Andrew's* (Dumfries, 1991).
McCartney, Crear, *The stained glass windows of St Machar's cathedral, Aberdeen.* Friends of St Machar's Cathedral, Occasional Papers, No. 5 (Aberdeen, 1979).
McCorry, J. Stewart, *The monks of Iona* (London, 1871).
Macfarlane, Leslie J, *St Machar's Cathedral in the later middle ages.* Friends of St Machar's Cathedral, Occasional Papers, No. 1 (Aberdeen, 1971).
Macfarlane, Leslie J, *St Machar's Cathedral, Aberdeen and its medieval records.* Friends of St Machar's Cathedral, Occasional Papers, No. 11 (Aberdeen, 1987).
Macfarlane, Leslie J and Short, Agnes, *The burgh and cathedral of old Aberdeen 1489–1989.* Friends of St Machar's Cathedral, Occasional Papers, No. 12 (Aberdeen, 1989).
MacGibbon, David, and Ross, Thomas, *The ecclesiastical architecture of Scotland from the earliest Christian times to the seventeenth century.* 3 volumes (Edinburgh, 1896).
Mackay, Hector M, *Old Dornoch: Its traditions and legends* (Dingwall, 1920).
McKean, Charles, *The district of Moray. An illustrated architectural guide* (Edinburgh, 1987).
McKean, Charles and Walker, David, *Dundee. An illustrated architectural guide* (Edinburgh, 1984).
Mackey, Donald J, *Bishop Forbes. A memoir* (London, 1888).
Mackie, Euan W, *Lismore and Appin. An archaeological guide* (Glasgow, 1993).
Mackintosh, Herbert B, *Elgin past and present* (Elgin, 1914).
Maclean, Allan (ed.), *Elgin Cathedral and the diocese of Moray 1224–1974* (n.d.).
Maclean, L, *An historical account of Iona from the earliest period* (Oban, 1841).
McLellan, Archibald, *Essay on the cathedral church of Glasgow; and a history of the see, as connected with the erection of the existing church: with a survey of its present condition, and plan for its repair and restoration, together with the general improvement of the ancient portion of the city* (Glasgow, 1833).
Macquarrie, Alan, and Macarthur, E Mairi, *Iona through the ages* (Argyll, 1992).
Macroberts, David, *The heraldic ceiling of St Machar's cathedral Aberdeen.* Friends of St Machar's Cathedral, Occasional Papers, No. 2 (Aberdeen, 1981).
Marshall, Elizabeth, *The Black Isle. Life and legend* (Fortrose, 1969).
Marshall, Jane, *A tour through Britain's abbeys and cathedrals* (London, 1964).
Mason, Arthur James, *Memoir of George Howard Wilkinson, bishop of St Andrews, Dunkeld and Dunblane, and primus of the Scottish Episcopal Church. Formerly Bishop of Truro.* 2 volumes (London, 1909).
Mason, Roger A, *The Glasgow assembly 1638* (Glasgow, 1988).
MCG–, J, *Cathedral church of Our Lady of Good Aid, Motherwell. Solemn re-opening and consecration of the altar by The Right Reverend Joseph Devine, PhD, Bishop of Motherwell. Second Sunday of Advent 9th December 1984* (Glasgow, 1984).
Miller, James F and Lusk, John C, *Dunblane cathedral* (Dunblane, n.d.).
Mooney, Harald, 'Some seventeenth century records of St Magnus Cathedral': In Thompson, W I L (1981).
Mooney, Harald, *St Magnus Cathedral Orkney* (Kirkwall, 1985).
Mooney, John, *Octocentenary of St Magnus Cathedral Kirkwall* (London, 1938).
Mooney, John, *The cathedral and royal burgh of Kirkwall.* 2nd edition (Kirkwall, 1947).
Morris, William J, *A walk through Glasgow cathedral.* 2nd edition (Glasgow, 1995).
Morrisson, A R and Turbet, R B, *The organ and organists of St Andrew's Cathedral, Aberdeen* (Aberdeen, 1981).
Morton, T Ralph, *The Iona community story* (London, 1957a).
Morton, T Ralph, *What is the Iona community?* (Glasgow, 1957b).
The murals of St Mary's cathedral, Glasgow. A visitor's guide.

Neale, John Mason, *The life and times of Patrick Torry, DD, bishop of Saint Andrews, Dunkeld and Dunblane, with an appendix on the Scottish liturgy* (London, 1856).

New, Anthony, *A guide to the cathedrals of Britain* (London, 1980).

Nicholson, Angela, and Nicholson, Keith, *Skye. The complete visitor's guide* (Insch, 1994).

Nicolson, Alexander, *History of Skye*. 2nd edition (Portree, 1994).

One hundred and seventy five years of St Mary's cathedral in the archdiocese of St Andrews and Edinburgh 1814–1989 (Edinburgh, 1989).

Orem, William, *A description of the chanonry, cathedral and King's College of Old Aberdeen, in the years 1724 and 1725* (Aberdeen 1791).

Pagan, James, *History of the cathedral and see of Glasgow* (Glasgow, 1856).

Paul, Sir James and Warrack, John, *The knights of the most noble and most ancient Order of the Thistle. A historical sketch of the Order by the Lord Lyon King of Arms and a descriptive sketch of their chapel* (Edinburgh, 1911).

Pennant, T, *A tour in Scotland, and voyage to the Hebrides; MDCCLXXII.* 2 volumes (London, 1776).

Perry, William, *The Oxford movement in Scotland* (Cambridge, 1933).

Perry, William, *Alexander Penrose Forbes. Bishop of Brechin. The Scottish Pusey* (London, 1939).

Peterson, M, *The restoration of Dunblane cathedral 1893. Centenary 1993* (Dunblane, 1993).

Pride, Glen L, *The kingdom of Fife* (Edinburgh, 1990).

Pringle, Denys, *Spynie Palace* (Edinburgh, 1996).

Radford, C Ralegh and Donaldson, Gordon, with revisions and additions by Fisher, Ian and Abraham, Christopher T, *Whithorn and the ecclesiastical monuments of the Wigtown district* (Edinburgh, 1984).

Richmond, James C, *A visit to Iona by an American clergyman* (Glasgow, 1849).

Ritchie, Anna, *Brough of Birsay* (Edinburgh, 1986).

Ritchie, Walter M, *The island of Lismore* (Lismore, 1995).

Robertson, Joseph, *Scottish abbeys and cathedrals* (Aberdeen, 1891).

Root, Margaret, *Dunkeld Cathedral* (Edinburgh, 1950).

Rose, D Murray, *The ancestry of St Gilbert of Dornoch* (1900).

Ross, Alexander J, *Memoir of Alexander Ewing, DCL, bishop of Argyll and the Isles* (London, 1879).

Royal commission on the ancient and historical monuments of Scotland (RCAHMS), *9th report with inventory of constructions in the Outer Hebrides, Skye and the small isles* (Edinburgh, 1928).

Royal commission on the ancient and historical monuments of Scotland (RCAHMS), *Argyll. An inventory of the monuments. Volume 4, Iona* (Edinburgh, 1982).

St Andrew's Cathedral Dundee (Dundee, 1986).

St Andrew's Cathedral Inverness (n.d.)

The St Columba Commemoration. Iona, 8th June 1897 (Edinburgh, 1897).

St Giles' Cathedral (n.d.)

St Giles' Cathedral, Edinburgh (Edinburgh, 1883).

St Mary's Cathedral (Edinburgh, 1992).

Scotus, *Glasgow Cathedral* (Glasgow, 1860).

Shanks, John, *Elgin: and a guide to Elgin Cathedral once denominated the lantern of the north, together with some pious and religious reflections within the old walls, evoked by the resident spirit of the ruins. By the old cicerone of Elgin Cathedral* (London, 1866).

Shaw, J A S, *In the end…the beginning. An account of St Mary's Cathedral, Edinburgh 1814–1964* (Edinburgh, 1964).

Short, Agnes, *The kirkyard of St Machar's cathedral, Aberdeen.* Friends of St Machar's Cathedral, Occasional Papers, No. 9 (Aberdeen, 1982).

Short, Agnes, *Old Aberdeen in the eighteenth century.* Friends of St Machar's Cathedral, Occasional Papers, No. 10 (Aberdeen, 1985).

Simpson, Grant G, *Old Aberdeen in the early seventeenth century: a community study.* Friends of St Machar's Cathedral, Occasional Papers, No. 3 (Aberdeen, 1980).

Simpson, James A, *Dornoch Cathedral. Glory of the north* (Derby, 1989).

Simpson, W Douglas, *Bishop's palace and earl's palace. Kirkwall, Orkney* (Kirkwall, 1989).

Skea, William, *Popular guide to Old Aberdeen* (Aberdeen, 1922).

Skrine, Henry, *Three successive tours in the north of England, to the lakes and great part of Scotland*. 2nd edition (London, 1813).

Southey, Robert, *Journal of a tour in Scotland in 1819* (London, 1929).

Stevenson, David, *St Machar's cathedral and the reformation.* Friends of St Machar's Cathedral, Occasional Papers, No. 7 (Aberdeen, 1981).

Sutherland, Elizabeth, Countess of (also Marchioness of Stafford, and later Duchess of Sutherland), *Views in Orkney and on the north-eastern coast of Scotland. Taken in 1805 and etched in 1807* (1807).

Swire, O F, *Skye: the island and its legends* (London, 1961).

Thomas, Charles, *Whithorn's Christian beginnings. 1st Whithorn lecture, 1st September 1992* (Whithorn, 1992).

Thompson, Paul, *William Butterfield* (London, 1971).

Thompson, William I L (ed.), *Orkney Heritage,* volume 1, 1981 (Kirkwall, 1981).

Thoms, David Boath, *Notes on the stained glass and the communion vessels in Brechin Cathedral* (Brechin, 1960).

Thoms, David Boath, *The kirk of Brechin in the seventeenth century* (Brechin, 1972).

Thoms, David Boath, *The Council of Brechin* (Brechin, 1977).

Thoms, David Boath, *Illustrated guide to Brechin cathedral* (Brechin, 1985).

Thorold, Henry, *Collins guide to the ruined abbeys of England,*

Wales and Scotland (London, 1993).

Tomes, John, *Blue Guide. Scotland* (London, 1996).

Towle, Eleaner A, *John Mason Neale, DD. A memoir* (London, 1906).

Trenholme, Edward Craig, *The story of Iona* (Edinburgh, 1905).

Turner, John, *The story of St Andrew's Cathedral Dundee 1836–1936* (Gloucester, 1935).

Vaassen, Elgin, *The makers of the 'Munich glass': the Munich Royal Glass Painting Works* (Glasgow, 1996).

Walcott, Mackenzie E C, *Scoti Monasticon. The ancient church of Scotland. A history of the cathedrals, conventual foundations, collegiate churches and hospitals of Scotland.* 2 volumes (London, 1874).

A walk-round guide to Saint Mary's cathedral. The mother church of the Diocese of Glasgow and Galloway in the Scottish Episcopal Church.

Ward and Lock, *Illustrated historical handbook to the Scotch cathedrals* (London, 1889).

Watson, T L, *The architectural history of Glasgow Cathedral* (Glasgow, 1911).

White, Gavin, *St Mary's Cathedral, Glasgow. A history* (Glasgow, 1995).

Williamson, Elizabeth, with Riches, Anne, and Higgs, Malcolm, *The buildings of Scotland. Glasgow* (London, 1990).

Wordsworth, Charles, *Annals of my life 1847–1856* (London, 1893).

Wordsworth, John, *The episcopate of Charles Wordsworth, bishop of St Andrews, Dunkeld and Dunblane 1853–1892. A memoir* (London, 1899).

Young, Andrew and Doak, A M, *Glasgow at a glance* (Glasgow, 1965).

Young, Robert, *The parish of Spynie in the county of Elgin* (Elgin, 1871).

Glossary

ABBESS: head of an abbey of nuns.

ABBEY: (i) a building occupied by monks or nuns under an abbot or abbess; (ii) also sometimes used to describe a church that was once part of an abbey, e.g. Westminster Abbey.

ABBOT: head of an abbey of monks.

AISLE: that part of a church, sometimes a later addition, running parallel with and divided from, the nave or the choir/chancel.

ALTAR: flat topped block, or table, used to consecrate the elements of bread and wine at the Mass/Eucharist/ Holy Communion.

ALTAR TOMB: raised monument resembling a solid altar.

AMBO: pulpit in the early Christian church.

AMBULATORY: aisle at the east end of a chancel, usually surrounding an apse and therefore semi-circular or polygonal.

APSE: large semi-circular or polygonal recess, arched or dome-roofed, especially at the east end of a church to house the altar.

APSIDAL: having the form of an apse.

ARCADE: range or arches supported by piers or columns; a blind arcade is one set in the surface of a wall.

ARCHBISHOP: the chief bishop of a province. There were formerly two archbishops in the Scottish Church: St Andrews (from 1472 to 1704) and Glasgow (from 1492 to 1708). The primate of the Roman Catholic Church in Scotland has been styled Archbishop of St Andrews and Edinburgh since 1878.

ARCHDEACON: cleric having defined administrative authority delegated to him by the bishop, generally the temporal administration of ecclesiastical property.

ARCHDIOCESE: diocese of which the holder has the ex officio title of archbishop.

ARCHPRIEST: from the early fifth century the term was applied to the senior priest of a city, either by years or appointment, who performed many of the Bishop's liturgical and governmental functions in his absence or during a vacancy; the title fell into disuse in the late Middle Ages.

AUGUSTINIAN: member of a religious order observing a rule derived from the writings of St Augustine of Hippo (d.430), they were otherwise known as the Black Canons. They were a preaching Order who, though living under a Rule and in community, worked in the world. Their more liberal ideals and more sociable way of life commended them to the people at large.

AUMBRY: small recess in the wall of a church or sacristy in which, in mediaeval times, sacred vessels and books were kept; now generally used to reserve the Blessed Sacrament or holy oils.

BALDACHINO: free standing canopy resting on columns over an altar. Also called a ciborium.

BALUSTER: pillar or pedestal swelling in the middle or towards the bottom.

BAPTISM: ceremony of admission to the Church, either by immersion in, or affusion with, water.

BAPTISTERY: part of a church containing the font used for the sacrament of baptism.

BARREL VAULT: vault with a semi-cylindrical roof.

BASILICA: an early form of building used for Christian worship modelled on civic buildings used for legal or commercial purposes. Basilicas were oblong halls with double colonnades. Although some cathedrals have been built in the basilical style, the title of "minor basilica" is now conferred by the pope on certain privileged churches in Rome and elsewhere in the world.

BATTLEMENTS: castellated parapet at the top of a wall for the defence of a building.

BENEDICTINE: member of a religious order founded in 529 at Monte Cassino by St Benedict, generally held to be the founder of western monasticism.

BENEFICE: ecclesiastical office which prescribes certain duties or conditions (spiritualities) for the due discharge of which it awarded certain revenues (temporalities).

BISHOP: deriving from the Greek word *episcopos* meaning 'overseer', the chief clergyman of a diocese, with powers of confirming, ordaining and instituting.

BISHOPRIC: the office of a bishop.

BLIND ARCADE: *see* ARCADE

BOSS: raised knob or projection usually covering the intersection of ribs in a vault.

BOX PEW: enclosed pew with door and high partition, much favoured in the eighteenth century.

BRIEF: letter from the Pope to a person or a community on a matter of discipline.

BROACH SPIRE: spire rising from a tower without parapet.

BULL: written mandate of the Pope, of a more weighty and serious nature than a *brief.*

BUTTRESS: support built against a wall.

CANON: priest who is a member of a cathedral chapter.

CANTOR: leader of singing in church.

CAPITAL: head or cornice, usually decorated, of a pillar or column.

CAPUCHIN: a more austere offshoot of the Franciscan Order, founded early in the sixteenth century, desiring to return to the primitive simplicity of the original Order.

CARTHUSIAN: the most austere religious order of all; founded by St Bruno of La Chartreuse in 1084. His rule was based on the concept of each monk living on his own as a hermit, grouped in little cells around a central cloister. They only met in church or for occasional gatherings in the chapter house or refectory.

CARTOUCHE: tablet with ornate frame, usually of elliptical shape.

CATHEDRA: the bishop's chair or throne. Its original position was in the centre of the apse behind the High Altar. In the Middle Ages it was placed on the south side of the chancel.

CHAMFER: surface formed by cutting off a square edge, usually at an angle of forty-five degrees.

CHANCEL: that part of a church housing the altar, usually an extension to the east end. The word is sometimes used interchangeably with choir.

CHANTRY: used to describe a priest, chapel or altar endowed to provide regular masses for the repose of the soul of an individual or family.

CHAPEL: part of a large church or cathedral with a separate altar; also used to describe Roman Catholic churches during the Penal Years.

CHAPTER: the priests attached to a cathedral or collegiate church.

CHAPTER HOUSE: the council chamber of the chapter, sometimes part of a cathedral, sometimes separate.

CHEVRON: Norman zigzag moulding.

CHOIR: (i) strictly that part of the chancel containing the seats of the clergy, but the word is often and erroneously applied to the whole chancel; (ii) a band of singers who lead services.

CHURCH: from the Greek word meaning 'Lord', a building for public Christian worship; there are many different types of church: e.g. parish, cathedral, abbey, priory, friary, conventual, collegiate.

CINQUEFOIL: *see* FOIL

CISTERCIAN: member of an order founded in 1098 by St Stephen Harding, Abbot of Citeaux. It was more austere than the Benedictine rule, forbidding unnecessary decoration of churches, and insisting that its houses should be founded in remote, wild places far from town and civilisation.

CLAUSTRAL: cloister, monastic buildings.

CLERESTORY: upper part of the nave walls of a church, containing a series of windows above the aisle roofs, usually the top stage of nave or chancel.

CLOISTER: (a) covered place for walking, often around a quadrangle with a wall on outer side and colonnade or windows on inner side, (b) the monastic life in general.

COADJUTOR: an assistant (bishop) to a diocesan bishop, generally with right of succession to the diocese.

COFFERING: sunken panels, square or polygonal, decorating a ceiling.

COIGN: projecting corner.

COLLEGIATE CHURCH: church which is endowed for a body of canons and/or prebendaries (a chapter), but is not the seat of a bishop.

COLONNADE: range of columns supporting an entablature.

COLONETTE: small column or shaft.

CONSISTORY COURT: Anglican bishop's court for ecclesiastical causes and offences.

CONVENT: building or buildings in which a body of religious live together, historically applied to houses of either sex, it tends now to be restricted to houses of nuns.

CONVENTUAL: less strict branch of the Franciscan Order which favoured the accumulation and common holding of property; founded early in the fourteenth century.

CORBEL: projection of stone, timber, etc., jutting out from wall to support the weight of an arch or vault.

CORNICE: decorative moulding in the angle between wall and ceiling.

COURSED: continuous range of stones or bricks of uniform height.

CREDENCE: small table at the side of an altar where the elements of bread and wine are placed before consecration.

CRENELLATION: stepped pattern in battlements.

CROCKET: small carved ornament on the side of a spire or pinnacle.

CROSSING: that part of a cruciform church where the nave, choir and transepts meet, often surmounted by a tower.

CROZIER: hooked pastoral staff of a bishop symbolising his territorial jurisdiction.

CRUCIFORM: built in the shape of a cross.

CRYPT: underground room below a church often used for the burial of the dead.

CUPOLA: small polygonal or circular domed turret crowning a roof.

CUSP: projecting point formed by the foils within the divisions of Gothic tracery.

CYCLOPEAN: large and irregular but smooth and finely jointed blocks of stone typical of ancient masonry.

DADO: plinth of column, or a linking design or pattern around the lower part of a wall.

DEAN: in England, the priest who heads the chapter of a cathedral or collegiate church; in Scotland and Ireland, the next senior priest to the bishop, equivalent to an archdeacon in England.

DECORATED: second phase of English Gothic, c.1290 to c.1350, marked by increasing decoration and geometrical or curvilinear tracery. Also used to describe that style when used in the nineteenth century Gothic Revival.

DIOCESE: territory or district under the jurisdiction of a bishop.

DIOCLETIAN WINDOW: semi-circular window divided by two mullions.

DOMINICAN: member of the order of preaching friars founded by St Dominic in 1215; officially known as the Order of Preachers (OP).

DORIC: oldest and simplest of the three Greek orders of column and entablature.

EARLY CHRISTIAN: term sometimes used to describe monastic architecture before the development of Romanesque c.1050, buildings generally of small and simple construction.

EARLY ENGLISH: first stage of English Gothic, c.1200 to c.1300, with pointed arches, lancet windows and simple tracery. Also used to describe that style when used in the nineteenth century Gothic Revival.

ENCAUSTIC TILES: glazed and decorated earthenware tiles.

ENTABLATURE: collective name for the architrave, frieze and cornice above a column.

EREMITIC: the life of a hermit or recluse.

FAIENCE: decorated earthenware.

FINIAL: topmost feature above a gable, spire or cupola.

FIRST FRUITS: the first year's revenue of a benefice, bishopric or other dignity.

FLECHE: a small slender spire.

FLORIATED: decorated with flower designs.

FLUTING: series of concave grooves cut perpendicularly in the surface of a column.

FOIL: the leaf shape formed by the cusping of Gothic tracery, as in trefoil (three-lobed), quatrefoil (four-lobed), cinquefoil (five-lobed), etc.

FONT: vessel to contain water used at baptism.

FRANCISCAN: member of a religious order founded by St Francis of Assisi in 1209. Officially known as the Order of Friars Minor (OFM).

FRATER: another word for refectory, deriving from the Old French *refraitour*.

FRIAR: a member of one of the four religious mendicant orders, from the French word for brother (Franciscans: Grey Friars or Friars Minor; Augustinians: Austin Friars; Dominicans: Black Friars or Friars Major; Carmelites: White Friars).

FRIARY: a house in which friars reside or have their headquarters. Unlike a monastery it is not a permanent residence for a friar and it has no enclosure.

FRIEZE: horizontal broad band of sculpture.

GABLE: the pointed end wall of a building, especially the triangular upper part, above the eaves.

GADROON: ribbed ornament, e.g on the lid or base of an urn, flowing into a lobed edge.

GALILEE: chapel or vestibule enclosing the porch. Also called narthex.

GLEBE: portion of land attached to a benefice and providing revenue.

GOTHIC: a word coined, it is thought by Sir Christopher Wren, to describe a form of architecture characterised by pointed arches and prevalent in western Europe (twelfth to sixteenth centuries). English Gothic architecture has been broadly divided into three phases: Early English, Decorated and Perpendicular. These divisions are not really appropriate to describe Scottish Gothic architecture, but are helpful in classifying the nineteenth century Gothic Revival buildings.

GROIN: the edge formed by the intersection of vaults, common from the Romanesque period. They were left plain at first but later they were invariably covered by ribs.

HARLED: roughcast with lime and small gravel.

HOOD-MOULDING: narrow band of stone projecting out over a door or window.

JACOBEAN: of the reign of King James VI of Scotland, I of England (1567-1625 in Scotland, 1603-1625 in England).

JAMBS: the upright sides of doors and windows.

LANCET: tall narrow arch or window with a pointed head, a feature of the Early English style.

LANTERN TOWER: tower of which a considerable portion of the interior is open to view from the ground and is lit by an upper tier of windows.

LECTERN: reading or singing desk in church.

LEGATE: ecclesiastic deputed to represent the Pope.

LIERNE: short rib, not connected to any of the springing points, connecting bosses and intersections of vaulting ribs.

LINTEL: horizontal timber or stone over door.

LITHIC: of stone.

LOUVRE: one of a series of overlapping boards placed in a window to allow ventilation but keep rain out.

LUCARNE: dormer window in a spire.

MACHIOLATION: a projecting parapet on a wall or tower, having openings in the floor between the supporting corbels.

MEDIEVAL: of the Middle Ages, fifth to fifteenth centuries.

METROPOLITAN: in the western church a bishop having authority over the bishops of a province, usually with the title of archbishop.

MENDICANT FRIARS: members of those orders forbidden to own property in common. Unlike monks they work or beg for their living and are not bound to one monastery by a vow of stability.

MISERICORD: hinged seat, carved on the underside, to give support to someone standing during a service.

MITRE: the double-pointed and arched hat of archbishops, bishops and some abbots.

MITRED ABBOT: an abbot with certain of the powers, functions and privileges of a bishop.

MONASTERY: the residence of a community of men living in seclusion under vows.

MONK: member of a community of men living apart from the world in a monastery under vows of poverty, chastity and obedience.

MORTUARY CHAPEL: chapel in which the bodies of the dead are kept before a funeral.

MOSAIC: *see* OPUS SECTILE

MOULDING: ornamental shaping as in the carving of an arch.

MULLION: slender vertical division between the lights of a window.

NAVE: the body of the church from the west door to the chancel, separated from aisles by arcades of pillars.

NICHE: recess in a wall or reredos for a statue, vase or other erect.

NORMAN: style of architecture with round arches and heavy pillars (known elsewhere as ROMANESQUE).

NUN: woman living in a convent under the vows of poverty, chastity and obedience.

NUNCIO: diplomatic representative of the Pope to countries where he is ex-officio Dean of the Diplomatic Corps.

OGEE: moulding showing in section a double continuous curve, concave below passing into convex above.

OPUS SECTILE: the name given to a form of marble inlay where pieces are cut into a shape which follows the line of a pattern or picture. It is to be distinguished from mosaic where pieces are cut to uniform size and where grouping and

not shape give the composition its form.

ORATORY: small chapel or place for private worship.

ORDER: one in a series of recessed arches and jambs surrounding a doorway.

PAPAL LEGATE: *see* LEGATE

PAPAL NUNCIO: *see* NUNCIO

PARAPET: part of the wall rising above the roof gutter used for protection or defence, often battlemented.

PARISH: an area having its own church and priest.

PENDENTIVE: spherical triangle formed by the intersection of a dome with two adjacent arches springing from supporting columns.

PERPENDICULAR: third phase of Gothic architecture, c.1330 to c.1530, characterised by vertical tracery in windows. Also used to describe that style when used in the nineteenth century Gothic Revival.

PILASTER: square pillar projecting from a wall.

PISCINA: recess with basin and drain, usually in the south wall of the sanctuary, for washing the sacred vessels.

PLINTH: the square base of a column.

PORTICO: large covered porch to a building fronted by rows of columns.

PREBENDARY: honorary canon of a cathedral formerly deriving income from an estate belonging to the cathedral.

PREMONSTRATENSIAN: member of an Order founded by St Norbert at Premontré in France in 1123. Otherwise known as the White Canons, they were a more austere offshoot of the Augustinians.

PRESBYTERY: (i) eastern part of the chancel, an alternative name for the sanctuary, (ii) priest's house.

PRIMATE: cleric with the rank of archbishop who presides over the church in a particular country.

PRIMUS: title of primate of the Scottish Episcopal Church, from the Latin *primus* meaning 'first'.

PRIOR: the head (conventual prior) or deputy head (claustral prior) of a monastery. During the early Middle Ages, the word was used in a very vague sense and might be applied to various secular officials. Under Benedictine influence, it came to denote the monk who ranked next to the abbot and deputised for him. Later it was applied to the heads of houses in mendicant orders and of the small houses dependent on an abbey.

PRIORESS: *see* under PRIOR

PRIORY: religious house presided over by a prior, in certain Orders, especially the Augustinians, the priory is the normal unit.

PRO-CATHEDRAL: a church used temporarily as a cathedral until another building can be acquired or constructed. Sometimes used to describe a building intended for cathedral status but not yet consecrated. (From the Latin *pro* – on behalf of.)

PROVINCE: territory, comprising a number of dioceses, under the jurisdiction of an archbishop as metropolitan.

PULPIT: raised enclosed platform from which the preacher delivers a sermon.

PULPITUM: screen, usually of stone, supporting a gallery between the nave and ritual choir of a cathedral or greater church.

QUOIN: external angle of a building.

REFECTORY: room in monastery used for meals.

RENAISSANCE: period of revival of art and architecture under the influence of classical models, in the fourteenth-sixteenth centuries.

REREDOS: ornamental screen, painted and/or carved, covering the wall at the back of an altar.

RESPOND: half pillar or half pier attached to a wall to support an arch.

RETROCHOIR: part of cathedral or large church behind the High Altar.

RETURN STALLS: seats set against a screen at the west end of the chancel or choir.

RIB: arch supporting vault.

RITUAL CHOIR: that part of a cathedral church not part of the architectural choir or chancel, but added to it by the use of screens or partitions. In the case of a short choir or chancel, the easternmost bay of the nave is sometimes used in this way.

ROMANESQUE: style of architecture prevalent in Romanised Europe between the Classical and Gothic periods, c.1050–1200, characterised by massive vaulting and round arches (known in England as NORMAN).

ROOD: crucifix, usually over the entry into the chancel.

ROOD SCREEN: ornamental partition dividing nave and choir in church surmounted by a rood.

ROSE WINDOW: circular window with patterned tracery about the centre.

ROUND TOWERS: tall, narrow towers built at the sites of Celtic monasteries, partly as belfries, partly as treasuries and partly as places of refuge. There are sixty-five identifiable towers in Ireland of which at least some part remains. Apart from one on the Isle of Man and two in Scotland (one attached to Brechin Cathedral), all built under Irish influence, Round Towers are an Irish phenomenon of the Romanesque period.

RUBBLE: masonry where stones are wholly or partly in a rough state, irregular in shape and size.

SACRISTY: building, usually part of a church where sacred vessels, vestments and other valuables were kept.

SAINT: man or woman, officially recognised by the church as having won by exceptional holiness a high place in heaven and veneration on earth.

SANCTUARY: part of the choir housing the altar, usually at the east end, sometimes called presbytery.

SCHIST: foliated metamorphic rock presenting layers of different minerals and splitting into thin irregular plates.

SEDILIA: series of seats (usually three: for priest, deacon and sub-deacon) set in the south wall of the chancel, often canopied and decorated.

SEE: from the Latin *sedes* meaning 'seat', used to describe the place in the diocese where the bishop has his residence and cathedral church, and from which he may take his geographical title.

SPANDREL: surface left over between an arch and its containing rectangle, or between adjacent arches.

SPRING: level at which an arch or vault rises from its supporters.

SQUINT: an opening through the wall of a church in an oblique direction enabling people to see the elevation of the Host at Mass.

STRING COURSE: projecting horizontal band or line of mouldings.

STUCCO: plaster or cement ornamental decoration of wall surface.

SUFFRAGAN: the word is used in two senses (i) to describe the bishop of a diocese in relation to the archbishop of a province, and (ii) a bishop who assists the bishop of a diocese.

SYNOD: ecclesiastical council attended by delegated clergy and laity.

TABERNACLE: receptacle (usually highly ornamented) containing the consecrated elements.

TAU: nineteenth letter of the Greek alphabet, a T-shaped cross.

TESTER: canopy or sounding board above a pulpit.

TITHE: tenth part of annual produce or labour taken for the support of the clergy and the church.

TRACERY: ornamental stone work in patterns in the upper part of Gothic windows, or the raised decoration on wall surfaces.

TRANSEPT: transverse part of a cruciform church.

TRANSITIONAL: period of architecture between Romanesque and Gothic and containing elements of both (twelfth-thirteenth centuries).

TRAVERTINE: white or light-coloured calcareous rock deposited from springs.

TREFOIL: *see* FOIL

TRIFORIUM: gallery or arcade above the arches of nave, choir and transepts.

TRIPLE-LIGHT: term used to describe windows of three divisions: typical of lancets.

TUSCAN: simplified form of DORIC.

TYMPANUM: space over door between lintel and arch, usually semi-circular or triangular.

VAULT: arched roof whose joints radiate from a central point or line, can be of stone, brick or wood, but usually stone: *see* also BARREL VAULT, LIERNE and GROIN.

VESICA: pointed oval shape.

VESTIBULE: the porch of a church.

VESTRY: (i) room or building attached to a church in which vestments are kept and put on, (ii) meeting of parishioners for parochial business.

WHEEL WINDOW: circular window with tracery radiating from the centre, giving the appearance of a wheel.